EZRA AMES OF ALBANY

1768–1836

EZRA AMES (1768–1836)
Self-portrait, *c.* 1800
Owned by the Albany Institute of History and Art

EZRA AMES OF ALBANY

PORTRAIT PAINTER

CRAFTSMAN · ROYAL ARCH MASON · BANKER

1768–1836

By Theodore Bolton and Irwin F. Cortelyou

And a Catalogue of His Works

By Irwin F. Cortelyou

With the collaboration of
Theodore Bolton

THE NEW-YORK HISTORICAL SOCIETY
170 Central Park West, New York 24, N.Y.
1955

PRINTED IN THE UNITED STATES OF AMERICA
Composition: The George Grady Press, New York
Lithoprinted by Edwards Brothers, Ann Arbor

A NOTE ON THE COLLABORATION

IN THE spring of 1949, Irwin F. Cortelyou (Mrs. George B. Cortelyou, Jr.) began a survey of the works of Ezra Ames and research on the artist's life. Later in 1949, after aiding her for several months, Mr. Theodore Bolton joined her in the work as a collaborator.

Mrs. Cortelyou is almost entirely responsible for the factual material in the biography and catalogue. She corresponded with or interviewed the owners of portraits; arranged and made most of the field trips; carried on the research at the Frick Art Reference Library and elsewhere for paintings by Ames misattributed to others, and for paintings hitherto unattributed to any artist but painted by Ames. She also photographed portraits, miniatures, and manuscripts which had not hitherto been photographed, many of which are now reproduced in this book; and searched manuscript as well as published sources.

Mr. Bolton is almost entirely responsible for placing this abundant material in literary and catalogue form for publication. He also verified many references; examined portraits; studied photographs of portraits at the Frick Art Reference Library; and throughout was influential in the organization of the book.

More specifically, the allocation of the responsibility for several sections of this work is as follows:

Mr. Bolton and Mrs. Cortelyou are jointly responsible for the chapters on the life and work of Ezra Ames. The preponderance of the writing was done by Mr. Bolton in a sentence-by-sentence collaboration with Mrs. Cortelyou.

In the chapter entitled "References to Paintings in the Account Books (1790–1834) of Ezra Ames," Mrs. Cortelyou took the initiative in relating known portraits by Ezra Ames to the entries in the Account Books. Mr. Bolton was mainly responsible for verification and much of the literary form. Mr. George B. Cortelyou, Jr., aided in the presentation of the statistical material.

Mrs. Cortelyou is responsible for the "Transcript of Entries for Portraits, Miniatures, and Paintings of Miscellaneous Subjects from Ezra Ames's Account Books." Although the transcript does not include the many references to craft work contained in the Account Books, these were thought to be of sufficient interest to present in a brief survey. Mrs. Cortelyou is responsible for this section, called: "Omissions from the Transcript: Craft Work."

Mrs. Cortelyou with the collaboration of Mr. Bolton compiled the catalogue of over five hundred paintings by Ezra Ames. The material for the catalogue, as stated above, was gathered almost entirely by Mrs. Cortelyou. The determination of uncertain attributions was made in consultation with Mr. Bolton, who is responsible for the pattern followed in the presentation.

Mr. David H. Wallace, Assistant Editor, The New-York Historical Society, designed and compiled the index.

Having thus allocated the responsibility for the more important sections of this book, it remains for the authors to state in conclusion that their work was inextricably interwoven throughout and that the collaboration has been a very happy one.

I. F. C.
T. B.

ACKNOWLEDGEMENTS

BEFORE joining Mr. Theodore Bolton in acknowledging the aid given us as collaborators I wish to make a brief statement of how this work began, and several acknowledgements of aid given personally to me. First of all my greatest debt of gratitude goes to Mr. Bolton, himself, for his early and continuing encouragement to me, a beginner in the field of early American art history.

I first heard of Ezra Ames four years ago from Dr. George Clinton Andrews who owns two portraits by Ezra Ames. He expressed the hope of finding a companion portrait to one of them and I decided to search for it myself. This led me inevitably to the Frick Art Reference Library where Miss Mildred Steinbach, Assistant Librarian, gave me intent and sympathetic attention. To her I am indebted for the idea and the confidence to tackle the larger work of compiling a catalogue of the paintings of Ezra Ames. Mr. James Thomas Flexner also encouraged me to proceed; and both he and Miss Steinbach, with great good will, have answered many questions and volunteered much helpful advice. To these three persons I herewith record my thanks.

The following sentence, written by Miss Dorothy C. Barck in her article on Ezra Ames in *The New-York Historical Society Quarterly Bulletin*, January 1927, also had its influence in my decision to attempt a catalogue of his paintings: "A valuable contribution to the history of American art," she said, "would be a search for, and a critical study of, all of Ames's portraits." I am grateful to Miss Barck for her challenging sentence, as well as her subsequent coöperation in the undertaking.

Early in the work I was also led, inevitably, to consult Mr. Bolton. I am indebted to him for informing me of the Account Book of Ezra Ames at the Albany Institute of History and Art; later for bringing my transcript of this Account Book, and already expanding catalogue, to the attention of Mr. Charles E. Baker, Editor of *The New-York Historical Society Quarterly;*

and for collaborating with me later on when my material required classification and literary form.

Mr. Baker's willingness to have me undertake the work has always seemed to me an extraordinary example of faith, and I have tried my best to live up to it. I wish to express my gratitude to him for it and for his sympathetic helpfulness throughout.

From this beginning the work grew into a three-part article on the Account Books and the life of the artist which appeared in *The New-York Historical Society Quarterly* for January 1951, July 1951, and January 1952. These articles, revised, and with the addition of many illustrations, of a bibliography and other reference sections, and of a catalogue of over five hundred of Ames's paintings, comprise the present volume.

During my research I paid many visits to the Albany Institute of History and Art, and I shall always remember with gratitude, the hospitality of its Director, Mr. Robert G. Wheeler, its Membership Secretary, Miss Margaret D. Robertson, and the entire staff. The most unusual aspect of this hospitality was the privilege accorded me by Mr. Wheeler of extending my working hours at the Institute beyond its formal time of opening and closing. I am grateful, too, for having been supplied with a very comfortable place in which to work; and, most important of all, for having been given free access to its valuable collection of manuscripts and other material on Ezra Ames.

I wish, further, to thank Mr. and Mrs. John C. Borden who, for several summers, were so generous as to provide me with a place to stay during my research trips to New York. Other friends who were also generous in this respect are: Mr. and Mrs. George N. Buffington; Mrs. Richard M. Hurd; Miss Clementine L. Miller; Mr. and Mrs. Hooker Talcott; and Mr. and Mrs. Greer Zachry. Similar aid was kindly offered by: Mr. and Mrs. Arthur W. Bingham, Jr.; Mr. and Mrs. Charles C. Lee; and Mr. and Mrs. Gardner D. Stout.

I am also grateful to Miss Iva Owens, not only for postponing her plans for several years in order to facilitate my work, but also for her good nature and coöperation during that period; to Mr. Charles T. Miller for training me in the mysteries of photographing portraits, miniatures, and manuscripts; and to my husband, George B. Cortelyou, Jr., for aid so often given of every possible kind.

And now joining Mr. Bolton, I wish to express our appreciation to all those who have granted permission to list and reproduce their pictures. Many of them have given us much helpful information, either in person or by letter. They are too numerous to be listed again here, but their names appear in the catalogue entries for their pictures and under the reproductions.

We also appreciate the hospitality extended to us by those who received us in their homes to view their paintings. They are: Dr. George Clinton Andrews; Mr. Thomas Barber; Mrs. Walter B. Binnian; Mrs. Marcus L. Blanchard; Mrs. Arthur W. Butler; Mr. George Agnew Chamberlain; Mrs. J. Chester Chamberlain; Mrs. Seth W. Cook; Mrs. J. Lewi Donhauser; Miss Louise S. Gilder; Mr. and Mrs. John Green; the late Frederick Hill; Mrs. John E. N. Hume; Mrs. Ellery S. James; Mrs. R. Keith Kane; The Misses Kellogg; Mr. and Mrs. Joseph Larocque; Miss Catharine Van Cortlandt Mathews and Mrs. William V. Mason; Mrs. William Ten Broeck Mynderse; Miss Evelyn Newman; Mr. and Mrs. Alonzo W. Paige; Mr. and Mrs. John De Witt Peltz; Miss Emily W. Rankin and Mr. Edward E. Rankin; Mr. and Mrs. Kenneth G. Reynolds; Miss Sarah Steward; Mrs. Weeks Stewart; Miss Cornelia L. Van Rensselaer Strong; Mr. John Bond Trevor; Miss Helen de Lancey Watkins; and Miss Eleanor B. Weir.

Next we wish to record our indebtedness to the following persons who have answered our letters or personal inquiries, sent us photographs, or given us various other aid: Mr. Harry MacNeill Bland; Mrs. S. V. R. Crosby; Mrs. Dora Lee Curtis; Miss Martha Donhauser; Mr. Albert Duveen; Mr. Edward Crosby Doughty; Mrs. Joseph S. Frelinghuysen; Dr. George C. Groce; Miss Agnes Halsey; Mr. Benjamin H. Haviland; Mrs. Livingston W. Houston; Mr. Robert A. Hug; Mrs. Joseph Jenkins; Miss Florence Chase Lamb; Mrs. James S. Malseed, Jr.; Mr. John M. Merriam; Mrs. Eleanor Melville Metcalf; Mr. Harry S. Newman; Miss Anna Wells Rutledge; Mr. Mitchell Samuels; Mr. Charles Coleman Sellers; Mrs. James Stoll; Mrs. Julian Street, Jr.; Mr. Howard Swiggett; Mr. Russell W. Thorpe; Mr. George S. Van Schaick; and Mrs. Alexander M. White.

Some persons have been of such great assistance to us that we would like to record our specific indebtedness to them. Thus we are grateful to: Mrs. Katharine M. McClinton whose mention of our work in her article on Ezra Ames in *The Magazine Antiques*, September 1951, resulted in the addition of at least two portraits to our catalogue; Miss Janet R. MacFarlane, who, besides giving us the utmost coöperation professionally, also sent us material whenever she thought it would benefit us; Mr. M. Halsey Thomas, who, likewise coöperating fully in all aspects of our work which involved him professionally, also volunteered information whenever he thought it concerned us; Mr. William C. Hook, Mrs. Edward L. Kernochan, Mr. Charles B. Lansing, Mr. Charles G. Loring, Miss Eleanor H. Lovett, Mrs. Stanley McCormick, Mr. Frederick McDonald, Mr. Douglas W. Olcott, Mr. Kenneth G. Reynolds, Miss Catharine Van Cortlandt Mathews, Mrs. Reginald P. Rose, and Miss Nina Romeyn—all of whom were indefatigable in answering our many questions; Miss Helen Burr Smith, who furnished us with genealogical and other material, including a valuable catalogue, and enlisted the aid of Miss Emily W. Rankin and Mr. Edward E. Rankin, in locating a number of portraits listed therein; Mr. Jay Leyda for supplying us with Beekman and Gansevoort references; and Mr. Mahonri S. Young, who discontinued his research into the work of Ezra Ames in favor of our investigations and who made available the results of his researches, unfortunately after we had in every case covered the same field.

To Mrs. William Sawitzky is due a special mention here because she so generously permitted us the full use of the notes, correspondence, and photographs relating to the paintings of

Ezra Ames, assembled by her husband, the late William Sawitzky. Examination of this material enabled us to add about a dozen portraits to our catalogue and also strengthened the attribution of many already known to us. Credit for each attribution is given in the catalogue entry.

We also thank all those persons associated with various institutions who have aided us in many ways. They are: Mr. Ledyard Cogswell, Jr., President, and Mr. Robert G. Wheeler, Director, Albany Institute of History and Art; Dr. Clarence S. Brigham, Director, American Antiquarian Society; Miss Gladys MacDonald, American Bible Society; Mr. John I. H. Bauer, Curator of Paintings and Sculpture, Brooklyn Museum; Mrs. Henry W. Howell, Jr., Librarian, Miss Mildred Steinbach, Miss Hope Mathewson, Mrs. Thurman Rotan, and Mrs. Thomas Edwards, Frick Art Reference Library; Mr. Theodore Heinrich, Curator, Henry E. Huntington Library and Art Gallery; Mr. Joseph Downs, Curator, Henry Francis Du Pont Winterthur Museum; Mr. Harold S. Sniffen, Curator of Prints, Mariners' Museum; Mr. Wendell Walker, Librarian, Masonic Hall, New York City; Mr. Chester A. Dolan, Jr., Clerk, Supreme Judicial Court, County of Suffolk, Commonwealth of Massachusetts; Mr. Douglas W. Olcott, President, Mechanics and Farmers' Bank, Albany, New York; Mr. Harry B. Wehle, Curator of Paintings, and Mrs. Josephine L. Allen, Metropolitan Museum of Art; Mrs. Frank J. Miller, Chairman, House Committee, Montgomery County Historical Society, New York; Mr. Joseph S. Trovato, Assistant to the Director, Munson-Williams-Proctor Institute; Mr. John Walden Myer, Director, Museum of the City of New York; Mr. Lester W. Herzog, Jr., Cashier, National Commercial Bank and Trust Company, Albany, New York; Mr. Ralph Thomas, Director, New Haven Colony Historical Society; Mr. Alexander J. Wall, Jr., Director, New Jersey Historical Society; Miss Marie F. Berry, New York Genealogical and Biographical Society; Dr. R. W. G. Vail, Director, Miss Dorothy C. Barck, Librarian, and Mr. Wayne Andrews, Mr. Charles E. Baker, Miss Geraldine Beard, Miss E. Marie Becker, Mr. Wilmer R. Leech,

Mr. Charles T. Miller, Mr. Michael Lazlo, The New-York Historical Society; Mr. Robert W. Hill, Keeper of Manuscripts, and Edward H. Morrison, New York Public Library; Miss Janet R. MacFarlane, Curator, New York State Historical Association; Mr. Charles G. Loring, Old South Association, Boston; Dr. Charles Francis Gosnell, State Librarian, and Miss Edna L. Jacobsen, New York State Library; Mrs. Barbara S. Roberts, Registrar, Pennsylvania Academy of the Fine Arts; Mrs. Mary Black Terwilliger, Historic Site Superintendent, Senate House Museum, Kingston, New York; Mr. Frederick McDonald, President, State Bank of Albany; Mr. Russell S. Coles, Director, and Mr. Gerald Bernstein, Staten Island Institute of Arts and Sciences; Miss Lillian Applegarth, Secretary to the President, Mrs. E. S. C. Smith, Acting Librarian, and Mr. H. L. Webb, Union College; Dr. Albert Corey, State Historian, Mr. William G. Tyrrell, University of the State of New York; and Mr. John Marshall Phillips, Director, Yale University Art Gallery.

To the following members of the Ames family we would like to express our gratitude for their helpfulness to us in this work. Without their coöperation it could not have been carried out so fully. Thus, our thanks go to Miss Elizabeth S. Edwards, great-granddaughter of the artist, for her patience and coöperation during the photographing of her portraits and miniatures; to Mrs. Franklin E. Everson, née Bette Bent Benedict, for her helpful letter; to Miss Gladys Ladu, great-great-great-grandniece of the artist, for bringing her miniatures to Albany for inspection; to Miss Mary L. Sutliff, great-grandniece and Miss Edith S. Wade, great-great-grandniece of the artist, for their many letters, for photographs and clippings sent to us, and for receiving us into their home to see their portraits. To Miss Sutliff, we express our esteem for her excellent genealogy of Betsy Mulford Sutliff, the artist's niece, which was an invaluable aid to us in writing our chapter on the family and background of Ezra Ames.

Rumson, New Jersey IRWIN F. CORTELYOU
December 10, 1952 (Mrs. George B. Cortelyou, Jr.)

CONTENTS

A Note on the Collaboration . . . iii

Acknowledgements . . . v

Illustrations (an alphabetical list) . . . xiii

Introduction . . . xvii

PART I: LIFE AND WORK

I Family and Background, 1768–1790 . . . 3

II Young Manhood, 1790–1793 . . . 9

III First Decade at Albany, 1793–1803 . . . 19

IV Rise as a Portrait Painter, 1804–1812 . . . 39

V First Success as an Artist, 1812–1816 . . . 63

VI Further Recognition, 1817–1825 . . . 87

VII Honors in Last Decade, 1825–1836 . . . 111

VIII Conclusion . . . 135

PART II: ACCOUNT BOOKS

IX References to Paintings in the Account Books (1790–1834) of Ezra Ames . . . 147

Description of the Account Books . . . 147

Entries Relating to Known Paintings . . . 153

Omissions from the Transcript: Craft Work . . . 170

Notes on the Transcript . . . 175

X Transcript of Entries for Portraits, Miniatures, and Paintings of Miscellaneous Subjects

From Ezra Ames's NYHS Account Books . . . 176

From Ezra Ames's Albany Institute Account Book . . . 178

PART III: CATALOGUE

Notes on the Catalogue 193

XI Portraits in Oil 201

XII Portraits in Miniature 314

XIII Landscapes, Figure Compositions, Still Life, and Drawings 318

XIV Prints after Portraits by Ezra Ames 337

XV Pictures Misattributed to Ezra Ames 344

XVI Pictures of Questionable Attribution. Unsettled Matters . . 348

Chronology of Residences and Places Visited 356

Bibliography of Sources Cited 359

Index 371

ILLUSTRATIONS

ALPHABETICAL LIST OF PORTRAITS

(All portraits are by Ezra Ames unless otherwise specified. The dates refer to the year or about the year in which each work was executed.)

Allen, Solomon, 1814 . . . 156
Ames, Angelo, *c.* 1818 (miniature) . . . 127
Ames, Angelo, *c.* 1827 (miniature) . . . 127
Ames, Ezra, *c.* 1790 (miniature) . . . 8
Ames, Ezra, *c.* 1800 . . . *frontis.*
Ames, Ezra, *c.* 1800 (miniature) . . . 8
Ames, Ezra, *c.* 1810 (miniature) . . . 127
Ames, Ezra, *c.* 1814 . . . 75
Ames, Ezra, silhouette by Henry Williams, *c.* 1805 . . . 42
Ames, Mrs. Ezra (Zipporah Wood), silhouette by Williams, *c.* 1805 42
Ames, Mrs. Ezra (Zipporah Wood), *c.* 1820 (miniature) . . . 137
Ames, Julius Rubens, *c.* 1826 . . . 125
Ames, Marcia Lucretia, *c.* 1820 (miniature) . . . 137
(?) Annesley, William, *c.* 1820 . . . 89
(?) Annesley, Mrs. William (Margaret La Casse), *c.* 1820 . . . 89
Bleecker, Harmanus, 1819 . . . 152
Bleecker, Leonard, *c.* 1805 . . . 37
Bloodgood, Francis, *c.* 1810 . . . 142
Brant, Joseph, (Thayendanegea) 1806 . . . 37
Brown, Mrs. Jacob Jennings (Pamela Williams), probably 1818 . 168
Burnham, Eleazer, 1826 . . . 121
Burnham, Mrs. Eleazer (Caroline Matilda Wood), 1830 . . . 121
Clinton, DeWitt, 1818 . . . 141
Clinton, Mrs. DeWitt (Catherine Jones), 1820 . . . 98
Clinton, George, 1813 . . . 76
Clinton, George, 1814 . . . 146
Clinton, George, 1818 . . . 62
Clinton, George Washington, *c.* 1813 . . . 78
Crolius, Clarkson, 1825 . . . 86
Cushing, Thomas Humphrey, *c.* 1815 . . . 81
Cushing, Mrs. Thomas Humphrey (Margaret Eleanor Norwood), *c.* 1815 . . . 81
Dwight, Theodore, 1817 . . . 90
Emes, Henry, *c.* 1832 (miniature) . . . 127
Emes, Jesse, *c.* 1790 . . . 2
Emes, Jesse, 1819 . . . 97
Emes, Mrs. Jesse (Mrs. Fanny Parminter), 1819 . . . 97

Fondey Family, 1803 . . . 18
Fowler, Samuel Stephenson, *c.* 1827 . . . 197
Gansevoort, Mrs. Peter (Catherine Van Schaick), 1824 . . . 98
Genet, Edmond Charles, *c.* 1809–1810 . . . xvi
Hamilton, Alexander, 1810 . . . 52
Hamilton, Alexander, engraved 1810 by Leney, 1810 . . . 51
Hamilton, Alexander, engraved (n.d.) by Hoogland, 1810 . . . 51
Hawley, Jesse, *c.* 1825 (miniature) . . . 109
Hillhouse, Thomas, *c.* 1817 . . . 90
Hills, Mrs. John (Huldah Mulford), *c.* 1831 (miniature) . . . 136
Hudson, Robert, *c.* 1820 . . . 94
Hudson, Mrs. Robert, *c.* 1820 . . . 94
James, Katharine Barber (so-called) . . . 128
James, William (1771–1832), 1822 . . . 106
James, Mrs. William (Catharine Barber), 1822 . . . 106
Jay, John . . . 141
Jones, Henry, Aged 20 Years, 1810 . . . 54
Jordan, Ambrose Latting, *c.* 1820–1825 . . . 101
Kane, John, *c.* 1804 . . . 41
Kent, James, *c.* 1812 . . . 75
King, Mrs. James (Ellen James), 1822 . . . 106
Mather, Elias, *c.* 1827 . . . 118
Meads, John, 1816 . . . 85
Meads, Mrs. John (Louisa Crane), 1816 . . . 85, 192
Melville, Mrs. Allan (Maria Gansevoort), *c.* 1814 . . . 82
Morris, Gouverneur . . . 160
Mulford, Mrs. Ezekiel (Sally Emes or Ames), *c.* 1804 . . . 2
Newman, Henry, 1810 . . . 57
Nott, Eliphalet, 1820 . . . 156
Paige, John Keyes, 1826 . . . 110
Paige, Mrs. John Keyes (Helen Maria Yates), 1826 . . . 110
Phinney, Elihu, 1799 . . . 26
Provost, George, 1805 . . . 168
Reynolds, Marcus Tullius, *c.* 1821 . . . 105
Reynolds, Mrs. Stephen (Lydia Bartlett), *c.* 1824 . . . 118
Rivington, James, 1806 . . . 165
Ruggles, Philo, 1822 . . . 93
Ruggles, Mrs. Philo (Ellen Bulkley), 1822 . . . 93
Spencer, Ambrose, 1811 . . . 158
Stafford, Spencer, 1805 . . . 45
Stafford, Mrs. Spencer (Harriet Romeyn), 1807 . . . 45
Strong, Theodore, *c.* 1820 . . . 105
Tallmadge, Benjamin, *c.* 1820–1826 . . . 155
Tallmadge, Mrs. Benjamin (Maria Hallett), c. 1820–1826 . . . 155

Tallmadge, Matthias Burnett, *c.* 1815 . . . 38
Tallmadge, Mrs. Matthias Burnett (Elizabeth Clinton), *c.* 1815 . 38
Tayler, John, 1816 . . . 78
Thorp, Aaron, 1826 . . . 117
Thorp, Mrs. Aaron (Mary Dunn), 1826 . . . 117
Throop, Enos Thompson, *c.* 1829– . . . 131
Tibbits, George, *c.* 1833 . . . 122
Tibbits, Mrs. George (Sarah Noyes), *c.* 1833 . . . 122
Tompkins, Daniel D., *c.* 1815– . . . 141
Tompkins, Mrs. Daniel D. (Hannah Minthorne), *c.* 1809 . . . 47
Tompkins, Children of Governor Daniel D., 1809 . . . 46
Townsend, Absalom, 1816 . . . 152
Tully, William, Jr., 1826 . . . 113
Van Buren, Martin, *c.* 1828– . . . 131
Van Cortlandt, Philip, *c.* 1809–1810 . . . xvi
Van Cortlandt, Pierre II, *c.* 1815 . . . 82
Van Rensselaer, Solomon, 1819 . . . 86
Van Rensselaer, Stephen III, probably 1819 . . . 86
Wade, James, *c.* 1822 (miniature) . . . 136
Walsh, Ann , 1807 . . . 48
Walton, Mrs. Jonathan (Margaret Ann Thatcher), *c.* 1830–35 . . 134
Washington, George, 1813 . . . 76
Watson, Elkanah, engraved *c.* 1820 by Balch, 1818 . . . 158
Watson, Elkanah, by J. S. Copley, 1782 . . . 139
Watson, Elkanah, *c.* 1809–1810 . . . 139
Yates, Joseph Christopher, *c.* 1823– . . . 141

SUBJECTS OTHER THAN PORTRAITS

Account Book No. 1 (1790–1797), first two pages of Ezra Ames's 174
Account Book No. 3 (1804–1834), section of a page of Ezra Ames's 185
Albany, View of State Street in 1805, by James Eights . . . 17
Albany, Official Map of 1794 . . . 31
Box made and decorated by Ezra Ames . . . 173
Catalogue Sale of Portraits, Albany, 1842 (handbill) . . . 132
Cigar Store Indian repainted by Ezra Ames, 1823 (woodcut) . . 358
Landscape, Perspective Painting of Lake George [with the fort], 1812, by Ezra Ames . . . 68
Landscape, A View of Lake George & Caldwell Village [without fort], *c.* 1812 and 1822, by Ezra Ames . . . 69
Landscape, Romantic, by Ezra Ames . . . 70
New York City, Robertson's View, 1793 . . . 17
Tobacconists' Signs, 1817: woodcuts after work by Ezra Ames . 173

PHILIP VAN CORTLANDT (1749–1831)

By Ezra Ames, *c.* 1809–1810

Owned by The Metropolitan Museum of Art

EDMOND CHARLES GENET (1763–1834)

By Ezra Ames, *c.* 1809–1810 (Photo by FARL)

Owned by the Albany Institute of History and Art

INTRODUCTION

EZRA AMES of Albany, prominent in his day as a portrait painter, is still remembered because his portraits have a local, a State and, sometimes, a national interest as records. Although he was born at Framingham, Massachusetts, in 1768, he settled at Albany as early as 1793, and lived there until his death in 1836. Except for a few early portraits, none of the pictures he painted before he moved to Albany has been identified, so that practically all his known portraits are of residents of New York State.

Since any portraits painted from life may be regarded either as personal records or as historical documents, and since Ames recorded the likenesses of about five hundred of his contemporaries, his portraits, many of which are still extant, constitute important documentary sources for the history of New York State during the early Republican Era. Nevertheless, despite the preponderance of interest in his work because of its historical significance, one should not overlook its solid artistic merits.

The fact that some of his portraits have been confused with the work of Gilbert Stuart, John Wesley Jarvis, John Vanderlyn, and Henry Inman gives an idea of their relative artistic quality. A number of his portraits, such as (among others) those of Julius Rubens Ames, Harmanus Bleecker, Francis Bloodgood, George Clinton (the version at The New-York Historical Society), Thomas Humphrey Cushing, Mrs. Thomas Humphrey Cushing, Samuel Stevenson Fowler, Edmond Charles (Citizen) Genet, Thomas Hillhouse, Henry Jones, Ambrose Latting Jordan, James Kent (the version at the Albany Institute of History and Art), Mrs. John Meads, Henry Newman, John Keyes Paige, Mrs. John Keyes Paige, Marcus Tullius Reynolds, Ambrose Spencer, Theodore Strong, Matthias Burnett Tallmadge, Absalom Townsend, William Tully, Jr., Philip Van Cortlandt, and Mrs. Jonathan Walton—all of which are reproduced in this volume—do rank with the work of those artists whose productions generally are of a high artistic excellence. However, although he sometimes reached their heights of artistry, Ames's average is not quite as high as theirs, for, like many of the portrait painters of his time, his purpose was less to produce an artistic result than it was to meet the demand for accurate likenesses—a demand met nowadays by photographers. Contemporary statements attest to Ames's particular ability in this respect. Ames also frequently made frames for his portraits to meet an additional requirement of his day that portraits with their frames serve as parts of the decorative furnishings of a room.

Besides achieving distinction as a craftsman and portrait painter, Ames became a prominent citizen of Albany, and the story of his life is an interesting part of the history of New York State. He was not only recognized as a portrait painter outside of his district, but he was also honored for over twenty-four years as the Grand High Priest of the Grand Chapter of Royal Arch Masons of the State of New York; and, besides, he was elected president of the Mechanics and Farmers' Bank of Albany after serving for twenty years as one of its directors. His record in all three activities—art, Masonry, and banking—will be included in the following biographical essay. There will also be some account of his forebears and his family. The emphasis, however, will be placed on his activity as a craftsman and as an artist. Obviously, not nearly all of the portraits painted by Ames will be mentioned in the biography; but the separate catalogue of his works will be as complete as the authors can make it.

Ezra Ames belonged to the generation of portrait painters residing in New York State during the first half of the 19th century who managed to compete successfully with the better-trained visiting artists. In his study of "New York Painting Before 1800," Dr. George C. Groce concludes that: "Resident artists fared badly in New York between 1751 and 1800." Among the artists who were unable to live by portrait painting alone and had to supplement their incomes by craft work and other means during the latter part of the 18th century he names Lawrence

Kilburn and Abraham Delanoy of New York City, and Ezra Ames of Albany.

Still referring to the latter part of the 18th century, Dr. Groce continues: "the visiting artist was not unlikely to take New York by storm." Among these visitors were: John Wollaston, the Englishman, who painted over fifty portraits during 1750–1752 alone; John Singleton Copley of Boston who visited New York City, Long Island, and Fishkill during July to December 1771, and earned over three hundred pounds at painting portraits; and Gilbert Stuart who, returning from Europe, landed in New York City in 1793 intending to proceed immediately to Philadelphia, but because he was rushed with orders delayed his departure until late in 1794.

In New England during the 18th century there had been an uninterrupted development of portrait painting from Smibert to Feke, to Copley, and to John Trumbull. In Pennsylvania and Maryland, likewise, a development may be traced, beginning with Engelhardt Kühn and Gustavus Hesselius, and extending to John Hesselius and Charles Willson Peale. But in New York State, until 1800, there had been no continuous tradition of painting as there had been in New England, Pennsylvania, and Maryland. After 1800 in New York State, however, a development of portrait painting began which flourished principally in New York City; and of the numerous artists in this movement John Wesley Jarvis, Henry Inman, and Charles Loring Elliott were, successively, the most distinguished. Outside of New York City, Ezra Ames achieved in upper New York State a position of similar importance in this trend.

THEODORE BOLTON

First of all, then, I have to tell you, as a fact of personal experience, that in all my poor Historical investigations it has been, and always is, one of the most primary wants to procure a bodily likeness of the personage inquired after; a good Portrait *if such exists. . . . Often I have found a Portrait superior in real instruction to half-a-dozen written 'Biographies,' as Biographies are written; —or rather, let me say, I have found that the Portrait was as a small lighted* candle *by which the Biographies could for the first time be* read, *and some human interpretation be made of them. . . .*

THOMAS CARLYLE

Chelsea, 3d May 1854.

PART I
LIFE AND WORK

MRS. EZEKIEL (SALLY EMES) MULFORD (1773–1861)
Sister of the artist
By Ezra Ames, *c.* 1804

Owned by Miss Edith S. Wade, Ames's great-great-grandniece

JESSE EMES (1739–1829), FATHER OF THE ARTIST
By Ezra Ames, *c.* 1790

Owned by Albany Institute of History and Art
Gift of Miss Mary L. Sutliff, Ames's great-grandniece

I

FAMILY AND BACKGROUND:

FRAMINGHAM, EAST SUDBURY, 1768–1790

EZRA AMES, portrait painter, was born on May 5, 1768, at Framingham, Massachusetts; and died on February 23, 1836, at Albany, New York. This information is inscribed on the handsome memorial to him, his wife, and two sons, in the Albany Rural Cemetery.

Ezra was the fourth child and third son of Jesse Emes and his first wife, Betty Bent, who married Jesse in 1761.[1] She was born on May 1, 1743,[2] and died on February 14, 1776.[3] She was the daughter of John Bent of Framingham, Massachusetts, and his wife, Betty Read of Sudbury.[4]

Although Ezra's father signed his will "Jesse Emes," and his name is thus spelled on his own and on other gravestones in his family plot at Staatsburg, New York, his name and that of his forebears is frequently recorded as "Eames" and "Emmes," and only rarely as "Ames." Other variations in the spelling of the name are "Eamms," "Eams," "Emms," and "Ems." Ezra himself, early in life, showed a preference for spelling his own name "Ames." Thus, he wrote "Ezra Ames" several times along the front cover and the flyleaf of his first Account Book (1790–1797). Inside the same booklet under the year 1792, he signed his name "Ezra Eames," but when he reverted to his earlier spelling and wrote "Ezra Ames" on the cover of his third Account Book (1804–1834), he never again deviated from this spelling of his name.

Ezra, a fifth-generation American, was descended in a direct line from Thomas Emes, apparently the first of the family in

[1] *MS Ames Family*. [All short-title citations in these footnotes will be described in full in the "Bibliography."]

[2] *Framingham V. R.*, 23; cf. Framingham V. R., 424, for gravestone record giving inferential birth date of "Bettey Eames," Ezra's mother; and *ibid.*, 23, recording the births of two children of John and Betty Bent, named Betty. The first presumably died young.

[3] *Ibid.*, 424.

[4] *Ibid.*, 239.

America, through John, Henry, and Jesse.[5] These men acquired and cleared land, developed homesteads, participated in community activities, and prospered in their small worlds. Ezra, in an urban setting, also acquired property, became a householder, took part in the civic affairs of his adopted city, and achieved fame and fortune in his larger sphere.

Thomas Emes (1618–1680/1), Ezra's great-great-grandfather, who settled in America about 1634, probably came from England.[6] In 1637 he fought in the Pequot Indian War. He was a brickmason. As a young man he lived in Dedham, Massachusetts; then in Medford, and in Cambridge, selling his property early in 1664/5, and moving to Sudbury where he leased "Mr. Pelham's Farm."[7] About 1670, Thomas settled in Framingham,[8] where: "He built his house on the southern slope of Mount Wayte, between the Sudbury river and Farm pond, at a distance of about seven miles S. W. from the ancient town of Sudbury. . . ."[9] He now became a farmer and landholder on a large scale,[10] and his holdings in 1677 are shown on a plan of Framingham Plantation, dated 1699.[11] He was "received as an Inhab. [Inhabitant] of Sherb. [Sherborn] Jan. 4, '74–5, and early chosen a Selectman; was on the Com. [Committee] for building the Meeting House, and received a grant for building the same.'"[12] In 1676, his farmhouse was attacked by a band of Indians. An inscription on a stone marking the site of this house at Mount Wayte, Framingham, reads: "Here stood the home of Thomas Eames, burned by the Indians in King Philip's War Feb. 1 1676. His wife and five children were slain and four carried

[5] Sutliff, 27–32. The name, standardized as "Emes" by Miss Sutliff, is retained in this account of the artist's forebears.

[6] *Ibid.*, 27.

[7] Temple, 531. On an excellent map of Middlesex County, Massachusetts, dated 1857, a "Pelham Pond" is shown in Wayland, which was once part of Sudbury. Because of its name the pond may have been on "Mr. Pelham's Farm" and, if so, this would definitely locate the land which Thomas Emes leased. See: *Middlesex County Map; Wayland V. R.*, Introduction.

[8] Barry, 227.

[9] *Ibid.*, 24.

[10] Temple, 531.

[11] *Framingham Memorial,* frontispiece.

[12] Barry, 227.

into captivity. This memorial is placed by his descendants A.D. 1900."[13]

One of Thomas's sons who escaped the massacre was John (1642–1733), Ezra's great-grandfather. John, also a brickmason, was born in Dedham, Massachusetts. He settled first at Watertown, and in 1678, at Framingham. He was a selectman of Sherborn in 1682, and of Framingham in 1701.[14] Thomas's grandson, Henry (1698–1761), Ezra's grandfather, was a member of a committee "to provide for the raising of the meeting house" at Framingham in 1735, a selectman of that town in 1740, 1744, and 1753, and a captain of the Framingham Militia in 1757.[15] Thomas and John each had two wives and ten children; Henry, one wife and eleven children; and Jesse, Ezra's father, three wives and nine children.[16]

Ezra's father, Jesse (1739–1829), the son of Henry Emes and his wife Ruth Newton, was born on July 14, 1739, at Framingham,[17] which is incorrectly spelled "Farming" on his gravestone in the Jesse Emes family plot at Staatsburg, New York. Josiah H. Temple, stating that Jesse "l[ived] on the Thomas place in Way [land]" and "came to Fram[ingham] 1764,"[18] lists him with a committee of four, chosen in 1770 to take care of the school houses,[19] and calls him a "captain" and "dentist."[20] Forty-three years later, Jesse in his will, dated March 24, 1813, styles himself a "gentleman."[21]

Answering the alarm of April 19, 1775, the day of the battles of Lexington and Concord,[22] Jesse Emes served as captain of a

[13] There are two markers at the site of the house of Thomas Eames on Mount Wayte in Framingham. One bears the inscription quoted above which is on a metal bronze tablet sunk into a stone; and the other is a metal marker nearby, with slightly different words, placed by the Massachusetts Bay Colony Tercentenary Commission in 1930. Mr. John M. Merriam in a letter of April 16, 1951, writes: "The most beautiful spot included within the Wayte grant was the little hill now known to us as 'Montwait,' a natural beauty spot which has been abused, misnamed and neglected by the later generation."

[14] Temple, 531.

[15] Temple, 531, 532, 197, 421, 222.

[16] *Ibid.*, 27–32.

[17] *MS Ames Family; Framingham V. R.*, 71.

[18] Temple, 533.

[19] *Ibid.*, 256.

[20] *Ibid.*, 533.

[21] *MS Emes, Jesse.*

[22] Temple, 275.

company of twenty-four men from Framingham who marched to Concord and Cambridge,[23] and served ten days.[24] From December 1, 1775, to January 15, 1776, he served as a subaltern in Captain Simon Edgel's company of militia.[25] At the end of this period his name appears on a pay abstract for travel allowance, dated Roxbury, January 14, 1776,[26] which he doubtless used in returning home. His return may have been caused by the illness of his wife. In any event she died a month later, on February 14, 1776,[27] leaving Jesse with six motherless children: Ezra, aged seven, Timothy (1762–1846), Jesse, Jr. (1764–1793), Bette (1766–1778), Polly (1771–1776), and Sally (1773–1861).[28]

On February 23, 1776, nine days after the death of his wife, Jesse Emes was commissioned a first lieutenant.[29] Finally on March 27, 1776, he was commissioned a captain in command of the 6th Company of the 5th Middlesex County Regiment of Massachusetts Militia, under Colonel Samuel Bullard.[30] On December 22, 1776, his daughter Polly died.[31] On February 17, 1777, he resigned from the army,[32] and on April 8, 1777, he married his second wife, Dorotha (Dorothy) Brown of Sturbridge.[33]

Judging from birth dates in the vital records of Wayland, Massachusetts, the family appears to have moved about 1778 from Framingham to that part of Sudbury which became East Sudbury and after 1835 was called Wayland. Ezra's half sisters and half brother are recorded as born there: Bette the second (1778–1825), born two months before the death of Bette the first, but presumably christened later; Polly (or Polle) the second (1781–1829); and Henry (1783–1833).[34] The family seems to

[23] *Ibid.*, 279.
[24] *Mass. Soldiers*, V: 362.
[25] *Ibid.*, 363.
[26] *Ibid.*, 368.
[27] *Framingham V. R.*, 424.
[28] Sutliff, 32. In *MS Ames Family*, Timothy was "still living in 1848," but *Framingham V. R.*, 425, gives the year of death as 1846.
[29] *Mass. Soldiers*, V: 368.
[30] *Ibid.*, 362–3.
[31] Sutliff, 32.
[32] *Mass. Soldiers*, V: 363.
[33] *Framingham V. R.*, 229; cf. also Sutliff, 32, and *MS Ames Family*.
[34] *Wayland V. R.*, Introduction, 20–21, gives birth dates; Sutliff, 32, gives both birth and death dates.

have remained there until they moved to New York State in 1790, because Jesse "Eames" is listed as still living in East Sudbury Town in the first Federal Census of Massachusetts, 1790.[35]

The story is told of Captain Jesse and of a friend, Captain Isaac Russel of Sherborn, Massachusetts, that after Burgoyne's surrender and as they marched homeward through Staatsburg, New York, in charge of some prisoners, "they were so charmed with the country that they decided to remove to it after the war."[36] However, Burgoyne surrendered on October 17, 1777,[37] eight months after Captain Jesse resigned, and no record has been found to show that he rejoined the army.

A different reason for Captain Jesse's move to Staatsburg is given in the account by the anonymous compiler of the unpublished record of the Ames or Emes family. This authority states, darkly, that Captain Jesse removed with his family to Staatsburg "from some freak of obstinacy."[38]

As a matter of fact and for whatever reason, the two captains each bought property on the Hudson River near the village of Staatsburg just above Hyde Park. The transcripts of a mortgage and three deeds on file in the Office of the County Clerk of Dutchess County, Poughkeepsie, New York, are the sources for the history of their land investments.[39] Their property was part of the land once owned by Gertrude Coeymans, née Staats,[40] who sold it to Christian Bergh, from whom it passed to his son John Bergh, and then to Charles Shaw. On August 28, 1790, Charles Shaw and Nicholas Hoffman "of the City of New York Merchants," and Nicholas De Peyster and Miles Sherbrooke, "of the City of New York Gentlemen," sold 65 acres of this property as Lot 1, and 130 acres as Lot 2, to Jesse Emes "of the County of Dutchess, Farmer," for 500 pounds. Then, on April 20, 1791, Charles Shaw and "three others" sold to Isaac Russel, 162 acres of property adjoining that of Jesse Emes for 325 pounds.[41]

[35] U. S. Dept. Comm. & Labor, *Census, 1790, Mass.*, 141.

[36] Smith, 236.

[37] Adams, I, 256.

[38] *MS Ames Family.*

[39] *MS Dutchess County.*

[40] Smith, 234.

[41] *MS Dutchess County.*

EZRA AMES, MINIATURE SELF-PORTRAITS ON IVORY

Left, *c.* 1790 Right, *c.* 1800

Owned by Miss Elizabeth S. Edwards, Ames's great-granddaughter (Photographed by Irwin F. Cortelyou)

On the property of Jesse Emes there was a stone house which had been built by Christian Bergh in 1771.[42] It is not certain just how soon after his purchase of the property on August 28, 1790, Captain Jesse moved his family into this house at Staatsburg. The family was certainly well established there by August 21, 1791, when his daughter Sally, Ezra's sister, was married to Ezekiel Mulford,[43] the youngest son of Captain David Mulford, a neighbor in Staatsburg.[44]

So far no record has been found to show that Ezra Ames accompanied the family on its move to Staatsburg. The earliest established date in the artist's chronology, aside from that of his birth, is May 1790, when he was working as a painter of all sorts at Worcester. He possibly did not see his family at Staatsburg until 1793. The chronicle of the intervening three years, based largely on the artist's Account Book for this period, is the subject of the next chapter.

[42] Smith, 236.
[43] Sutliff, 20.
[44] *Ibid.*, 31.

II

YOUNG MANHOOD, 1790–1793:

WORCESTER, POUGHKEEPSIE, NEW YORK, ALBANY

WORCESTER, Massachusetts, was the scene, and 1790 was the time, of the artist's earliest recorded activity. This record is found in the first of the artist's three Account Books which together cover, intermittently, the period from 1790 through 1834.* These books and sixteen small Expense Books which cover the period, also intermittently, from 1799 through 1826, constitute the chief sources for his chronology. As records of his work, the Account Books are not complete, for in them the artist does not list a large number of portraits he is known to have painted during the period they cover. Because of these omissions it seems evident that he did not record any work for which he received immediate payment. But he was eventually paid by nearly all his patrons, for he indicates payments received on all but a few of his entries.

On the front wrapper of the earliest Account Book which covers, in unchronological fashion, the period from May 1790 through July 8, 1797, and includes several entries for 1800 and 1802, the artist has inscribed the name of the town "East Sudbury." However, the names of all but two of the first nine patrons listed (the second and seventh) appear in the first Federal Census of 1790 as residents of Worcester Town. The second patron, a "Mr. Buckminster," may be either the Thomas or Lawson Buckminster included under Framingham Town which adjoined East Sudbury Town. The name of the seventh patron, entered as "Seymore," does not appear in the census list for any of these three towns.[1] It seems highly probable that the artist first recorded his craft and artistic work only after he moved to or obtained his first jobs in Worcester.

* For a full description of the Account Books, with a transcript of the entries which refer to paintings, see pp. 147–190.

[1] U. S. Dept. Comm. & Labor, *Census, 1790, Mass.*, 141, 244, 245.

Ames records his first patron under May, 1790, in which month he celebrated his 22d birthday. He notes that for painting Esquire Allen's chaise payment was due him from Joseph Torrey, who was presumably Esquire Allen's agent. Under July and October he notes that Mr. Buckminster owed him for painting three chaises, one of them a "common" chaise. Then the artist records the indebtedness to him of a well-known citizen of Worcester, Stephen Salisbury, who came to Worcester in 1767, built a mansion there in 1772, and a store in 1790—structures still standing on the block bounded by Highland, Lancaster, and Harvard Streets.[2] It is doubtless to one of these that Ames refers in his entry, dated December 4, 1790: "D[ebto]r Step Salisbury To painting a chimney piece / red Seader [cedar] paints & glue 0 6 0." He then notes the painting of a sleigh for Abner Child at 12 shillings; next a sign ordered by Daniel Waldo for which he was to receive a pound and 2 shillings; and then again the painting of a sleigh, this time for Elias Mann.

Under the same date, December 4, 1790, Ames enters his first record as an artist, noting the payments due him on four miniatures, for three of which he charged 18 shillings each, and for one of which he charged a pound. The patrons for these works were the person named Seymore previously mentioned; "Theopelous Whealer," and Joseph Wheeler, both of Worcester; and an unidentified lady named Polly Dixon. There is no trace of these miniatures today.

On the other hand, there are two miniatures and a portrait in oil (by Ames of this period) which have been located but are not recorded in the Account Book. They are family portraits so that there was, obviously, no need to record them. One of them, a dim little miniature of an unidentified girl of the Ames family, is assumed to be the earliest because the least skillfully painted. The second miniature is a self-portrait thought to have been painted about 1790 because of the apparent age of the sitter and also because his costume is of that period. In this miniature, which resembles miniatures by Ramage, the artist represents himself

[2] Sawyer, 65–92.

with a brush poised in his hand before a canvas on an unseen easel to the right. Both of these small likenesses are owned by Miss Elizabeth Seelye Edwards, great-granddaughter of the artist. The oil portrait is a primitive painting, said by the family to represent Jesse Emes, father of the artist, once owned by Miss Mary L. Sutliff, great-grandniece of the artist, and presented to the Albany Institute of History and Art.

For the year 1791 the artist records in his Account Book the painting of only three miniatures, for at this period and, indeed, for years to come, he was far less occupied with portraiture than he was with miscellaneous craft work. One type of small work he mentions for the first time in an entry dated December 1791: "D[ebto]^rs Engine company [of Worcester, Mass.] To painting twelve buckets a[t] - 1/4 - is - 0:16:0." Besides painting fire buckets for the town, Ames also mentions the painting for individuals of a few fire buckets which he sometimes "lettered." He may have painted and lettered many more than he recorded, for practically everyone in town was provided with a fire bucket. According to a reference reprinted in the *Albany Chronicles* one learns that at Albany in 1793, the year Ames was to settle in that city, "each house [was] required to hang three buckets in its hallway and attend fires."[3] Conditions were presumably similar in Worcester during 1791.

Ames recorded numerous other types of work for 1791. The decipherable part of the record for that year appears to be: the painting of thirteen signs, three stands of colors, two sleighs, four chaises, three clockfaces, two fences, a sun blind, a looking glass, and a chimney back; the painting and papering of two rooms, and the varnishing of four bedposts, as well as the painting of a floor, a door, a carpet, a wagon, a chest of drawers, two "cherubs," the alphabet, and some flowerpots. He also records "Days Labour" for Benjamin Willard, Nathaniel Patch, and others at five shillings per day.

Ames apparently spent the entire year of 1792 at Worcester, except for three horseback trips which he noted in an Expense

[3] Reynolds, 382.

Book. One of his trips was to Leicester, another was to Lancaster, while the third was to a town the name of which is indecipherable. In his Account Book the artist records payments due him, during 1792, for three miniatures at his customary price of 18 shillings each; and for a "portrait" priced at "1:10:0" which he charged to a Mr. Draper. If by writing the word "portrait" for the first time, instead of the word "miniature," the artist meant to distinguish between a likeness on canvas and one on ivory, then this would be the first portrait in oil recorded by him. That the portrait was *for* Mr. Draper does not necessarily mean that the portrait was *of* Mr. Draper, though it may well have been.

In the same Account Book, and dated "September ye 20 1792," the artist records: "D[ebto]r Thomas Sheppard To painting a Landscape & cyphers on the back and Sides of a chaise—3/." The entry is interesting because it is one of the few references to the painting of landscapes found in the artist's memoranda. A partial list of Ames's other miscellaneous work during the year 1792 includes the painting of signs, stands of colors, window shades, drums, clockfaces, chaises, a piece of hair work, a penknife, the numbering of a meetinghouse pew; and the gilding of a "blaze"—the flame-shaped ornament on top of a banner staff[4]—for "Captain Edgeall," who was possibly the Captain Simon Edgel under whom Ames's father had served during the Revolution.[5]

In the same year the young artist received a delightful and friendly letter from his sister Sally who, it may be recalled, had married Ezekiel Mulford at Staatsburg the year before. The letter, dated August 25, 1792, Clinton, New York, is addressed to "Mr. Ezra Eames in Worcester," whom she entitles "the painter." In it the nineteen-year-old girl complains of poor health due to her "foolishness in trying to please her," doubtless their

[4] Information supplied by Mrs. Katharine M. McClinton. An Account Book entry, dated 1797, is interesting because it itemizes the component parts of a "stand of colours," including the blaze:

Dereck [Dirck] Ten Broeck Dr	
To painting a Stand of Colours	2:16
To—Silk—for Do	1:16
To—fringe	10:6
To—Brass Blaze & ferril [ferrule]	12
To—Staff	5
To—Case	4
	£ 6: 3:6

[5] *Mass. Soldiers*, V: 368.

stepmother, who, she confides, "now Despises me and treats me with Disdane because I got married and left her to[o] Soon to her mind." Both Sally and her husband wish that the artist would make his home at their "house this winter."[6]

Ames did not accept the invitation. He remained, instead, at Worcester, at least until January 17, 1793, for on that day he records the last and only work done at Worcester that year for which payment was due him:

Mr Stephen Harris D^r^	
To Painting his Miniature	18/
and a piece of heir work	6
	1.4.0

After this he records no payments due until July 5, 1793, the date of his first entry made at Albany. Because of this blank period, and also because of an advertisement which Ames inserted in the Albany newspapers on August 1, 1793, a journey, recorded in an undated list of expenses more detailed than any other in the artist's Account Books, may be assigned to this year. The trip took him to Poughkeepsie, where he is known to have been in April of that year, then to New York, and at last to Albany. The journey was a momentous one in the artist's life: he left Massachusetts and, at the age of twenty-five, settled permanently in New York State.

Although he does not specify when he went or how long he stayed, his whereabouts he states precisely. The first section of his itinerary reads:

my trunk from the warf up town	1/
for wood	8/
To Shoes	13/
Linine for Maj^{r} Lives^{n}	30/6
Honey for Seize [sizing]	/9
1 point of Oyl	1/
making ye Linen for Lik^{n}	1/
To making ye frames for Mj^{r} L	5/
Board & washing a fortknight	18/

[6] *MS Ames & Others,* No. 1, August 25, 1792.

from poughkeepsie to Maj[r] Livingstons	2/
En—at vandue	2/
To picture frame	1/6
To Linen ¾ y[d]	2/6
For Maj[r] L. Pictures to y[e] warf	1/6
Board a[t] poughkeepsie	12/

One may infer from this record that, embarking from some still-unidentified riverside town, possibly Staatsburg, Ames took a voyage along the Hudson—in a sloop, during those days before the advent of steamboats; got off at Poughkeepsie, where he remained about a month; and, while there, painted some "pictures" for a certain Major Livingston. This patron might have been Major Henry Livingston, Jr. (1748–1828), whose home called "Locust Grove" was about two miles south of Poughkeepsie Courthouse. The "pictures," now unlocated, were possibly companion portraits of the Major and his second wife-to-be, whom he married in September of that year.[7]

During his sojourn at Poughkeepsie Ames visited a Masonic Lodge. This, the earliest reference to the artist's Masonic activity, one finds in the long and distinguished record of his membership in that fraternal society which has been assembled by Mr. E. T. Reid. The reference reads: "The lodge that made Ezra Ames a Mason can indeed be proud. But long and patient research has so far failed to bring to light the place and the lodge that made him a Mason. We are confident, however, that he was made [a Mason] between 1789 and 1793 because on April 1, 1793, he is recorded in the Minute book, still preserved, as a visitor to the famous old Solomon's Lodge No. 1 of Poughkeepsie, N. Y."[8]

Having finished his painting at Poughkeepsie, Ames boarded a sloop, taking with him the Livingston "pictures," and sailed for New York. His expenses he records as follows:

Passage to N York	10/	Tuseday noon
Maj[r] L. Pictures freight	6/	
Heir dressings	1/	
Oyl turpintine	1/	
To the theatre	6/	

[7] Thomas, 32, 37, 45, 42.

[8] Reid, 11.

freitage from the warf to my lodgings	1/
heir pow[d]er	1/
Book of knowledge	1/3 [?]
to the Museum	/6
passage to L. Isleand	/6
For Board	1– 4–0
To Washing	0– 2–
To Mattrass bed	0–17–
To Blanket	0– 7–6
To quire of paper	0– 2–
Jug of gin	0– 3–6

From this list of expenses one is able to trace the continuation of the artist's odyssey: disembarking at New York, he paid freight on the Livingston "pictures" and rented lodgings which he furnished with a bed, mattress, and blanket. After he had his hair dressed, he attended the theater, and one may imagine that he went there on the first night of this, presumably his first, visit to the big city. During his sojourn he also visited a museum, and likewise treated himself to a six-penny ferry voyage to Long Island.

One might infer, since he bought a Book of Knowledge, that he began a homestudy course at this time. However, the volume was probably nothing weightier than a small pamphlet by Abraham Weatherwise entitled: *The Book of Knowledge: or, Wheel of Fortune. Shewing The Signification of Moles, and the Interpretation of Dreams. The various and wonderful operations of the Signs & Planets on the Human Body. The Art of Physiognomy & Palmistry.—The Wheel of Fortune, and several Solutions in matters of Love.* The great public need for guidance on these subjects is revealed by the fact that a copy of the book at The New-York Historical Society, dated 1806, is the fifty-fifth edition of the work. Possibly the section on the reading of character by the location of moles on the body led Ames to portray so painstakingly these blemishes on the faces of his sitters.

In view of the fact that Ames was beginning his career as a portrait painter, it is interesting to speculate as to the possibility of his seeing the portraits of Gilbert Stuart. That celebrated painter had but recently arrived in the city from Ireland, and although one objective of his return to this country was to paint a portrait of George Washington, so rushed was he with orders to paint the prominent citizens of New York that he remained more than a year in that city before he finally left for Philadelphia where he painted Washington's portrait. William Dunlap who visited Stuart's studio at this time writes of it as a fashionable gathering place. He states that in New York, Stuart "opened an attelier in Stone-street near William-street, where all who admired the art or wished to avail themselves of the artist's talents, daily resorted."[9] Although there is no proof, one cannot help wondering: was Ames among those who "admired the art" of portrait painting and who "daily resorted" to the pictorial reception room of Gilbert Stuart?

How long Ames remained in New York City cannot be reckoned precisely. His expense account for board indicates a stay of about a month. After whatever period of time it was, he sailed for Albany. His own undated record reads: "Passage from N. York to Albany," then "passage from Albany to Staats[burg]," and at last "Passage back again." It was doubtless to Albany that Ames returned because, as it has been previously stated, the undated entries relating to his voyage down and up the Hudson fit into his Account Book only during the otherwise unaccounted for time-period between January 17, 1793, Worcester, and July 5, 1793, Albany.

The next reference to the artist in point of time is August 1, 1793, Albany, when Ames inserted an advertisement in the newspapers announcing his advent in that community as an artist and craftsman. In the advertisement, which will presently be quoted in full, the artist enumerated his abilities first as an artist, and then, in detail, as a craftsman. He obviously foresaw a greater demand for his abilities as a craftsman than as a portrait painter. With this public bid for patronage Ezra Ames began life anew at Albany.

[9] Dunlap (1834), II: 229–30.

VIEW OF NEW YORK, AUGUST 20, 1793

Hand-colored print, "Arch^{d} Robertson, fecit," 1793

Owned by The New-York Historical Society

THE ALBANY OF EZRA AMES

View of State Street in 1805, by James Eights (1798–1882)

Courtesy of the Albany Institute of History and Art

THE FONDEY FAMILY

By Ezra Ames, signed and dated, 1803

Owned by Dr. Charles K. Winne, Jr., on permanent loan at the Albany Institute of Hisory and Art

III

FIRST DECADE AT ALBANY, 1793–1803:

CRAFT WORK, PORTRAIT PAINTING, MARRIAGE, MASONIC ACTIVITY

WHY DID Ames select Albany as a place in which to settle rather than New York City? Although his motives are not known, one may imagine that he considered Albany an expanding commercial center which would afford more opportunities for his employment, and less competition, than he would find in New York City. The Census of 1790 shows 30,148 free persons and 2,180 slaves in New York City. The directories for 1790 and 1794 show an increase in the number of "householders, persons occupying stores, shops &c," from 4,500 to 9,000,[1] and the city was still the capital of the State.[2]

But Albany was also expanding rapidly. In 1789, four years before Ames arrived there, Albany was a hamlet of about 600 houses "built mostly by trading people on the margin of the river."[3] In 1784 the post office had only just been established.[4] There was no theater until 1785.[5] The streets were not lighted until 1795.[6] Nevertheless, after exploring the navigable rivers, Elkanah Watson, the banker and philanthropist who later became one of Ames's patrons, forecast correctly "that Albany is one of the most favorable positions in America for the future enjoyment of a vast internal commerce."[7]

The passage of the Canal Act in 1792[8] foreshadowed the expansion of Albany as a transportation center; and the establishment of the Bank of Albany in the same year was an indication of the increasing financial prosperity of the citizens. One learns from a contemporary notice that: "Subscription books for the proposed Albany Bank opened at the City Tavern, with deposits of $15 per share, which are over-run in less than three hours."

[1] Scott, *U. S. Gazeteer.*
[2] Adams, IV: 118.
[3] Munsell, I (1850): 314.
[4] Reynolds, 363.
[5] *Ibid*, 365.
[6] *Ibid*, 386.
[7] Watson, 318.
[8] *N. Y. State Laws, 1792*, II: Chapter 40, p. 427.

Of the first directors appointed, Stephen Van Rensselaer, John Maley, James Caldwell, and John Stevenson,[9] became patrons of Ames. The incorporation of another institution in 1792 was the result of a meeting the year before of citizens who each subscribed $25 for the establishment of the Albany Library.[10] Of the trustees, James Van Ingen, treasurer and first librarian, Stephen Van Rensselaer, James Fairlie, and Hunloke Woodruff,[11] were among those who became the artist's patrons.

The next year on February 11, 1793, a constitution was adopted for The Albany Mechanics' Society,[12] of which Ames later became an incorporator and member. Then, also in 1793, The Society for the Promotion of Agriculture, Arts and Manufactures was incorporated.[13] This Society, founded in New York City, moved to Albany in 1800[14] where, in 1804, it was reincorporated as The Society for the Promotion of Useful Arts.[15] Combining with two other organizations in 1900, the Society became the Albany Institute and Historical and Art Society. The name was shortened in 1926 to the Albany Institute of History and Art,[16] which is the present title. In the building of this institution there are today over thirty works of art by Ezra Ames—the largest collection of his pictures so far assembled.

It was, therefore, at a propitious time in the history of Albany that Ames selected this city as a desirable place in which to make his way in the world. He arrived there on, if not before, July 5, 1793, the date alluded to heretofore as the first recorded in his Account Book under the heading of Albany. But this entry and the one which follows are not records of work, but records of the sales of some of the artist's personal belongings. In the entry of July 5th, he charged a Mr. Tiffeny 12 shillings for a pair of "paist kneebukles"; and in the entry of July 9th, he charged the same person 4 shillings for a "Shaving Box." A little later he was to sell more of his small possessions.

[9] *N. Y. State Laws, 1792,* II: Chapter 61, p. 468. Reynolds., 381.

[10] Reynolds., 380.

[11] *N. Y. State Laws, 1792,* II: Chapter 13, p. 391.

[12] Munsell, VII (1856): 240.

[13] *N. Y. State Laws, 1793,* III: Chapter 59, p. 38–39.

[14] Hatch, *Albany Institute,* 316.

[15] *N. Y. State Laws, 1804,* III: Chapter 41, p. 604.

[16] Hatch, *Albany Institute,* 325.

He was obviously low in funds. To remedy this condition he lost no time in calling the attention of the citizens to his abilities. He inserted an advertisement in the Albany newspapers for August 1, 1793:

> In Mark Lane, just below Bloodgood & Follet's store. *Painting.*—Portrait and Sign Painting, Gilding and Limning. The subscriber solicits the patronage of the admirers of the Fine Arts of Painting, Portraits, Miniatures, and Hair Devices. From the encouragement he has already received, he flatters himself of giving general satisfaction. Those who are not satisfied with his performances will not be compelled to have the work when it is finished. Gentlemen and ladies will be waited upon in any part of the city. Signs, Coaches, Chaises, Sleighs, Standards, &c., painted in the best manner. Orders from the country will be received and attended to—and all favors gratefully acknowledged by their humble servant,
>
> EZRA AMES[17]

If one may judge by the artist's Account Book record alone, no "admirers of the Fine Arts" in Albany responded to this ingratiating bid for patronage. That may be why, on September 14th, he sold his penknife with "two blades" for 4 shillings to the Mr. Tiffeny who had already bought the knee buckles and shaving box; and, on September 18th, sacrificed "one Neckless" for 12 shillings and his "Best penknife" for 8 shillings, to a Mr. Quackenbush. He does not record any oil portraits or miniatures until the following year; and, further, there were but few listed patrons who employed him either as a journeyman-painter or a craftsman. Beginning with the next year, however, the tide turned in his favor.

The amount of miscellaneous work for which Ames recorded payment due him during 1794 was quite as large and as surprisingly varied as it was at Worcester during 1791 and 1792. His record includes: the painting of twelve signs, six sleighs, seven buckets, a signboard, a table, a water tub, two chests, some chair curtains, a stand of colors, three window cornices, a bread trough, a tea cannister and chest, and a Masonic apron; the varnishing of six chair bodies, a sulkey, and four timepiece cases; the gilding of a looking-glass frame, a picture frame, and three clock balls; the

[17] Munsell, III (1852): 157–158.

papering of a room (for 8 shillings); and the lettering of some oyster kegs.

As for his portraiture during 1794, he boldly doubled his prices. That they were not deemed excessive is revealed by his record from January through May, 1794. During these months he was called upon to paint a dozen miniatures at 2 pounds each, and two portraits, one of which was undoubtedly in oil because his charge for it was 4 pounds, or twice as much as that for a miniature. To estimate his success as an artist at this time in comparison with his former output and financial return, so far as these are revealed by his own records, it may be pointed out that within the first five months of the year 1794 at Albany the artist had painted as many miniatures at an advanced price as he had painted, all told, during the previous years, from 1790 to 1793, in Worcester; and that for a portrait in oil for a Mr. Glen he had received more than double his former price.

Of the miniatures he recorded in 1794, two were of very prominent citizens. These miniatures, now unlocated, were of "Mrs. [George] Clinton" and of "his Excel[l]ency," George Clinton, then Governor of the State.[18] This is the first record of work for the Clinton family of whose members Ames was to paint so many portraits. Other miniatures of the same year were for Dr. D. Treat, John Hayke, John Hooker, Mr. Spalding, M. Dewett, and Levi Willard. Mrs. Ya[tes] and Miss Cornelia Yates each ordered two. Ames also listed a portrait for Thomas Diamond and the "Painting & finishing the Drapery of Maj^r Fairleys Portrait" for Mrs. Fairley.

During the same year the artist recorded his expenses for making five trips. On April 1, 1794, he went to Staatsburg, obviously to see his family; on April 13th, he went to Pittstown, New York, presumably to visit his sister Sally who had recently settled there;[19] on May 4th, he visited Troy; on May 24th, he went to "Sohoes"—meaning Cohoes, a town near Albany; and later in the year he made an extended trip to Massachusetts. The reason for this trip to Massachusetts is indicated in an entry dated March

[18] *DAB*, IV: 227.

[19] Sutliff, 21

6, 1794: "For a locket Miss Z. Wd." This locket, which cost him a pound, was destined for the young woman who was soon to become his wife. After a visit to Boston, in September, he went to Northbridge; and there, on October 6, 1794, he married Zipporah Wood, who had been born at Uxbridge, Massachusetts, April 5, 1775, and was to die at Albany, April 8, 1836, a month and a half after her husband. She was the daughter of Josiah Wood (1732–1815) of Upton, Massachusetts, and Zipporah (Wheelock) Wood, of Mendon, Massachusetts; and the granddaughter of Jonathan and Margaret (Thayer) Wood.[20] Soon after the wedding, Ames and his wife went to Albany to live.

They must have arrived some time before October 25, 1794, because on that day Ames wrote a long letter from Albany to his friend Dr. Hiram Walker of Staatsburg. The letter contains more about its author's state of mind than about his state of affairs. Having announced the fact of his marriage, Ames writes: "I have lately been in New England, where I spent about Four weeks with my friends," among them a Mr. and Mrs. Rice who "send their best regards to you." He reminds his friend Hiram that "you are indebted to me for a letter" but excuses the young doctor because "I am informed that you are in pursuit of a Dulceinea"—a "Laudible" activity which would naturally "engage all your leisure moments." Then, in an outburst of confidence, he gives a humorous account of his own experiences in search of a wife. Writing as if his experiences were Homeric voyages of discovery, he uses such obscure figures of speech that it is often as difficult to chart his course as it would be to trace the precise dimensions of a cloud. The following summary, with quotations taken from the letter, is an attempt to follow him on his metaphorical sea-faring.

During the first of three voyages, and while "Coasting on the Seas of love," Ezra "had Several views of the Land" which were fair to see. But the "rocks of phrenzy" were so "numrous" that he decided not to attempt a landing, consoling himself with the thought that it was difficult for even "the best pilot to escape

[20] *MS Ames Family.*

the whirlpools of passion." He therefore prudently rested on the "Sea of diliberation for Several days." This spirit of procrastination apparently incensed the lady, because the artist then writes that "the wind Shifted to an unfavorable Quarter and Blew up a terible Storme" from which he was rescued only by the kind "hand of providence." Shaken but undismayed he soon "renewed" his "Corrage," set sail on his second voyage, and sighted land for a second time, but a land so dreadful that, deterred by the "horrows of the place," he did not even attempt a landing.

Notwithstanding these disastrous experiences the artist writes: "I could not bear the tho^{t} of being an Old Batchelor, nor that of being an henpek[ed] Husband.—Those Ideas was So near[ly] balanced in the Scale of reason than one Ten Thousandth part of a grain would have turned the Scale. However, finding myself unhappy in my present Sittuation, I determined to make myself happy, or Compleat my misery."

He therefore set sail on his third voyage, sighted land, and this time attempted and made a successful landing. He concludes his letter with a comparison between the third discovery and the other two: "I soon came in sight of land which appeared agreeably diversified with hills and vallies, though not so ravishing as at first, nor miserably wreathed as the Second discovery.—I was determined to land at all events, which [I] effected without much difficulty. What I have discovered Since I have been there will remain forever concield with me.—All I shall Say upon the Subject is! that I am happy at present, and have no desire to return to the Land of Celibacy."[21]

A year after the writing of this letter, sometime in 1795, a child was born to the Ames couple. The child, named Lucretia, died in infancy.[22] In the meanwhile, Ames had transferred his Masonic interests to his adopted community, and started on his distinguished career in Masonry.

Concerning the beginnings of the artist's rise to prominence as a Freemason in Albany, Mr. E. T. Reid writes that Ames "was

[21] *MS Ames and Others,* No. 1, October 25, 1794.

[22] *MS Ames Family.*

admitted a member on December 30, 1794, of Union Lodge No. 1, now Mt. Vernon Lodge No. 3. He withdrew from this lodge on November 17, 1795, apparently for the purpose of helping to found Temple Lodge No. 53 (now No. 14) of which he was a Charter member. This lodge was duly organized in 1796. The petition for this lodge was endorsed by Masters Lodge No. 2 (now No. 5)."

The next year he took the first of the degrees which led him at last to one of the most exalted positions in Freemasonry. "Now for the first time," Mr. E. T. Reid writes, "we can state positively where and when he received a degree of Masonry. From the minute book of the Temple Chapter No. 5, of Albany, N. Y., we find that he was received and acknowledged a Most Excellent Master on February 14, 1797. After the Lodge of Most Excellent Masters was closed, a Chapter was opened and he was exalted a Royal Arch Mason on the same day. Immediately he became active in the Royal Arch and served Temple Chapter as Principal Sojourner in 1797."[23]

The artist's admission into Union Lodge in 1794 marks the beginning of what became his extensive employment (which was to reach its peak in 1800) as a painter of Masonic regalia and engraver of Masonic medals and certificates. Just two days after his induction, Ames specifies the following Masonic work in his Account Book: "Capt Moullen D[ebto]^{r} January ye 1—1795 To painting a Carpet for Pittstown Lodge—:7:4." The record of his other miscellaneous work for the year 1795 is small and contains no unusual items.

On the other hand, his record of miscellaneous work for the years 1796–1797 is large and varied. Besides the painting of five Masonic aprons, the engraving of two Masonic certificates (at 36 shillings), and entries for other usual types of his craft work, one finds in his Account Book the mention of such unfamiliar employments as "paintin Sunders hear devices," one of them for a ring (at 3 shillings); the painting of a few "mourning pieces" (at 24 shillings each), a fanlight, a watering pot, and a trumpet; the

[23] Reid, 11.

lettering of a "border for a rug"; the making, painting, and gilding of a tin chandelier; and the lettering of a sloop for which he charged a Mr. Guest 3 shillings. In contrast, his recorded art work for the years 1795–1797 includes the painting of only five

ELIHU PHINNEY (1756–1813)

By Ezra Ames, 1799
(Dated by Ames's NYHS Account Book)

Owned by Mrs. Alexander S. Phinney

miniatures: one each for Francis Follet, Mrs. Samuel Hawkins, Hezekiah Sharliff, James Rogers, and a miniature and hair work as well as a portrait, presumably in oil, for a Mr. Ellis—all unlocated.

During these years one finds numerous entries in his Account Book showing that to increase his income he sold artists' materials, picture frames, pictures, and prints. The picture frames he apparently either made himself and gilded, or bought ready-made for gilding. As for the many "pictures" and "mezzitints prints" which he recorded, these he sold at so low a price that one may surmise that they were not his original work but rather prints which, since there are no known prints by Ames, were the work of other men. Thus in an entry dated May 19, 1796, Ames records the sale of "2 pictures Solomon's Temple & City Jerusalem" for a pound and 12 shillings to William James.

William James (1771–1832), the debtor for these pictures, was an Irishman who arrived at Albany in 1793, the same year that Ames moved there; established himself as a merchant; and in time, became the second-wealthiest man in the State, the first being John Jacob Astor.[24] That James was a friend as well as a customer of Ames is indicated by an entry appearing in the Account Book on the day following James's purchase of the two prints. On May 20, 1796, the artist, coupling his name with that of the merchant apparently because the rhyme pleased him, notes that "Mr James to Ezra Ames" is debtor to the amount of 8 shillings for Ames's "Painting a Sign," and to a similar amount for "lettering his Store."

Years later a son of William James was to marry the daughter of Ezra Ames. The daughter, and second child born to the Ames couple, named Marcia Lucretia, was born in 1798 and died in 1886, according to the gravestone in the James family plot at the Albany Rural Cemetery. Mrs. Russel Hastings, in her monograph on the James family, gives Marcia's birth date as "August 2, 1797, about"; and the date of her death as March 2, 1886. In 1824 Marcia Lucretia Ames married the Reverend William James (1797–1868),[25] a twin son of the elder William by his first wife.[26] It is interesting to note, in passing, that Henry James (1811–1882), the son of William James the elder (1771–1832) by his third wife,[27] was to become the father of Henry James the novelist and of William James the philosopher.[28]

[24] Matthiessen, 4.
[25] Hastings, 108.
[26] *Ibid.*, 104.
[27] *Ibid.*, 106.
[28] *Ibid.*, 112–113.

During the years of 1798–1800 Ames made a number of entries in his second Account Book recording his work for his fellow Masons. Thus, on May 12, 1798, he charged Thomas Smith Webb, " who is supposed to be the father of American Rite in Masonry,"[29] $1.50 for "painting and varnishing a harpsichord." Other references to Ames's work for his Masonic brethren during these years are:

[May 20, 1798]	M[r] John Eames of Whitestown D[ebto][r]	
	To 1 Masonic Sattan apron R A	$ 4
May 20, 1798	To engraving a M[ar][k] Meddel	$ 2
Dec 23 [1799]	Elihu Phinney Esq[r][30] D[ebto][r]	
	To Painting his portrait	$15
	To a Frame for d[itt]o— & box	2
May 3, [1800]	Elijah H. Metcalf 1—medal Gi[lt] Otsego M[aste][r] M[ar][k] Lodge N° 5	
[June] 17, [1800]	Doc[t] [Jonathan] Eights D[ebto][r]	
	To a Masonic apron	14/
[June] 27, [1800]	To Gilt Masonic Meddel	1:16

During the year 1798, Ames also recorded the painting and gilding of two sloop heads, one at a price which he omitted to mention, for a Captain Height, and the other for a Captain Donneley, for which he charged $3.50; and the painting of a still-unidentified miniature for John M. Dole.

A large amount of engraving was recorded by Ames during 1798–1800 for a Mr. J. Macauly who may have been the John Macauly listed in the earliest Albany Directories, 1813–1815, as an artist living at No. 1, Beaver Street. The work consisted of the ornamenting and engraving of "cyphers," probably meaning initials or monograms, on sixty or more spoons, about nine rings, three pairs of sugar tongs, seven whips, a few sleeve buttons and clasps, a snuffbox, a watch key, a needle case, and some Masonic jewels. He also did similar work for S[ilas W.] Howell.[30a]

During this time Ames was also employed by N. B. Bassett, who is listed as a watchmaker in the Albany Directory for 1815.

[29] Reid, 10.

[30] Elihu Phinney was First Master, Otsego Lodge, Cooperstown.—*Idem.* The portrait of Elihu Phinney reproduced here, from a photograph furnished by Miss Janet R. MacFarlane, is doubtless the portrait mentioned in the entry.

[30a] Expense Book for 1799–1800.

For him, in entries extending from March 1799 through January 1800, Ames recorded the ornamenting of two clockfaces, the painting of two others, and the lettering of another two; the engraving of about sixty spoons, and a few sleeve buttons and clasps. By 1802, N. B. Bassett had become partner in the firm of Bassett and Warford, and for this partnership Ames lettered three clockfaces, at 2 shillings each, during that year.

Unusual items in his repertoire during 1798–1800 were the painting of a chequerboard, the engraving of a brass knocker, the "gilding a Cross & letters I H S," and the "Shadeing of a weather vain." Of his usual items during the same period, he painted about thirty signs, ranging in price from 50 cents to $15. Thereafter he was less and less occupied as a craftsman and job painter.

During 1799–1801 he also added to his income by renting one of his rooms and taking in boarders. Under the date of January 21, 1799, he noted in the earliest of his Expense Books that he charged "M^ssrs^ Warner & Forbs," $18.50 for a bed, a bedstead, and table. Mr. Warner stayed for a short time only; but Mr. Forbs, except during the summer months, remained several years. He paid an average rate of $14 a month until a certain "Mr Ennis came to board," on March 1, 1800, when Mr. Forbs's rent dropped to $9, Mr. Ennis paying $10 a month, possibly because the two men shared a room. Although Mr. Ennis left after a five-months stay, he is heard of once more when he presented an account to Ames on January 29, 1801, for "monies" belonging to their Masonic Chapter paid him by Brothers Crocker, Macauley (also spelled Macauly), Bunnel, and Penniman.[31] The less transient Mr. Forbs remained with the Ames family into 1801.

The artist's shop and presumably his studio during the first half-dozen years of his residence in Albany were on Mark Lane. In *The Albany Register*, of November 25, November 29, and December 10, 1799, he announced his removal from Mark Lane to Washington Street, in an advertisement which reads as follows:

[31] *MS Ames and Others,* No. II, January 29, 1801.

Painting and Engraving. The subscriber begs leave to inform his friends and the public, that he has removed his shop from Mark-Lane, to Washington-Street, at the sign of Raphael's bust, and solicits the patronage of the admirers of the fine arts.

The painting of Portraits, Miniatures, Hair Devices, Standards, &c. will be executed in the most elegant taste and style—also Freemasons aprons, sashes, and ornamental paintings in general, done in the best manner, and on the most reasonable terms.

Seals, M[ar]k. M[aste]r. Mason's Medals, &c. engraved neatly and elegantly.

Orders from the country will be punctually attended to: and all favours gratefully acknowledged, by the public's humble servant.

EZRA AMES

Albany, Nov. 25, 1799.

Some of his "hair devices" and "ornamental paintings" were possibly based on designs in a volume of plates entitled *New & Allegorical Devices for Artists in General & Particularly for Jewelers & Enamel Painters,* engraved by Garnet Terry, and issued in 1795. Ames's copy of this book is now at the Albany Institute.

As for his new address, it is not known if the house on Washington Street, marked by the "Sign of Raphael's Bust," into which Ames moved his shop in 1799, was number 41 Washington Street, listed as the address of Ezra Ames in the first Albany Directory, dated 1813.[32] On the other hand it is definitely known that 41 Washington Street was the same location as 41 South Pearl Street, listed as the address of Ezra Ames in the directory for 1814.[33] The number was the same. The name of the street had been changed during the year 1814.[34]

Although Ames probably did not own his place during this period of his early struggles, as time went on he became the owner not only of this but also of other property in the block. A chart, among the Ames papers at the Office of the Surrogate, Albany, shows the extent of his holdings. On the chart one can see that the Ames home stood on the west side of South Pearl (a street running parallel with and about four blocks from the

[32] *Albany Directory, 1813,* p. 9.

[33] *Albany Directory, 1814,* p. 14.

[34] *Ibid.,* 3.

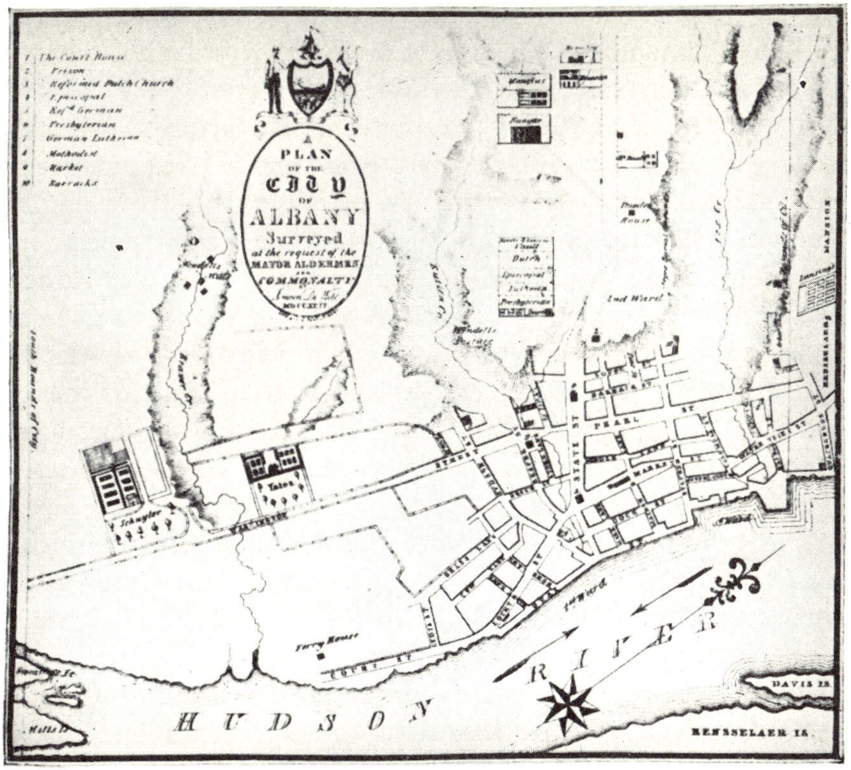

OFFICIAL ALBANY MAP OF 1794

Made by Surveyor Simeon De Witt in 1794

From *Albany Chronicles* (Albany: 1906), opp. page 384

Hudson River), and was midway between Hudson and Plain Streets. The rest of his property consisted of lots with houses, at least two of which he rented to tenants.[35] Looking at a map of Albany, engraved in 1794 after a survey by Simeon DeWitt,[36] one finds that the property which Ames was to acquire was situated on the same street as, and just north of, the Yates and Schuyler mansions.

In 1796 there were 1,093 houses in Albany,[37] five hundred of which had been built since 1789. By 1800 street lights, first installed in 1795, extended "at no spot further than half a mile back

[35] *MS Ames, Ezra, Estate*, No. I.

[36] Reynolds, map opp. 384.

[37] *Ibid.*, 355.

of the river, the rest of the land being unsettled upon."[38] The property on which the Ames house stood was just on the fringe of this lighted area.

During the year 1800, the first in his new quarters, Ames recorded the payments due him for the painting of Masonic aprons, signs, and looking-glass frames; the gilding and varnishing of picture frames; and the engraving of probably a name or an initial on a brass knocker, a pair of sugar tongs, a clasp, a clockface, a seal, several Masonic medals, a coffin plate, and spoons. He also noted a charge "To painting a Lion" which must have been a sizable beast, because the price was 5 pounds 4 shillings, which was more than he charged for a portrait. He does not record any portraits for this year, which, of course, is not proof that he painted none.

Reviewing the artist's output of paintings as recorded in his Account Books from the time of his arrival at Albany in 1793 through the year 1800, it will be found that he painted eighteen miniatures and four portraits, only one of which is located. Only in a few instances has the sitter's name been specifically given in the entries. It should be remembered, however, that the artist painted other portraits during the same period which he did not record in his Account Books.[39]

Two located but unrecorded paintings of this period are self-portraits. One is a bust portrait in oil, at the Albany Institute of History and Art, given by Miss Mary L. Sutliff. Not only is it well drawn and carefully painted, but there is also an attempt at characterization in the likeness. The likeness is that of a handsome young man who looks confidently yet pleasantly at the spectator. A miniature in the Edwards collection greatly resembles the oil portrait, and for this reason the writers have called it, too, a self-portrait. Both the miniature and the portrait in oil are assigned to about the year 1800.

Two personal references to the artist relate to the year 1800.

[38] *Ibid.*, 392.

[39] A complete record of the paintings of Ezra Ames as presently known will be given in the catalogue of his works to follow.

One is a record of the fact that the artist was in Framingham in this year. On the cover of an Expense Book the artist notes, briefly: "Framingham, June 7, 1800." There is no evidence to show why he went or how long he stayed.

The other reference is to the artist's Masonic activity. In 1800, Ames was elected High Priest of Temple Chapter. He was appointed Grand Visitor the same year, and again in 1801. At last, in 1802, for "his consistent, loyal and brilliant work in Royal Arch Masonry," he was "awarded" the high office of the Most Excellent Grand High Priest of the Grand Chapter of New York. To this exalted position he was reëlected annually until 1826,[40] when, after holding the office for twenty-four years, he declined the nomination.[41]

Another institutional connection of Ames's which brought work to his shop was The Albany Mechanics' Society, already mentioned as having been organized in 1793. When the Society was incorporated, Ames's name appeared on the first page of the Act of Incorporation which passed the State Legislature on March 6, 1801,[42] in response to a petition made by "Bernardus Evertson and others, Mechanics and Tradesmen of the city of Albany and its vicinity," associated "for the laudable purpose of protecting and supporting such of their brethren as by sickness or by accident may stand in need of assistance, and of relieving the widows and orphans of those who may die in indigent circumstances; and also of providing means of instruction for their children."[43] In a sketch of The Mechanics' Society, signed "E. W. S.," one learns that: "The Society as incorporated consisted of 64 members—comprising at the time the prominent leading mechanics and tradesmen of this city to which were subsequently added many others, and swelling the aggregate number of its members to 150."[44]

Although Ames's name appears on the front page of the Act of Incorporation, it does not appear in the pages of a possibly earlier

[40] Reid, 11.

[41] *Ibid.*, 13.

[42] *New York State Laws, 1801*, Chapter 15, p. 18–19.

[43] *MS Mechanics' Society;* also *New York State Freedom Train Document Book*, 53.

[44] Munsell, VII (1856): 241, 242.

document, the signed register of members of The Mechanics' Society. On the other hand, a number of Ames's patrons are listed in both records. One of these, Philip Hooker (1766–1836), who is specified as the second vice president of the Society in the Act of Incorporation,[45] was the most prominent architect in Albany,[46] although he modestly gives his occupation as "carpenter."[45] There are several references to Hooker in the artist's first Account Book, and also to Hooker and his partner in the second. Ames noted in an entry dated May 7, 1802, that the firm of "Hooker & pulman" [Putnam][47] owed him 4 pounds; and in another entry, dated June 24, 1802, he recorded a charge against the same firm of 10 shillings for some "composition moulding" which was possibly of plaster. Another patron and fellow member of The Mechanics' Society was Isaac Hutton (1767–1855), the first treasurer of the incorporated Society,[45] who was partner in the firm of Isaac & George Hutton, jewelers and silversmiths of Albany, whose silverware is treasured to this day.[48] In his first Account Book, Ames noted in an entry dated August 1, 1794, that for 8 shillings he gilded and varnished "4 timepiece cases" for Isaac Hutton. Other references to Isaac Hutton occur for the years 1794 and 1796; and a reference to the partnership of I. & G. Hutton is dated March 1801. Besides Hooker and Hutton, there are, on the register of the Society, the names of the following members whom Ames likewise recorded as among his patrons: William Fryer, painter and glazier; James Hodge, stone cutter, first vice president of the Society;[45] Ira Porter, tailor; and John W. Fryer, gold and silversmith,[49] who was the first secretary of the Society.[45]

But Ames did not have to depend entirely on orders from fraternal sources. In his second Account Book he noted in May 1801 that for 20 shillings he gilded the clock hands of the "D[utch] Church" of which he was later, and possibly then, a member;

[45] *N. Y. State Laws, 1801*, Chapter 15, 21.

[46] *DAB*, IX: 198.

[47] Reynolds, 357.

[48] Hatch, *Magazine Antiques*, January 1945, p. 32–35.

[49] *MS Mechanics Society*.

while in August he made two picture frames, with glass, at 10 shillings each for "His Excel[l]ency Geo–Clinton." Among the other jobs that the artist recorded for 1801 are about thirty pertaining to picture frames and framing; the gilding and lettering of five signs; the gilding of five clock balls; the varnishing of a phaeton body; and the painting and gilding of twelve window "cornishes" for Peter Gansevoort, Abraham Ten Eyck, Richard Allanson, and Sanders Lansing. He recorded no portraits for the year, but, again, this must not be taken as proof that he painted none.

During the early years of the century two sons were born to the Ames couple. In 1801 their third child, Julius Rubens, was born—on January 1st, according to the manuscript record of the "Ames or Emes Family,"[50] but on May 1st, according to the inscription on the monument in the family plot at the Albany Rural Cemetery. According to the inscription, he died on June 5, 1850. Both of these sources give his name as Julius R. Ames. The authority for his full name is the Library of Congress card recording the second edition of a pamphlet which he wrote, entitled *Liberty*, published in 1839 by the Anti-Slavery Society in New York. He became a miniature painter but never rose to more than local fame. Some of his miniatures are at the Albany Institute.

It is impossible to say exactly when Angelo, the younger son of the Ames couple, was born. The anonymous author of the manuscript account of the family, writing before Angelo's death, states that he was born on January 29, 1803.[50] A second source, a card at the Albany Rural Cemetery, states that he died on May 26, 1886, at the age of eighty-two years, two months, and twenty-seven days, which would establish his birth date as February 29, 1804.[51] A third source, the inscription on his gravestone, gives the same date for his death, May 26, 1886, as that recorded on the cemetery card, but it gives his age as eighty-one which would make his birthday fall some time during the year 1805. Curiously enough a search of the extensive collection of church

[50] *MS Ames Family.*

[51] Albany Cemetery Association card.

records of Albany, at the New York State Library, has failed to reveal the birth date of Angelo, or of any of the other children of Ezra Ames.

Returning to the year 1802, a few of the small jobs which he noted were: the painting of a sign for 12 shillings; the gilding and enameling of five picture frames, three at 36 shillings each and two for a total of 24 shillings; the gilding of a looking glass frame for 28 shillings; and the painting of a gig carriage with "Jappan varnish" for Mr. Kane for 1 pound, 8 shillings.

The artist also recorded the painting of a portrait with a frame on August 18, 1802, for Leonard Gansevoort. It is the first portrait recorded in the Account Books after 1799. At present the writers must leave open the question of identifying the entry with any of the extant portraits by or attributed to Ames of the two Leonard Gansevoorts, cousins, who were born within a few years of each other.[52]

The artist's Account Book for the year 1803, if kept, is lost. In his Expense Book for the year one learns that Ames visited New York in June. An important pictorial document which fits into his chronology at this time, is a group portrait of members of the Fondey family inscribed with the names of all the sitters, and signed and dated 1803, on loan at the Albany Institute of History and Art. A miniature on ivory of John Fondey, Jr., also at the Albany Institute, similar to that person's portrait in the group picture, may be attributed to Ames as of the same year.

The setting for the figures in the conversation piece of the Fondey family is a tiled and balustraded terrace. John Fondey, Jr., and his wife are seated on a sofa at the left, while surrounding them are four of their children, not to mention their dog; and before them stands their son Isaac, with upraised arm, delivering an oration for their benefit. It is a large, quaint, interesting work, but primitive in its composition and technique; and it in nowise foreshadows the skilled painting which Ames was to accomplish six years later.

[52] *Appletons' Cyclopaedia of American Biography*, II: 589–590.

LEONARD BLEECKER (1755–1844)

By Ezra Ames, *c.* 1805

Formerly owned by Ehrich Galleries

(Photo by courtesy of Mrs. William Sawitzky)

JOSEPH BRANT, THAYENDANEGEA (1742–1807)

By Ezra Ames, dated by a receipt, 1806

Owned by the New York State Historical Association

(Photo by FARL)

MRS. MATTHIAS BURNETT TALLMADGE (1780–1825)

By Ezra Ames, *c.* 1815

Owned by Yale University Art Gallery
Mabel Brady Garvan Collection

MATTHIAS BURNETT TALLMADGE (1774–1819)

By Ezra Ames, *c.* 1815

Owned by Yale University Art Gallery
Mabel Brady Garvan Collection

IV

RISE AS A PORTRAIT PAINTER, 1804–1812:

ALBANY, VISIT TO NEW ENGLAND, MASONIC ACTIVITIES

EARLY in the year 1804, Ezra Ames acquired a ledger-sized volume in which to keep his accounts; and in this, the third of his extant Account Books, he has left a record of work for which he had not been paid at the time of delivery, from May 4, 1804, through December 28, 1834. It is the chief source for tracing the chronology of the artist's later years.

In the first entry the artist charged James Hodge $2.50 for gilding a "Blaze for an Urn for Ye Bank." Other entries of 1804 for ornamental painting include one for a Masonic apron, two for stands of colors, and twelve for signs. The Account Book record of artistic work includes the painting of a miniature for James Hodge, and the painting of a portrait in oil for Mrs. McGourk, and the painting of another for Solomon Southwick. The artist also listed a portrait for Matthias B. Tallmadge. His portraits of Mr. and Mrs. Matthias B. Tallmadge, owned by Yale University and on loan at The English-Speaking Union, New York City, are considered, because of the technique and costume, as well as of the ages of the sitters, to have been painted later than 1804, so that neither could be the portrait referred to in the entry. The portrait painted for Southwick has been tentatively identified as the portrait of him at the Mechanics and Farmers' Bank of Albany.

Some unrecorded but extant portraits which have been assigned to this period are the unfinished group portrait of the artist's children, Marcia, Julius, and Angelo, in the Edwards collection; the portrait of the artist's sister, Sally Emes Mulford, owned by Miss Edith Sutliff Wade, a great-great-grandniece of the artist; and the portrait of John Kane. In the latter portrait there is more color-variety than is usual in the artist's early work. The cool blue of the coat collar and the green table corner are pleasantly contrasted with the warm light-yellow waistcoat and the patch of red on the arm of the chair. In assigning a date for these portraits, the apparent ages of the sitters has been the chief guide. It was an experimental period; and the artist was emerging from his primitive methods of painting, employing techniques too varied for reliance to be placed on any one of them as exclusively characteristic of any particular year.

Aside from the above-mentioned artistic and miscellaneous works, the artist also recorded in his Account Book for 1804 a "picture of the happy old Cople or Darby & Joan," which he sold on August 8th for $5. Twice during the following years he sold "pictures" of the same couple: one on July 18, 1806, for $5, and another on July 20, 1811, for $6. It is impossible to tell whether these were prints by some other artist, or paintings by Ames. His sign "Darby and Joan" which he recorded in 1817 was undoubtedly a painting, and perhaps based on a print.

In 1805 Ames made a two-months visit to New England. The bare record of this trip, entered in his third Expense Book, reads:

1805 July	
Horse & Chair	£ 50
hey 24/–Oats 6/	1–10
Shoeing horse 10/6	10–6
Bridle & halter 12/	12
16—July went to New England	
Returned 16 September	
Expenses to New England etc	£ 40–0–0

Two silhouettes, one of Ames and the other of his wife, may be mementos of this trip. They have always remained in the possession of members and descendants of the artist's family, and are now in the Edwards collection. They are stamped "Williams," indicating that the artist was Henry Williams of Boston.[1] The costumes and the apparent ages of the artist and his wife as shown in the silhouettes make it possible to assign the profiles to the year of this visit to New England.

The record of the trip is interesting, for in addition to giving a

[1] Wehle, 64, 112. Several silhouettes by Williams are reproduced in Alice Van Leer Carrick's *Shades of Our Ancestors.*

JOHN KANE (1734–1808)
By Ezra Ames, *c.* 1804
Owned by Mr. R. Keith Kane (Photo by FARL)

EZRA AMES (1768–1836) MRS. EZRA AMES (1775–1836)

Silhouettes on paper by Henry Williams, Boston, *c.* 1805

Owned by Miss Elizabeth S. Edwards, their great-granddaughter (Photographed by Irwin F. Cortelyou)

specific reference to time and place for his chronology, it shows that the artist was rising in his community as a substantial citizen who could afford a horse and carriage. He could also afford small gifts. He records, during the September after his return from New England, and in his Expense Book, that he gave two pounds "Cash to Mulford," who was doubtless Ezekiel Mulford, the husband of his sister Sally, "for children." This probably means that he wished the two pounds to be distributed among his six nephews and nieces. One of the nephews, the youngest child, was named Ezra Ames Mulford.[2] The artist's name persisted in the family. The nephew, later on, christened one of his sons Ezra Ames,[3] and there were besides, in the family and up to 1867, an Ezra Ames Jordan,[4] two Ezra Ames Sutliffs,[5] and an Ezra Ames Spencer.[6]

Returning to the year 1805, and to the artist's Account Book,

[2] Sutliff, 24.
[3] *Ibid.*, 25.
[4] *Ibid.*, 24.
[5] *Ibid.*, 34, 37.
[6] Roosevelt, 296.

there is a record of two miniatures. On February 14th, he listed one for Mr. Bulkey at $15; and on March 2d, he listed another at the same price for Smith Thompson. They are the last miniatures recorded in his Account Books. A number of extant miniatures of a later date show that he did not relinquish entirely the painting of small portraits. About a dozen of these are family portraits: likenesses of his wife and children, and of members of the Emes, Mulford, and Wade families, both old and young, including one self-portrait.

During 1805, there is also a record of ten portraits in oil at an advanced price of $20 a li' eness: a portrait for Smith Thompson, two each for Zebulon R. Shepherd and James Caldwell; and one each for Jacob Vander Heyden, Thomas Barry, and William P. Beers, all of which remain unidentified, as do the two recorded miniatures. Ames also recorded the painting of two portraits *for* George Provost, one of which has been located and identified as *of* that patron. For seven of these ten portraits the artist supplied the frames, which he probably made himself, at $10 each.

During the same year, the artist's record of work other than portraiture was for a Masonic "Piece," a Masonic carpet, and six signs. This short list of journeyman activity is typical of the lists of similar employments for 1806 and 1807. Though diminishing year by year in quantity, he was to carry out such small painting jobs, in conjunction with the more congenial and remunerative work of painting portraits, for many years to come.

Although five years were to pass before Ames received more than local fame as a portrait painter, his Masonic activity had, in the meanwhile, brought him national recognition. On January 9, 1806, Ames was elected the General Grand Scribe of the General Grand Chapter of Masons of the United States, an office he held until June 6, 1816.[7] In 1807 another Masonic honor was bestowed upon him. A warrant was issued for the establishment of an Ames Mark Lodge at Schoharie, N. Y., which, according to Mr. Wendell Walker, the librarian of the Masonic Library in New York

[7] Reid, 11.

City, was undoubtedly named for Ezra Ames. The lodge no longer exists because, according to Mr. Walker, all Mark lodges in New York State had disappeared by about the year 1830.[8]

In 1806 the artist recorded five portraits charged to Lieutenant Thorne, James Rivington, Mr. Germain, Mrs. Diamond, and Dr. Samuel Stringer. Of these only one, the portrait listed for James Rivington, has been identified. It is a copy, now at The New-York Historical Society, by Ames of a portrait of James Rivington, senior, by Gilbert Stuart.[9]

The foregoing list of portraits is not a complete record of Ames's portraits for the year, because there is an unrecorded likeness of Colonel Joseph Brant, at the Ticonderoga Museum of the New York State Historical Association, which is documented and dated as of 1806 by a framed receipt kept at Fenimore House, the Museum and Executive Office of that Association, at Cooperstown, New York. The receipt reads: "August 27th 1806/ Receivd of Mr Wm Caldwell/ Thirty Dollars in full for/ Painting a Portrait & frame/ of Col. Brandt—/ EZRA AMES."

This strengthens the inference, which has heretofore and frequently been made, that the entries in the artist's Account Book are memoranda merely of the work for which he had not been paid at the time of delivery. Almost invariably Ames has written the abbreviation for the word "debtor" after the names of the patrons recorded. Furthermore, the artist's record of his miscellaneous work may be as incomplete as his record of artistic work has just been shown to be—an inference all the more plausible when one considers the very small amounts of money involved in these transactions. Many small jobs were probably paid for in cash as a matter of course, and hence there was no need to record them.

To about 1807 may be assigned an original but unrecorded portrait of Harmanus Ten Eyck. Of the recorded portraits for 1807, two were for James La Grange (unlocated), and two for

[8] Ross, I: 744; *MS Walker.*

[9] For a discussion of this portrait see pp. 163–166. For Lt. Thorn's portraits see Catalogue nos. 333, 333a.

MRS. SPENCER STAFFORD
(1792–1849)

SPENCER STAFFORD
(1772–1844)

By Ezra Ames, 1807 and 1805

Owned by Miss Louise S. Gilder (Photos by FARL)

Benjamin Knower. One of these was of Mrs. Knower (unlocated). The other was of Knower, himself, and is either the one at the Mechanics and Farmers' Bank of Albany, or a similar one privately owned. Two unrecorded portraits of Spencer Stafford and of his wife are definitely dated as of 1805 and 1807.

For the next year, 1808, the artist's record of work unpaid at the time of entry comprised the painting of seven portraits (and their frames), fourteen signs (including a large watch sign which he gilded and lettered for $2.50), a stand of colors for Leonard Gansevoort, and two picture frames. In May 1808 Ames noted that a Mrs. Banyard owed him $6 for "Cleaning and repairing" Governor Jay's portrait; and on September 3, 1808, that he painted "a letter box on his office door" for Solomon Southwick, the State Printer[10] and later the first president of the Mechanics and Farmers' Bank,[11] and charged fifty cents for the work.

[10] *DAB*, XVIII: 414.
[11] Mechanics and Farmers' Bank, *Span of a Century*.

CHILDREN OF GOVERNOR DANIEL D. TOMPKINS

By Ezra Ames, signed and dated, 1809

Owned by Staten Island Institute of Arts and Sciences
(Photographed by Irwin F. Cortelyou)

Considering this and similar items recorded in the Account Book during the period, one gathers that the artist accepted any work, however small, to make his financial ends meet. Indeed, the items taken from his Account Books seem trifling matters of fact when they are examined for any one year; but when they are viewed as a sequence over a period of years, they constitute part of the inspiring story of the slow but steady rise of a highly industrious artist to affluence and recognition.

The artist's recorded but unlocated portraits for the year 1808, include seven portraits *for* and possibly *of* Isaac Hansen, John Van Schaick, Garret Van Wie, Dr. Hunloke Woodruff, Captain Solomon Townsend, and Robert Dunbar for whom two portraits were painted. On May 16, 1808, the artist noted that he had painted a portrait of Mrs. Rivington for Mrs. Van Cleek.

For the year 1809, the artist's record of miscellaneous work in-

MRS. DANIEL D. TOMPKINS (1781–1829)
By Ezra Ames, *c.* 1809
Owned by The New-York Historical Society

ANN WALSH (1800–1811)
By Ezra Ames, 1807 (Photo by FARL)
Owned by Mr. John DeWitt Peltz

cluded the painting of six signs, a stand of colors, and two "Sattain fancy pieces"; and the gilding of a weathervane. As for the portraits recorded during that year, one was for Theodore Sedgwick, another for Dr. Hunloke Woodruff, and still another for Solomon Southwick of a Mr. Barber. None of these has as yet been located.

A most interesting unrecorded painting, signed and dated by Ames as of the year 1809, is owned by the Staten Island Institute of Arts and Sciences. This is a group portrait that shows the five children of Daniel D. Tompkins, who had been elected Governor of New York State in 1807.[12] The painting shows a reversion by the artist to his earlier methods. This authentic early American primitive, painted in 1809, resembles in its artless composition and hard technique the Fondey family portrait, painted by Ames in 1803. Indeed, without the irrefutable dates one would be inclined to assign the later picture to about the time that the earlier was painted. In fact, the artist's techniques were so varied and fluctuating throughout his early period—that is to say during the first two decades of his professional career—that in an attempt to assign a tentative date to a portrait one must have recourse to other considerations, such as the probable age of the sitter at the time the picture was painted and the possible date of his or her costume.

After seeing the primitive painting of the Tompkins children, one views with surprise certain other portraits painted during the same period. Thus the portraits of Ezekiel Mulford, known only in a reproduction; of Edmond Charles Genet, at the Albany Institute; and of Philip Van Cortlandt, owned by the Metropolitan Museum (which all may be assigned to the years 1809 or 1810 because of the ages of the sitters in conjunction with their costumes and the manner of brushing their hair *au coup de vent*), are accomplished works of art, whereas the group portrait of the Tompkins children painted in 1809 has just been noted as a veritable primitive conversation piece.

A letter of 1810 shows that Ames by this time, if not earlier,

[12] *DAB*, XVIII:583.

had gained some slight recognition in New York City for his artistic work. In the letter, headed "N. York 11 January 1810," Williams and Whiting, publishers, inform the artist that they have gone to press on a book and wish that he would send them his drawing of "Gen[l] Hamilton's Portrait."[13] We know that the drawing, a bust portrait now unlocated, was finally sent, because an engraving made after it by Leney is dated "September 1810." It appears as the frontispiece to the first of three volumes entitled *The Works of Alexander Hamilton . . . An Improved Edition of the Federalist*, published by Williams and Whiting in 1810. An undated engraving by Hoogland is based either on the engraving by Leney or on the drawing which is lost.

It seems not implausible that the lost drawing, obviously not made from life because it dates six years after Hamilton's death, was based on a bust in plaster of Hamilton owned by Ames and listed in the inventory of his estate.[14] This practice was not unknown. John Trumbull, for example, based a number of his portraits in oil of Hamilton on one of the marble busts of the statesman by Giuseppe Ceracchi.[15]

Two bust portraits in oil by Ames of Hamilton, unlike each other and also unlike the engravings after the lost portrait drawing, have been located. One, long owned at Union College, New York, is recorded in a letter of presentation, dated 1875, as having been painted from life.[16] The portrait, however, is doubtless the one recorded by Ames in his Account Book under the date of 1810 and thus obviously not a life portrait.[17] The other portrait of Hamilton attributed to Ames is in Kentucky. This the writers have, unfortunately, not been able to examine.

Recorded but now-unidentified paintings of the year 1810 included portraits charged to Joseph Warford, Isaac Hansen,

[13] *MS Ames and Others*, No. I, January 11, 1810.

[14] *MS Ames, Ezra, Estate*, No. I.

[15] Sizer, 29.

[16] *Union Alumni Monthly*, January 1928, p. 71.

[17] A full-page reproduction of this portrait, in color, appeared in *Fortune*, February 1951. A further discussion of the portrait is given in this volume on p. 157.

ALEXANDER HAMILTON (1757–1804)

Engraving by Leney, 1810

After a drawing by Ezra Ames, 1810

ALEXANDER HAMILTON (1757–1804)

Engraving by Hoogland, undated

After either the Leney engraving or the Ames drawing, 1810

ALEXANDER HAMILTON (1757–1804)
By Ezra Ames, dated by Account Book, 1810
Owned by Union College (Photo by FARL)

Thomas Livingston, Charles Z. Platt, Dr. Pomeroy, and Mr. Gourlay; and a picture entitled "the asalt of the Ile of [?]" charged to James Caldwell. The record of ornamental painting for the year includes two signs for the New York State Bank; two stands of colors for I. & G. Hutton, and another stand for the Washington Benevolent Society charged to Charles Z. Platt, S. Brown, and H. Lansingh; and thirteen banners for the same three men.

Four entries dated June 22d, 26th, July 9th, and August 6th, give an idea of the prices Ames obtained for his decorative painting. He painted three fancy pieces at 16 shillings each; a mourning piece which was a composition with "7 figers" at 40 shillings; and a mourning piece for which he charged 12 shillings, doubtless because this composition contained fewer figures than the first. These decorations were commissioned by a generous Mrs. Tompson, who presented the fancy pieces to Miss Briton, Miss Little, and a certain lady whose name is indecipherable; and the mourning pieces to Miss Bassett, and to Miss Little who, since she was already favored with a fancy piece, must have been an especial favorite of Mrs. Tompson.

Unrecorded but extant portraits tentatively assigned to the year 1810 are: two self-portraits, one at the Albany Masonic Temple and the other in the Edwards collection; a portrait of Francis Bloodgood, and one of his wife, who wears a flower-bordered shawl, which is a characteristic accessory found in many of Ames's portraits of women. The splended portrait of Francis Bloodgood shows a greater breadth of handling than that used in the self-portraits.

Two unrecorded portraits, both signed and dated 1810, are the exceptionally strong characterizations of Henry Newman, a bust portrait privately owned, and of Henry Jones, a half-length standing portrait with an elaborate and colorful background, at The New-York Historical Society. The sophisticated technique and the highly artistic effect of these portraits make it difficult to believe that they were painted by the same artist who

HENRY JONES AGED 20 YEARS

By Ezra Ames, 1810

The New-York Historical Society

had painted the primitive group portrait of the Tompkins children just the year before.

The portrait of Henry Jones is comparable with the best American portraiture of the period. Henry Jones, a young man of twenty years, stands boldly with one hand on his hip, against a green curtain overlapping most of a gray column and the sky beyond. In his right hand he holds a pair of gloves; in his left, a cylindrical hat. The gloves are a grayish tan tint, the lining of the hat is of a bright scarlet hue, color notes which produce effective contrasts with the black costume and enhance the color scheme of this, one of the most artistic of all the artist's portraits.

That the artist was able to produce such a striking composition and convincing characterization, and with such an assured technique, only a year after he had painted the primitive group portrait of the Tompkins children, presupposes a period of intensive self-training. To account for this surprising improvement in so short a time leads one to infer that as a preliminary exercise for the painting of his elaborate composition of Henry Jones, Ames, about 1809–1810, made his extremely accurate copy, now owned by the Albany Institute of History and Art, of Copley's large portrait of Elkanah Watson. When the copy and the original were placed side by side in the Ames Exhibition of 1946, at the Albany Institute, it was impossible, at a first glance, to tell which was the original by Copley and which the copy by Ames. Having gained some insight into the management of a figure with a setting, and having improved his technique during the process of copying the picture, Ames probably next painted his half-length standing portrait of Simeon De Witt, owned by Rutgers University, for in this painting (judged from a photograph) the artist so obviously, and successfully, imitates the style of Copley. Then shortly after, in 1810, Ames painted his portrait of Henry Jones.

To this period of self-improvement one may safely assign some copies which the artist made after the portraits of Gilbert Stuart, because the influence of that artist, already apparent in his bust portraits of Francis Bloodgood and Henry Newman, is pronounced in the case of the portrait of Judge Ambrose Spencer which is dated precisely as of the year 1811 by an entry in the artist's Account Book. In this portrait, the influence of Stuart's half-length seated portraits is apparent. Ames has placed his sitter in a setting of accessories such as Stuart used, and painted them in Stuart's manner. The table, the ink stand, the quill pen, and especially the curved arm of a chair, with a pad of red plush, are all accessories found in some of Stuart's portraits. They are conventional studio properties found in the work of other portrait painters of the day, but Ames has followed Stuart's manner of placing and painting them.

Most of his copies of portraits by Stuart, and the copy which he made after Copley's portrait of Elkanah Watson, always remained in the artist's studio. They formed part of a collection of paintings which he increased over the years. A handbill of the sale of his pictures, dated 1842 and thus six years after his death, lists seventy paintings, including Ames's copies of portraits by Stuart of Washington, Adams, Jefferson, Madison, Theodore Sedgwick, Peter Gansevoort, and Robert R. Livingston. He owned the original by Stuart of James Rivington of which he had made a copy already mentioned. He also owned a portrait by John Wesley Jarvis of Gideon Fairman, the engraver, which is unlocated. Besides the handbill, a manuscript inventory of the paintings in the artist's possession at the time of his death is another source for information concerning the artist's pictures.[18]

The copies, the original portraits by Stuart and Jarvis, and numerous examples of his own work, formed a gallery of showpieces which had, by 1810, become one of the sights of the city. The gallery is mentioned in an article on "Improvements in Albany," by an anonymous observer in the *Medical Repository* for July 1810: "In the fine arts, Mr. Ames, merits the highest eulogy for his gallery of paintings, which are worth the attention of every sensible traveller."

[18] [Ames, Ezra], *Catalogue Sale of Portraits*, 1842; *Ms. Ames, Ezra, Estate*, No. 1.

HENRY NEWMAN (1780–1874)

By Ezra Ames, dated on back, 1810

Owned by Miss Evelyn Newman (Photo by FARL)

To complete the information concerning the artist during 1811: Ames recorded in his Account Book a sale entered as "To a Picture of the Happ[y] Old Couple"—the second mention of "Darby and Joan"—which may have been a print or a painting; and the painting of "A Masonic Carpet for Temple Lodge & Chapter," at Albany, for which he charged Dr. C. C. Yates $70, and an additional $3 for the frame. The unlocated portraits of this year included those painted for Lawrence Van Cleek, Caleb Russell, and Matthew Trotter. In addition, Obadiah Penniman was charged for a portrait of Mrs. Penniman, and William McHarg was charged for "2 Portrait[s] & Frames viz Genera[l] King & Lady."

By 1811 the artist's Masonic duties had become so time-consuming that his brothers wished to express their appreciation. Mr. E. T. Reid writes: "On February 7, 1811, a laudable resolution was adopted testifying to his merits as the leader of Grand Chapter and he was presented with a service of silver plate valued at $150.00." Mr. Reid then quotes the text of the resolution which reads in part as follows:

> Whereas, Our Most Excellent Grand High Priest, Ezra Ames, from an ardent and highly laudable anxiety to promote the welfare of Masonry, and the interests and well being of this Grand Chapter in particular, has for a long period consented to officiate in the station he now holds, to the manifest injury of his professional avocations and real detriment to his individual interests, and
>
> Whereas, it is evident that this institution owes much of its present respectibility, harmony, and general usefulness to his fostering care and assiduous attention, therefore
>
> Resolved, That the thanks of this Grand Chapter be presented to our Most Excellent Grand High Priest, Ezra Ames, for his having generously preferred the welfare of this institution to his own personal emolument, [*and so forth; and that*]. . .the Grand Secretary and Grand Treasurer be, and they are hereby authorized and required to procure and present him immediately with a service of plate, of the value of a sum not exceeding $150.00. . . .[19]

Possibly as a result of this resolution the artist had fewer administrative duties at his lodge and had more time to develop

[19] Reid, 12.

his artistic talents. Ames also had the opportunity of displaying his work prominently, and of gaining consideration as an artist beyond the city limits of Albany. This opportunity arose when a group of artists held the First Annual Exhibition of the Society of Artists of the United States in Philadelphia during 1811. To this exhibition Ames sent a portrait which was accepted.

But before recording his contribution to that display, two examples of his miscellaneous work, which the artist noted in entries written during March and April, 1811, should be mentioned. The entries relate to an episode in the early history of Hudson River steamboats:

March 20 [1811]
James Van Ingen Esqr D[ebto]^r
To painting figure of Hope for steamboat 8.00
April 24 [1811]
James Van Ingen Esqr D[ebto]^r
To painting the Beaver assiduity for steamboat 7.00

The steamboats mentioned were among the earliest on the Hudson River. The first was the famous *North River*, which was built in 1807, and known also as the *Clermont* by 1810.[20] The second was the *Car of Neptune*, built in 1809. The third and fourth were the *Hope* and *Perseverance*, both built in 1811,[21] and were obviously the boats for which Ames painted the "figure of Hope" and "the Beaver assiduity." The paintings were not for the paddle boxes, for this type of decoration was not introduced until after 1835.[22] Nor were they figureheads, according to Mr. Harold S. Sniffen who suggests that they might have been pictures to adorn the cabins of the boats.[23] Possibly "the Beaver assiduity" was the oil painting, at the Albany Institute, of the coat of arms of the city of Albany.[24] It represents two men seated on either side of a shield on which there is a beaver cutting down a tree. Under the beaver is the word: "Assiduity."

The *Hope*, launched March 19, 1811, and the *Perseverance*,

[20] Flexner, 318, 319.

[21] Munsell, VI (1855): 40.

[22] Brown, *American Neptune*, January 1943, 38.

[23] *MS Mariners' Museum*, letter from Harold S. Sniffen, Curator.

[24] Munsell, I (1850): 138, vignette of Albany coat of arms.

began running as companion vessels in July 1811.[25] These boats, owned by the James Van Ingen Company, ran in competition with the Livingston and Fulton Company's boats, whose owners had obtained monopolistic rights in 1803 from New York State to operate boats on the Hudson River for twenty years.[26] The firm of Robert R. Livingston and Robert Fulton accordingly applied to the Circuit Court of the United States for the District of New York for an injunction to restrain the Van Ingen Company from "constructing or using Steam Boats on the waters of the Hudson."[27] The injunction was granted,[29] but in the meanwhile the first steamboat race in history was run by the rival companies between the *Hope* and the *Clermont* (or *North River*) on July 27, 1811, starting at Albany. The race resulted in a collision about two miles above the town of Hudson, but neither boat was damaged.[28]

In 1813, after the injunction was granted, the *Hope* and the *Perseverance* were delivered to the Livingston and Fulton Company for confiscation.[29] The boats were broken up at Albany in the presence of their builders.[30] The strong probability that the paintings by Ames were destroyed at this time would be an argument against the attribution to Ames of the painting at the Albany Institute as being one of the paintings he made for the steamboats.

But these decorative paintings were minor works. The next reference to the artist relates to a work of major importance. This was a portrait with which Ames made his first bid for consideration as an artist in competition with other artists. The portrait was displayed at the First Annual Exhibition of the Society of Artists of the United States, held at Philadelphia during 1811. In the catalogue of the exhibition the artist is classed with the "†American Artists, whose works came too late to be inserted

[25] Reynolds, 409–410; Munsell, V (1854): 28.

[26] *New York State Laws, 1803*, Chapter 94, p. 295–296.

[27] *Balance & State Journal*, August 6, 1811, p. 254.

[28] Bullock, *Journal of American History* (1907), 421.

[29] Morrison, 39.

[30] Bullock, *op. cit.*, 421.

in their proper places," and his painting is thus listed: "327 Portrait of a Youth . . . . †Ames."[31] The portrait has not been certainly identified.

There is no contemporary notice of the portrait probably because, no matter how well it might have been painted, it was a likeness of a person of no importance. Is it possible that the picture was the portrait of Henry Jones, now at The New-York Historical Society, painted in 1810? The suggestion arises because that portrait, so obviously painted as a show-piece to display the artist's skill, is a portrait of a 20-year-old youth.

After the acceptance of his work at the First Exhibition of the Society of Artists, Ames prepared to display his work at the Second; and this time, to attract public attention, instead of submitting a portrait of a person of so little importance as to be entitled simply "Portrait of a Youth," he painted a likeness of the most prominent citizen of Albany who was likewise a national figure. This was George Clinton, a military hero, a friend of Washington, and the first Governor of New York State, a position to which he had been elected seven times. He died, in office, on April 20, 1812, as Vice-President of the United States.[32]

Although it is not known exactly when Ames painted his portrait of George Clinton, at least it was finished in time to be shipped and submitted for the exhibition held during June 1812 at Philadelphia. With this second show-piece Ezra Ames, who was now beginning his forty-fifth year, at last gained all the recognition for which he could possibly have wished. His portrait of George Clinton was accepted for the exhibition, noticed by the public, praised in the press, purchased by the Pennsylvania Academy[33] as its first acquisition; and, finally, it led to several commissions for replicas of the picture. It marks the point when it may be said that Ames was now firmly established in his profession. The history of this unusual success begins the next chapter in the artist's career.

[31] *First Annual Exhibition of the Society of Artists of the United States*, catalogue 1811, p. 16.

[32] *DAB*, IV: 226–228.

[33] *Port Folio*, 1813, p. 127.

GEORGE CLINTON (1739–1812)
By Ezra Ames, dated by Account Book, 1818
Owned by Dr. George Clinton Andrews

V

FIRST SUCCESS AS AN ARTIST, 1812–1816:

PORTRAITS OF GEORGE CLINTON, A FEW LANDSCAPES, BANK DIRECTOR

AT THE Second Annual Exhibition of the Society of Artists of the United States and the Pennsylvania Academy, held at Philadelphia in 1812, Ezra Ames exhibited two portraits:[1] No. 24, "Portrait of a Gentleman," which has not been identified; and No. 193, "George Clinton Esq late Vice-president of the United States," which is no longer extant for reasons presently to be discussed.

To judge from the supposed replicas, the portrait of George Clinton was a veritable show-piece. It represented a very prominent citizen of forceful character; and it must have been a striking likeness and a fine artistic work because of the impression it made on the officers of the Academy, and on the critics. In a critical review of the exhibition, dated June 15, 1812, and appearing in *The Port Folio* for July 1812, the writer, who identifies himself only with the initials "G.M.," paused at length before the picture painted by Ames:

"No. 193, *is a portrait of the late vice president, by Ames of Albany*. In reviewing this picture we are equally pleased and astonished, as well at the excellence of the picture, and the correctness of the likeness, as that it was painted by a person little known as an artist, and who has never had any regular instructions in his art, and but few opportunities of even seeing the works of others. The genius and strength of his own mind have, however, produced a picture that no artist need be ashamed of; and it may not be improper to remark, that he only exhibits this as an earnest of what he intends to do hereafter. This artist adds one star more to the constellation of American genius."[2]

[1] Society of Artists of the United States and the Pennsylvania Academy, *Second Annual Exhibition*, catalogue 1812, pp. 17, 35.

[2] *Port Folio*, 1812, p. 25.

A brief but no less laudatory notice appeared in the *Philadelphia Gazette:* "In reviewing this picture the friends of the deceased will be gratified with the correctness of the likeness and will be no less delighted with the beauty of the painting."[3]

The result of these, and doubtless other, favorable impressions of the portrait was an unusual action, at that time, on the part of the officials of the Pennsylvania Academy: they bought the picture for their permanent collection. In a letter to Ames, dated July 6, 1812, John Vallance, the Keeper of the Academy, wrote, in part: "A circumstance extremely flattering to you is, that this is the *first* picture the Academy ever purchased. . . . This will read well on there [*sic*] minutes and will tell well among your friends. . . ."[4]

Curiously enough, in the letter there is no mention of the title of the picture. However, it is specifically recorded in the minutes of the Academy for July 13, 1812: "Messrs Rush and Gibson were appointed a committee to purchase the portrait of Mr. Clinton, now in the Academy, at the price fixed by Mr. [Bass] Otis, said to be $80."[5]

The portrait, although then the property of the Academy, was listed in the catalogue of the annual exhibition held during the next year. A reviewer in *The Port Folio*, for August 1813, signing himself "M" and presumably the same "G.M." who had reviewed the exhibition for the same magazine in 1812, made this report: "24. *The portrait of George Clinton, esq. late vice-president of the United States.*—Ames. This very excellent picture was exhibited and much admired in the last exhibition. It has been since purchased from the artist, by the Pennsylvania Academy of Fine Arts."[6]

Thereafter the portrait is listed in many of the exhibition catalogues up to and including the one for the year 1845 when it was

[3] Munsell, V (1854): 33.

[4] Wheeler, *American Collector*, August 1947, p. 7.

[5] *MS Pennsylvania Academy of the Fine Arts, Correspondence*, letter from Mrs. Barbara S. Roberts, Registrar, to Dr. George Clinton Andrews, March 22, 1949.

[6] *Port Folio*, 1813, p. 127.

in the "Directors' Room."[7] In 1845 the Academy building was destroyed by fire. According to the Registrar of the Academy in a letter dated March 22, 1949: "A partial search of later catalogues after 1845 shows no mention of the painting being in the collection of the Academy. It has been presumed, (although it is not specifically mentioned in any lists so far found of works destroyed in the fire) that it must have been lost in the fire of 1845."[8]

Despite this reasonable assumption, claims have been made for two very similar half-length standing portraits of George Clinton, both undoubtedly by Ames, that each is the original of the portrait sent to the exhibition of 1812. One is privately owned in New York City; and the other is at The New-York Historical Society. Both claims are based on undocumented statements. The claim made for the version at The New-York Historical Society, published in the 1941 catalogue of American portraits at the Society,[9] has recently been withdrawn since the present writers have identified the portrait with the one recorded by the artist in his Account Book during 1814.[10] A third half-length standing portrait of George Clinton, similar in most respects to the other two, painted for the Common Council of the City of Albany, is now on loan at the Albany Institute of History and Art.[11]

The portrait of George Clinton exhibited in 1812 and presumably destroyed by fire in 1845, has often been referred to as a full-length picture,[12] but after considerable search no document has been found which would prove that this is correct. It has also been recorded as a bust portrait in an old acquisition book of the Pennsylvania Academy, entitled Academy Records, No. 6, as follows: "Bust of George Clinton [acquired] by B[ass] Otis purchased of the artist [Ezra Ames] price $80. July 16, 1812."[13]

[7] Pennsylvania Academy of the Fine Arts, *Catalogue*, 1845, p. 13.

[8] *MS Pennsylvania Academy of the Fine Arts, Correspondence, op. cit.*

[9] Shelley, 57.

[10] A discussion of this portrait is given on pp. 154, 157.

[11] *Magazine of Art*, Albany Institute Edition, April 1948.

[12] *DAB*, I: 243.

[13] *MS Pennsylvania Academy of the Fine Arts, Correspondence, op. cit.*

However, it is difficult to believe that the portrait was either a bust or a full-length. It was probably not a bust portrait because, with one exception, the price was over three times as much as Ames had recorded for a picture up to that time, which indicates something over a bust-sized likeness. On the other hand, it was probably not a full-length because the artist's only portraits of this size located so far, are the two in the Executive Chamber of the New York State Capitol, and these reveal the artist's ineptitude rather than his ability as an artist. It seems highly probable that in selecting a size for a picture to display his talents, he would have decided upon neither a bust portrait, which would not make much of a showing at an exhibition, nor a full-length portrait, which he would find difficult to manage; but, rather, a half-length standing portrait. In short, having painted such a show-piece as the half-length standing portrait of Henry Jones, it may be imagined that he then went on to paint another show-piece the same size, but, as it has been suggested, of an important person: George Clinton whose services to the nation made him a prominent character, and whose recent death made the portrait of him a timely picture for exhibition purposes. Therefore, the portrait exhibited in 1812 was presumably similar to the several extant half-length standing portraits of the statesman.

One of these, owned by The New-York Historical Society, is a striking artistic performance in spite of its conventional background. It is skillfully painted, the pose is natural, and the characterization is lifelike and convincing. If the portrait exhibited at the Pennsylvania Academy was indeed the prototype of this painting, then it must have made a handsome showing at the exhibition.

Since it was not a commission, the portrait of George Clinton, exhibited in 1812, is not listed in the artist's Account Books, where he recorded only those items for which payment was due him at the time of entry. These Account Books are, as it has frequently been remarked, incomplete as lists of the artist's work; nor is a complete listing of all his paintings attempted in this biographical essay. A complete tabulation of his work is attempted in the Catalogue at the end of this study.*

Here, as heretofore and hereinafter, the attempt is made simply to present a survey of the artist's work. Therefore, it is sufficient, usually, to state only the number of portraits which he recorded each year in his Account Books; and to refer only in a general way to the work which he did not record, but which has been identified. However, here and there, certain paintings which serve to illustrate some characteristic of the artist's work will be noted more or less in detail.

In 1812, Ames noted the painting of eight portraits, but he did not record four extant portraits belonging to this year or to this period. Two of them, bust portraits of John Maley and his wife which form part of a collection of several portraits by Ames decorating the walls of the owner's handsome drawing room in Loudonville, near Albany, N. Y., are specifically dated 1812. The other two unrecorded portraits, exceptionally fine character studies of James Kent, may be assigned to this period because the heads in these portraits, almost identical likenesses, are of a man about forty-nine years old which was the judge's age in 1812.

We now come to a discussion of the rare landscapes of Ezra Ames. During the year 1812, he recorded, in his third Account Book, the painting of two views of Lake George: one for James Kane, which has not come to light; and the other for John Tayler, a wood panel which has recently been located. Later on in his Account Book, in 1822, he recorded altering a view of Lake George for James Caldwell, which has been identified as a wood panel, privately owned.

The recently located view of Lake George painted for John Tayler, shows, in the foreground, a fort built on a hollow square design; and a lake, with a village, mountains, and sky in the background. On the ramparts of the fort are some small figures. The other located view of Lake George, altered in 1822, is similar to the panel painted in 1812, except that it does not have the fort in

* Page 193.

PERSPECTIVE PAINTING OF LAKE GEORGE [WITH THE FORT]
By Ezra Ames, dated and titled by Account Book, 1812

(Photographed by Irwin F. Cortelyou)

Owned by Mrs. Weeks Stewart

the foreground. The discovery of the view with the fort reveals the nature of the alteration. Comparing photographs of the two views it is obvious that the fort was originally in both pictures and was painted over in the Caldwell version. Dim perspective lines of the fort show through the overpainting.

The lower margin of the Caldwell picture is lettered: "A VIEW OF LAKE GEORGE & CALDWELL VILLAGE taken from the west side of the fort." An inscription is on the back of the panel: "Wm Caldwell / A[l]bany / Taken by Ezra Ames / from Fort George / By request of my Father who took him / to the Lake to make this view." Since the picture was painted on the site, possibly the other two views, recorded in

A VIEW OF LAKE GEORGE & CALDWELL VILLAGE [WITHOUT FORT]
By Ezra Ames, *c.* 1812 (Photo by FARL)
[Fort overpainted, presumably the "alteration" noted in Account Book, 1822]
Owned by Miss Catharine Van Cortlandt Mathews and Mrs. William V. Mason

1812, were based on this direct transcript from nature. If this be true, then the picture must have been painted during, or even before, the year 1812.

An unrecorded landscape of a different type is at the Albany Institute. It was presented by Miss Elizabeth S. Edwards, the artist's great-granddaughter, who entitled it "The Lady of the Lake." However, when it was exhibited at the Chicago Art Institute and the Whitney Museum of American Art during 1945, it was listed in the catalogues as a "Romantic Landscape."[14] It is a picture of a woman draped in white who stands at the prow of a boat floating on a mountain lake or stream. In the middle distance

[14] Sweet, 115.

ROMANTIC LANDSCAPE

By Ezra Ames

Owned by the Albany Institute of History and Art

there is a Gothic castle on top of a cliff; in the background, a mountain range. The painting cannot be dated by its technique because there are no dated paintings by Ames of a similar type with which it may be compared. A tentative date has been suggested by Mr. Frederick A. Sweet who mentions the picture as one of the "occasional examples" of landscape painting "produced under the unsympathetic conditions which prevailed in this country before 1825. . . ."[15]

In his recent book on the American arts, Mr. Oliver W. Larkin refers to the "Romantic Landscape" when he writes: "Ezra Ames of Albany seems to have anticipated Cole's *Voyage* [*of Life*] with a rather crudely painted allegory. . . ."[16] This conjec-

[15] *Ibid.*, 28.

[16] Larkin, 203.

ture is more than probable. The four small panels at the Albany Institute, comprising the preliminary sketches for the "Voyage of Life" by Thomas Cole, were painted in 1839–1840,[17] whereas a painting entitled "Voyage of Life" is listed in the tabulation of Ames's work found in the inventory of his estate made in 1836, after his death. Indeed, the picture, variously called "Romantic Landscape" (the title used by the writers in their Catalogue), "Allegorical Landscape," and "The Lady of the Lake," may at one time have been called "Voyage of Life" by Ames himself. Mr. Sweet, in a sentence following immediately after the one previously quoted, states: "Thomas Cole's Voyage of Life elaborates on the theme used in Ames' Romantic Landscape." Assuming that the picture was painted "before 1825," and accepting the date, 1812, for the views of Lake George, then these landscapes have an historic significance: they are anticipations, respectively, of the romantic and realistic paintings of the Hudson River School.

Three other allegorical pictures are listed in the tabulation of the artist's paintings in the inventory: an "Allegory of Providence," an "Allegory of Faith & Death," and an "Allegory present past & future."[18] Still another allegorical landscape is listed in the artist's Account Book, during 1819, entitled "alegorical Painting," and charged to William Barclay for Temple Lodge. These are all as yet unlocated.

Turning now to the artist's miscellaneous and ornamental work, dated 1812, which he recorded in his third Account Book: after an examination of the entries one gains the impression that by this time Ames was inclined to accept such commissions only from friends, or societies in which he had a personal interest, unless they involved returns large enough to be an incentive. Thus he recorded the payments due him for five stands of colors, one of them for I. and G. Hutton; a stand of colors and thirteen banners for the Washington Benevolent Society of Washington County; three portrait frames, two for "P. S. Van Rensselaer,"

[17] Sweet, 118.

[18] *MS Ames, Ezra, Estate,* No. 1.

and another for "P. Van Cortlandt"; and fifteen sashes for the St. Andrews Society.

The next reference to the artist in point of time is found in a letter of the year 1813 to the artist from a friend named Benjamin Armitage, who lived in New York City. This letter, and another dated 1816 which will be quoted later on, reveal him as a man very actively interested in the artist's work. Armitage in his letter headed New York, January 21, 1813,[19] begins:

> I have often wished to have a line from you since your return to Albany and having an opportunity of forwarding a line to you I embrace it with pleasure.
>
> Pray how are you coming on in Albany? Mr. Waldo is (I understand) painting Naval Heroes and you ought to be painting Army Heroes.

The painter to whom Armitage refers is Samuel Lovett Waldo (1783–1861),[20] with whose work some of the portraits by Ames have been confused.

"There is no foreseeing what is to come," Armitage continues, "but several of your well wishers are of opinion had you staid here you would by this time have been as Waldo is viz you would have had as much work as you could wish for." This leads Armitage to speak of the War of 1812, then still waging; and of the chances one had of earning a living as an artist during war-time conditions:

> At first view it would appear that at a time of War no reasonable man would (in such a place as New York) lay out his money for pictures, portraits &c but when you come to consider how few men in a Community are men who merit the title of *Reasonable Men* & that if all men were truly under the direction of Reason there would be very few Wars; I say when you take these things into consideration, is it to be wondered at that when the first apprehension we experienced in New York from the War was a little worn off & we had seen a few valuable Ships bro^{t} in as Prizes we began to hug ourselves as being in little danger & all our old habits returned upon us as if Peace was returned to us & the War at an end.

[19] *MS Ames and Others*, No. 1, January 21, 1813.

[20] *DAB*, XIX: 333–334.

Armitage concludes:

> I occasionally fall in with Sylvanus Miller the Surrogate & some days ago he asked me if I tho^{t} you would ever send him the portrait of the Vice President [George Clinton] he ordered & I told him I tho^{t} you would send it to him:—If you send it to my care in the Spring please write to him stating the price and ordering the Amt. paid to me on your Acct. and send the letter under cover to me & I will deliver the letter and (if you say so will) keep the portrait until it is paid for—

One gathers from this letter that Armitage and Ames were friends of long standing; that Armitage out of admiration for Ames and his work acted as a self-appointed agent for the artist in New York City; and that he was regretful because Ames had not settled in New York. But Ames, once having made the decision to settle in Albany, probably never gave a second thought to leaving his adopted city where he was well established and busy filling out commissions. Two of these were public commissions for full-length portraits: one of George Washington, the other of George Clinton, and they were destined for the State House. Both were painted in 1813, and both are today in the Executive Chamber of the State Capitol at Albany.

A transcript of the resolution adopted by the State Assembly authorizing the appointment of a committee to call on Ames and then report to the House concerning the "propriety" of having him paint the portrait of Washington, is found in a letter written by James Van Ingen to Ames dated April 3, 1813.[21] The document dated April 2, 1813, states in part:

> Resolved unanimously, that a Committee of seven members be appointed to confer with our ingenious and accomplished fellow-citizen and artist Mr. Ezra Ames, and report to this House, their opinion on the propriety of procuring from him, a full length portrait of General George Washington late President of the United States, for the purpose of having the same placed above the Speaker's Chair; and that Mr Taylor, Mr Jones, Mr Sears, Mr Cady, Mr Dox, Mr E. Williams, and Mr Van Vechten be the said Committee.

On the same sheet with this transcript Van Ingen addresses himself to Ames: "I deem it proper to apprize you that the fore-

[21] *MS Ames and Others,* No. I, April 3, 1813.

going resolution passed the house of assembly yesterday and I expect the Committee appointed thereby, will call on you this afternoon–[April 3]."

The full-length portrait of George Washington, painted as a result of that call, may have been based on the engraving by Heath after the "Lansdowne Portrait" of Washington by Gilbert Stuart.[22] This is more plausible than assuming that Ames made a direct copy of the painting itself which was then, and is now, in Philadelphia.[23] In fairness to Stuart and to Ames it should be stated that the Heath engraving is an indifferent copy of the portrait.

Authorization for the "purchase of a full length portrait" of George Clinton, as well as for the portrait of George Washington, is found in the "Laws of the State of New York," 1813, of the 36th Session of the Legislature, begun November 2, 1812, passed April 13, 1813.[24] The portrait of Clinton was paid for by the Comptroller during that year and hung in the State House in December 1813.[25] The two portraits are companion paintings of the same size.

The portraits were more than satisfactory. In 1823, when they were no longer novelties, they still held the public attention, and Horatio Gates Spafford felt impelled to write with uncritical enthusiasm that "in the Assembly Chamber, there is an admirable full length portrait of Washington, by Ames, of Albany, and in the Senate Chamber, one of George Clinton, unrivalled in faithfulness, and unexcelled in execution."[26] In *The New York Times* for November 28, 1937, the late Edward Alden Jewell, a less enthusiastic reviewer than Horatio Gates Spafford, wrote of the artist and of the picture of George Clinton, at the time it was shown at a loan exhibition of portraits at the Corcoran Gallery of Art:

[22] Frankenstein and Healy, *Art in America*, February 1950, p. 26.

[23] Park, II: 854–855.

[24] *N. Y. State Laws, 1813*, Chapter CCIII, p. 326; Section XXXVIII, 335, for Washington portrait; XLVII, 337, for Clinton portrait.

[25] Bowen, 439.

[26] Munsell, I (1850): 308–309.

JAMES KENT (1763–1847)

By Ezra Ames, *c.* 1812

Owned by the Albany Institute of History and Art

EZRA AMES (1768–1836)

Self-portrait, *c.* 1814 (Photo by FARL)

Owned by the Mechanics and Farmers' Bank of Albany

GEORGE CLINTON (1739–1812)
By Ezra Ames, 1813 (Photo by FARL)
Owned by the State of New York (in the Capitol)

GEORGE WASHINGTON (1732–1799)
By Ezra Ames, 1813 (Photo by FARL)
Owned by the State of New York (in the Capitol)

. . . take an American artist who whole-heartedly and lavishly subscribes to the English rococo manner and see what can happen. Take the huge portrait of George Clinton by Ezra Ames. Here is an American artist who, helped to some extent, no doubt, by fortune, but also depending optimistically upon his own bootstraps, rises above the profession of coach painter to that of the painter of important official portraits. His opulence with respect to embellishment is almost staggering. The property room of a provincial artist's mind has been completely denuded for the occasion. And it looks as if a last-minute pinch of snuff had blown the whole elaborate mise-en-scene into a state bordering on bright chaos.

The artist fell down lamentably in his painting of the legs and feet, identically placed in both portraits although the figures face in opposite directions. Nevertheless, they gave satisfaction to the citizens; gained prestige for the artist; and brought him commissions so that now, in his forty-sixth year, he was able to turn down small painting jobs. The only large order for ornamental painting which he recorded in his Account Book, during 1813, was the painting of eight banners, at $5 each, for a branch of the Washington Benevolent Society in Pittsfield; and two for each branch in the counties of Albany and Ontario. The painting of a frame; and a stand of colors for Philip Van Rensselaer, completes his record for the year. His record of miscellaneous work for the ensuing years is even smaller. In 1814 the only small work he recorded is a frame charged to Ambrose Spencer for a portrait of General Armstrong; and in 1815, a frame, a sign, and a coat of arms—the latter for a family named Platt.

By the year 1813, then, one may infer that Ames considered himself primarily a painter of portraits. Indeed, his name, profession, and address appear in the first Albany Directory, published in 1813, doubtless as he himself reported this information to the compilers of that work, as "Ames, Ezra, portrait painter, 41 Washington." The name of the street, as noted earlier, was changed in 1814 to South Pearl. His profession is given as "portrait painter" in all the directories of the city thereafter as long as he lived.

During 1813, besides the seven portraits he recorded in his

GEORGE W. CLINTON (1778–1818)
By Ezra Ames, *c.* 1813
(Photo: Irwin F. Cortelyou)
Owner: Dr. George Clinton Andrews

JOHN TAYLER (1742–1829)
By Ezra Ames, signed and dated 1816
(Photo by FARL)
Owner: Historical Society of the Tarrytowns

Account Book, he probably painted some of the located portraits which he did not record. He certainly painted the two full-length portraits of Washington and George Clinton for the city in that year. However, there is no telling when he painted the extant bust and half-length standing portraits of George Clinton which he did not record. If they were based on the likeness painted in 1812 for the Pennsylvania Academy of the Fine Arts exhibition, they may have been painted any time during or after that year.

There is a bust portrait of George Clinton's only son, George Washington Clinton, formerly attributed to Vanderlyn, which Ames painted about 1813, judging from the apparent age of the sitter. Ames did not record the portrait in his Account Book of this period, but it is listed in the certified inventory of his estate[27] and in the handbill of the sale of his portraits in 1842, several years after his death.[28]

[27] *MS Ames, Ezra, Estate*, No. 1.
[28] [Ames, Ezra], *Catalogue Sale of Portraits*, 1842.

In this portrait the artist has placed the sitter within a very faintly indicated oval which forms a painted mat, a substitute for the gilt mat used in framing pictures. This conventional device is employed to center the attention of the spectator on the head and shoulders of the sitter. Ames had used the device before this time, as for example in his portraits of Elihu Phinney, in 1799; of Solomon Southwick, painted about 1804; of Spencer Stafford, painted in 1805; and, at times, he used it later on, as for example in his portrait of Marcus Tullius Reynolds, painted about 1821, which the portrait of George Washington Clinton greatly resembles.

In 1814 the artist entered the banking business. According to the minutes of the Mechanics and Farmers' Bank of Albany, on June 6, 1814, at the annual meeting of the stockholders, Ezra Ames was elected one of the thirteen directors.[29] It is possible that the bust portrait he painted of himself, owned by the bank, was painted this year.

In 1814 the bank, chartered in 1811 and the third to be established at Albany, had moved into a handsome marble building on the northeast corner of Court and Exchange Streets where it remained until 1875. It was then installed in its present quarters on State Street. Solomon Southwick had served as the first president of the bank from 1811 to 1813, and Isaac Hutton was serving as second president when Ames became one of the directors in 1814.[30] Twenty years later Ames himself rose to the position of president of this bank.

Beginning in August of the year before, 1813, Ames raised his price for a bust portrait with its frame from $45 to $50. For the half-length standing portrait of George Clinton with its frame, painted in 1814, he charged $150.[31] It is true that the price was large but so was the portrait. Furthermore, only once thereafter

[29] *MS Mechanics and Farmers' Bank, Minutes*, consulted by Mr. George B. Cortelyou, Jr.

[30] Mechanics and Farmers' Bank, *Span of a Century*.

[31] This is the portrait at The New-York Historical Society and is discussed on pp. 154, 157.

did the artist record a charge of $150 for a portrait with its frame, and this was in 1818 when he painted the half-length standing portrait of Governor DeWitt Clinton for the City of Albany. After 1813, his average price was $50 for an average-sized portrait with its frame.

A receipt documenting a portrait for which Ames received $60, including the frame, is dated September 18, 1815, and is made out to Pierre Van Cortlandt II for a portrait painted of his "Lady," presumably his second wife, who was Anne Stevenson. It is a family tradition that Anne Stevenson sat for the artist while he finished the bust of the profile portrait of Van Cortlandt's first wife, Catharine Clinton, who had died in 1811 before her portrait was finished.[32] This profile is now at the Museum of the City of New York, where there is also a profile miniature of her by Ames which resembles the oil portrait. A portrait of Pierre Van Cortlandt II, himself, by Ames may also belong to the year 1815 because the costume of the sitter dates from about that year.

Portraits of or about this year, which Ames did not record, include: portraits of Thomas Humphrey Cushing and of his wife, privately owned; of Matthias B. Tallmadge and of his wife, owned by Yale University and on loan at the English Speaking Union, New York City; of John Hankinson and of his wife, who was the daughter of Mrs. Thomas Humphrey Cushing; and of Mrs. Ebenezer Foot. Then there is a copy, at the Albany Institute, which Ames made of the original portrait of Robert R. Livingston by Gilbert Stuart, which dates from this period. A resolution to have the copy painted is mentioned in the minutes, March 10, 1814, of The Society for the Promotion of Useful Arts, a forerunner of the present Albany Institute of History and Art. Livingston had been president of the Society. In the minutes of February 28, 1815, the portrait is referred to as having been "procured."[33] Although Ames is not mentioned in the minutes in

[32] Information supplied by Miss Catharine Van Cortlandt Mathews.

[33] *MS The Society for the Promotion of Useful Arts, Minutes,* consulted by Mr. Ledyard Cogswell, Jr.

THOMAS HUMPHREY CUSHING (1755–1822)

By Ezra Ames, *c.* 1815

Owned by Estate of Frederick Hill

MRS. THOMAS HUMPHREY CUSHING

By Ezra Ames, *c.* 1815 (Photo by FARL)

Owned by Estate of Frederick Hill

PIERRE VAN CORTLANDT II (1762–1848)
By Ezra Ames, *c.* 1815 (Photo by FARL)
Owned by Miss Catharine Van Cortlandt Mathews and Mrs. William V. Mason

MRS. ALLAN MELVILLE (1791–1872)
By Ezra Ames, *c.* 1814 (Photo by FARL)
Owned by Dr. Henry Alexander Murray

this connection; he is mentioned in the minutes under the date of March 2, 1814, as elected chairman of the Fine Arts Committee of the Society,[34] which supports the assumption that it was Ames who painted the copy. But no such documentary support is actually needed because the portrait is quite evidently the work of Ames.

Reverting to his original work at this time: although for a number of years he had not recorded the painting of any miniatures, a miniature on an oval-shaped piece of ivory of his wife Zipporah, owned by Miss Elizabeth S. Edwards, may be assigned to about 1815 to 1820, because of the apparent age of the sitter. Age and costume are the only criteria available for dating his miniatures because the techniques used by the artist in miniature painting are not sufficiently known to assign his miniatures to specific dates for technical reasons.

Aside from these artistic occupations, Ames, who never forewent his Masonic activities, continued to receive demonstrations of esteem from the members of this fraternity. According to Mr. E. T. Reid, he was: "chosen as the Grand Captain General of the Grand Encampment of the State of New York in June 1816, and reelected in 1817, 1818 and 1819. In the General Grand Encampment of the United States of America he was elected General Grand Captain General in June 1816, and reelected on September 16, 1819. Thus the Knights Templar demonstrated their respect for his skill and ability."[35]

A novelty appears in the artist's Account Book records for 1816: a lottery sign for S. & M. Allen whom he charged $100 for the work. The firm of S. & M. Allen managed all kinds of lotteries at their "Allen's Truly Lucky Lottery Office" which they advertised prominently in *The Albany Register* for April 29, 1817, and numerous other issues of that newspaper during the period.

During the year 1816, Ames also recorded in his third Account Book the painting of eight portraits. Several of these have been

[34] *MS The Society for the Promotion of Useful Arts, Minutes*, consulted by Mr. Robert G. Wheeler.

[35] Reid, 11–12.

located. Two of them, one of John Tayler at the Philipse Castle Restoration, Tarrytown, and the other of Absalom Townsend, privately owned, are boldly painted against simple backgrounds. Two others, in contrast, the privately owned portraits of John Meads and Mrs. John Meads, are meticuluously painted with background accessories. The portraits of Absalom Townsend and Mrs. John Meads are especially fine characterizations and rank with the best of the artist's productions.

In 1816, Ames was in his forty-eighth year. That he was now active as a banker, Freemason, and artist, is not surprising, for men in those days were apt to have more than one active interest. What is noteworthy in the case of Ezra Ames is that he finally reached the top in all three of his main interests. It is especially remarkable that he continued to develop his abilities as a painter. That he might have gained wider recognition as an artist had he so desired, one may deduce from an invitation to display his work in New York City which he received in 1816. This invitation came in the form of a letter, now at the Albany Institute, from his friend Benjamin Armitage in New York City,[36] who, it may be recalled, had previously interested himself in the artist's behalf.

New York Sepr 27th 1816

Mr Ezra Ames
Dear Sir

You no doubt have seen in our New York Papers that the Academy of Fine Arts are going to have an Exhibition in their New Rooms next month & invite Artists to send Specimens of their works to be shewn.

I trust you will make up your mind to send something of yours amongst other works of this State & that you will at once send me down the sizes of Paintings which you will furnish & I will without loss of time make application for Room to be reserved for them & wait their arrival here, and this done wait for the pleasure of seeing you as one of my family, that you may see & be seen amongst the Artists of our State, for Pennsylvania has too long boasted of being the only one in the Union that had any Painters in it to boast of—

Give my Compliments to all your Family & believe me yours truly

BENJ^n ARMITAGE

[36] *MS Armitage, Benjamin,* letter to Ezra Ames, September 27, 1816. Reference and photostat of letter supplied by Miss Helen Burr Smith.

MRS. JOHN MEADS (b. 1785) JOHN MEADS (1777–1859)

By Ezra Ames, Acct. Bk. dates, 1816 (Photos: Irwin F. Cortelyou)

Owner: Mr. Joseph Larocque, Jr.

P.S. Mr Oakey desires me to say that if you conclude to come down, he wishes you to bring with you your Box of tricks, Palletts, Brushes &c &c so as to be prepared for Action as Mrs Oakey wants her Portrait & he thinks he can get one or more Good, hard, Strong Faces amongst his Friends; he wishes you to write me saying what you determine upon—

Yours &c

B. A———.

Ames's reply to this letter has not been located which is unfortunate because the artist failed to display his work at the first exhibition of the revived American Academy of the Fine Arts which opened on October 25, 1816,[37] and it would be interesting to know why. Nor did he display his work at any of the subsequent exhibitions although, as hereinafter related, he was elected a member of the American Academy in 1824. At present the matter remains a mystery; and the only other reference worth recording for the year 1816 is the artist's memorandum that $720 covered his entire expenses for the year extending from January 1, 1816, to January 1, 1817.

[37] Cummings, 7.

CLARKSON CROLIUS (1773–1843)

By Ezra Ames, signed and dated, 1825

The New-York Historical Society Gift of Clarkson Crolius, Jr., 1863

SOLOMON VAN RENSSELAER (1774–1852) (Photo by FARL)

By Ezra Ames, Acct. Bk. date, 1819

Owners: Miss Emily W. and Mr. Edward E. Rankin

STEPHEN VAN RENSSELAER (1764–1839)

By Ezra Ames, probably 1819 (Photo by Macbeth Gallery)

Owned by New York State Historical Association

VI

FURTHER RECOGNITION, 1817–1825:

WORK FOR JOSEPH DELAPLAINE, PORTRAIT OF DEWITT CLINTON, AMES AT ERIE CANAL CEREMONIES

AMES began the year 1817 by painting some Masonic regalia for which he was very well paid. According to his entry in the Albany Account Book, dated January 16, 1817, he charged John T. Dotty $260 for a breastplate, mitre, crown, and robes "Compleat for the High Priest, King & Scribe," for the Richmond Chapter. Then, on April 22, 1817, he noted that he charged A. Clark, Charles White, and Warner F. Hitchcock the same amount for a similar outfit, for the Glens Falls Chapter.

In 1817, as in 1816, he painted a lottery sign for S. & M. Allen, at his customary price of $100. He also painted two signs for tobacco shops. One of these, entered in his Account Book on May 20, 1817, and entitled "Old Darby and Joan" he painted for Joseph Fry at a charge which is indecipherable. It may be recalled that he sold "pictures" with this title in 1804, 1806, and 1811, which were likely prints by another artist; so that, perhaps, the sign he painted for Joseph Fry was a copy of one of these prints. A wood engraving probably after the sign is used in an advertisement of Fry's tobacco shop in *The Albany Gazette* for June 3, 1819, January 13, 1820,[1] and numerous other issues of the paper. It is an especially good advertisement for a tobacco shop appealing as it does to women as well as men, because in the engraving Darby and Joan are shown holding hands and both happily smoking their pipes.

The other sign Ames painted for a tobacconist was entitled "Sign Pocahuntas," for which he charged George Pearson $40 on February 13, 1817. A wood engraving, doubtless after this sign, appears in *The Albany Gazette & Daily Advertiser* for November 11, 1818, above an advertisement with the caption:

[1] Reference for January 13, 1820, and photostat, supplied by Mrs. Katharine M. McClinton.

"At the sign of Pocahontas," inserted by Walter Van Veghten and Mathias Kline who "occupy the store and factory of the late Mr. G. Pearson, State-street. . . ."

Besides these references to his ornamental painting, there are entries in the third Account Book, also dated 1817, which give a partial record of his artistic work for that year. In them the artist noted the indebtedness to him of six patrons for portraits: three, with frames, at $50 each; one, without a frame, at $30; and two at $75 each, with their frames.

One of those priced at $75 has been identified as a portrait of Gouverneur Morris, now on loan at Columbia University, which is an ambitious attempt to show a man seated at half-length and extending one hand toward the spectator. A duplicate of this portrait, which the artist did not record, is at The New-York Historical Society.[2] Ames painted two more portraits of Gouverneur Morris, both at present unlocated. One is listed in the inventory of the artist's effects, 1836,[3] and also in the handbill of the sale of his paintings, 1842.[4] The other he recorded in his Account Book in 1818 for Joseph Delaplaine.

Unrelated to the artist's work but fitting into his chronology at this time are two references to trips which he made and recorded in his Expense Book for 1817. He paid two visits to Schenectady, one in May and the other in July.

In 1818, Ames painted some portraits for the publisher Joseph Delaplaine of Philadelphia which were destined for a projected portrait gallery of "Distinguished Americans" advertised as a "Panzographia" to be opened on the first day of January, 1819. There were to be over two hundred portraits in the collection.[5]

Of the eighteen portraits which Ames listed in his Account Book during 1818, nine were painted for Joseph Delaplaine. Five of them—"Doct^{r}" Livingston (a copy), Gouverneur Morris, George Clinton, Solomon Van Rensselaer, and the Reverend

[2] A discussion of these portraits is given on pp. 159–63.

[3] *MS Ames, Ezra, Estate*, No. 1.

[4] [Ames, Ezra], *Catalogue Sale of Portraits*, 1842.

[5] Delaplaine, 15, 16.

(?) MRS. WILLIAM ANNESLEY (1800–1832)
By Ezra Ames, *c.* 1820
Owned by Mrs. Seth W. Cook

(?) WILLIAM ANNESLEY (1793–1862)
By Ezra Ames, *c.* 1820
Owned by Mrs. Seth W. Cook

THOMAS HILLHOUSE (1766–1834)

By Ezra Ames, *c.* 1817

Owned by Mrs. John T. E. Hillhouse

THEODORE DWIGHT (1764–1846)

By Ezra Ames, dated by Account Book, 1817

Owned by Mr. C. K. Johnson

Hooper Cumming (crossed out and here assumed not to have been painted)—were to be paid for by Delaplaine himself at $15 a portrait. The remainder—portraits of the first Mrs. DeWitt Clinton (Maria Franklin), a copy, former Acting Governor John Tayler, Solomon Southwick, and Stephen Van Rensselaer —were to be paid for, respectively, by Governor Clinton, who ordered the copy of a portrait of his wife; and the others by the sitters themselves, at a cost of $30 a portrait.

Delaplaine's Gallery was bought in 1825 by Rubens Peale for Peale's Museum, New York, which failed in 1837. At the sale of this museum that year, P. T. Barnum bought most of the collection for his American Museum.[6] One of the portraits which Barnum presumably did not acquire was the striking bust portrait of George Clinton, now owned by Dr. George Clinton Andrews, which has a history of having been bought by a private individual at the Peale sale.[7] Another portrait, that of Solomon Van Rensselaer, is known to have been acquired by P. T. Barnum, and was destroyed by fire when Barnum's American Museum burned down[8] on July 13, 1865.[9]

In 1818, Ames painted a number of other pictures for DeWitt Clinton besides the portrait of Mrs. Clinton intended for Delaplaine's Gallery. Two of them were portraits of the Governor's sons George and Franklin. The other three were still-life paintings of fish, for the Governor was a naturalist of standing. But Ames, a portrait painter, did not list them as still-life paintings. One he recorded as a "Portrait of a White Lake Fish," another he listed as a "Portrait of a Lake Herring," and the third, of an unidentified sitter, he recorded simply as "Fish."

A year earlier, in 1817, Ames began to paint the official portrait of DeWitt Clinton as Governor of New York State for the Corporation of the City of Albany. Of other portraits of the statesman, a number were painted about this time; for DeWitt Clinton, having failed to be reappointed as Mayor of New York City in

[6] *MS Sellers, Charles Coleman*, letter dated May 31, 1949.

[7] Bowen, 439.

[8] Bonney, I: 400–401.

[9] *Harper's Weekly*, July 29, 1865, pp. 473–474.

1815, immediately began his campaign for the Governorship of the State, and it was thought necessary that his likeness be kept before the public for political purposes. Clinton recorded the names of a number of artists in his still unpublished diary during the years 1816 and 1817. It is interesting to mention their names here because it will give an idea of Ames's position in the chronology of American art history.

During the year 1816, DeWitt Clinton recorded calls, in New York City, on Cooper, Parisen, Jarvis, Trumbull, Vanderlyn, and Milbert, and twice mentioned specifically sitting to Jarvis. In 1817, he recorded frequent calls on and sittings to Vanderlyn, Jarvis, Dunlap, and Coffee the sculptor, also in New York City; and in several entries he wrote that he had sat to "Dunlap and Vanderlyn," probably meaning he sat to both at the same time.

Later in 1817, after he had taken up his duties as Governor at Albany, Clinton began sitting for his official portrait to Ames. On December 4, 1817, Clinton notes "E. Ames" in his diary. Then on December 8, 1817, he writes, specifically, that he "called at Ames for a sitting." In entries for December 24, 1817, and January 6, and 23, 1818, he again notes that he "sat for Ames." Four entries for January 5, 19, and 31, and February 28, read merely "Ames's or Mr. Ames."[10] The portrait must have been finished before March 8, 1818, which is the date on which Ames recorded it in his Account Book. The charge was $100 for the portrait, and $50 for the frame.

After the painting of this portrait, Clinton entered the name of the artist in his diary on March 25 and 31; June 5, 10, 25, and 27; September 4 and 5; October 12; and December 16, 1818; and February 2, 1819. Since merely the name is given in the entries, one can only guess at the nature of these visits. One visit was on March 25. This was the same day that Ames noted in his Account Book the Governor's indebtedness to him for "Painting a Portrait of a Lake Herring," which permits one to surmise that on this and perhaps on some of the other visits the artist called for his

[10] *MS Clinton, DeWitt.*

PHILO RUGGLES (1765–1829)
By Ezra Ames, signed and dated, 1822
Owned by Columbia University (Photo by FARL)

MRS. PHILO RUGGLES (1779–1865)
By Ezra Ames, signed and dated, 1822
Owned by Columbia University (Photo by FARL)

ROBERT HUDSON (*c.* 1785–1825)
By Ezra Ames, *c.* 1820
Privately owned

MRS. ROBERT HUDSON
By Ezra Ames, *c.* 1820
Privately owned

marine subjects, or painted them on the premises. Perhaps, again, he and the Governor discussed Masonic matters. On one of the visits, September 5, 1818, he was among an interesting group of callers at the Governor's mansion: the Secretary of State, Miss Spencer and her niece, and Citizen Genet and his wife with their son.

To this period belong some of the portraits by Ames which have been confused with the work of other artists. One, the portrait of Mrs. Hooper Cumming and her daughter, presented to The New-York Historical Society in 1896 as the work of Rembrandt Peale, was attributed to Ames by William Sawitzky in 1944. Another, the portrait of her husband owned by The New Jersey Historical Society, formerly attributed to John Vanderlyn, was recently attributed to Ames by the writers, judging from a photograph. The attribution was made because the portrait is a companion portrait to that of the sitter's wife (that is, the portraits are the same size and the sitters face each other); and because it has mannerisms found in the work of Ames such as the placing of the high lights in the eyes; and the bold painting of the background similar to that found in the portrait of Absalom Townsend. It is here assumed that this portrait of Hooper Cumming is not the portrait recorded by the artist in his Account Book as painted for the Joseph Delaplaine Gallery (crossed out, and thus possibly never painted), because it is a family picture and not a gallery piece.

A privately owned portrait of Mrs. Jacob Jennings Brown, painted about 1818, formerly attributed to Jarvis, was attributed to Ames in 1940 by William Sawitzky. Another and different portrait of Mrs. Brown, owned at the Munson-Williams-Proctor Institute, was attributed to Ames in the same year by Miss Hope Mathewson.

Of the six portraits which the artist recorded in his third Account Book as of the year 1819, one has been identified as the bust portrait of Harmanus Bleecker which is now at the Harmanus Bleecker Library, Albany. A replica of the portrait is privately owned. The one at the Harmanus Bleecker Library, rather dark perhaps because of the need for cleaning, is an especially fine characterization. Painted with extreme care, it is one of the best examples of the artist's work. Another recorded and located portrait by the artist during this year is the convincing likeness of General Solomon Van Rensselaer which remains today in the house in Albany for which it was intended. Two portraits, unrecorded in the Account Book but signed and dated 1819, are of the artist's father, Captain Jesse Emes, at the age of 80, and of the Captain's third wife, who was then 70, and whom he married in January of that year.[11]

The artist's recorded miscellaneous work for 1819 includes the "alegorical Painting for T[emple] Lodge," Albany, previously mentioned; a portrait frame for Ambrose Spencer; another for the Reverend John Chester; a fancy piece to be used as an embroidery design; and two signs. One of the signs, recorded July 16, 1819, is entitled "Eagle Sign." It is charged to H. Bamman who had advertised in *The Albany Gazette* for June 3, 1819, the opening of his Eagle Tavern, and it was for this caravansary that the sign was undoubtedly painted. It cost Mr. Bamman $13. The other sign was likewise for Mr. Bamman, and cost him $7.

Other references to the artist at this time are found in his Expense Book for 1819. During June, Ames visited New York City, a trip which cost him $30; his expenses for the calendar year of 1819 amounted to $900; and $52.29 was what he had to pay in taxes.

There are only a few entries listing unpaid-for ornamental and artistic work accomplished during the next year 1820. The artist constructed three frames, one of them charged to Ambrose Spencer "for his Lady's portrait"; painted two stands of colors for the Albany Regiment; and made a "lottery sign for Richmond" for which he charged S. & M. Allen $80. With the painting of this sign Ames brought to a close his record of sign painting —an activity he had first recorded in 1791, twenty-nine years

[11] Reynolds, Helen Wilkinson, 41.

MRS. JESSE EMES, STEPMOTHER OF THE ARTIST

By Ezra Ames, 1819

Owned by Miss Edith S. Wade

JESSE EMES (1739–1829), FATHER OF THE ARTIST

By Ezra Ames, signed and dated, 1819

Owned by the Albany Institute of History and Art

MRS. DEWITT CLINTON (1783–1855)

By Ezra Ames, dated by Account Book, 1820

Owned by the Long Island Historical Society

(Photo by FARL)

MRS. PETER GANSEVOORT (1752–1830)

By Ezra Ames, dated by a receipt, 1824

Owned by the Albany Institute of History and Art

(Photo by courtesy of Mrs. William Sawitzky)

earlier. His prices had ranged from as low as two shillings in 1791 to $100 each for lottery signs painted in 1816, 1817, and in 1818.

His artistic work for the year 1820 includes the painting of a "Pike fish" and two portraits of the second Mrs. DeWitt Clinton (Catherine Jones), one an original and the other a "copy," all for Governor Clinton. In this instance Ames used the word "copy" to mean a replica of his own portrait. Entries for portraits of the Reverend Doctor "Blackford" in 1818, and his wife in 1820, probably refer to those of Doctor Blatchford and his wife (reproduced in the Blatchford family genealogy), still unlocated.

One of the portraits of Mrs. Clinton, either the original or the replica, is at The Long Island Historical Society. The portrait is characteristic of a group of Ames's portraits of women which he painted early and late. In this group, some of the women wear turbans, some wear caps, some are bareheaded, and some wear frills of lace about the throat; but whatever the costume, they are all draped with similar flower-bordered shawls. In a portrait of Mrs. Thomas Jones (Margaret Livingston), which was possibly painted at the same time as that of her daughter, Mrs. DeWitt Clinton, the shawl is also introduced.

A picture belonging to the period about 1820–1825 is the handsome portrait of Ambrose Latting Jordan at the New York State Historical Association, Cooperstown, N. Y. It was once attributed to Morse and, more recently, tentatively attributed to Jarvis. A portrait of Jordan is listed in the inventory of the artist's estate, 1836, and also in the handbill: *Catalogue Sale of Portraits* [in the artist's estate], 1842, which is documentary evidence for the attribution to Ames. Artistic reasons for the attribution are: the dark vertical strip at one side of the picture; the faint diagonal at one of the upper corners; and the placing of the high lights in the eyes on the inside of both pupils—three characteristics of many of Ames's portraits.

There is an interesting document of the year 1820 which shows how far the artist's reputation had by now penetrated into upstate New York. It is a letter, dated July 20, 1820, Ovid, New

York, in which William Thompson requests of Ezra Ames that he take as a pupil a young man of exceptional character named John Morehouse, who would "furnish himself with board by his industry."[12] To this young aspirant there is no further reference.

The next year there is another reference to an aspiring young man who visited Ames's gallery and later on made a name for himself as an artist. He was born in 1806 at Lennox, Madison County, New York; and when he was fifteen years old his father took him on a visit to Albany. There the boy "saw for the first time a gallery of portraits: they were the works of Mr. Ames."[13] The boy was Frederick R. Spencer who became a well-known painter of the next generation.[14]

In his Expense Book for the same year, 1821, during May, the artist recorded a trip he took to New York. In his Account Book during the year he noted the painting of seven portraits, and also a still-life picture of an apple and a pear, the latter for DeWitt Clinton. The next year he continued to work for this patron and friend. On April 23, 1822, he recorded the painting of a "Silver Lake White Fish" for the Governor; and on June 11, 1822, he recorded that the Governor owed him $10 for cleaning and gilding a frame for a portrait of Judge Ambrose Spencer. Another small job of this year was the "altering a painting of Lake Georg[e]" at a charge of $2 for James Caldwell, a landscape of which mention has already been made. He also recorded payment due him on three portraits, which suggests not so much that he painted only a few portraits this year, but that other portraits of this year were so promptly paid for that they did not have to be recorded.

One learns from his Expense Books that during the next two years the artist took a number of outings. In June of 1822, he recorded that he spent $50 on a trip to New York. On August 1, 1822, he noted that $4.25 covered his "Expenses in vewing" the "Cannal" without, however, recording the point of vantage from

[12] *MS Ames and Others,* No. 1, July 20, 1820.

[13] Dunlap, II: 436.

[14] *Appletons' CAB,* V: 629.

AMBROSE LATTING JORDAN (1789–1865)

By Ezra Ames, *c.* 1820–1825

Owned by Mr. Stephen C. Clark
On permanent loan to the New York State Historical Association

which he made this observation of what was doubtless the Erie Canal then under construction. The following year in June, 1823, he spent $60 on a visit to New York and Philadelphia; and in August of the same year he spent another $60 on a trip to Buffalo, and "Niageria."

Since Buffalo was the western terminus of the Erie Canal, one may assume that Ames spent some of his time in "vewing" the canal construction from there during this last trip. The eastern section of this great undertaking was completed on October 1, 1823. Referring to the Erie and Champlain Canals, Cadwallader D. Colden wrote: "... when the lock which forms the communication between the Canals, and the artificial basin in the Hudson River, at Albany, was opened on the eighth of October, eighteen hundred and twenty-three, there was a continuous Canal navigation from the Genesee River, and from White Hall, at the head of Lake Champlain, to Albany." He continues: "Such an auspicious event as the passage of the first boats from the west, and the north into the tide waters, was celebrated with some ceremony." In the celebration of this event held at Albany, on October 8, 1823, Ezra Ames took a prominent part.

Colden records that, on the appointed day, the canal boats arrived at Albany "with colours flying, bands of music, and crowded with people...." He continues: "The first boat which entered the lock was the De Witt Clinton, having on board Governor Yates, the Mayor and Corporation of Albany, the Canal commissioners and engineers, the committees, and other citizens. Several other boats succeeded. One, (not the least interesting object in the scene), was filled with ladies. The cap-stone of the lock was laid with masonic ceremonies, by the fraternity who appeared in great numbers and in grand costume."[15]

The Masonic ceremonies were described by the editor of *The Albany Argus* in the issue for Friday, October 10, 1823:

> On Wednesday the 8th inst. the thunder of artillery and the pealing of bells announced the arrival of the day which will ever be held

[15] Colden, 59–61.

memorable by the inhabitants of this city, and form an important era in the annals of the state.... At this time, the ceremony of laying the top-stone of the lock, was performed by Ezra Ames, Grand High Priest of the Grand Chapter of the state of New-York, dressed in his official robes, and attended by his subordinates, arrayed in the insignia of their respective offices, in the following order:—

The procession opened to the right and left, and the grand officers passed through to the front, and once around the lock to the north side.

The companions formed on each side of the grand officers with the grand marshall on the left.

Prayer by the Rev. Grand Chaplain.

Exhortation by the Grand High Priest [Ezra Ames].

Celebration ode chanted while the procession moved three times around the lock under the arches.

The engraved plate was then examined and placed under the cape stone by the Grand Scribe.

The cape stone was laid by the Grand High Priest [Ezra Ames] assisted by the Grand Architects.

Corn, wine and oil were consecrated on the cape stone by the presiding officer [Ezra Ames].

Benediction by the presiding officer [Ezra Ames].

Closing ceremonies. The procession passed three times round the lock under the arches.

Final close by the discharge of nine cannon, by three times three—flourish of music between each three.

The editor then went on to say that the "Final Close" consisted in another ceremony "no less novel and interesting" than the others: "Dr. Mitchell" poured bottles of water from "two oceans"—one from the mid-ocean of the Atlantic, and the other from the Pacific—into the lock. This was Dr. Samuel L. Mitchill who, after the ceremony of mingling the waters: "pronounced an epithalamium upon the union of the River and the Lakes, after which the lock gates were opened, and the [canal boat] De Witt Clinton majestically sunk upon the bosom of the Hudson."[16]

Reverting to the Masonic ceremonies, Mr. E. T. Reid writes that: "Afterward DeWitt Clinton wrote to Grand Chapter commending the Grand High Priest [Ezra Ames] for his skill and dignity in conducting the work and he also stated that the cere-

[16] Colden, 61, 273.

monies made a most favorable impression on the assembled multitude."[17] This was the first of the Erie Canal Celebrations. At the second Canal Celebration, held in 1825 upon the completion of the Erie Canal for its entire length from Lake Erie to the Hudson River, Ezra Ames was again to take a prominent part in the ceremonies.

In October 1823, Ames recorded in his Expense Book that he paid a visit to Waterford. Earlier in the same year, he recorded in his Account Book, two small but unusual jobs: the painting, or repainting, of two tobacco-store Indians. The charges were against a Mr. Solomon, both for "painting an Indian statue." The first charge was for $6, the second for $5. They are the last records of miscellaneous and ornamental work found in the artist's Account Books. A wood engraving, presumably after one of the Indian statues, appears in an advertisement of "Caldwell & Solomons Tobacco and Snuff Store" published in *The Albany Gazette* for January 13, 1820.[18]

Turning from the artist's Masonic activities and his miscellaneous job-painting, to continue his chronology as an artist: a number of portraits may be assigned to the years 1820–1826 One of these is a bust portrait of Colonel Benjamin Tallmadge, in his later years; and another is a bust portrait of his son, Lieutenant Benjamin Tallmadge, Jr., a handsome portrait of a young man in naval uniform which afforded Ames the opportunity of introducing some pleasing color contrasts. Both are said to have been painted in 1820. Another portrait of about this year is that of Theodore Strong, carefully drawn and colorfully painted. Equally well-drawn but thinly painted is the excellent character study of Marcus Tullius Reynolds, painted *c.* 1821. Bust portraits of Dr. Stephen Reynolds and his wife were painted *c.* 1824.

The portrait of William James (1771–1832) at Union College is definitely dated: the year 1822 appears clearly on a letter which he holds in his hand. It was formerly attributed to Stuart, and then

[17] Reid, 13.

[18] Photostat of advertisement supplied by Mrs. Katharine M. McClinton and reproduced with her article on "Ezra Ames, Ornamental Painter," in *The Magazine Antiques*, September 1951.

THEODORE STRONG (1790–1869)
By Ezra Ames, *c.* 1820
(Photo by FARL)
Owner: Mr. Theodore Strong, Jr.

MARCUS T. REYNOLDS (1788–1864)
By Ezra Ames, *c.* 1821
(Photo by FARL)
Owner: Mr. Kenneth G. Reynolds

to Waldo and Jewett. Finally it was attributed to Ames by the late William Sawitzky. A portrait of Mrs. James King (Ellen James), daughter of William James (1771–1832) by his second wife, Mary Ann Connolly; and a portrait of the third wife of William James, Catharine Barber, formerly attributed to Waldo, are contemporaneous. The portraits of father and daughter have backgrounds which are much alike, and the hands of all the sitters are painted in a similar manner. The two women hold handkerchiefs, and Mrs. James wears the characteristic flower-bordered shawl. The handwriting in the letter which William James holds in his hand, clearly addressed: "Wm James, E[sq.,]/ Albany," resembles the handwriting of Ezra Ames in his Account Books. The three portraits are reproduced herein.

Soon after the painting of the James family portraits an important event took place in the Ames household: the marriage of the Reverend William James (1797–1868), a son of the artist's patron, William James (1771–1832) and his first wife, Elizabeth

MRS. WILLIAM JAMES (1782–1859)
By Ezra Ames, 1822 (FARL photo)
Owned by Mr. A. Coster Schermerhorn

WILLIAM JAMES (1771–1832)
By Ezra Ames, 1822 (FARL photo)
Owned by Union College

MRS. JAMES (ELLEN JAMES) KING
(1800–1823)
By Ezra Ames, 1822 (FARL photo)
Owned by Mrs. Reginald P. Rose

Tillman, to the artist's daughter Marcia. The reporter in *The Albany Argus,* Friday, November 26, 1824, announced it as follows: "Married–On Wednesday evening [November 24] last, by the Rev. Mr. Weed, Rev. William James to Marcia L. the daughter of Ezra Ames, Esq. all of this city." The witnesses were Dr. Chester and J. V. Henry. The ceremony took place in the First Presbyterian Church, Albany,[19] probably because four years earlier, in 1820, the groom had been ordained by the Presbytery at Albany.[20] The wedding was thus recorded in his Expense Book by the father of the bride: "Marcia 50.00" and "Weding Expenses 30.00."

Although the wedding took place in the Presbyterian Church, at this time Ezra Ames probably belonged to the Dutch Church. It is true that in 1794 he had contributed 12 shillings to the "Presperterian Church," but for the next twenty years there is no mention in either his Account Books or Expense Books of any other such contribution. Then, beginning in 1815 and continuing intermittently through his Expense Books, until the last one dated 1826, he made entries for pew rent in an unspecified church. The amount he mentions as paid yearly was usually "16/." The church was probably the one referred to in the executors' accounts of the artist's estate as the "2nd Dutch Church," in which, according to them $5.00 was the charge for pew No. 36 on the second floor;[21] or, as specified on page three of the certified inventory of his estate, "pew No. 36 in the N. E. Corner Gallery of S. Dutch Church."[22] The edifice referred to was no doubt the one then on Beaver Street known at various times as the Second, South, and Middle Dutch Church. It was replaced in 1881 by a building on the corner of Madison Avenue and Swan Street.[23]

Returning to the year 1824: in that year Ames was elected a member of the American Academy of the Fine Arts, the associa-

[19] *MS First Presbyterian Church,* typewritten Register.

[20] Hastings, *New York Genealogical and Biographical Record,* April 1924, p. 108.

[21] *MS Ames, Ezra, Estate,* No. V, Item 5.

[22] *Ibid.,* No. I, Item 1.

[23] Howell and Tenney, 771.

tion to whose exhibition, held in 1816, Benjamin Armitage had urged him to send his work. This second reference to the American Academy, found in the minutes of the association, is dated May 29, 1824:

> The following gentlemen were nominated and elected Academicians of this Institution. [*There then appear the names:*] Messrs William Jewett, E. Metcalf, N. Rogers, J. Milbert, A. B. Durand, W. W. Wall, John Frazee, C. Ingham, Henry Inman, Enrico Causicci, William Main and E. Ames of Albany—and the following gentlemen were proposed as Associates Messrs Bisbee, Paradise, De Rose, Wright, Marsiglia, and R. W. Weir—at the same time the following gentlemen were proposed as Honorary Members—Charles Leslie, [William] Strickland, S. F. B. Morse, Charles Fraser, G. Fairman, J. Wood, N. Joscelyn.[24]

In the exhibition catalogues for 1825, 1826, and 1827, Ames is listed as an Honorary Member. Although his membership obviously gave Ames the privilege of sending his work to the American Academy exhibitions, an examination of the exhibition catalogues fails to show that Ames ever exhibited his work at any of their displays. Furthermore, an examination of the exhibition catalogues of the National Academy of Design, organized in 1825 as a rival association to the American Academy of the Fine Arts,[25] likewise fails to show that Ames was ever an exhibitor with this group of which he was not a member.

An invitation from the American Academy sent to Ames announcing an exhibition is at The New-York Historical Society. It is a printed form from the secretary with "E. Ames Esq" handwritten at the top of the sheet, and dated December 12, 1831, inviting him "to exhibit some specimens" of his art " at the annual Exhibition" of that association.

About 1825, Ames painted a miniature of Jesse Hawley, now at The New-York Historical Society. It was Jesse Hawley who, on the morning of October 26, 1825, addressed the crowds assembled at Buffalo during the gala day set aside for the celebration of the opening of the "Great Erie Canal." These festivities cen-

[24] MS *American Academy of the Fine Arts, Minutes*, III: 144–145.

[25] Cowdrey, *National Academy of Design Exhibition Record.*

tered around a flotilla of five boats destined to depart that day on an epoch-making first voyage on the entire length of the canal from Lake Erie to the Hudson River; and thence to the sea. The passengers in the first boat, the *Seneca Chief*, were Governor DeWitt Clinton, the Lieutenant Governor, and numerous delegates from cities along the waterway. When the festivities were over at Buffalo, the *Seneca Chief* "led off in fine style, drawn by four grey horses, fancifully caparisoned," and all the boats in the flotilla followed after.[26]

JESSE HAWLEY (1773–1842)
Miniature on ivory
By Ezra Ames, *c.* 1825
The New-York Historical Society
Gift of Jesse Hawley

In the meanwhile a celebration was being prepared for the reception of the passengers when the boats reached Albany. Governor Clinton "who so ably served the Craft as its Grand Master," had "asked the Masons of the State to take part in the imposing ceremony when the waters of Lake Erie first mingled with the ocean." Ezra Ames was selected to act as master of ceremonies[27] at this second Canal celebration, as he had been asked to act at the first held in 1823.

Levi Beardsley, a recently elected member of the State Assembly[28] who came to Albany for the celebration, recalls in his Reminiscences that on the evening of November 1, 1825, the city was crowded with "citizens from every part of the state."[29] The celebration which attracted this multitude to Albany was to begin on the morning of the following day.

[26] *The Albany Argus & City Gazette*, November 4, 1825, (article dated November 1, 1825, quoted from *The Buffalo Journal* of October 25, 1825).

[27] Bresee, *Masonic Family Magazine*, July–August 1950, p. 11. Reference supplied by Mr. Charles T. Miller.

[28] *Appletons' CAB*, 207.

[29] Beardsley, 213, 216.

MRS. JOHN KEYES PAIGE (1797–1829) JOHN KEYES PAIGE (1788–1857)

By Ezra Ames, both dated by Account Book, 1826

(Photographs by FARL)

Owned by Dr. J. Lewi Donhauser

VII

HONORS IN LAST DECADE, 1825–1836:

AMES AT THE ERIE CANAL CELEBRATION, LATER WORK AS AN ARTIST, BANK PRESIDENT

ALTHOUGH the sky over Albany was ominously dark on the early morning of November 2, 1825, a cold northwest wind soon blew the clouds away; and the day was memorably fair when, at half past ten o'clock, the flotilla reached the last lock where the boats were to be lowered and passed through to the Hudson River.[1] On the shore, by a monument in which the records of the event were to be sealed, stood a group of Freemasons with Ezra Ames at their head as master of ceremonies. Standing in the bow of the *Seneca Chief* were Governor DeWitt Clinton, who was to conduct the formal opening of the canal, General Stephen Van Rensselaer, and other Canal Commissioners. Levi Beardsley recalls:

> Several boats were in the procession, all of them loaded with passengers containing as many as could be safely on them. As they approached the lock, a deposit was made in the monument, of papers, manuscripts, and other articles, giving a history of the work. The acting grand master [Ezra Ames] then proceeded in the presence of the fraternity and thousands of spectators, to adjust and place the "cap stone," in masonic forms. He finally gave three emblematic knocks, declaring it finished. The brethren passed round, as if to inspect and verify the truth of the annunciation, performing their part of the ceremony; the cannon announced the completion; and the boats glided through the lock into the Hudson.[2]

A reporter for *The Albany Argus* noted that the announcement of the completion was a grand salute from twenty-four cannon mounted on the pier.[3]

The festivities continued throughout the day, and ended in an entertainment at the Albany Theatre. The theatre managers issued an advertisement, dated November 2, 1825, announcing the

[1] Colden, 308–309.

[2] Beardsley, 213–214.

[3] *The Albany Argus & City Gazette,* Tuesday, November 8, 1825, XIII, No. 1335 (article dated Friday, November 4, 1825).

attractions for the evening: a play, a farce, and the reciting of an "Ode" composed especially for the Erie Canal Celebration. In their advertisement there is a reference to the work of Ames:

> The evening's Entertainment to conclude with a splendid transparency, in honor of the CANAL CELEBRATION, representing the Genius of America supporting the portraits of Mr. Clinton and Mr. Fulton, painted by Mr. Sera; the portrait of Mr. Clinton from a painting of Mr. Ames. In the background a view of the Hudson, with the steam boat Fulton in perspective. A view of the CANAL with boats passing and repassing.[4]

The completion of the inland waterway was eventful because New York rather than New Orleans would thereafter become the chief port of trade with the Northwest Territory.[5] From then on the larger part of the commerce of the Mississippi Valley moved through the Valley of the Mohawk, then down the Hudson River. Thus began the great economic development of New York State.[6]

Among the portraits that Ames painted many are of the men who were prominent during this expansion. For this reason, aside from their artistic merits, they are important historical documents of that era. As for their artistic merits: the best of Ames's later work shows an increasing skill in characterization and technique. However, as Mr. Robert G. Wheeler has pointed out: "Often we find a late painting which seems quite similar to an early one in technical ability and approach."[7]

In his third Account Book, during 1823, the artist listed no portraits for which payments were due him. In 1824 he listed six. Among the nine portraits listed during 1825, he did not list the excellent portrait of Clarkson Crolius, at The New-York Historical Society, which is signed and dated on the back as of this year. Also unrecorded in the Account Book are the portraits of William Tully, Jr., 1826, and Julius Rubens Ames, about 1826. The portrait of Tully is characteristic of Ames's work except

[4] Munsell, *Collections*, II (1867): 47?

[5] DAB, IV: 224.

[6] Bresee, *Masonic Family Magazine*, July–August, 1850, p. 15.

[7] Wheeler, *American Collector*, August 1947, p. 8.

WILLIAM TULLY, JR. (1785–1859)
By Ezra Ames, 1826

Owned by Yale University Art Gallery

for the boldly painted buff-colored overcoat and mantle. In contrast, the portrait of the artist's son is meticulously painted throughout. The portrait of Tully is an exceptionally convincing characterization.

Several references in the artist's Expense Book for the same year, 1826, relate to his travels. In June he visited Staatsburg, obviously to see his father, spending $4; in July he visited New York, his expenses coming to $25; and the same month, perhaps on his return trip from New York to Albany, he revisited Staatsburg, his expenses this time coming to $8, which indicates a longer stay than his visit in June.

Thirteen letters at The New-York Historical Society, to and from Ames, relate to his official duties as a Mason. They cover the period from 1810 to 1826.[8] During the latter year Ames retired from his position as Grand High Priest. Of his retirement, Mr. E. T. Reid writes:

> After twenty-four years' service as Grand High Priest Ezra Ames was again tendered the nomination, but he believed he had been in office long enough and should now retire, and accordingly he declined the nomination. On February 10, 1826, a resolution was adopted as follows:
>
> "Resolved, That the thanks of this Grand Chapter be presented to M. E. Ezra Ames, Past Grand High Priest, for his long, able and satisfactory discharge of the duties of his office, and the officers were authorized to prepare a suitable testimonial to be presented to him at the next annual meeting of the Grand Chapter, the expense not to exceed $250.00."
>
> This was done on February 10, 1827, by M. E. Asa Fitch and M. E. Companion Ezra Ames made a suitable speech of acceptance.

In 1828 Ames again attended the Grand Chapter, and for the last time in 1829. Mr. Reid concludes: "Thus we come to the end of the active career of one of the most remarkable companions who ever wore the Mitre and the Breastplate."[9]

A reference to another of the artist's group participations is vague as to time, but it is placed here because it reveals him in a position of leadership in artistic as well as Masonic circles. Jonathan Tenney wrote in 1883:

[8] *MS Ames and Others*, No. 1.

[9] Reid, 13.

At one time Albany had a "Gallery of Fine Arts," where were collected quite a display of good pictures by such artists as Durand, Sully, Peale, Chapman, Carleton, Weir, the Harts, Ames and others. But most of the artists sought more favored homes and the treasures of the gallery were scattered. Ames, who was the founder and leading spirit, had died.[10]

One of the rare references to the artist's home life is found in a letter of the year 1827, from Caroline Spencer, presumably the daughter of Polly (Emes) Spencer who was the half-sister of Ezra Ames,[11] addressed to "Mon Cher Julius," her cousin and a son of Ezra Ames. Writing from Jersey City, July 23, 1827, Caroline begins by telling of the bizarre exploits of Julius' brother Angelo who had gone to sea in a pilot boat with the idea that seasickness would cure him of what Caroline hoped was an imaginary ailment. She also reports that "Uncle Harry," alluding to Henry Emes, a half-brother of Ezra Ames,[11] and "Aunt Rachel talked of visiting Delhi this summer." Then she writes: "I learn by your letter that Uncle [Ezra] Ames has returned from Rochester since you give us news from Marcia, I am happy to hear that she is again settled in good health." Of Captain Jesse Emes, Ezra's father, and of his third wife, Caroline writes: "Old Grandpa and Grandma are very much the same. Grandpa fails from year to year but gradually. . . ."[12]

Not quite two years after this intimation of his declining health, Captain Jesse Emes died on May 7, 1829, at the age of ninety.[13] In 1949 two visitors to Staatsburg,[14] searching for gravestones of members of the Emes family, found the family burying ground. It was hidden in a clump of trees on a hill west of the New York Central tracks near the railroad station. There is now no right of way to the plot, and its existence is not generally known to the local residents. The gravestones are overgrown with grass and poison ivy. The trunk of a large oak, which has grown up on the plot since the tablets were placed, has tilted the

[10] Tenney, 62.
[11] Sutliff, 31, 32.
[12] *MS Spencer, Caroline.*
[13] Gravestone.
[14] Irwin F. Cortelyou, and her husband, Mr. George B. Cortelyou, Jr.

gravestone of Captain Jesse Emes to a sharp angle. Other gravestones in the plot which the visitors recorded are those of Dorothy Emes (Captain Jesse's second wife); and those of his sons Jesse, Jr., and Henry.[15]

In a transcript of the Captain's will, dated March 24, 1813, among the records at the Surrogate's Court, Poughkeepsie, there is a note stating that the original will was delivered to the Captain's son Henry who was appointed the executor of the estate. Captain Jesse left forty pounds each to his daughters Sally Mulford, Polly Spencer, and Betty Silknegg [*sic*], a codicil dated Staatsburg, August 29, 1825, being inserted after Betty's death; and fifty pounds each to his sons Timothy Emes and Ezra "Emes." To the children of Jesse Emes, Jr., he left one shilling, "they having received their part."[16]

Reverting to an earlier year, and specifically to the artist's record of portraits unpaid for at the time of completion: a number of the twelve portraits which he listed in his Account Book during 1826 have been located. One is a copy he made of his bust portrait of Colonel Tallmadge. Three others are of Aaron Thorp, his wife, and their daughter. In the first two of these, the artist took his usual care in the painting of the likenesses. On the other hand, in his portrait of the Thorps' daughter, the artist reverts to his earlier methods, which he invariably used in his portraits of children. It has little of the skilled artistry of the portraits of Aaron Thorp and his wife, and is simply a delightful primitive painting. Bust portraits of John Keyes Paige (formerly attributed to Francis Alexander) and of his first wife, Helen Maria Yates, noted in the Account Book this year, have also been located. Both are excellent characterizations, painted with great assurance.

The portrait of Samuel Stevenson Fowler, unrecorded in the

[15] The foregoing tombstones were also recorded in 1913 by George S. Van Vliet, who in addition recorded those of Betsey Selkreg [sic] (Jesse's daughter by his second wife); her husband, John Selkreg; John W., and Mary L. Selkreg, infants; Angelo Hughes, Jr., infant; Eliza Abby Hughes Cox; and John Wooldridge. Poucher and Reynolds, 124. The name Selkreg is spelled "Silkregg" by Sutliff, 32; and "Silknegg" in the will of Jesse Emes.

[16] *MS Emes, Jesse, Will.*

AARON THORP

By Ezra Ames, dated by Account Book, 1826

Owned by Miss Eleanor B. Weir (Photo by FARL)

MRS. AARON THORP

By Ezra Ames, dated by Account Book, 1826

Owned by Miss Eleanor B. Weir (Photo by FARL)

ELIAS MATHER (1776–1843)
By Ezra Ames, *c.* 1827 (Photo by FARL)
Owned by Miss Gertrude Robinson Smith

MRS. STEPHEN REYNOLDS (1770–1843)
By Ezra Ames, *c.* 1824 (Photo by FARL)
Owned by Mr. Kenneth G. Reynolds

Account Books, but painted about 1827, judging from the apparent age of the sitter, is one of Ames's most attractive works. The figure is well drawn, well placed, and tastefully related to a background of pleasing color.

The record of the artist's portraits as found in his third Account Book during the four years from 1827 through 1830 may be summarized in a paragraph. He recorded three portraits in 1827; one in 1828; nine in 1829; and eight in 1830. Of several which have been located, one, a portrait of Eliphalet Nott painted for three students of Union College, is owned by that institution. Another is a portrait of Gerrit Yates Lansing, recorded in 1830, which is privately owned.

In a letter of the following year, one finds another of the few references which have been discovered, relating to the artist's family life. The letter is from the artist's daughter, Marcia Lucretia Ames, who was then Mrs. William James, to her brother Angelo, who, by this time, was a voyager in search of his health. The letter, dated Albany, January 6, 1831, is addressed to Angelo; and the forwarding addresses, including Mobile and Charleston (both crossed out), and New Orleans, indicate three of the young man's ports-of-call. Marcia begins:

> We had the pleasure of receiving your favour of the 24 yesterday. I read it over and over to all the family they listened to every word with the deepest interest. Ma [Mrs. Ezra Ames] said she was glad to hear her Son Angelo was alive yet. Pa [Ezra Ames] says the poor boy must have had a hard time of it—even Poll turned her head and looked as if she felt sorry—but she is in fine spirits this morning just now she is sitting on her pole laughing very heartily.

Although the precise nature of Angelo's hardships are only hinted at, they must have been hard indeed, for in the course of the long and pious passage which follows, the clergyman's wife hopes that her "Dear brother" feels "Grattitude to your Creator for preserving your life, when no human aid could be obtained." She then writes:

> Our family affairs go on much as usual. I have occupied the parlour all winter. Anna goes to school at [the] young Ladies Seminary. Emeline

is housekeeper and Ma is the lady New Years day we had a number of calls Dr Meigs Mr Fowler Mr Allcott Mr Marvin Mr King and Mr James seigniour—there were several more of your friends whose names I do not remember—Mr Dunn sends his best respects to you he wishes you to write him immediately, business has been very dull, we have not had any sleighing and very little cold weather, the franklin [stove] has kept the parlour pleasant and comfortable—

Further on she writes: "Julius continues in his own room painting Miniatures." She continues: "the cats and Parrot are in perfect health. The family all send their love—Ma sends her love in particular she says you must bring her a present and come home in the spring in good health. . . ." She concludes: "from your affectionate Sister Marcia L. James." Then, in a postscript, there is the only reference found thus far to the artist's feelings for any of the members of his family. "Write to Pa immediately," she implores, "You cannot show us a greater favour."[17]

The next month, on February 1, 1831, there is a final reference to the artist as a Freemason. In the report of the trustees of the Grand Chapter for that date, there is a record of the sale of stock of the Mechanics and Farmers' Bank of Albany which Ames had bought for the Chapter in 1820 for $1,590.00. The stock was sold in 1831 at an advance of fifty percent.[18]

This purchase, made six years after he had been elected one of the board of directors of the Merchants and Farmers' Bank, is an indication of that business acumen which gained Ames the respect of his associates in the banking business. Three years after the sale of the stock which he had purchased for the Grand Chapter, Ames attained the highest possible position of confidence in the bank: he was elected president of the bank at the annual meeting of the board held on June 3, 1834.[19] Benjamin Knower had resigned as president on February 3, 1834; and Charles Dudley, a former mayor of the city, was acting as president when the meeting took place.[20] Of the twelve directors, ten were pres-

[17] *MS James, Mrs. William.*

[18] Reid, 13.

[19] *MS Mechanics and Farmers' Bank, Minutes*, consulted by Mr. George B. Cortelyou, Jr.

[20] Mechanics and Farmers' Bank, *Span of a Century*.

ELEAZER BURNHAM (b. 1780)
By Ezra Ames, signed and dated, 1826
Owned by Mr. William C. Hook

MRS. ELEAZER BURNHAM (d. 1832)
By Ezra Ames, signed and dated, 1830
Owned by Mr. William C. Hook

MRS. GEORGE TIBBITS (1767–1846)
By Ezra Ames, *c.* 1833 (Photo by FARL)
Owned by Mr. George Dudley Tibbits

GEORGE TIBBITS (1763–1849)
By Ezra Ames, *c.* 1833 (Photo by FARL)
Owned by Mr. George Dudley Tibbits

ent; and, according to the minutes of the meetings: "there was one blank ballot and nine votes for Ezra Ames."[21]

There is an interesting reference to the qualifications for this office as bank president found in the centennial booklet *Span of a Century* issued by the Mechanics and Farmers' Bank: "That year [1834] Mr. Ames, who had risen from an artisan to an artist, and his brother officers, secured an amendment to the charter which removed the Mechanics and Farmers restrictive clause requiring that the president must be chosen from one of these classes, and allowed the choice of any one irrespective of his profession or employment."[22] As the president of the bank he attended all the board meetings except the one on January 20, 1835; and the few held early in the next year, before his death in February.[23]

In 1834 Ames also received recognition of a different kind: a paragraph about him appeared in the *History of the Rise and Progress of the Arts of Design in the United States*, by William Dunlap, the well-known work which was published in two volumes and which bears the same relation to the history of American artists as does the biographical work of Giorgio Vasari to that of the Italian painters and sculptors. In his history Dunlap noted that:

> Mr. Ames was a coach painter in Albany; but attempting portraiture, so far succeeded, that, in 1812, his portrait of Governor George Clinton was exhibited, much to the painter's credit, in the Pennsylvania Academy of Fine Arts. He, for many years, painted portraits of most of the western members of the legislature, and of many others: and I have reason to believe, that in old age he enjoys the blessings of competency, derived from his enterprise and industry. He has a son who paints miniatures.[24]

Julius was the son, doubtless trained by his father, who painted miniatures; and his name appears, with that of his father and brother, in the Albany Directories for the period 1832–1836:

[21] *MS Mechanics and Farmers' Bank, Minutes.*

[22] Mechanics and Farmers' Bank, *Span of a Century*.

[23] *MS Mechanics and Farmers' Bank, Minutes*, consulted by Mr. George B. Cortelyou, Jr.

[24] Dunlap, II: 258.

Ames, Angelo, 41 s. Pearl
Ames, Ezra, portrait painter, 41 s. Pearl
Ames, Julius R. miniature painter, 41 s. Pearl

Besides following his father's profession, Julius also became an active member of his father's Masonic lodge. Both brothers, indeed, were members of Temple Lodge, but Julius was the more active, for he was elected Master of the lodge in 1831 and 1834.[25]

There is little known about Ezra Ames at this time. In his Account Book under the date of September 3, 1831, he noted that Henry Shaw owed him for "Painting his daughters Portrait," which is the only portrait which he recorded for that year. There is then an hiatus in his Account Book until December 28, 1834, when he noted that Mrs. Cooper was his debtor "To Painting a Portrait of Doct^r Cooper her Deceased Husband." This portrait has recently been identified as of Dr. Charles DeKay Cooper. A photograph of an unlocated portrait of Mrs. Cooper (Margaret Tayler), daughter of John Tayler, was found in the same collection.

This entry for December 28, 1834 is the last in the Account Books. The artist had now but a little over a year to live. He did not attend several meetings of the Board of Directors of the Mechanics and Farmers' Bank during January–February, 1836.[26]

He died in office as president of the bank on February 23, 1836. Thus ended the successful career as an artist and banker of the boy who forty-three years earlier had settled in Albany and sold his small belongings to make ends meet. On the day of his death, a notice appeared in the *Albany Evening Journal:*

> Died. This morning at 3 o'clock Ezra Ames in the 68th year of his age. The relatives, friends & acquaintances of the deceased are invited to attend his funeral to-morrow at 3 o'clock from his residence 41 So. Pearl Street.

A similar notice appeared in *The Daily Albany Argus* on the following day.

That Dr. A[lden] March was the physician in attendance one

[25] Reid, 13.
[26] *MS Mechanics and Farmers' Bank, Minutes,* consulted by Mr. George B. Cortelyou, Jr.

JULIUS RUBENS AMES (1801–1850), ELDER SON OF THE ARTIST

By Ezra Ames, *c.* 1826

Owned by Miss Edith S. Wade

learns from his receipted bill;[27] from another receipted bill, it is evident that Richard Merrifield arranged the funeral ceremonies.[28] It was an old custom in Albany that: "None attend" a funeral "without a previous invitation,"[29] which may explain why Richard Merrifield charged for "Inviting & Attending Funeral." The funeral took place on February 24, 1836. Snow must have been on the ground because Richard Merrifield arranged for twenty sleighs to form the funeral procession.

Zipporah Ames did not long survive her husband. She died that spring, April 8, 1836.[30] Again Richard Merrifield arranged for the funeral ceremonies. In his itemized bill he charged for ten carriages which formed the funeral procession.[31]

The remains of Ezra Ames, his wife and their sons Julius and Angelo, now rest at the Albany Rural Cemetery in a large, well-kept oval plot surrounded by a driveway. This cemetery, however, was not consecrated until 1844,[32] and could not have been the original place of burial of the artist and his wife. At what time and from what cemetery their remains were removed to this plot is not noted in the cemetery records, the earliest of which are dated 1869. In that year only Angelo was still living, Julius having died in 1850. The cemetery records list the plot as the Angelo Ames lot indicating that Angelo was the purchaser.

The original place of burial of Ezra Ames and his wife, and also their son Julius, must have been the cemetery once on State and Knox Streets, established in 1806 on ground now a part of Washington Park,[33] because, according to a map of this cemetery at the Albany Institute, it was divided into sections for the various denominations including the Dutch Reformed Church of which the Ames family were presumably members. In 1868, this burial ground was closed and the bodies removed to St. Agnes Cemetery and to the Rural Cemetery.[34] The year 1868, then, was doubtless the time, and the old cemetery on State and Knox

[27] *MS Ames, Ezra, Estate,* No. V, Item 4.

[28] *Ibid.,* No. II, Item 1.

[29] Munsell, I (1850): 315.

[30] *MS Ames Family.*

[31] *MS Ames, Ezra, Estate,* No. II, Item 2.

[32] Phelps, 42.

[33] *Ibid.,* 33.

[34] *Ibid.,* 79.

EZRA AMES (1768–1836)

Self-portrait, *c.* 1810

ANGELO AMES (1803–1886)

Son of the artist, *c.* 1818

Owned by Miss Elizabeth S. Edwards

HENRY EMES (1783–1833)

Half brother of artist, *c.* 1832

Miss Elizabeth S. Edwards

ANGELO AMES (1803–1886)

Son of the artist, *c.* 1827

Owned by Albany Institute

FOUR MINIATURES ON IVORY BY EZRA AMES

(Photographed by Irwin F. Cortelyou)

[SAID TO BE] KATHARINE BARBER JAMES (1834–1890)
GRANDDAUGHTER OF THE ARTIST
By Ezra Ames, date uncertain
Owned by Miss Elizabeth S. Edwards

Streets was the place from which the remains of Ezra Ames, his wife, and their elder son were removed to the present plot in the Albany Rural Cemetery.

A handsome family monument in the center of the Ames plot is incised on three faces: on the front face appear the names of Ezra Ames and his wife; on the right face, the name of Julius; and on the left face, that of Angelo. Four small stones to the east of the monument are incised with the same names. The stone dedicated to Ezra Ames bears, besides his name, the emblem of the Freemasons.

There is another stone in the plot, placed horizontally, which is also dedicated to Ezra Ames and his wife. It was probably removed from the old cemetery with their remains in 1868. At the top is carved the emblem of the Freemasons; at the bottom, this inscription: "In their death they were not divided."

In the records of the Albany County Surrogate's Court, Albany, there is a typewritten copy of the artist's will and numerous other papers relating to his estate.[35] Among these is an inventory assembled by appraisers who valued the artist's personal estate at $65,953.61.[36] Another version of the inventory, at the Albany Institute, gives the valuation as $65,835.36.[37] Other papers relating to the estate are at The New York State Library, Albany.[38]

The artist left about a third of his estate to each of his three children. Two maps of his real estate[39] show the practically even division of his property into three parts, one for each of his heirs.

Julius Ames and Angelo Ames, the executors of the estate, kept their accounts in a book now at The New York State Library.[40] Other documents relating to their joint transactions are among the papers in the Surrogate's Court.[41] One, dated May 2, 1838, is a power of attorney given by Angelo Ames to Julius Ames to act as sole executor of the estate.[42] The reason Angelo

[35] *MS Ames, Ezra, Estate*, No. V, Item 2.

[36] *Ibid* No. I, Item 2; and No. V, Item 1.

[37] *Ibid.*, No. I, Item 1.

[38] *Ibid.*, No. II; and No. III.

[39] *Ibid.*, No. I, and No. V, Item 1.

[40] *Ibid.*, No. IV.

[41] *Ibid.*, No. V.

[42] *Ibid.*, No. V, Item 6.

gave up his duties as an executor was that he was about to leave Albany and resume his quest for a climate suitable for his health, a quest which was to last a number of years.

If Angelo did not leave immediately, he left shortly thereafter because he is mentioned in a letter as rambling about Europe in search of his health by a visitor who saw Julius over five months later. In a letter filed with the Duyckinck Papers at The New York Public Library, James William Beekman writes to his friend Evert A. Duyckinck as follows:

> Albany October 20th 1838 Saturday night. My dear Evert I am just returned from the Studio of an Albany artist—Mr Ames—quite a curious genius—to whom I was introduced by a friend—we found our man up two pair of stairs in a back room to which we made our way through picture frames and old lumber—A large rocking chair was hauled down from a semicircular screen of black—wherein *Sitters* went to recline—for me, and my friend accommodated with the only other chair in the room while the artist squatted down on the corner of a chest, and ever and anon picking up into momentary life a dim lamp by way of keeping time, entertained us right well—presently conversation turned on an absent brother of his—who had been in Madeira for his health—Our host spoke of some of the *fruits* of that famous island—that his brother had sent him—some wine actually put up there by him and therefore undoubtedly the real juice—to offer us some was of course the next thing—and ushering us into a large room hung round with many portraits of great men and women, celebrated & ignoble—but all original and acknowledged likenesses, he left us to our meditations for a time—Directly he returned, and led us into a Cabinet about ten feet square shelved to the ceiling, and dusky with books on two sides, while several choice pictures from Italy hung on the other walls. Beneath a fine Sketch of Old Charon ferrying over the Styx one of the loveliest of souls, was a little stand & thereon, true classic supper, wine nuts & apples—here were *chairs* for all—and our rusty looking open collared friend seemed just in the right place—he is an artist and a bookworm of snug fortune, but retiring habits—very much like Hawthorne, lives with an old aunt here, and reigns supreme in the upper stories of her house among easels, pallettes and canvases—His brother has a fantastic name rather Pealeian—namely "*Carlo Angelo*"—but is nevertheless described to be a very clever fellow—He is rambling about Europe, a confirmed Dyspeptic in search of comfort—chasing the climate that he fancies wherever he fancies it to be—he will be at Paris this winter and talks of Constantinople, or his brother here does for him—To this genius I am promised a letter and it may be worth taking—at all events I have had a rare evening.

MARTIN VAN BUREN (1782–1862)
By Ezra Ames, *c.* 1828–

ENOS T. THROOP (1784–1874)
By Ezra Ames, *c.* 1829–

Two of the "Portraits of Seven Governors of New York" by Ezra Ames
Owned by the City of Albany, at the Albany Institute of History and Art

The studio in which this "rare evening" took place was, obviously, the former studio of Ezra Ames at 41 South Pearl Street; and the host, Julius Rubens Ames. The pictures on the walls, and the books on the shelves reaching up to the ceiling were among those listed in the inventory made of the artist's estate in 1836.

Among the books were the Encyclopaedia Britannica; Delaplaine's Repository; Lavater's Physiognomy; The National Portrait Gallery; Ferguson's Astronomy; and some volumes on medicine and Freemasonry. Besides these reference books, there were: Fielding's Works; Homer's Iliad and Odyssey; Cervantes' Don Quixote; Milton's Paradise Lost; The Arabian Nights; The Spectator Papers; and the British Classics. The assessed value of the library, including a collection of drawings and engravings, was $264.77.[43]

A number of the pictures are listed in a handbill, dated July 26, 1842, advertising a "Sale of Portraits" in the estate of Ezra

[43] *MS Ames, Ezra, Estate*, No. I.

CATALOGUE SALE OF PORTRAITS.

By order of the Executors, to close an estate, will be offered for sale at No. 41 South Pearl-street, 2d story, until the 1st of October. The collection of

PORTRAITS IN OIL

by the late EZRA AMES, comprising about 50 likenesses of some of the most eminent Statesmen, Clergymen, &c., of this country. Also, several Portraits of Ladies, Fancy Pictures, &c. These paintings are principally originals, with a few copies from Stuart. Many of them are suitable for the rooms of public institutions. Such an opportunity to obtain authentic likenesses of our most celebrated public characters, has rarely, if ever been presented.

PRESIDENTS.

1. George Washington, copy from G. Stuart.
2. Head of John Adams, " " "
3. " Thomas Jefferson, " "
4. " James Madison, " "
5. " Martin Van Buren. "

GOVERNORS.

6. George Clinton.
7. De Witt Clinton.
8. Joseph C. Yates.
9. Enos T. Throop.

---

10. Hon. Stephen Van Rensselaer, Lt. Gov.
11. " do. do. do. in early life.
12. " John Taylor, Lt. Gov.
13. " Theodore Sedgwick, from Stuart.
14. General Peter Gansevoort, from do.
15. " Alexander Hamilton.
16. " Jacob Brown.
17. Col. ——— Lamb.
18. " ——— Williams.
19. Chancellor James Kent, 2 feet 4, by 3 feet.
20. Judge Smith Thompson, in early life.
21. " Wm. W. Van Ness, 2 ft 4 by 3 ft
22. Hon. Governeur Morris. " " "
23. " Samuel L. Mitchell, L. L. D. F. R. S.
24. " John W. Yates.
25. " James Strong, Esq.
26. " John I. De Graff.
27. " Ambrose L. Jordan.
28. George W. Clinton, Esq.
29. Thomas P. Jones, Esq.
30. William L. Stone, Esq.
31. Thomas H. Wentworth, Esq.
32. Timothy Dewey, Esq.
33. S. J. Penniman, Esq.
34. ——— Watkins, Esq.

William Robertson.

CLERGYMEN.

35. Rev. Dr. Timothy Dwight, 3 feet 5, by 4 feet 5.
36. " " Timothy Dwight, 2 feet 8, by 3 feet.
37. " " John H. Livingston.
38. " " Eliphalet Nott.
39. " " do. do. (duplicate.)
40. " " do. do. in early life.
41. " " Edward D. Griffin.
42. " " Andrew Yates.
43. " " B. T. Welch, 2 feet 8 by 3 feet.
44. " " Isaac Ferris.
45. " " ——— Forman.

---

46. Group. Likeness of a mother and child.
47. Portrait of a lady.
48. " "
49. " "
50. " "
51. " "
52. " "
53. " "
54. " "
55. " "
56. " "
58. Elkanah Watson, Esq. copy from Copely, 4 feet by 5.
59. Chan. Robert R. Livingston, from Stuart.
60. James Rivington, painted by G. Stuart, 2 feet 4 by 3 feet.
61. Gideon Fairman, head by J. W. Jarvis.

HISTORICAL PICTURES.

62. Murder of the Princes in the Tower, 4 feet 9 by 7 feet 3.
63. Shipwreck scene from the Tempest, 4 feet by 5.
64. The Last Supper, (original,) 3 feet 5 by 4 feet 5.
65. Sampson and the Philistines, 3 feet by 4 feet 5.

66, 67, Groups of Heads.

68. Venus and Cupid, 2 feet 4 by 3 feet.

69, 70. Two Landscapes by A. R. Gutowski.

Also a few fancy pictures, busts, &c.

Pictures ready for examination. Those not previously disposed of, will probably be offered at public sale on the 1st of October. The size of portraits are 2 feet, by 2 feet 6 inches, except when specified.

Albany, July 26, 1842.

RARE BROADSIDE, ALBANY, JULY 26, 1842

As reproduced in *NYHS Quarterly Bulletin*, July 1931, p. 67

Ames. According to this handbill, reproduced on the page opposite, the pictures were then "ready for examination. Those not previously disposed of, will probably be offered at public sale on the 1st of October."[44]

Little remains to be told of the immediate family and home of Ezra Ames. According to the Albany Directories, Angelo and Julius continued to live at the home on 41 South Pearl Street until 1846/47, when they moved to 3 Plain Street, just around the corner, and on part of the property in Ezra Ames's estate. Here they lived for the rest of their lives.

Julius Rubens Ames died on June 5, 1850, and Angelo died on May 26, 1886, according to the inscriptions on their gravestones in the Albany Rural Cemetery. Marcia Lucretia Ames (Mrs. William James) died, March 2, 1886,[45] and was buried nearby in the James family plot.[46] She was an aunt by marriage of William James, the philosopher, and Henry James, the novelist.[47]

Julius is remembered as an artist; Angelo, as a philanthropist. It is as a philanthropist that Angelo is mentioned in the editorial entitled "Death of Angelo Ames" in the *Argus*, May 27, 1886:

> Angelo Ames, one of the oldest and best known residents of Albany, died yesterday of old age. He was eighty-four years old and was born in this city being the son of Ezra Ames the famous artist. At his father's death he inherited a very large fortune in real estate. The deceased was an uncle of Mrs. Isaac Edwards. He was never married. Mr. Ames was very charitable and gave large amounts to deserving institutions, well earning the title of public benefactor.

During 1857: "In taking down the building in South Pearl Street formerly occupied by Ezra Ames as a portrait gallery, a part of the wall fell, injuring several persons. . . ."[48] This demolition, in 1857, ends the history of Ezra Ames, and of the house into which he had moved during the last decade of the 18th century.

[44] [Ames, Ezra], *Catalogue Sale of Portraits*, 1842.

[45] Hastings, *New York Genealogical and Biographical Record*, April 1924, p. 108.

[46] Gravestone.

[47] Hastings, *New York Genealogical and Biographical Record*, April 1924, pp. 104–114.

[48] Munsell, IX (1858): 341.

MRS. JONATHAN WALTON (d. 1843)
By Ezra Ames, *c.* 1830–35
(Photo by FARL)

Owned by Miss Helen de Lancey Watkins

VIII

CONCLUSION

THE PORTRAITS painted by Ezra Ames constitute the most important part of his artistic activity. He painted only a few landscapes, still-life pictures of which none are located, and figure compositions. His portraits, like any portraits, may be considered as to their value as historical documents, or as to their artistic merits; and it is interesting to discuss them from both these points of view.

Living before the days when the portrait photographer became an active competitor of the portrait painter, Ezra Ames produced a larger number of portraits of people in Albany and the surrounding district than any other painter of his day. Speaking of the historical importance of these pictorial records, the late William Sawitzky wrote: "during the first three decades of the last century he [Ames] recorded the physiognomies of so many prominent and more or less interesting people, that his work deserves to be better known than it actually is."

Historically considered, his portraits have the merits of accurate likenesses painted from life. Concerning the merits of life portraits as historical documents, Thomas Carlyle wrote, to his friend David Laing, his thoughts at the time of a projected exhibition of Scottish portraits:

> . . . I have to tell you, as a fact of personal experience, that in all my poor Historical investigations it has been, and always is, one of the most primary wants to procure a bodily likeness of the personage inquired after; a good *Portrait* if such exists; failing that, even an indifferent if sincere one. In short, *any* representation, made by a faithful human creature, of that Face and Figure, which *he* saw with his eyes, and which I can never see with mine, is now valuable to me, and much better than none at all. This, which is my own deep experience, I believe to be, in a deeper or less deep degree, the universal one; and that every student and reader of History, who strives earnestly to conceive for himself what manner of Fact and *Man* this or the other vague Historical *Name* can have been, will, as the first and directest indication of all, search eagerly for a Portrait, for all the reasonable Portraits there are; and never rest till he have made out, if possible, what the man's natural face was like.

MRS. JOHN HILLS (1806–1878)
(Ames's niece, Huldah Mulford)
Miniature on paper, *c.* 1831
Owned by Miss Gladys Ladu

DR. JAMES WADE (1789–1868)
(m. Ames's niece, Sally Mulford)
Miniature on paper, *c.* 1822
Owned by Miss Edith S. Wade

Often I have found a Portrait superior in real instruction to half-a-dozen written "Biographies," as Biographies are written. . . .

The fidelity of Ames's portraits are vouched for by contemporary statements. Recording so many of the men who were prominent in shaping the events of their time and place, Ames's portraits are therefore historical documents of prime importance.

Turning from the historical to the artistic aspects of the portraiture of Ezra Ames: for convenience his portraits in miniature and those in oil may be separately discussed because two media are involved. His miniatures, in turn, may also be considered under two heads: those painted in watercolor on paper, and those painted on ivory.

A number of family miniatures are painted in watercolor on paper. Two of them, portraits of Dr. Wade and his small son Ezekiel, are painted in monotone with considerable dash, and

MRS. EZRA AMES (1775–1836)
(Zipporah Wood)
Miniature on ivory, *c.* 1820
Owned by Miss Elizabeth S. Edwards

MARCIA L. AMES (1797/8–1886)
(Artist's daughter, m. William James)
Miniature on ivory, *c.* 1820
Owned by Miss Gladys Ladu

without backgrounds. Another, of Mrs. John Hills wearing a cap, is carefully painted, and except for some slight shading around the head and shoulders, the background is untouched. There are also a number of family miniatures painted on ivory. They are all carefully painted. Among them are three self-portraits: one an oval, painted about 1790; another oval painted about 1800; and the third, a rectangle painted about 1810. A miniature of the artist's wife is painted on an oval ivory. Miniatures of the artist's daughter Marcia, and of the artist's half-brother Henry, are painted on rectangular pieces of ivory.

Very few professional miniatures by Ames have been located. One is a miniature painted on an oval ivory of John Fondey, Jr. Another is of Jesse Hawley which is painted on a somewhat larger piece of ivory, and is rectangular in shape. In all, not many miniatures by Ames have been located, and for the purposes of this survey the ones mentioned are sufficient to show that they vary greatly in size, shape, and technique. They are above the work of the average miniature painter of that day; but clearly the artist was more interested in the, for him, more congenial, and certainly more remunerative, work of portrait painting in oil.

Surveying his portraits in oil in the order of their production, and tracing his development chartwise, it will be found that the artist's development was very gradual. Indeed, judging from photographs of his portrait of his father, painted about 1790, and of Elihu Phinney, 1799, the artist made no appreciable artistic progress during the first decade of his career. If one then glances at photographs of his portrait of John Kane, *c.* 1804, of George Provost, 1805, and of Joseph Brant, 1806, one sees a slight advance in the artist's ability at characterization. In the same respect, however, there is little difference between the Fondey family group, 1803, and the Tompkins family group, 1809. They are primitive paintings.

However, before he painted the Tompkins family group, Ames had already painted two portraits which foreshadowed his mature style, those of the Staffords painted in 1805 and 1807. In them, the spandrels—that is to say the corners of the canvas which have been brushed in to form an imperfect oval—are more pronounced than the faint indications of these decorative elements in the likenesses of himself about 1800, and of Elihu Phinney, 1799. In the portrait of Spencer Stafford, too, the artist has introduced a sky background for probably the first time. Finally, there is more expression in these than one finds in the earlier portraits. His portraits of Ezekiel Mulford, of Citizen Genet, and of Philip Van Cortlandt, painted during 1809–1810, show still further advance in technique and characterization.

This improvement has been accounted for elsewhere by the fact that Ames trained himself by making copies after the portraits of Copley and Stuart: one after Copley and a number after Stuart. These, as well as an original portrait by Stuart and another by John Wesley Jarvis, Ames kept in his gallery, probably as

ELKANAH WATSON (1758–1842)

By John Singleton Copley, 1782

Photo: Metropolitan Museum

Owned by Trustees, Thomson Hall Princeton, N. J.

COPY AFTER COPLEY (AT LEFT)

By Ezra Ames, *c.* 1809–10

Photo: Albany Institute

Owned by Albany Institute of History and Art

guides for his own procedure. Certainly the influences of these artists are apparent in Ames's portraits.

Despite these influences, Ames gradually evolved his own style, which after 1810 is usually so personal that his work, when a sufficient amount of it has been studied, is fairly easy to distinguish. Throughout his career he retained some very definite mannerisms. One, easily recognizable, and first noticed by Mr. Charles E. Baker, is the placing of the high lights in the eyes of the sitters. They are dot-like high lights, and are placed not on the same sides of both eyes, as they would be if the artist regarded the source of light on the sitter, but at the upper and inner edges of the pupils.

Another distinct mannerism found in some portraits, as for example that of Absalom Townsend, and one of the two portraits of Mrs. Jacob Jennings Brown, is a dark diagonal area brushed in at the upper right of the canvas. It is as if the artist, tired of painting the drapery in detail, had painted it abstractly, in order to focus the attention on the heads alone. On the other hand, the costumes in the portraits by Ames are carefully painted, and in the case of stocks and laces great attention is given to detail. In contrast: Ames was careless about the painting of hands, and showed as little of them as possible.

He never overcame his primitive manner in the painting of children, invariably giving them a look of maturity far beyond their years. His few landscapes are also primitively executed.

There is a group of portraits by Ames which may be discussed without regard to the order of their painting, not only because it would be difficult to establish all of their dates, but also, because they are well known as the "Portraits of Seven Governors of New York," and it is thus convenient to think of them as a series. They are the property of the City of Albany and had been in storage for some time when they were loaned to the New York State Historical Association Museum, Ticonderoga, N. Y. There they remained until 1946, when they were placed on permanent loan at the Albany Institute of History and Art. They are all large-sized canvases and make a handsome showing as a group in one wing of the building.

The portrait of George Clinton, similar to the portrait at The New-York Historical Society, and that of John Jay, which is a copy of a portrait by Gilbert Stuart, cannot be dated. However, the remaining portraits were presumably painted during or after the terms of office of the various Governors represented. Indeed, the one of DeWitt Clinton was painted in 1818 on commission from the Corporation of the City of Albany, and was begun shortly after that statesman assumed his duties as Governor in Albany. The other four portraits are of Daniel D. Tompkins, whose term of office extended from 1807–1817; of Joseph C. Yates, whose term extended from 1823–1824; of Martin Van Buren, who became Governor at the end of 1828, and resigned in March 1829, to become Secretary of State of the United States; and of Enos T. Throop, who succeeded Van Buren and was Governor of the State from 1829–1832.

JOHN JAY (1745–1829)
After original by G. Stuart

DEWITT CLINTON (1769–1828)
Dated by Account Book, 1818

DANIEL D. TOMPKINS (1774–1825)
By Ezra Ames, *c.* 1815–

JOSEPH C. YATES (1768–1837)
By Ezra Ames, *c.* 1823–

FOUR OF THE "PORTRAITS OF SEVEN GOVERNORS OF NEW YORK" BY EZRA AMES
Owned by the City of Albany, at the Albany Institute of History and Art

FRANCIS BLOODGOOD (1768–1840)
By Ezra Ames, *c.* 1810 (Photo by FARL)
Owned by Mr. Alonzo W. Paige

In conclusion, a few of the many portraits by Ames once attributed to better-known artists, but quite typical of his other work, should be mentioned again because their misattributions show the relative merit of Ames's work. Among these portraits are likenesses of: William James, formerly attributed to Gilbert Stuart and, more recently, to Waldo and Jewett; George Washington Clinton, formerly attributed to Vanderlyn; Reverend Hooper Cumming, also at one time attributed to Vanderlyn; Mrs. Hooper Cumming, once attributed to Rembrandt Peale; Gouverneur Morris (at Columbia University), attributed in several publications to Thomas Sully, and elsewhere to Charles Willson Peale as copied from Ezra Ames; Ambrose Latting Jordan, formerly attributed to Morse and, later, tentatively to Jarvis; Mrs. Jacob Jennings Brown (privately owned), once attributed to Jarvis; Francis Bloodgood, once attributed to Inman; and John Keyes Paige, formerly attributed to Francis Alexander.

It is important, in estimating Ames's position as an artist, also to recall the several portraits heretofore unattributed to any artist but now attributed by the writers to Ames. Among the best of these are the well-painted and convincing likenesses of Samuel Stevenson Fowler, Mrs. John Meads, and Mrs. Jonathan Walton.

Artistically speaking: the portraits of Fowler and Jordan, both characteristic works by Ames, are as fine as any of the men's portraits painted by Jarvis and Inman; and the portrait of Mrs. John Meads is a noteworthy performance recalling the women's portraits by Gilbert Stuart, though entirely typical of the work of Ames.

The noticeable influence of Stuart in the works of Ezra Ames, already mentioned as the result of copying that artist's work, may also have been due to the direct assistance from Stuart himself, for there is a clipping, undated, from the Albany *Argus* which reads:

That famous old Albany artist, Asa W. Twitchell, who represents in the largest sense the past and present of art in Albany . . . has given the following interview to the Argus on "Albany's Contribution to Art." The interview, in part, reads: "When I came to Albany in 1861 . . . I found in this city an excellent exhibition of portraits painted from time to time for Albany people by Ezra Ames, the first portrait painter of note in the northern part of New York State. Ezra Ames was a Mason, and he found some of the earliest employment for his talent in the painting of the symbols for Masonic lodges. Later in life he went to Boston, and there he studied under Stuart, then the foremost American portrait painter.*

If Ames did study in Stuart's Boston studio, it must have been in the summer of 1805, when he visited Boston with his wife, unless he made a later visit to Boston of which he left no record. However, there is a possibility (pointed out in the second chapter of this book) that when Ames and Stuart were both in New York in May of 1793, the younger artist may have met the older artist, and studied his work. Indeed, since Ames and Stuart arrived in New York at about the same time in 1793, and also in Boston at about the same time, in 1805, it may be that Ames planned his trips to coincide with those of Stuart.

As a result of the foregoing survey, it may be said that Ames, painting in the general style of Stuart, Jarvis, Vanderlyn, Inman, and Waldo, produced a number of portraits which have the excellent artistic qualities found in the work of these men. His portraits, then, are important not only as pictorial records of men and women in New York State during the early decades of the 19th century, but also as works of art many of which rank with those of the first painters of his time.

* *Ms. Gansevoort-Lansing Collection.*

PART II

ACCOUNT BOOKS

GEORGE CLINTON (1739–1812)

By Ezra Ames, 1814

[Now correctly dated from Ames's Albany Institute Account Book]

Gift of George Clinton Tallmadge, his great-grandson, 1858, to The New-York Historical Society

IX

REFERENCES TO PAINTINGS IN THE ACCOUNT BOOKS (1790–1834) OF EZRA AMES

DESCRIPTION OF THE ACCOUNT BOOKS

EZRA AMES (1768–1836), portrait painter of Albany, left three manuscript Account Books which date from 1790 through 1834 and therefore span virtually his entire professional career. In them, he records those paintings, and other work, for which he was not immediately paid. These references to his paintings, though an incomplete record, approach in number the whole body of his otherwise-known work. Even the Account Book entries which relate to already known paintings add considerably to our knowledge of them. It is obvious, then, that these manuscripts are important sources for the study of one of the most significant artists active in New York State during the first third of the 19th century, one whose work has artistic as well as wide historic interest. Like many of the early American painters, little has been written about either this artist or his work.

Two of the Account Books kept by Ames, covering intermittently the earlier and shorter period between May 1790 and October 1802, have been for many years in the possession of The New-York Historical Society. The third and latest Account Book covering the more than thirty years from May 4, 1804, to December 28, 1834, while the artist's productivity was at its height, was presented by an anonymous donor to the Albany Institute of History and Art as recently as November 1946. Four times as contributive of new material on the artist's work as the earlier two Account Books combined, this important manuscript has not hitherto been published either in full or in part. By courtesy of the Board of Directors of the Albany Institute and its Director, Mr. Robert G. Wheeler, permission has been granted to the writers to publish under the auspices of The New-York Historical Society numerous extracts from this new material, including all references by the artist to his own paintings.

The two earliest of Ames's Account Books relate to work done during his youthful residence (1790–1793) at or near Worcester, Massachusetts, as well as to his early efforts (1793–1802) in the environs of his chosen home, Albany, New York. The material in these two Account Books was first drawn upon by Miss Dorothy C. Barck for her article on the artist in *The New-York Historical Society Quarterly Bulletin* of January 1927; more recently, by Mr. Hermann Warner Williams, Jr., for an alphabetical list of portraits and of "fancy" subjects by Ames mentioned in these two Account Books, in *Art in America* of October 1942; later, by Mr. E. T. Reid for his article on the artist's Masonic activities in *The Royal Arch Mason* of March 1943; and finally, by Mr. Robert G. Wheeler for his article on the artist and his work in the *American Collector* of August 1947. In none of these articles is there a full transcript of the entries relating to the artist's paintings.

The extracts at the end of this essay are full transcripts of all the original entries in which Ezra Ames referred to his own easel paintings and miniatures in all three of his Account Books. By "original entries" is meant the first recorded entries without later notations or marks of cancellation indicating payment. These extracts include the many hitherto unpublished entries taken from the third Account Book at the Albany Institute as well as those already drawn upon from the two earlier books.

The Account Books contain by no means a complete record of Ames's paintings. As will be seen from the table (p. 150) and the accompanying text explaining the tentative nature of the totals presented, there are at least 383 extant or previously located paintings known or believed to have been executed by Ames. Only 48 of these can, at the present time, be related by the writers definitely or tentatively to any of the paintings recorded in the three Account Books. The absence of the remaining 335 extant or previously located paintings from the Account Book entries supports the inference that, except for a few references to expenses or to cash sales in the first two manuscripts, all three of

Ames's Account Books are records of accounts receivable only. Moreover, the almost invariable appearance of the abbreviation "D^r^" (for debtor) in each entry, as well as the bookkeeping phraseology and system of entry, points strongly to the conclusion that Ames recorded in his Account Books only those items, including his paintings, for which he had not received payment in full upon delivery.

The total number of paintings listed in the three Account Books is approximately 229. Of these about 40 are listed in the two earlier manuscripts and have thus for many years been included among the recorded paintings. Only one of these forty has as yet been located. In the third Account Book approximately 189 paintings are listed and of these, as previously indicated, 47 have been definitely or tentatively identified. The remaining 142 paintings recorded in the third book are still unlocated.

Breaking down the total number of 229 paintings recorded in the three Account Books into classifications according to subject matter: the earlier two Account Books, at The New-York Historical Society, contain references to 9 portraits in oil, 30 portraits in miniature, and one painting of a lion; and the third Account Book, at the Albany Institute, contains references to 173 portraits in oil, 3 in miniature, 3 landscapes, 6 still-life pictures, and 4 pictures of miscellaneous subjects.

At present the approximate total of the located and unlocated paintings, both easel paintings and miniatures, including all those recorded in the three Account Books, is 564. Of this grand total, the two Account Books at The New-York Historical Society are the sole source of 39 and the third Account Book at the Albany Institute of History and Art is the sole source of somewhere near 142. And these 142 subjects have not previously been included among either the known or the recorded paintings of Ezra Ames. This numerical approximation is within three or four pictures which will presently be discussed.

The statistics discussed above are summarized in the table following. This table includes all the easel paintings and minia-

TENTATIVE TOTALS OF PAINTINGS BY EZRA AMES

	Source of Statistics	*Location Category*	*Ports. in Oil*	*Miniatures*	*Landscapes*	*Figure Comps.*	*Still Life*	*Miscel. Subjects*	*Totals*
1.	First Two Account Books	Extant[1]	1	0	0	0	0	0	1
2.	First Two Account Books	Unlocated[2]	8	30	0	0	0	1	39
3.	First Two Account Books	Total	9	30	0	0	0	1	40
4.	Third Account book	Extant[1]	38	0	2	0	0	0	40
5.	Third Account book	Once Located[3]	7	0	0	0	0	0	7
6.	Third Account book	Unlocated[2]	128	3	1	0	6	4	142
7.	Third Account book	Total	173	3	3	0	6	4	189
8.	Not in the Account Books	Extant[1]	157	26	1	3	0	0	187
9.	Not in the Account Books	Once Located[3]	119	2	0	15	3	9	148
10.	Not in the Account Books	Total	276	28	1	18	3	9	335
11.	All Three Account Books	Total (lines 3+7)	182	33	3	0	6	5	229
12.	Sub-Totals from All Sources: Lines 1, 4, 8	Extant[1]	196	26	3	3	0	0	228
13.	Sub-Totals from All Sources: Lines 5 and 9	Once Located[3]	126	2	0	15	3	9	155
14.	Sub-Totals from All Sources: Lines 2 and 6	Unlocated[2]	136	33	1	0	6	5	181
15.	All Sources: Grand Totals[4]	All Categories	458	61	4	18	9	14	564

December 1, 1953

Arranged by George B. Cortelyou, Jr.

[1] "Extant" includes only those paintings whose present locations are known to the authors and are given in the Catalogue, p. 191 ff.

[2] "Unlocated," for the purposes of this table, includes only paintings recorded in the Account Books for which the authors have found no subsequent record.

[3] "Once Located," for the purposes of this table, includes paintings known to the authors by records other than, or in addition to, entries in the Account Books but which are not extant to their knowledge. Many of these are from the Inventory, 1836, and the handbill: *Catalogue Sale of Portraits*, 1842, of the Ezra Ames estate.

[4] These totals comprise all the paintings listed in the first three sections of the Catalogue: XI, XII, and XIII. Four extant drawings and one once-located drawing are also listed in the latter section. The grand total, therefore, of all paintings and drawings—extant, once located, and unlocated—known to and accepted at this date by the authors as by Ezra Ames, is 569.

tures by Ezra Ames which diligent search has brought to the attention of the writers. It does not include four extant drawings and one recorded drawing. The Account Books list no drawings.

The totals presented are only tentative. Subsequent research, new-found paintings, and possible changes in attribution will undoubtedly alter most of the totals. Thus, a greater number of Account Book entries may later be related to known paintings. The discovery of more relationships of this kind would reduce the total of 564 paintings. On the other hand, the discovery of additional canvases which cannot be related to entries in the Account Books would increase the total. The increase may well be larger than the decrease.

Another reason that some of the totals must be considered as only tentative is the obscurity of several of the Account Book entries which refer to paintings. For example, one long entry presumably of 1793 records the purchase of materials for painting "pictures" *for* Major Livingston. Were these portraits *of* Major Livingston? And how many were there? It is here assumed that there were two portraits as the custom was to have companion portraits painted. Another obscure entry refers to several portraits including one of the Reverend Hooper Cumming. This entry, dated September 8, 1818, was crossed out and marked "Erat." A corrected entry under the same date was then written but did not include the name of the Reverend Mr. Cumming. It is here assumed that his portrait was not painted, although it might have been painted and the reference to it deleted from the entry because payment had been received. Two other entries, one dated 1790 and the other 1791, record miniatures for Joseph Wheeler, and it is here assumed that two miniatures were painted, although the second entry may possibly be merely a record of payment for the miniature recorded in the first.

There is a gap consisting of an unrecorded period of eighteen months from October 1802 to May 4, 1804, between the second and third Account Books; another gap in the latter book of equal length from August 26, 1822, to March 4, 1824, broken only by

HARMANUS BLEECKER (1779–1849)
By Ezra Ames, 1819
Owned by Harmanus Bleecker Library, Albany

ABSALOM TOWNSEND (1786–1861)
By Ezra Ames, 1816
Owned by Mrs. Van Santvoord Merle-Smith

[Both of these portraits, here reproduced from FARL photographs, are dated and the attributions confirmed by entries in the Albany Institute Account Book of Ezra Ames] two entries for miscellaneous work in May 1823; and still another seven years later when the aging artist seems to have painted little. These, however, are the only long gaps in Ames's three Account Books which record so much of his activity as an artist. These, and sixteen manuscript Expense Books (1799–1826) owned by The New-York Historical Society, constitute the most important documents for establishing the record of the artist's life and work.

The main interest in the Account Books from the standpoint of this chapter is indicated by its title, and only references to paintings which may be termed works of art are included in the transcript of entries. Not transcribed are the many entries relating to Ames's odd jobs and miscellaneous work; these too have their value as biographical data and as evidence of the economic status of early-19th-century American artists outside the metropolitan centers, and so will be summarized in a later section of this essay. The entries transcribed, besides enlarging the corpus of Ames's otherwise recorded work, throw considerable light on a number of his previously known paintings, and this aspect of the subject will now be discussed.

ENTRIES RELATING TO KNOWN PAINTINGS

Besides their contribution of some 142 otherwise unrecorded subjects by Ames, the importance of the extracts taken from the Albany Institute Account Book is fourfold: some of the entries confirm former attributions of paintings to Ames; some for the first time establish the dates of known portraits; and still others aid in the identification of unattributed works of the artist, or provide further documentation of authentic works already known. By the word "known" three conditions relative to the existence of portraits are meant: a portrait may be known only through an engraving, as for example the portrait of Elkanah Watson; or it may be known only by a record of its previous location, such as the portrait of General Solomon Van Rensselaer painted for Delaplaine, destroyed by fire, and of N. Allen, now unlocated; or it may be an authentic and located painting.

Because of the prominence of the subject, a most interesting example of the dating and documenting of an undoubted Ames portrait by an entry in the Albany Institute Account Book is that of Governor George Clinton (1739–1812), owned by The New-York Historical Society. In the 1941 *Catalogue of American Portraits* owned by the Society the Clinton canvas is recorded as being "the portrait Ames exhibited at the Pennsylvania Academy in Philadelphia, 1812, and by which he achieved his first success." But the portrait there exhibited (according to a recent letter from Mrs. Barbara S. Roberts, Registrar of that institution) was purchased by the Academy for its own permanent collection soon after the exhibition. (Her letter refers to the minutes of the Board of Directors dated July 13, 1812, in which is recited the decision to make the purchase; and she further notes that this is the first purchase of a painting recorded in their minutes.) The acquisition of the portrait by the Academy is confirmed in a review of its Third Annual Exhibition (1813) in *Port Folio* for August 1813, page 127. Thereafter the portrait is listed in most of the catalogues of the annual exhibitions of the Academy up to 1845 when the Academy building burned. Since the portrait has not been found listed in later exhibition catalogues and cannot otherwise be accounted for by the Academy, it was presumably lost in the fire. It is therefore difficult to suppose that this was the portrait acquired by George Clinton Tallmadge and presented by him to The New-York Historical Society in 1858 as stated in the 1941 *Catalogue* of the Society.

There is, on the other hand, very strong reason to think that George Clinton Tallmadge (whose family name is also spelled Talmadge) acquired a portrait painted by Ames of his great-grandfather, George Clinton, for his grandfather, Mathias B. Talmadge, which was recorded by Ames in his Account Book under the date of May 1814, as follows: "Mathias B. Talmadge Esq[r] D[r] To Painting a half length Portrait of the late Vice presi-

BENJAMIN TALLMADGE (1754–1835)
By Ezra Ames, *c.* 1820–26 (Photo by FARL)
Owned by Mrs. Charles Lassell

MRS. BENJAMIN TALLMADGE (d. 1838)
By Ezra Ames, *c.* 1820–26 (Photo by FARL)
Owned by Mrs. Charles Lassell

SOLOMON ALLEN (1751–1821)

By Ezra Ames, dated by Account Book, 1814

Owned by the Museum of the City of New York

(Photo by FARL)

ELIPHALET NOTT (1773–1866)

By Ezra Ames, dated by engraving, 1820

Owned by Old South Association

On permanent loan to Union College

dent George Clinton"; and further that it was this 1814 portrait —not the one exhibited in 1812—that George Clinton Tallmadge presented to The New-York Historical Society.

Another instance of a portrait which can be dated and identified as to the artist by reference to the Account Book is that of Alexander Hamilton (1757–1804), at Union College, Schenectady. The portrait has a history to fit the entry in Ames's Account Book dated April 25, 1810, listing a portrait of Alexander Hamilton as charged to Elijah Thomas and delivered to Dr. C. C. Yates. In the *Union College Portrait Index* (June 1950), numbered 103, it is unattributed as to artist. According to *The Union Alumni Monthly*, January 1928, the portrait hung for some time in the President's Office also unidentified as to subject, until the discovery of a letter to President Potter from General Alexander Hamilton, a grandson of the subject, dated December 8, 1875, in which the writer states, in part:

> I beg you to accept for Union College the accompanying original portrait of my grandfather, Alexander Hamilton. This portrait was given me in 1833 by my late friend Mr. Winfield Scott Yates, formerly of Albany. Mr. Yates informed me that he received the picture from his uncle, Gov. Joseph C. Yates for whom it had been painted from life, shortly before my Grandfather's death. The elder members of our family, and friends, who recollected my Grandfather, have regarded this picture as an excellent likeness.

Because the portrait mentioned by Ames in his entry was delivered to Dr. C. C. Yates, the father of Winfield Scott Yates (the nephew of Governor Yates), the entry must refer to the portrait now at Union College. Thus the entry dates the portrait, identifies the artist, proves the identity of the subject as Alexander Hamilton, and confirms William Sawitzky's attribution of the picture to Ezra Ames. Finally, it proves that the portrait was not painted from life as stated in the letter, but dates from the year 1810, which was six years after the death of Alexander Hamilton.

The specific history of another portrait at Union College, also of a well-known person, is established by an entry in the

AMBROSE SPENCER (1765–1848)
By Ezra Ames, 1811
Owned by Mr. John De Witt Peltz

ELKANAH WATSON (1758–1842)
"E. Ames Pinx^t. [1818] V. Balch Sculp^t."
from Watson's History of N. Y. Canals, 1820

[Both of these portraits are dated by Ames's Albany Institute Account Book. The Spencer portrait is reproduced from a FARL photograph.]

Albany Institute Account Book. In the entry, dated November 18, 1828, Ames records the painting of a portrait of Dr. Nott for Jesse W. Goodrich, E. H. Blatchford, and S. R. Wynkoop. Three very similar portraits of Dr. Eliphalet Nott (1773–1866), are listed in the typewritten *Union College Portrait Index* (1950). All resemble an engraving by A. B. Durand after a portrait of Dr. Nott by Ezra Ames. All three have been examined. One, No. 87, attributed to Ames with a question mark, seems to be a replica. Another, No. 22, on loan from Old South Association, Boston, unidentified as to artist in the *Index*, is known to be by Ames, and is thus attributed on the Frick Art Reference Library photomount because of its resemblance to the Durand engraving. The third portrait, No. 84, which hangs over the President's desk at Union College and has always been in the possession of the institution so far as is known, is certainly by

Ames and presumably the portrait recorded in the entry. The reasons for reaching this conclusion are these: Dr. Nott was president of Union College from 1804 to 1866, and Goodrich, Blatchford, and Wynkoop were students in the class of 1829, as recorded in Raymond's history of *Union University*. The portrait was commissioned in November of their senior year. It is possible that these three seniors were chosen by their class to make the arrangements with Ezra Ames for painting this portrait of President Nott for presentation to Union College. It seems hardly possible that they kept it for themselves.

Another Account Book entry clears up the confusion in attribution which surrounds the portrait of Gouverneur Morris (1752–1816) owned by Mr. Gouverneur Morris, a great-grandson of the subject. The portrait is now on loan at Columbia University and bears the label: "Copy of a portrait by Thomas Sully." The portrait is reproduced in C. W. Bowen's *The Centennial Celebration of the Inauguration of George Washington*, 1892, facing page 160, and erroneously attributed to Thomas Sully. It is also attributed to Sully in the *Life and Works of Thomas Sully*, 1921, by E. Biddle and M. Fielding, No. 1279, in an entry repeating Bowen's error and transcribing incorrectly the record as given by Sully in his manuscript Register.

This portrait is also attributed to Charles Willson Peale on the photomount of the photograph at the Frick Art Reference Library with the caption: "Copy after Ezra Ames." This attribution is based on an interpretation of a diary entry supplied by Mrs. McCook Knox, written by Mrs. Stephen Bonsal (Henrietta Morris), a great-granddaughter of the subject, on December 11, 1893, stating in part that "old Mrs Sayre . . . brought Miss Peale from Philadelphia to look at her grandfather's portrait, [of] my great-grandfather." Of this attribution, Mr. Charles Coleman Sellers, author of *Charles Willson Peale*, states in a letter to the writers:

> I do not believe the copy from Ezra Ames is by Peale, and have not included it in my list. Peale generally added something of his own touch to

GOUVERNEUR MORRIS (1752–1816)

By Ezra Ames

Gift of Stephen Van Rensselaer, 1817, to The New-York Historical Society

a copy, and I cannot see his hand in this picture. I think the evidence of the diary very tenuous. If the ladies of 1893 thought this picture a Peale, it still leaves one unconvinced. The "Peale" tag was supplied very liberally at this time.

Another portrait of Gouverneur Morris bearing a striking resemblance to the one owned by his great-grandson was presented to The New-York Historical Society, November 11, 1817, by Stephen Van Rensselaer, a fitting memorial to the second President of the Society. The idea of having a portrait painted for the Society is recorded in the Minutes, December 6, 1816: "Resolved that a portrait of the late Hon. Gouverneur Morris dec^d president of this Society be procured at the expense thereof, and that the Recording Secretary [John Pintard] be charged with carrying this resolution into affect." Several letters relating to the project are at The New-York Historical Society. One shows that John Pintard wrote to William T. Meredith of Philadelphia, who married a niece of Gouverneur Morris, requesting a replica of their portrait of Morris by Thomas Sully. Meredith's reply to Pintard, dated January 2, 1817, is as follows:

> My friend, Mr Sully, has just now left me your letter of 23^d December, with the subjoined resolution, and a letter to himself from Dr Hosack requesting that, besides the copy of Mr Morris' portrait desired by you, another may be taken for his own gratification.
>
> I can assure you, Sir, with sincerity, that it is extremely painful to convey through you to your highly respected Institution any other reply than one of a chearful and respectful acquiessence to their request; and the more so, because the declining it may postpone the honour which is contemplated to the memory of a man toward whom I have ever entertained sentiments of profound respect and affectionate esteem. But the Portrait in question is peculiarly the property of Mrs Meredith; and as she has very lately felt herself obliged by reasons which cannot find a proper place in this communication but which were entirely approved by me,— to refuse an application for a copy from another quarter, with which I presume Dr. Hosack is acquainted,— I cannot with consistancy or self respect, yield to an endeavour to obtain one indirectly by using the liberal purpose of the New York Institution and the weighty influence which on every occasion must accompany the request of its Members.

The reason not given by Meredith is divulged in a letter by

Thomas Sully who wrote to Dr. Hosack, then Second Vice-President of the Society, from Philadelphia, January 9, 1817, as follows:

Dear Sir

Mr. Meredith has replied to the letter from the Historical Society of New York which contained a request to have the portrait of the late G Morris Esqr copied for their Hall by which you will learn his objection to their wishes—The true reason of his withholding the picture is to prevent Mrs Morris having a copy of it; for reasons which do not at all concern me: I think, if after the lapse of some time M^{rs} M would herself make the application; it would not be refused.

With respectful regard to Mrs Hosac and your daughter

I am dear Sir

Yr friend & obt Svt.

Tho[mas] Sully

Dr Hosac

B Delaplaine has promised me to write to you.

On January 18, 1817, Meredith wrote to Dr. Hosack: ". . . I am sincerely sorry that this *Feeling* has required me to refuse at all,—& even to delay my assent to a request coming from the Historical Society [to have a replica of the Sully portrait made]."

Whether or not this refusal of the Merediths to allow the copying of their Sully portrait of Gouverneur Morris in order to thwart the subject's widow from obtaining one was the reason, it is clear that shortly afterwards she commissioned Ames to paint a portrait of her husband, for on June 21, 1817, the artist recorded the completion of such a portrait, as follows:

Mrs Morris D^{r}	
To a Portrait of the late Govn^{r} Morris Esqr	$50.00
To a Burnished Gilt Frame	25.00
" a Packing Box	1.00

This entry documents and dates the portrait which has remained in the Morris family to this day, and confirms the attribution of William Sawitzky that the portrait is by Ames, though not from life. In the meanwhile Dr. Hosack, who had failed to obtain a copy of the portrait of Gouverneur Morris by Sully for the Society, apparently took advantage of a visit to the Society by Charles Willson Peale on June 10, 1817, when its minutes record him as being made an Honorary Member, to apprise him of its desire for a likeness of its late president. Just two weeks later, on June 24, 1817, Peale wrote to David Hosack:

> . . . I have employed some agents to find out a Portrait of Gouverneur Morris, which I painted when he was connected with Robert Morris in financing. If I succeed in obtaining it, and it is deserving a place amongst the other Portraits [at the Society], I shall have a pleasure in sending it, or a copy, as soon as possible. The least chance of obliging the Historical Society will be grateful to the feelings of
>
> Your friend
>
> C. W. Peale

An entry in the minutes for July 8, 1817, states that Dr. Hosack reported the contents of Peale's letter to the Society. However, C. W. Peale apparently never found the portrait, and the Society's desire for a likeness remained still unfulfilled. Finally, in the minutes of the Society for November 11, 1817, one learns from the entry, in ink, that: "The Portrait of Gouverneur Morris Esq. by [Ames of Albany *and* Ezra Ames *written in pencil*] was presented by Stephen Van Rensselaer Esq. of Albany." The pencilled words are written in the same handwriting as that of those in ink. This is, then, a contemporary record of the receipt of the portrait of Gouverneur Morris by Ames which is listed as such in the *Catalogue of American Portraits* issued by the Society.

The portrait at Columbia University, which is documented by the entry in the Account Book, is further documented by its resemblance to the portrait of Gouverneur Morris by Ames at The New-York Historical Society. One question now arises: was The New-York Historical Society picture painted from life? At present the question remains unanswered.

One of the Account Book entries identifies a copy of a portrait by Gilbert Stuart as by Ames. In the entry, dated July 5, 1806,

Ames records the painting of "a Portrait" for "Mr Ja^{s} Rivington." Since the patron could not have been James Rivington the elder—one-time merchant, bookseller, and newspaper publisher, who died in 1802, the reference must be to his son James Rivington whose name had appeared in the New York Directory for 1802 as his father's partner. The son's name disappears from the New York Directory in 1806, the year the Account Book entry was made, and appears in the first Albany Directory in 1813. Thus he could have been in Albany in 1806. After careful consideration of this entry in the light of what is known of a portrait of James Rivington the elder by Gilbert Stuart, now lost, the writers conclude that this entry must refer to a copy of the original portrait by Stuart. That the original was owned by Ames, then or later, is indicated by the listing of a "Portrait of Rivington by Stuart" in the certified inventory of the paintings in the estate of Ezra Ames, dated April 1836, now at the Albany Institute.

A portrait said to be by Stuart of Rivington is listed by G. C. Mason in his life of the artist, 1879, as owned by William Henry Appleton; but this portrait, later owned by Percy Rivington Pyne, is recorded by Lawrence Park in his four-volume work on Stuart, 1926, as a copy. Park stated that "it cannot be accepted as the original work which is still unlocated." He also mentions the copy at The New-York Historical Society, which was a gift of Dr. Samuel C. Ellis, grandson of Mrs. James Rivington and her first husband, Cornelius Van Horne, in 1858, and which is listed in the Society's 1941 *Catalogue* as by an unidentified artist after Stuart. This copy greatly resembles the work of Ames in its clear hard attention to detail; the precise lettering on the newspaper is similar in its precision to the lettering on papers introduced by Ames into his original portraits such as that of Simeon DeWitt. Again in painting the highlights of the eyes the copyist used small dots placed at the tops of the pupils in the manner so characteristic of Ames, whereas most of Stuart's highlights are dashes placed almost invariably at the upper left of the pupils. Like many artists

JAMES RIVINGTON (1724–1802)

By Ezra Ames, July 5, 1806, after the original by Gilbert Stuart

[Here first attributed and dated from data in Ames's Albany Institute Account Book]

Gift of Dr. Samuel C. Ellis, 1858, to The New-York Historical Society

of his day Ames admired Stuart's portraits, and as exercises to benefit him in his own work he copied several of them. Some of these are listed in his inventory. This fact, plus the estate inventory record of Ames's ownership of Stuart's Rivington, plus the stylistic resemblances of the Society's copy to Ames's known handywork, plus the Account Book entry of a portrait painted by Ames for the younger James Rivington after his father's death, adds up to a strong confidence that the Society's painting may now be attributed to Ezra Ames, as a copy after the original by Gilbert Stuart.

A portrait of General Solomon Van Rensselaer (1774–1852), known to have been painted by Ames, is exactly dated by an entry in the Albany Institute Account Book. Ever since the artist painted it in 1819 it has been in the possession of the family and has hung on the walls of "Cherry Hill" at Albany, New York, a house built in 1768 by Colonel Philip Van Rensselaer, uncle and father-in-law of the subject and now the residence of his descendants, Miss Emily W. Rankin and Mr. Edward E. Rankin. In an entry dated December 6, 1819, Ames charges General Solomon Van Rensselaer for "Painting his Portrait" which thus dates the likeness to the day. An earlier portrait of General Solomon Van Rensselaer is recorded on September 8, 1818, as painted for Joseph Delaplaine. This portrait was destroyed by fire. Mr. and Miss Rankin, in a letter to the writers, have traced the history of this portrait as follows:

In *A Legacy of Historical Gleanings*, volume I, pages 400–401, by Mrs. Bonney, a daughter of Solomon Van Rensselaer, there is set forth a letter from Joseph Delaplaine to Gen. Van Rensselaer, dated Philadelphia Feb. 28, 1822, in which occurs the following sentence: "It gives me pleasure to mention that *your Portrait* in my Gallery is recognized by all who know you." Mrs. Bonney then writes: "The above mentioned portrait was the most strikingly correct likeness ever taken of Gen. Van Rensselaer and for many years was in Philadelphia, but subsequently purchased by P. T. Barnum, Esq. Different members of Gen. Van Rensselaer's family, when in New York, repeatedly tried to obtain possession of this valuable picture, but they were told by the proprietor that 'money could not buy it.' A few years since, when 'Barnum's Museum' was destroyed by fire, unfortunately this cherished portrait, with the rest of his truly valuable collection, was reduced to ashes."

It has already been stated that the late William Sawitzky attributed portraits of Hamilton and Morris to Ames, and that his attributions are confirmed by entries in the Albany Institute Account Book. In four other instances the attributions of portraits to Ames by this, the most distinguished of all historians of early American art, are now confirmed by entries in the same Account Book. The portrait of Ambrose Spencer owned by John DeWitt Peltz, attributed in 1942, is recorded January 9, 1811. Portraits of Aaron Thorp and his wife owned by Miss Eleanor B. Weir, also attributed in 1942, are recorded May 1826. And the portrait of Gerrit Yates Lansing owned by Gerrit Yates Lansing, attributed in 1932, is recorded February 19, 1830.

Either of two portraits of Mrs. Jacob J. Brown, one owned by Harold T. Patterson, and one by the Munson-Williams-Proctor Institute, Utica, is probably the portrait recorded in the Account Book, March 12, 1818. The Patterson portrait, formerly attributed to John Wesley Jarvis, was attributed to Ames by the late William Sawitzky in 1940. The portrait owned by the Munson-Williams-Proctor Institute was attributed to Ames by Miss Hope Mathewson in 1940.

Four more attributions made by Miss Hope Mathewson to Ames of known portraits are confirmed by entries found in the Albany Institute Account Book. One of the portraits, attributed in 1937, and owned by Miss Eleanor B. Weir, is of a small girl, Frances Mary Thorp, the portraits of whose father and mother were attributed to Ames by William Sawitzky. In his entry in the Account Book, dated May 1826, Ames lists all three portraits. Other portraits attributed to Ames by Miss Mathewson, of subjects now found recorded in the artist's Account Book, are: the portrait of Mrs. John Keyes Paige, owned by Dr. J. Lewi Donhauser, attributed 1945, recorded October 1826; the portrait of Major George Provost, owned by Mrs. Stanley McCormick, attributed 1950, recorded October 29, 1805; and the portrait of

MAJOR GEORGE PROVOST

By Ezra Ames, 1805

Owned by Mrs. Stanley McCormick (Photo by FARL)

MRS. JACOB JENNINGS BROWN (1785–1878)

By Ezra Ames, probably 1818

Owned by Mr. Harold T. Patterson (Photostat by FARL)

[The attributions and dating of both these portraits are supported by entries in Ames's Albany Institute Account Book]

Absalom Townsend, owned by Mrs. Van Santvoord Merle-Smith, attributed 1935, recorded March 13, 1816. In this wise attributions on technical grounds to Ames are here confirmed by actual documentation.

Other portraits which are dated by entries in the Albany Institute Account Book are those of: Harmanus Bleecker, owned by The Harmanus Bleecker Library, Albany, recorded June 1819; DeWitt Clinton, on indefinite loan at the Albany Institute of History and Art, recorded March 8, 1818; John Keyes Paige, owned by Dr. J. Lewi Donhauser, recorded October 1826; John Tayler, now at Philipse Castle Restoration, which is inscribed on the back and dated 1816, and must be either of the portraits recorded August 14 or 28, 1816; and Elkanah Watson, known only in an engraving dating from 1820, recorded September 15, 1818.

A number of known portraits are less positively dated or identified. Thus the portrait of N. Allen, formerly owned by Dr. G. L. Laporte, which can be safely attributed to Ames, may be the portrait of Nathaniel Allen recorded April 15, 1817, in the Albany Institute Account Book. A portrait of Solomon Allen, now at the Museum of the City of New York, is probably the one recorded May 1814 as charged to "Mr. Solomon Allen To painting a portrait of his father," if we can assume that father and son had the same Christian name. A portrait of Solomon Southwick which may be the portrait recorded November 2, 1804, in an entry charging Solomon Southwick "To painting a portrait," is now in the Board Room of the Mechanics and Farmers' Bank, Albany. In an entry for September 8, 1818, Ames charges Southwick for a portrait destined for Joseph Delaplaine, but this could not be the portrait under discussion, because the sitter represented is much younger than Southwick was in 1818.

Three portraits and a landscape—all located—remain to be mentioned because they are also tentatively dated by entries in the Albany Institute Account Book. The portraits of Benjamin Tal[l]madge and his wife, formerly in the collection of Mrs.

Charles Peace Roy who bequeathed them to her daughter Mrs. Charles Lassell, may be those recorded on April 6, 1826, as copies, charged to "Cushman Esq[r] Troy [N. Y.]." The portrait of Stephen Van Rensselaer, at the New York State Historical Association, Cooperstown, New York, may be the portrait referred to in an entry of October 14, 1818, in which Van Rensselaer is charged for a portrait of himself for Joseph Delaplaine; or it may be the portrait referred to in an entry of April 24, 1819, which reads: "To Painting the portrait for your son. . . Delivered to your son S.V.R. Jun[r]," and charged to Stephen Van Rensselaer; or it could be the copy noted by Ames, June 3, 1825, for General Dunbar, Van Rensselaer's agent. The landscape, a "View of Lake George and Caldwell Village," owned by Miss Catharine Van Cortlandt Mathews and Mrs. William V. Mason, was probably painted long before the entry in the Account Book dated August 26, 1822, which is a note of a charge for "altering" the picture.

The documentation of the twenty-eight known paintings discussed in the present essay, made possible because the Albany Institute Account Book of Ezra Ames is now available for study, is an indication of the possibilities for a further study of the artist's work. In time other paintings by Ames may be located, dated, or otherwise documented by a study of the Account Books.* It is for this reason that a transcript of all the entries relating to the artist's paintings have been extracted from the artist's records and made available here in printed form.

OMISSIONS FROM THE TRANSCRIPT: CRAFT WORK

Numerous entries in the Account Books relating to the artist's work as a craftsman and journeyman painter, and thus falling

* Indeed, since the above account was written, the authors themselves have located or found other record of twenty additional paintings which they can now document as to painter and date through references in the Account Books. Though these discoveries were made too late for incorporation into the above discussion along with the twenty-eight which *are* discussed, they have been embodied in the Catalogue with their Account Book references and included in the revised table on p. 150.

outside the scope of the following transcript, are summarized here. This partial revelation of the remaining contents of the Account Books will indicate, comparatively, how much of the artist's work was artistic and how much of it was of a miscellaneous nature. Further, the great variety of work produced by Ames will give a general idea of the activities of other artists of that period and of a provincial portrait painter's status during the early years of the Republic.

Miscellaneous Jobs: Entries relating to miscellaneous jobs comprise by far the greater part of the first two Account Books and about half of the third. This type of work ranged from such day labor as papering rooms and painting fences, sleighs, and chaises, to painting signs, clockcases and clockfaces; making and painting "stands of colours" and Masonic regalia of all kinds; engraving and initialing spoons, rings, coffin plates, and other articles; and producing hair work and mourning pieces, as well as painted fancy pieces for embroidery.

Hair Work, etc.: Of hair work, Ames records seven orders between 1792 and 1796, three of which were included with orders for miniatures; of mourning pieces, he records four between 1796 and 1810; of fancy pieces, he records eight between 1809 and 1819, two of which are described as "for embroidery."

Signs: The artist records payment due him for about 162 signs between 1791 and 1820. In 1823 he records the painting of two "Indian statues" for a tobacco-shop proprietor. After that his painting was devoted exclusively to easel pictures. In eight cases only did Ames indicate the subject of his signs. They are as follows: a "Saw Sign" in 1797; "a large watch sign" in 1808; a "Sign Pocahuntas" in 1817; "a sign of Old Darby & Joan" in 1817; and an "Eagle Sign" in 1819. In each of the years 1816, 1817, 1818, and 1820 he records the painting of a lottery sign.

"Pictures": In all three Account Books there are entries which may or may not refer to original work by Ames. In this category there are three which refer to "pictures" of "Darby & Joan," two of which he sold for $5.00 in 1804 and 1806, and one for $6.00 in 1811. Inasmuch as these prices were higher than for

other so-called "pictures," these entries may possibly refer either to original oil paintings by Ames, perhaps copied from a print, or to prints, not by Ames, which he sold. Although he painted a sign of "Darby & Joan" in 1817, as previously noted, this does not mean that the earlier pictures were necessarily paintings. Indeed, from 1797 through 1811 references appear in the Account Books to "pictures" at so low a price that one can more readily infer them to have been prints. Thus in 1797, "2 Pictures Solomons Temple, & City Jerusalem," which were sold for 32 shillings for the two, might well have been prints.

Prints: There are four other entries between 1798 and 1800 which give a descriptive title but no mention of the medium employed and which are thought to refer to prints, thus: In 1798, "To a frame & Glass for [*?*] Liberty" for $2.00; in 1800, "To framing the Lawyers agent" for 10 shillings, "To 2 Caricatures of England & Scotland" for 9 shillings, and "To 4 Sea peices [*sic*] framed & glazed" for 3 pounds 12 shillings for the lot.

Then there are twelve references between 1797 and 1811, covering over 46 items, which refer specifically to prints: In 1805, "To Several ages d[*itt*]o [*mezzotinto print*] Colored 5/6"; in 1808, "To a Large print Golden Chain of Salvation," for 50 cents; and during the period seven references to mezzotinto prints, sometimes referred to by Ames as "mezzitints prints," and three references simply to prints. Since there is no known pictorial work engraved by Ames one may assume that none of these prints was by Ames.

Unclassified: Two baffling entries defy classification. In 1791 Ames records that he charged J. Thomas 1 pound 16 shillings "To painting 2 Cherubs etc."; and in 1798, he charged P. S. Van Rensselaer 14 shillings "To painting & a Glass."

Purchases: In a group of entries which appear to list expenses there are three entries which possibly refer to purchases by Ames of paintings which he may have bought to serve as models. The entries are for a miniature and setting in 1792; "1 Picture Sea Piece," and a miniature and hair work in 1794.

"AT THE SIGN OF POCAHONTAS"
For George Pearson, 1817

"OLD DARBY AND JOAN"
For Joseph Fry, 1817

WOODCUTS OF TWO TOBACCONISTS' SIGNS PAINTED BY EZRA AMES
From the *Albany Gazette* of Nov. 11, 1818, and June 3, 1819

BOX MADE AND DECORATED BY EZRA AMES
Owned by the Albany Institute of History and Art

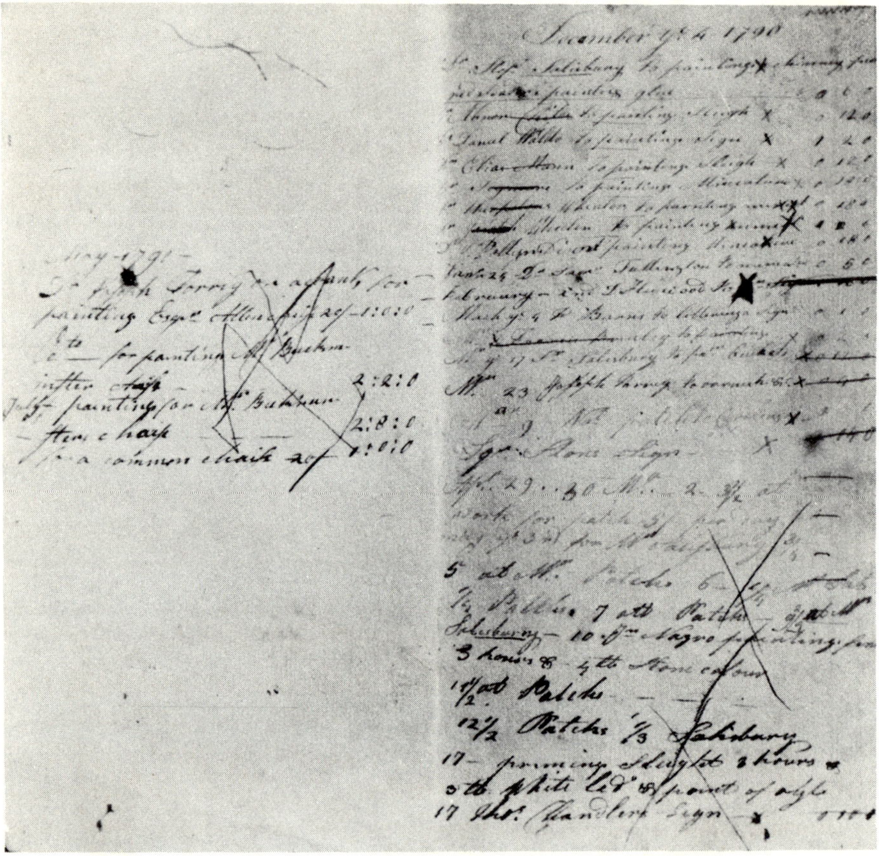

FIRST TWO PAGES OF AMES'S ACCOUNT BOOK NO. I (1790–1797)

Listing earliest miniatures and miscellaneous odd jobs

Owned by The New-York Historical Society

(Photographed by Irwin F. Cortelyou)

NOTES ON THE TRANSCRIPT

The following entries relating to Ames's paintings are published practically as the artist recorded them in his Account Books. They are, however, arranged in chronological order, which involved the transposition from the actual order of many of the entries in the first two Account Books, and a few in the third. The compilation includes the dates of the entries, the names of the patrons who commissioned the paintings, the names of the sitters whenever Ames recorded them, the references to the frames which he generally supplied, and the amounts charged. Except for the slight standardization in the form of dates, amounts charged, and a few abbreviations, the entries as printed reproduce the text of the manuscript even to the misspelling of names.

The dates have been standardized in the following manner: the years, frequently repeated by Ames before each entry, are given but once, at the beginning of each year; and the months, although variously spelled in full or abbreviated, have been uniformly contracted. The amounts charged have likewise been printed in a uniform manner. A final standardization is the invariable use of the abbreviations "M^r^" and "M^rs^" and "M^essrs^" as the artist almost invariably wrote them. "D^r^," of course, stands for debtor. When it was omitted by Ames, [*No D^r^*] is inserted.

Indications of payments received have been omitted. These consist of the word "paid," or the cancellation of the entry by a line running through the words, or by a cross mark. No transcript is made of entries for balances due except when they are the only indication that a portrait was painted.

No attempt has been made to preserve the original alinement of dashes following the abbreviation "do" [for "ditto"] or to reproduce those which appear as flourishes. Otherwise, the transcript following is a faithful chronological reproduction of all the data contained in Ames's three Account Books relating to his easel paintings and miniatures.

X

TRANSCRIPT OF ENTRIES FOR PORTRAITS, MINIATURES, AND PAINTINGS OF MISCELLANEOUS SUBJECTS FROM EZRA AMES'S NYHS ACCOUNT BOOKS

Date		Entry	Price
1790		[*Worcester, Mass.*]	
Dec	4	Dr Seymore To painting Miniature	£0:18:0
Dec	4	Dr Theopelous Whealer To painting miniat.	0:18:0
Dec	4	Dr Joseph Wheeler To painting miniat.	1: 0:0
Dec	4	Dr Polly Dixon painting Miniature	0:18:0
1791		[*Worcester, Mass.*]	
Jan	29	Dr Sam^{el} Fallington to mineature	0: 5:0
Sep		D^{r} phillips miniature	0:18:0
Oct		[*No D^{r}*] Joseph Wheeler miniature [*possibly payment for the miniature in entry of Dec. 4, 1790, under same name*]	1: 0:0
		Locket & setting	0: 8:0
1792		[*Worcester, Mass.*]	
Mar	27	Dr Mr Draper To painting a portrait 30/	1:10:0
Apr	21	D^{r} M^{r} harris to painting miniature	0:18:0
Jul	13	[*No D^{r}*] Sanford for his miniature	[*Not given*]
Sep	14	Dr A. D. To painting a Miniature	0:18:0
Oct	17	Dr Doct^{r} Wm Lanton To painting a Miniature	0:18:0
1793		[*Worcester, Mass., and Poughkeepsie, N.Y.*]	
Jan	17	Mr Stephen Harris D^{r} To Painting his Miniature	0:18:0
		and a piece of heir work	0: 6:0
[*c. Apr–May*]		[Maj^{r} Livingston pictures]	[6:15:0]
		[Note: In several undated entries, here assigned to *c.* April–May 1793, Ames records his expenses for materials for painting pictures for Major Livingston, and for payment received from him of £6:15:0]	
1794		[*Albany, N.Y.*]	
Jan		Doc^{t} D. Treat D^{r} To Painting his Miniature	0:40:0
Feb	10	M^{rs} Y^{a} [Yates] [*No D^{r}*] For 2 Miniatures	4: 0:0
Feb	22	of Mr Glen [*No D^{r}*] for Portrait painting	4: 0:0

Date	Entry	Price
1794 (cont'd)		
Feb 25	Dr Mr John Hayke	
	To painting Miniature	£0:40:0
Mar 3	Mr John Hooker [*No Dr*]	
	To Painting a miniature	0:40:0
Mar 26	Mr Spalding Dr	
	To Painting a Miniature	0:40:0
Mar 28	[*No Dr*] for Mrs [George] Clinton miniatr	2: 0:0
	for his Excel[l]encys Do	2: 0:0
Apr 1	[*No Dr*] for Mr M. Dewetts mr [miniature]	2: 0:0
Apr 24	Miss Corn Yates Dr	
	To Painting 2 miniatures	4: 0:0
May 1	of Mr Levi Willard [*No Dr*]	
	for a miniature	0:40:0
May 3	Mr Thomas Diamond Dr	
	To Painting a portrait	0:48:0
Jun 19	Mrs Fairley Dr	
	To Painting & finishing the Drapery of Majr Fairleys Portrait	1:12:0
	To the Frame	0:12:0
	To Gilding the frame	0: 8:0
1795		
Mar 26	Mr Francis Follet Dr	
	To Painting a Miniature	0:40:0
	To a heir plat	0: 6:0
Aug 8	Dr Mrs Samuel Hawkins	
	To painting a Miniature	0:40:0
1796		
Feb 26	Mr Hezah Sharliff Dr	
	To Painting a Miniature	0:40:0
Jul 22	Mr Ellis Dr	
	To painting a portrait	3: 4:0
	To painting a Miniature & heir work	0:48:0
1797		
[*No date*]	Mr James Rogers [*No Dr*] To Painting a Mineature	0:40:0
	To a Glass for Do	0: 6:0
1798		
Jul 30	John M. Dole Dr	
	To painting a miniature	$ 5.00

Date	Entry	Price
1799		
Dec 23	Elihu Phinney Esq[r] D[r]	
	To Painting his portrait	$15.00
	To a Frame for do & box	2.00
		1.00
1800		
Dec 22	M[r] [*no name given*] D[r]	
	To painting a Lion	£5: 4:0
1802		
Aug 18	Leonard Gans[e]voort Esq[r] D[r]	
	To 1 Portrait	4: 0:0
	To a Frame for do	4: 0:0

TRANSCRIPT OF ENTRIES FOR PORTRAITS, MINIATURES, AND PAINTINGS OF MISCELLANEOUS SUBJECTS FROM EZRA AMES'S ALBANY INSTITUTE ACCOUNT BOOK

1804		
May 22	Matthias B. Tallmadge Esq[r] D[r]	
	To painting a portrait	$ 20.00
	To a Frame for do	10.00
Jul 20	M[r] James Hodge D[r]	
	To painting a miniature	15.00
Nov 2	M[r] Solomon Southwick D[r]	
	To Painting a Portrait	18.00
	To Frame for do	10.00
Dec 16	M[rs] McGourk D[r]	
	To painting a portrait	20.00
	To a Frame for do	10.00
1805		
Feb 14	M[r] Bulkey D[r]	
	To painting a Miniature	15.00
Mar 2	The Hon[bl] Smith Thompson Esq[r] D[r]	
	To painting a portrait	20.00
	To painting a Miniature	15.00
Apr 17	Zebulor Shepherd Esq[r] D[r]	
	To painting 2 portraits $20 each	40.00
	To 2 Frames for do $10 each	20.00

Date	Entry	Price
1805 (cont'd)		
Jun	Mr Jacob Vanderhyden D^r	
	To Painting a Portrait	$20.00
	To Frame for do	10.00
Jun 29	Mr Thomas Barrey D^r	
	To Painting a Portrait	20.00
	To a Frame for do	10.00
Jul	Mr James Caldwell D^r	
	To Painting Two Portraits $20 each	40.00
Oct 29	George Provost Esqr D^r	
	To Painting 2 Portraits at $20	40.00
	To Two Frames for do at $10	20.00
Oct 30	William P. Beers Esqr D^r	
	To Painting a Portrait	20.00
	To a Frame for do	10.00
1806		
May	Leu^t Thorne Esqr D^r	
	To Portrait & Frame	30.00
Jul 5	Mr Ja^s Rivington D^r	
	To a Portrait & Frame	30.00
Oct 13	Mr Germain D^r	
	To a Portrait & Frame	30.00
Oct 27	Mrs Diamond D^r	
	To Portrait & Frame	30.00
Dec 27	Doct^r Saml Stringer D^r	
	To a Portrait & Frame	25.00
1807		
Dec 24	Mr James Lagrange D^r	
	To painting Two portraits & Frames	60.00
Dec 25	Mr Benjn Knower D^r	
	To Painting Two portraits & Frames	60.00

[*Note: According to a bill dated December 25, 1807, laid in the Account Book, receipted by Ames, more details are given as follows:*]

To Painting a Portrait	$25.00
To –do– – do his Lady	25.00
To Two gilt frames–$10 each	20.00
	70.00

Date	Entry	Price
1808		
May 16	M[rs] Van Cleek D[r]	
	To a Frame & portrait of M[rs] Rivington	$30.00
Jul 28	Isaac Hansen Esq[r] D[r]	
	To a portrait & Frame	30.00
Aug 10	M[r] John Van Schaick D[r]	
	To a portrait & Frame	30.00
Aug 13	M[r] Garret Van Wie D[r]	
	To a portrait & Frame	30.00
Nov 1	Doct[r] H. Woodroof D[r]	
	To Portrait & Frame	30.00
Nov 7	Cap[t] Solomon Townsend D[r]	
	To Ballance due on a portrait & Frame	15.00
Nov 22	M[r] Robert Dunbar D[r]	
	To 2 Portraits & Frames $30 each	60.00
1809		
Mar 24	Solomon Southwick Esq[r] D[r]	
	To a Frame & Portrait of M[r] Barber	30.00
Jul 13	T. Sedgewick Esq[r] D[r]	
	To Painting a Portrait	20.00
Jul	Doct[r] H. Woodroof D[r]	
	To Painting a Portrait & Frame	30.00
1810		
Apr 25	Elijah Thomas Esq[r] D[r]	
	To Portrait & Frame of Genr[l] Hamilton delivered to Doct[r] C. C. Yates	25.00
May 4	M[r] Joseph Warford D[r]	
	To a Portrait & Frame	35.00
Jun 16	Isaac Hansen Esq[r] D[r] To Portrait & Frame	35.00
Jul 3	M[r] James Caldwell D[r]	
	To Painting the asalt of the Ile of [*?*]	10.00
	To a Frame for do	10.00
Aug	M[r] Thomas Livingston D[r]	
	To a Portrait & Frame	35.00
Oct 3	M[r] C. Z. Platt D[r]	
	To a Portrait & Frame	35.00
Oct 29	Doct[r] Pomeroy D[r]	
	To Portrait & Frame	30.00
	To Box for do	.75
Nov 22	M[r] Gourlay D[r] To a Portrait & Frame	40.00

Date	Entry	Price
1811		
Jan 9	His honor Ambrose Spencer Dr	
	To a portrait $30	
	To a Frame for do $15	$45.00
Jan 31	Mr Lawrence Van Cleek Dr	
	To a Portrait & Frame	35.00
Mar 20	James Van Ingen Esqr Dr	
	To painting figure of Hope for steamboat	8.00
Apr 24	James Van Ingen Esqr Dr	
	To painting the Beaver assiduity for steamboat	7.00
Jun 13	Mr Caleb Russell Dr	
	To Portrait & Frame	30.00
Aug	Mr Obadiah Penniman Dr	
	To a Portrait of Mrs Penniman	25.00
Nov 6	Mr Wm McHarg Dr	
	To 2 Portrait & Frames viz Genera[l] King & Lady	76.00
Dec 13	Mathew Trotter Esqr Dr	
	To a Portrait & Frame	38.00
1812		
Mar 4	Mr Wegdon Dr	
	To Portrait 25 Dol & Frame 20 Dol	45.00
Mar 13	Mr James Kane Dr	
	To one View of Lake George	25.00
	To 4 Large Frames $25 each	100.00
Apr 1	Lawrance L. Van Kleeck Esqr Dr	
	To Painting a Portrait of Miss Van Rensselaer 25 Dols Frame 20 Dols	45.00
May 8	Mr Gilbert Stewart Dr	
	To painting a portrait	25.00
	To a Frame for do	13.00
May 8	John Bogart Esqr Dr	
	To painting a Portrait	25.00
	To a Frame for do	20.00
[*No date*]	Mr John C. Cuyler Dr	
	To a Ballance due acct a portrait	5.00
Sep 9	Mr John Randel Dr	
	To Painting a Portrait of his sister, Mrs Weeks	25.00
	" a Burnished Gilt Picture Frame	21.00
	To Painting a portrait of his Mother & sister	35.00
	" a Frame for do	21.00

Date		Entry	Price
1812 (cont'd)			
Sep		John Tayler Esqr D^{r}	
		To a Perspective painting of Lake George	$25.00
		To a Frame for do	25.00
Nov	21	Direct Ten Broek Esqr D^{r}	
		To Painting a Portrait	30.00
1813			
Mar	18	Mr Sedgewick D^{r}	
		To Painting a Portrait	25.00
Apr	5	Mr John Randel, Junr D^{r}	
		To painting a portrait of his father	25.00
		To Burnished Gilt Frame for do	21.00
May	14	Mr I. M. Wells D^{r}	
		To Ballance due on a Portrait	10.00
		To a Portrait frame	18.00
Aug		Doct^{r} John Stearns D^{r}	
		To a Portrait	30.00
		To a Burnished Gilt Portrait Frame	20.00
Oct		Mr Ira Porter D^{r}	
		To Painting a Portrait	30.00
		" 2 Burnished Gilt Portrait Frames $20.00	40.00
		Cr—one portrait returned $15.00	
Nov		M^{r} E[b]enizer Smith D^{r}	
		To Painting 2 Portraits $30 each	60.00
		2 Burnished Gilt Frames for the above	40.00
1814			
May		Mathias B. Talmadge Esqr D^{r}	
		To Painting a half length Portrait of the late Vice president George Clinton	100.00
		" a Burnished Gilt Frame for do	50.00
May		Mr Solomon Allen D^{r}	
		To painting a portrait of his father	30.00
		—a frame for do	20.00
May		Doct^{r} Romyne Beck D^{r}	
		To a Portrait of Doct^{r} Romeyn	30.00
		To—Frame for do	15.00
Dec	5	Robert L. Livingston Esqr D^{r}	
		To Painting a Coppy of Mrs Stevens	40.00
1815			
Feb		Mr Dela Van D^{r} To Painting a Portrait	30.00
		To a Burnished Gilt Frame	20.00

Date	Entry	Price
1815 (cont'd)		
Mar 3	Mr Thomas Mounsey D^r^	
	To Painting a Portrait	$30.00
	To Burnished Gilt Frame	20.00
Mar 17	James Gourlay Esqr D^r^	
	To Painting a full length Portrait of a Child	30.00
	To a Burnished Gilt Frame for do	25.00
Jul 21	Isaac Hamilton Esqr [*No D^r^*]	
	To Painting 2 Portraits $30	60.00
	" Two Burnished Gilt frames for do	40.00
1816		
Mar 13	Mr Absalom Townsend D^r^	
	To Painting a Portrait	30.00
May 31	Aaron Hackley Esqr D^r^	
	To a Portrait $30 & Burnished Gilt Frame	50.00
Aug 14	John Tayler Esqr D^r^	
	To Painting a Portrait	30.00
	To a Burnished Gilt Frame	20.00
Aug 28	John Tayler Esqr D^r^	
	To Painting a Portrait for Lynot Bloodgood	30.00
Nov 25	Mr George B. Spencer D^r^	
	To Painting Two Portraits $30	60.00
	" Two Burnished Gilt frames $20 ea	40.00
Dec	Mr John Meads D^r^	
	To painting Two portraits $30 each	60.00
1817		
Apr 4	John F. Bacon Esqr D^r^	
	To Painting a Portrait	30.00
	To a Burnished Gilt Frame	20.00
Apr 15	Nathl Allen Esqr D^r^	
	To Painting a Portrait	30.00
Apr 18	Theodore Dwight Esqr D^r^	
	To Painting a Portrait	30.00
	To Burnished Gilt Frame	20.00
Jun 21	Mrs Morris D^r^	
	To a Portrait of the late Govn^r^ Morris Esqr	50.00
	To a Burnished Gilt Frame	25.00
	" a Packing Box	1.00
Sep 13	James Van Ingen Esqr D^r^	
	To painting a portrait of his son	30.00
	To a Burnished Gilt Frame for do	20.00

Date		Entry	Price
1817 (*cont'd*)			
Sep	15	Mr James Davis D^r	
		To Painting his portrait & son	$50.00
		To a Burnished Gilt Frame	25.00
1818			
Jan	10	Elkanah Watson Esqr [*No D^r*]	
		To painting a Portrait of his Daughter	30.00
		To a Burnished Gilt Frame	20.00
Mar	8	Govn^r [DeWitt] Clinton D^r	
		To Painting a Portrait of a White Lake Fish	2.50
Mar	8	Elisha Jenkins Esqr D^r	
		To Painting a Half length Portrait of Govn^r Clinton (for the Corporation)	100.00
		To a Burnished Gilt Frame for do	50.00
Mar	12	Maj^r General Brown D^r	
		To Painting a Portrait of his Lady	30.00
		" a Burnished Gilt Frame for do	20.00
Mar	25	Govn^r [DeWitt] Clinton D^r	
		To Painting a Portrait of a Lake Herring	2.00
Jul	31	Govn^r [DeWitt] Clinton D^r	
		To painting a Coppay of a Portrait of his Lady For Joseph Delaplain	30.00
Sep	5	Govn^r [DeWitt] Clinton D^r	
		To Painting a Portrait of his son George	30.00
		To–do–do – –his son Franklin	30.00
		To 2 Burnished Gilt Frames $20 each	40.00
Sep	8	Mr Joseph Delaplaine D^r	
		To Portrait of the late Vice presid^t Clinton	15.00
		To Genl Sol Van Rensselare	15.00
		[To do–Rev. H. Cumming, *crossed out*]	15.00
		[Note: In an entry, same date (Sep 8), the portraits of Clinton and S. Van Rensselaer are listed with a portrait of Rev. Hooper Cumming. All three names are crossed out. The first two are re-entered, the third omitted, in the final entry. Thus the third, the portrait of Cumming, may never have been painted, or it may have been omitted because paid for on delivery.]	
Sep	8	Govn^r Tayler D^r	
		To a Portrait for Delaplaine's Gallery	30.00
Sep	8	Solomon Southwick Esqr D^r	
		To his Portrait for Delaplaine's N-Gallery	30.00

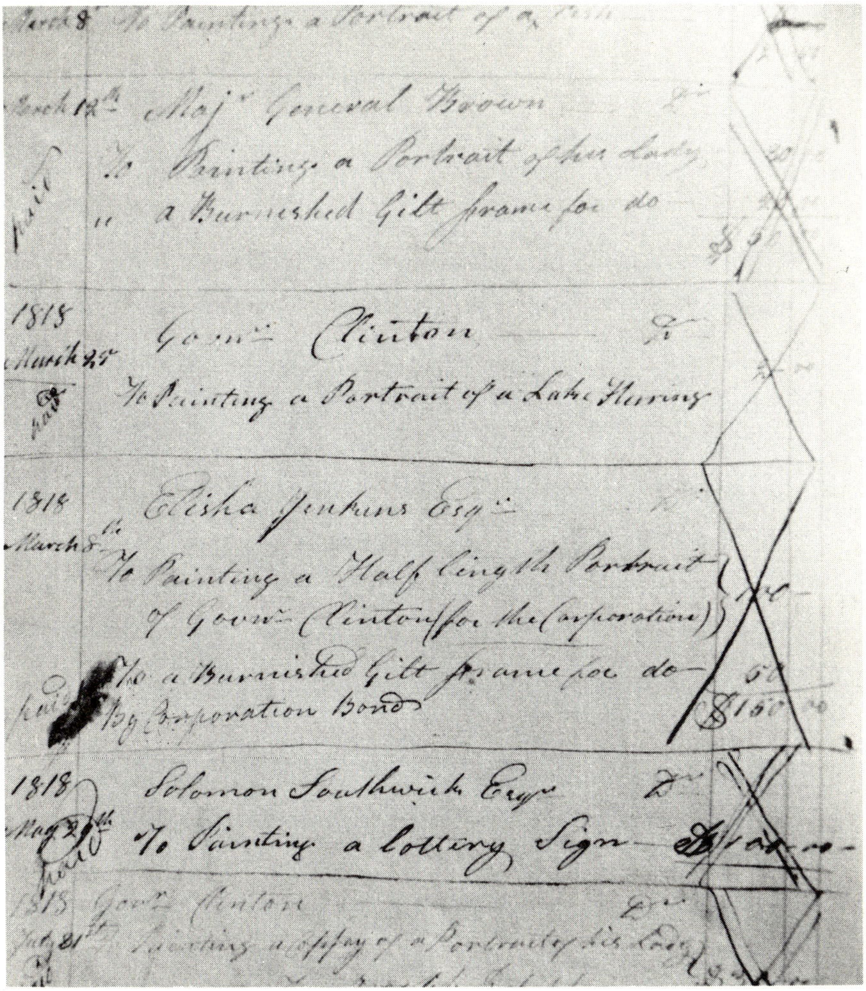
March 8th To Painting a Portrait of a Fish

March 12th Majr General Brown Dr
paid To Painting a Portrait of his Lady
" a Burnished Gilt frame for do

1818 Govr Clinton Dr
March 25th
paid To Painting a Portrait of a Lake Herring

1818 Elisha Jenkins Esqr
March 8th To Painting a Half length Portrait
of Govr Clinton (for the Corporation)
paid To a Burnished Gilt frame for do 50
By Corporation Bond $150

1818 Solomon Southwick Esqr Dr
May 29th
paid To Painting a lottery Sign

1818 Govr Clinton
July 21st To Painting a Coppy of a Portrait of his Lady

SECTION OF A PAGE FROM AMES'S ACCOUNT BOOK NO. 3 (1804–1834)

Listing portraits of people and fish and a lottery sign

Owned by the Albany Institute of History and Art

(Photographed by Irwin F. Cortelyou)

Date		Entry	Price
1818 (*cont'd*)			
Sep	15	Elkanah Watson Esqr D^{r}	
		To a Portrait of Himself	$30.00
		To a Burnished Gilt Frame	20.00
Oct	8	Mr Giles Spencer D^{r}	
		To Painting a Portrait of his Daughter	30.00
		To a Burnished Gilt Frame	20.00
Oct	10	Govn^{r} [DeWitt] Clinton D^{r}	
		To Painting a Fish	2.50
Oct	14	[Joseph Delaplaine D^{r}]	
		To Copy of a Portrait of Doct^{r} Livingston	15.00
		To do—Gov^{n} Morris	15.00
Oct	14	Stephen Van Rensselaer Esqr D^{r}	
		To a Portrait for J. Delaplain, Philadelphia	30.00
Oct	31	Mr John Meads D^{r}	
		To Painting a Portrait of Mrs Crane	30.00
Dec	28	Revd Arthur I. Stansbary D^{r}	
		To Painting a Portrait of his Mother	30.00
		To Burnished Gilt Frame	20.00
Dec	29	Revd Doc^{t} Blackford D^{r}	
		To Painting his Portrait	30.00
		To Burnished Gilt Frame	20.00
1819			
Jan	13	F. [*possibly* J *or* G] Humphery D^{r}	
		To Balance on a Portrait &c	25.00
Mar	1	Wm Barclay D^{r}	
		To an alegorical Painting for T[emple] Lodge &c	10.00
Apr	24	Stephen Van Rensselaer Esqr D^{r}	
		To Painting a Portrait for your son	30.00
		To a Burnished Gilt Frame	20.00
		Delivered to your son S.V.R. Junr	
Jun		H. Bleeker Esqr D^{r}	
		To Painting his Portrait for Mrs Sedgwick	30.00
		To Gilt Frame for do	10.00
		To Portrait for the Revd Broadhead, Phi^{l}	30.00
		To Burnished Gilt Frame	20.00
Jul	27	Mr James Caldwell Esqr D^{r}	
		To a Portrait & white Frame	35.00
Dec	6	Genl Solomon Van Rensselaer D^{r}	
		To Painting his Portrait	30.00
		To a Burnished Gilt Frame	20.00

Date	Entry	Price
1820		
Jan 28	Gov^{n} [DeWitt] Clinton D^{r}	
	To Painting a Portrait of Mrs Clinton }	
	To Burnished Gilt Frame for do }	$60.00
	To a do—a—Coppy—do	30.00
Sep 7	Revd Doct^{r} Blackford D^{r}	
	To Painting a Portrait of his Lady	30.00
	To a Burnished Gilt Frame	20.00
Dec 23	His Excellency Gov^{n} [DeWitt] Clinton D^{r}	
	To Painting a Pike—fish—	1.50
1821		
Apr 3	Guint Van Schoonhovn Esqr D^{r}	
	To Portrait of his Lady	30.00
	To a Frame for do	14.00
Sep 18	Mr George W. Stanton D^{r}	
	To Painting his Portrait	30.00
	To—do—his Lady	30.00
Oct 3	Peter Gansevoort Esqr D^{r}	
	To Painting a Portrait of his father	30.00
Oct 17	Wm Wilkinson Esqr (Providence) D^{r}	
	To Painting his Portrait	30.00
	Delivered to Mr Mather	
[*No date*]	Thomas R. Gold Esqr D^{r}	
	To Painting his Portrait	30.00
[*No date*]	R. Temple Esqr (Rutland, Vermont) D^{r}	
	To Painting a Portrait of his father	30.00
Dec	His Excellency Govr [DeWitt] Clinton D^{r}	
	To Painting an Apple & a Pear	[*Not given*]
1822		
[*No date*]	Alexander O. Spencer Esqr D^{r}	
	To painting a Copy of Judge Spencers Lady	30.00
	To a Burnished Gilt Frame	13.00
Mar 19	John Townsend Esqr D^{r}	
	To Painting a Portrait of Judge Spencer son	30.00
	To a Burnished Gilt Frame for the above	13.00
Apr 9	Barnum Whiple Esqr D^{r}	
	To Painting his Portrait	30.00
Apr 23	Goven^{r} [DeWitt]Clinton D^{r}	
	To Painting a Silver Lake White Fish	[*Not given*]
Aug 26	James Caldwell Esqr [*No D^{r}*]	
	To altering a paintg of Lake Georg[e]	2.00

Date	Entry	Price
1824		
Mar 4	Cushman Esqr D^{r}	
	To Painting a Portrait of his Father	$25.00
	To – Do – do – his mother	25.00
Apr 17	Aaron Huckley Esqr D^{r}	
	To a Portrait of his lady	30.00
	To a Frame $8	8.00
May 10	Doct^{r} Megs D^{r}	
	Portrait of his mother	30.00
May 16	Revd G. [*possibly* J.] Hurlbert D^{r}	
	To Painting his Portrait	30.00
	To a Frame for do	13.00
Oct 19	Mrs Davinson D^{r}	
	To Painting a Portrait of her Husband	30.00
	To Burnished Gilt Frame	18.00
1825		
Mar 12	Mrs Mancius D^{r}	
	To Painting her Husbands Portrait	30.00
	To Burnished Gilt frame–Do	12.00
	" a Coppy of a portrait	25.00
	" a Frame for do	7.00
Jun 3	Genl Dunbar D^{r}	
	To Painting a Copy of General S. Van Renns-selaer's portrait	30.00
Jul	Mr Tilly Allen D^{r}	
	To Painting his Portrait	30.00
	To–do–his Ladys–do	30.00
Oct 14	Mrs Pain (Troy) D^{r}	
	To Painting her Portrait Kit Cat Size	40.00
Oct 14	Mr D. Williams D^{r}	
	To Painting portrait his Lady & Child	50.00
	To–do–his Portrait Kit Cat Size	40.00
Nov 10	Mr James B. Duglass D^{r}	
	To Painting his Lady's Portrait and Daughters	50.00
	Picture Returned 1834	
1826		
Apr 6	Cushman Esqr Troy [N. Y.] D^{r}	
	To a Copy of a Portrait of Col. Talmage	30.00
	To–do–of his Lady	30.00

Date	Entry	Price
1826 (cont'd)		
May 18	John Brinckerhoff Esqr D^{r}	
	To Painting his Ladys Portrait	$30.00
May 29	Mr Valentine W. Rathbone D^{r}	
	To Painting a Portrait of his Child	30.00
May	Mr Aaron Thorp D^{r}	
	To Painting a Portrait of his Child	30.00
	To—do his do	30.00
	To—do do Ladys Portrait	30.00
Oct	John K. Page Esqr D^{r}	
	To Painting his Portrait	30.00
	" do his Ladys Portrait	30.00
Oct 9	Mr Egberts D^{r}	
	To Painting his Portrait	30.00
Oct 9	Mr Chandler Starr D^{r}	
	To Painting his fathers Portrait	30.00
Oct 9	Mr James Hunter D^{r}	
	To Paintin[g] his Portrait	30.00
1827		
Oct 16	Mr Mills D^{r}	
	To Paintin[g] a Portrait of his Son	30.00
Oct	Mr Hatch (of Troy) D^{r}	
	To a Portrait of Randel Rice Deceased Returned	15.00
Oct	Mr Mandevell (Waterford) D^{r}	
	To Painting his Portrait	30.00
1828		
Nov 18	Messrs Jesse W. Goodrich, E. H. Blatchford, & S. R. Wynkoop D^{r}	
	To a Portrait of Doct^{r} Nott	30.00
	" " Frame for do	12.00
1829		
Jan 7	Govn^{r} Taylors Portrait [*No D^{r}*]	30.00
Feb 6	Mrs Levy Solomans D^{r}	
	To Painting a Portrait of her son Levy	30.00
	To — do — do — do Samuel	30.00
Jun 20	John Trotter Esqr D^{r}	
	To Painting his Portrait	30.00
	"—do—his sons do	30.00

Date		Entry	Price
1829 (cont'd)			
Jul	24	Mr J. Ten Eyck D^r	
		To Painting a Coppy of his fathers portrait	[*illegible*]
Aug	21	John S. Van Rensselaer Esqr D^r	
		To Painting his Portrait	$30.00
		To—do—do—Ladys—do	30.00
Nov	20	Judge Southerland D^r	
		To a Portrait of Chan^r Lansingh	30.00
1830			
Feb	19	Garret Y. Lansingh Esqr D^r	
		To Painting his Portrait	30.00
Jun	19	Willard Walker D^r	
		To Painting his Portrait	30.00
		To—do—his Ladys	30.00
Jun	19	Mrs Stuart D^r	
		To Painting her Deceased Husbands Portrait	30.00
Jun		Doct^r R. Forsyth D^r	
		To Painting Portraits of his Two sons $30 each	60.00
Nov	30	Mr S. Penniman D^r	
		To Painting his Portrait	30.00
		To—do—his Ladys	30.00
1831			
Sep	3	Henry Shaw Esqr D^r	
		To Painting his daughters Portrait	30.00
1834			
Dec	28	Mrs Cooper D^r	
		To Painting a Portrait of Doct^r Cooper her Deceased Husband	30.00

[*Last Entry*]

[The above transcript was made and arranged by Irwin F. Cortelyou.]

PART III
CATALOGUE

MRS. JOHN MEADS (b. 1785)
By Ezra Ames, dated by Account Book, 1816
Owned by Mr. Joseph Larocque, Jr.
(Photographed by Irwin F. Cortelyou)

NOTES ON THE CATALOGUE

THIS IS THE FIRST attempt to assemble an extensive catalogue of the portraits and other pictorial works of Ezra Ames. The writers have tried to make the list as complete as possible. They have investigated all likely sources; have tried to examine all portraits which could be located, indicating the fact of such examination in the catalogue entries; and have weighed all available evidences for and against the attributions as to artist and the identifications as to sitter. If some mistakes have been made (as is probable) or when additional pictures by Ezra Ames come to light (as is certain), the authors and publisher will appreciate having these matters brought to their attention.

The Catalogue lists 569 pictures by Ezra Ames. It also lists 23 prints after portraits by Ames, 19 pictures misattributed to Ames, and 29 pictures of questionable attribution. The Catalogue as a whole, therefore, comprises 640 entries. These are numbered consecutively (including six lettered insert-entries) and are arranged in the following sections, each section containing the inclusive entry-numbers shown:

XI Portraits in Oil (1–452, and 6 lettered insert-entries)

XII Portraits in Miniature (453–513)

XIII Landscapes, Figure Compositions, Still Life, and Drawings (514–563)

XIV Prints after Portraits by Ezra Ames (564–586)

XV Pictures Misattributed to Ezra Ames (587–605)

XVI Pictures of Questionable Attribution. Unsettled Matters (606–634)

In Sections XI, XII, and XIII, which record the pictures by Ezra Ames, 228 paintings and four drawings are catalogued as located, and 336 paintings and one drawing are listed as still unlocated. Many of these unlocated pictures no doubt still exist, as presumably do other paintings and drawings by Ames of which no record at all has come to the writers' attention. Some of these will surely one day be found and identified.

It is for the reasons just mentioned that the statistical table on page 150* is captioned "Tentative Totals of Paintings by Ezra Ames." The table, which excludes the five known drawings, does comprise, however, every painting, whether located or not, which is listed in the Catalogue as by Ames. The totals shown are: 458 portraits in oil, 61 miniatures, 4 landscapes, 18 figure compositions, 9 still life pictures, and 14 paintings of miscellaneous subjects—a sum total of 564 paintings. Adding the five drawings, the grand total of all pictorial works of art presently known to and accepted by the authors as by Ezra Ames—and thus recorded in the catalogue entries—is 569.

Within the entries, the pertinent information (whenever ample enough to warrant segregation by subheadings) is arranged in the following order: (1) sitter or subject, (2) description, (3) date of painting, (4) inscription, (5) owner(s), (6) photograph(s), (7) reproduction(s), (8) exhibition(s), (9) attribution(s), (10) notes of explanation when necessary, (11) whether unlocated and, if located, whether examined by one or both of the authors, and (12) whether and where illustrated in the present volume.

Within each catalogue section the entries are arranged alphabetically by sitter's name or subject title. The same sitter may be found in several sections of the catalogue as well as mentioned in the text, so the index should be consulted to catch all references to portraits of a given person. Portraits of women are listed in the catalogue either under their maiden names or under their married names according to whether the portraits were painted before or after marriage. The index in each case carries cross-references from one name to the other. Variant spellings, or incorrect spellings by Ezra Ames, of sitters' names and variant

* This table is arranged not only by three location-categories from the point of view of time, but also by six picture-subjects and by three classifications of the sources from which the paintings are known.

titles of pictures will be found in the index with a reference to the correct spelling or the listed title. For example, the picture entered as No. 538 below appears in the index under its variant titles of Lady of the Lake, Allegorical Landscape, and Voyage of Life, with a *see* reference from each to Romantic Landscape—the title by which it is listed in the Catalogue.

When a name (with or without date-span) in the first two alphabets is followed by the word "Patron" in brackets, the meaning is that the name is recorded in the Account Books or elsewhere as the person charged for a portrait of which the sitter as such has not been identified. In such cases the patron may or may not be the sitter. The probability, however, is that either the patron or a member of his family was the sitter, for which reason portraits not otherwise identifiable are listed by the names of the respective patrons when these are known.

In order to avoid duplication of entries for identical pictures, the writers have attempted to relate known paintings to those mentioned in the Account Books, 1790–1834, in the Inventory of Ames's estate, 1836, and in the *Catalogue Sale of Portraits* by the artist's executors, 1842. Since many of these relationships have been established by the process of elimination, the discovery of new pictures may quite possibly upset some of them. In allocating the entries from the above three sources, it has been assumed that paintings mentioned in the Account Books were delivered to the persons charged for them (unless otherwise stated in the Account Books) and therefore would not be found still in Ames's possession at the time of his death or in the sale of paintings from his estate in 1842. It has been further assumed that the listings in the 1836 Inventory and the 1842 Sale duplicate each other when the sitters' names or picture titles are alike in both.

In describing the pictures, the support is mentioned only if other than canvas; the size is given in inches, height before width. The word "sight" used to qualify a measurement means the size of the picture as seen when framed; that is, it does not include the unseen portion of the canvas fitting into the grooves of the frame. The phrases "head to right" and "head to left" mean to the viewer's right and left. The following descriptive terms (based on Charles Henry Hart, "Thomas Sully's Register of Portraits," *Pennsylvania Magazine of History and Biography*, October 1908, p. 395, with "half-length standing" and "full-length" added) are used consistently:

BUST: includes the arms but not the hands.

HALF-LENGTH: includes the hands but not the legs.

KIT-KAT: a half-length larger than ordinary.

HALF-LENGTH STANDING: includes the legs above the knees.

THREE-QUARTER LENGTH: includes the legs below the knees but not the feet.

FULL-LENGTH (OR WHOLE-LENGTH): includes the feet.

Although the authors have taken notes on color and composition for every picture examined by them and have solicited such information for pictures they could not examine, these notes have been omitted from the catalogue entries because: (1) merely for the purpose of identification they are usually unnecessary; (2) in some instances color and/or composition are described in the text; (3) a study of the many illustrations in this volume will provide a more concrete understanding of Ames's compositional practices than a series of descriptions possibly could; and (4) such information will be made available to students either at the Frick Art Reference Library or upon application to Irwin F. Cortelyou, Rumson, N. J.

In general it may be said that a majority of the oil portraits have plain dark-brown backgrounds, either red-brown, gray-brown, or olive-brown. A few have gray backgrounds; and a very few have sky and landscape backgrounds. In his earlier period Ames occasionally painted spandrels on his bust portraits in imitation of the wooden mat sometimes used for centering the attention on the face. Devices most frequently used for decorative backgrounds are plain perpendicular strips of shadow placed at one edge of the canvas; and diagonal shadows, draperies,

SAMUEL STEVENSON FOWLER (1799–1850)
By Ezra Ames, *c.* 1827
(Photo by FARL)

Owned by Mr. Marcus L. Blanchard

and columns, used separately or together. The draperies or diagonal shadows, as the case may be, are often placed so as to frame the head in a diagonal, triangular, or diamond-shaped area of light. The columns, sometimes placed at one side of the canvas or back of the sitter's head almost like a panel, are often used with drapery. The draperies are almost invariably crimson or cold vermilion. In only about half a dozen portraits are the draperies green, and in only two or three, yellow. The costumes of both men and women are usually black. About a dozen portraits of women show white dresses; and about four blue and four gray. The introduction of a flower-bordered shawl is noticeable at various periods in a number of the portraits of women. The heads in the portraits are always well placed. And in many —so many, indeed, that the idiosyncrasy becomes a veritable signature—Ames places the highlights of the eyes at the inner upper rims of both the pupils. The reader may easily make further generalizations from a study of the numerous illustrations.

When two or more portraits are said to be similar, very similar, or almost identical, without specifying that one is the original of the other(s), it should be understood that no priority has been established between or among them.

In establishing the year when a picture was painted, the "circa" (*c.*) dates were approximated by judging the apparent ages of the sitters and by comparing their costumes and the artist's style of painting with those of dated portraits. Definite dates of painting (those without the *c.*) were in every case established by documentary evidence—an inscription, a receipt, a dated engraving, a letter, or an Account Book entry. Whenever a reference is made from the Catalogue to an Account Book entry, additional information, such as the price of the portrait and frame, may be found by turning back to the Account Book transcript under date of the entry cited. Such prices, however, and others mentioned herein from the early records must not be taken to reflect in any way the present value of those pictures—first, because the purchasing power of the dollar has greatly decreased since then—by at least 75 percent—and, second, because the pictures have gained in value both as historical records and, with the growing appreciation of Ames's productions, as works of art.

A number of pictures by Ezra Ames bear inscriptions on the back, sometimes by the artist, sometimes by another hand. These are all recorded. However, no certainly authenticated portrait by Ezra Ames, excepting the self-portrait of *c.* 1814 at the Mechanics and Farmers' Bank, Albany, has been found to bear the signature of the artist on the face of the canvas.

In listing the ownerships of a picture, the entry begins with the first certainly known owner; but this, obviously, is not necessarily the first owner. Occasionally, too, there is a gap between the owners listed which could not be supplied.

For the convenience of those who wish to see or obtain photographs of paintings, the writers have given, wherever able, the location of negatives, photographic prints, or photostats. The first phrase, name, or abbreviation following the subheading "Photograph" indicates where, or through whom a negative is available. When this is not known, the location of a print, or photostat is substituted. "Photograph: AIHA; print at FARL," means that a negative is at or available through the Albany Institute of History and Art, and a print is at the Frick Art Reference Library.

The sources of information in the Catalogue appear within the entries immediately following the statements of fact to which they relate. None of the references used solely in the catalogue entries are listed in the Bibliography, because they pertain only to individual sitters or pictures and so have no bearing on the work at large. Most of the sources used in the Catalogue are cited by full or adequate partial title, with place and date of publication. Titles of sales catalogues are given in descriptive rather than literal form. A few frequently used references are cited by abbreviations, or names of authors, only. These and the other abbreviations or contractions used in the entries are listed with their meanings in the NOTE ON ABBREVIATIONS AND CONTRACTIONS on page 200. (The source references in the following list may be found in full in the Bibliography.)

Note on Abbreviations and Contractions

AIHA: Albany Institute of History and Art, Albany, N. Y.

BDAC: *Biographical Directory of the American Congress*, 1774–1927.

CAB: *Appletons' Cyclopedia of American Biography*.

DAB: *Dictionary of American Biography*.

Exhibition AIHA 1934: Exhibition of Paintings by Ezra Ames Owned by Albanians, November 1934, Albany Institute of History and Art, Albany, N. Y. (See Ms. section of Bibliography under "Ames Exhibition. Albany, N. Y., November 1934.")

Exhibition AIHA 1936: Exhibition of American Portraits and Landscapes, June 2–September 20, 1936, Albany Institute of History and Art, Albany, N. Y. (See Miscellaneous section of Bibliography under "Albany Institute of History and Art, *Exhibition . . . 1936*.")

Exhibition AIHA 1946: Exhibition of Paintings by Ezra Ames, November 1946, Albany Institute of History and Art, Albany, N. Y. (See Ms. section of Bibliography under "Ames Exhibition. Albany, N. Y., November 1946.")

FARL: Frick Art Reference Library, New York City.

IFC: Irwin F. Cortelyou.

Metropolitan Museum: The Metropolitan Museum of Art, New York City.

Munsell: *Annals of Albany*.

NYHS: The New-York Historical Society, New York City.

NYSHA: New York State Historical Association, Cooperstown, N.Y.

Reynolds: *Albany Chronicles* (1906).

TB: Theodore Bolton

December 1, 1953 IRWIN F. CORTELYOU

XI

PORTRAITS IN OIL

THIS SECTION includes both the portraits whose ownership is known, and those of which there is a record but which have not been located. The portraits are painted on canvas unless otherwise noted. Those not painted on canvas are painted on wood panels.

The fact that a portrait is listed here indicates that the writers accept it as by Ezra Ames, whether or not a notation to that effect appears in the entry.

[1] ADAMS, JOHN (1735-1826), second President of the United States. A portrait of "John Adams" is listed with other portraits described as "heads from Stuart" and is appraised at $30.00 in the Inventory, 1836, of the Ezra Ames estate. This is doubtless the portrait painted by Ezra Ames, listed as No. 2, "Head of John Adams, copy from G. Stuart," [30 x 24 inches] in the handbill: *Catalogue Sale of Portraits*, 1842, in the Ezra Ames estate.
Unlocated.

[2] ALETHIA, probably a niece or great-niece of Ezra Ames, referred to in a letter at NYHS, dated January 6, 1831, from Marcia L. (Ames) James to Angelo Ames. A painting entitled "Alethia, unfin." is listed and appraised at $10.00 in the Inventory, 1836, of the Ezra Ames estate.
Unlocated.

[3] ALEXANDER, JOSEPH (1765-1855), merchant, first president, 1826-1832, of the Commercial Bank of Albany, changed to National Commercial Bank and Trust Company of Albany in 1920 *(One Hundred Twenty-Fifth Anniversary, 1825-1950,* booklet issued by the bank).
Description: 30 x 24 inches. Bust, head and eyes to left. Restored 1951.
Date: c. 1820.
Inscription on paper found when restored: "Joseph Alexander / First President of the / Commercial Bank Albany / Born May 20, 1765 / Died Dec. 17, 1855 / Aged 90 yrs. 6 mos. 27 days / This portrait was painted by the / Elder Ames about the year 1820 when / the subject was 56 years old."
Owner: National Commercial Bank and Trust Company of Albany, Albany, N. Y.

Photographs: FARL 15447, before restoration; the owner, after restoration, print at FARL.

Exhibition: AIHA 1934.

Attribution: The artist was unknown in 1932 at which time William Sawitzky was "inclined" to attribute it to Ezra Ames, judging from a photograph. This tentative attribution is confirmed by the inscription.

[4] ALLEN, N., possibly Nathaniel Allen (1780-1832), Member, State Assembly, New York, 1812; Representative from New York, U. S. Congress 1819-1821 *(BDAC).*

Description: 30 x 24 inches. Bust, head to right.

Date: Possibly the portrait recorded in Account Book, April 15, 1817, for Nathaniel Allen.

Owners: (1) Frank Bulkeley Smith, Worcester, Mass.; (2) F. B. Smith Sale, Plaza Hotel, New York City, February 22-23, 1920; (3) bought for $80 by Dr. G. L. Laporte, New York City.

Photograph: FARL 40148

Reproduction: Catalogue, F.B. Smith Sale, Plaza Hotel, New York City, 1920.

Unlocated.

[5] ALLEN, SOLOMON (1751-1821), born in Northampton, Massachusetts; died in New York City; Major in the Massachusetts troops during the Revolution; was in charge of Major André at the time of his removal to West Point; became a missionary preacher; married Beulah Clapp (1750-1813) (*CAB*; and *DAR Lineage Book,* Vol. 29, p. 298, and Vol. 127, p. 117).

Description: 29¾ x 23¾ inches. Half-length, head to right.

Date: Probably the portrait recorded in Account Book, May 1814, for Solomon Allen [Jr.?] for a "portrait of his father."

Owner: Museum of the City of New York, presented by Mrs. Frank Allen, 1932.

Photograph: FARL 18723.

Attribution: To Ezra Ames by the late William Sawitzky, according to a note in his file on Ezra Ames lent to the writers by Mrs. Sawitzky.

Examined by IFC and TB. [Illustrated p. 156]

[6] ALLEN, TILLY, merchant, broker (*Albany Directory*, 1815, 1821). A portrait painted of him and for him is recorded in Account Book, July 1825.

Unlocated.

[7] ALLEN, MRS. TILLY. A portrait painted of her for Tilly Allen is recorded in Account Book, July 1825.

Unlocated.

[8] AMES, EZRA (1768-1836).
Description: 30½ x 24½ inches. Bust, head to right.
Date: *c*. 1800.
Owners: (1) William Kirby Sutliff (or Sutliffe), great-grandnephew of Ezra Ames; (2) Miss Mary L. Sutliff, great-grandniece of Ezra Ames; (3) presented by her to AIHA.
Photograph: AIHA; print at FARL.
Reproduction: Mary L. Sutliff, *A Record of the Ancestors and Descendants of Betsy Mulford Sutliff*, facing p. 30.
Exhibition: AIHA 1946.
Note: Presumably the "Ancient portrait of E. Ames" listed and appraised at $10.00 in the Inventory, 1836, of the Ezra Ames estate.
Examined by IFC and TB. [Illustrated: frontispiece]

[9] AMES, EZRA (1768-1836).
Description: 30 x 23¾ inches. Bust, head to right.
Date: *c*. 1810.
Owner: Albany Masonic Temple, Albany.
Photograph: AIHA.
Exhibition: AIHA 1946.
Examined by IFC and TB.

[10] AMES, EZRA (1768-1836).
Description: 29¾ x 23½ inches. Bust, head to right.
Date: *c*. 1810.
Owners: (1) Mrs. William James, daughter of Ezra Ames; (2) her daughter Mrs. Isaac Edwards; (3) her daughter Miss Elizabeth S. Edwards, Albany, on loan at AIHA since 1951.
Exhibition: AIHA 1946.
Note: Probably the portrait of Ezra Ames listed and appraised at $30.00 in the Inventory, 1836, of the Ezra Ames estate.
Examined by IFC and TB.

[11] AMES, EZRA (1768-1836).
Description: 30 x 24 inches. Bust, head to left.
Date: *c*. 1814.
Inscription: Signed lower right, "E. Ames / Albany."
Owner: Mechanics and Farmers' Bank, Albany.
Photograph: FARL 15438.
Reproductions: *American Collector*, August 1947, p. 8; Mechanics and Farmers' Bank, *Span of a Century*, 1811-1911.
Exhibitions: AIHA 1934, 1946.
Examined by IFC and TB. [Illustrated p. 75]

[12] AMES, EZRA (1768-1836). Unfinished. A portrait of "Ezra Ames unfinished" is listed and appraised at $25.00 in the Inventory, 1836, of the Ezra Ames estate.
Unlocated.

[13] AMES, JULIUS RUBENS (1801-1850), miniature painter, elder son of Ezra Ames.
Description: 29¾ x 23¾ inches. Bust, head to left.
Date: *c*. 1826.
Owner: Miss Edith S. Wade, Cohoes, N.Y., great-great-grandniece of Ezra Ames.
Photograph: AIHA; print at FARL.
Exhibition: AIHA 1946.
Examined by IFC and TB. [Illustrated p. 125]

[14] AMES, MARCIA LUCRETIA (1797/98-1886), daughter of Ezra Ames; married in 1824 to the Reverend William James (1797-1868), half brother of the father of Henry James the novelist and William James the philosopher (Mrs. Russel Hastings, "William James of Albany," *New York Genealogical and Biographical Record,* April 1924, pp. 104-113). A painting entitled "Marcia L. Ames in ... blue" is listed and appraised at $15.00 in the Inventory, 1836, of the Ezra Ames estate.
Unlocated.

[15] AMES, MARCIA LUCRETIA, in ALLEGORY: PRESENT, PAST, AND FUTURE. A painting entitled "Marcia L. Ames Allegory present past & future" is listed and appraised at $15.00 in the Inventory, 1836, of the Ezra Ames estate. Possibly based on the composition of "The Hours: Past, Present and Future," a miniature by Edward Greene Malbone (1777-1807).
Unlocated.

[16] AMES CHILDREN: MARCIA LUCRETIA (1797/98-1886), JULIUS RUBENS (1801-1850), ANGELO (1803/5-1886), children of Ezra Ames and Zipporah (Wood) Ames.
Description: 36 x 27¼ inches, sight. Unfinished. Group of three children.
Date: *c*. 1805.
Owner: Miss Elizabeth S. Edwards, Albany, great-granddaughter of Ezra Ames.
Photograph: By Irwin F. Cortelyou.
Examined by IFC and TB.

[17] (?) ANNESLEY, WILLIAM (1793-1862), born in England; died in Albany. In business in Montreal as a looking-glass maker and print seller; son of William Annesley (1768-1848); married (1) Margaret La Casse (1800-1832), (2) Margaret Ç. Miller (1816-1853) (letter to IFC from Miss Nina Romeyn, 3/9/52).

Description: Panel, 29¼ x 23½ inches. Bust, head to left.

Date: *c.* 1820.

Owners: (1) Mr. George Agnew Chamberlain, custodian of Annesley estate, grandnephew of the sitter; (2) Miss Nina Romeyn, great-granddaughter of the sitter; (3) presented by her to Mrs. Seth W. Cook, New Castle, Delaware, great-granddaughter of the sitter.

Photograph: The owner; print at FARL.

Attribution: The artist was unknown to the owners. Attributed to Ezra Ames by Mrs. Thomas Edwards (FARL), 1951.

Note: The identity of the sitter is not certain (letter to IFC from Miss Romeyn, 3/9/52).

Examined by IFC. [Illustrated p. 89]

[18] (?) ANNESLEY, MRS. WILLIAM, née Margaret La Casse (1800-1832), French Canadian, died in Montreal (letter to IFC from Miss Nina Romeyn, 3/9/52).

Description: Panel, 29¼ x 23½ inches. Half-length, head to right.

Date: *c.* 1820.

Owners: (1) Mr. George Agnew Chamberlain, custodian of Annesley estate, grandnephew of the sitter; (2) Miss Nina Romeyn, great-granddaughter of the sitter; (3) presented by her to Mrs. Seth W. Cook, New Castle, Delaware, great-granddaughter of the sitter.

Photograph: The owner; print at FARL.

Attribution: The artist was unknown to the owners. Attributed to Ezra Ames by Mrs. Thomas Edwards (FARL), 1951.

Note: The identity of the sitter is not certain (letter to IFC from Miss Romeyn, 3/9/52).

Examined by IFC. [Illustrated p. 89]

[19] BACON, MRS. A portrait of "Mrs. Bacon" is listed and appraised at $5.00 in the Inventory, 1836, of the Ezra Ames estate.

Unlocated.

[20] BACON, JOHN F. (*c.* 1789-1860). [Patron]. Attorney (*Albany Directory*, 1817); Clerk of the N.Y. State Senate, 1814-1840; U.S. Consul at Nassau, where he died February 25, 1860, aged 71 years (Munsell, X, 1859, p. 302; Jonathan Tenney, *New England in Albany*, Boston, 1883, p. 66). A portrait painted for him is recorded in Account Book, April 4, 1817.

Unlocated.

[21] BARBER, JOHN (died 1808) or possibly ROBERT (*c.* 1770-1812). A portrait painted of a Mr. Barber for Solomon Southwick is recorded in Account Book, March 24, 1809. This entry possibly refers to Robert Barber (*c.* 1770-1812) (Munsell, V, 1854, p. 33) who established the *Albany Register* in 1788; or more probably to his brother John (died 1808) who published the paper in partnership with Solomon Southwick after Robert Barber retired and left Albany in 1792. The partnership was dissolved in 1800 (Clarence S. Brigham, *History and Bibliography of American Newspapers 1690-1820*, Worcester, 1947, I, p. 539). Solomon Southwick married a sister of John and Robert Barber (*DAB*, XVII, 413, 414).
Unlocated.

[22] BARREY, THOMAS, probably Thomas Barry (*c.* 1738-1813). [Patron]. He was "for a long period a respectable merchant and worthy citizen," of Albany, who died January 17, 1813, aged 75. "His funeral sermon was preached at the Catholic Church by the Rev. Mr. McQuade." (Munsell, V, 1854, p. 38). A portrait painted for "Mr. Thomas Barrey" is recorded in Account Book, June 29, 1805.
Unlocated.

[23] BAYARD, WILLIAM, 2d (died 1826), partner in the mercantile firm of Bayard, Leroy & McEvers, New York City; third son of William Bayard (1729-1804) *(CAB).* The sitter's daughter, Harriet Elizabeth, married Stephen Van Rensselaer IV (*Daughters of the American Revolution Magazine,* August 1917, p. 75).
Description: 30 x 24 inches. Bust, head to left. Very similar to No. 24.
Date: 1819.
Inscription on back of canvas: "Albany / E. Ames Pt 1819."
Owners: (1) The Misses Catherine and Marie Campbell, granddaughters of the sitter; (2) purchased from them at a family auction in 1913 by Thomas H. Barber, New York City, great-great-grandson of the sitter.
Photograph: FARL 50578.
Examined by IFC.

[24] BAYARD, WILLIAM, 2d (died 1826).
Description: Bust, head to left. Very similar to No. 23.
Date: *c.* 1819.
Owner: Mrs. Theodore Vernon Boynton, 1917.
Photograph: Edmonston, Washington, D. C.
Reproduction: *Daughters of the American Revolution Magazine,* August 1917, p. 75.
Unlocated.

[25] BEEKMAN, CUNEIRA.
Description: 30 x 24 inches. Bust, head to right.
Date: *c.* 1804.
Owner: Van Cortlandt House Museum, New York City.
Photograph: FARL 31008.
Attribution: To Ezra Ames by Miss Hope Mathewson (FARL), 1941.
Examined by IFC.

[26] BEERS, WILLIAM P. (died 1810). [Patron]. City Clerk of Albany (Reynolds, 408). A portrait for him is recorded in Account Book, October 30, 1805.
Unlocated.

[27] BLATCHFORD, SAMUEL (1767-1828), clergyman, born in England; settled in Albany 1795; pastor of Lansingburgh Presbyterian Church, 1804-1828 (Eliphalet Wickes Blatchford, *Blatchford Memorial II, A Genealogical Record of the Family of Rev. Samuel Blatchford, D.D., 1912, p. 63).* Preached the first annual sermon of the Albany County Bible Society, February 12, 1811, in the North Dutch Church, Albany (Munsell, I, 1869, p. 255).
Description: Bust, head to left.
Date: Possibly the portrait painted of and for "Revd Doct Blackford" recorded in Account Book, December 29, 1818.
Reproduction: *Blatchford Memorial II,* frontispiece.
Attribution: To Ezra Ames by Irwin F. Cortelyou and T. Bolton, 1951, judging from the reproduction.
Unlocated.

[28] BLATCHFORD, MRS. SAMUEL, née Alicia Windeatt (1767-1846), born in England; wife of Reverend Samuel Blatchford, married in 1788 (Eliphalet Wickes Blatchford, *Blatchford Memorial II,* 1912, p. 63).
Description: Half-length, head to right.
Date: Possibly the "Portrait of his Lady" painted for "Revd Doctr Blackford" recorded in Account Book, September 7, 1820.
Reproduction: *Blatchford Memorial II,* facing p. 46.
Attribution: To Ezra Ames by Irwin F. Cortelyou and T. Bolton, 1951, judging from the reproduction.
Unlocated.

[29] BLEECKER, HARMANUS (1779-1849), lawyer; Representative from New York, U. S. Congress, 1811-1813; Member, New York State Assembly, 1814-1815 *(BDAC).* Partner of Theodore Sedgwick (1780-1837) *(CAB).*

Description: 30 x 24 inches. Bust, head to right. Almost identical with No. 30.

Date: 1819. This is doubtless the portrait of "H. Bleeker Esqr" recorded as painted for "Mrs. Sedgwick" in Account Book, June 1819, just above the entry there for No. 30, and so presumably is the original of that portrait.

Owners: (1) Mrs. Sedgwick; (2) Miss Maria Sedgwick; (3) Young Men's Association, Albany; (4) Harmanus Bleecker Library, Albany.

Photograph: FARL 15457.

Reproduction: Harriet Langdon Pruyn Rice, *Harmanus Bleecker*, New York, 1924, frontispiece.

Exhibitions: AIHA 1934, 1936, 1946.

Attribution: To Ezra Ames by William Sawitzky and Mrs. Laurence Barretto (FARL), 1932; attribution confirmed by a letter dated 1889, found in 1932, quoting Miss Maria Sedgwick, and noted on FARL photomount, and by the entry in Account Book, June 1819.

Examined by IFC and TB. [Illustrated p. 152]

[30] BLEECKER, HARMANUS (1779-1849).

Description: 34 x 24 inches. Bust, head to right. Almost identical with No. 29.

Date: 1819. This portrait is doubtless the one charged to "H. Bleeker Esqr" as painted for the "Revd Broadhead, Phil." It is recorded in Account Book, June 1819, below the entry for No. 29 and so presumably is a replica.

Owners: (1) Mrs. John Romeyn Broadhead; (2) her brother Robert Fanshaw Bloodgood; (3) his daughter Mrs. Delavan B. Downer; (4) her daughter Mrs. William C. Cate, Belmont, Massachusetts.

Photograph: FARL 17107.

Attribution: To Ezra Ames by William Sawitzky, and Mrs. Laurence B. Barretto (FARL), 1932.

[31] BLEECKER, LEONARD (1755-1844), born in New Rochelle, N. Y., son of James L. Bleecker; merchant; Major in the Continental Army; one of the founders of the Society of the Cincinnati; died in Newtown, Long Island, N. Y.

Description: 44 x 29½ inches. Bust, head to right.

Date: *c.* 1805.

Owners: (1) Mr. Bleecker Bangs, Brooklyn, N. Y.; (2) Ehrich Galleries, New York City, in 1933.

Attribution: To Ezra Ames by William Sawitzky. This portrait was brought to the attention of the writers by a photograph, along with all information given above except for the date of painting, found in the

late William Sawitzky's file on Ezra Ames lent to them by Mrs. Sawitzky.
Unlocated. [Illustrated p. 37]

[32] BLOODGOOD, FRANCIS (1768-1840), lawyer; Mayor of Albany, 1831, 1833; married (1) Eliza Cobham, 1792, (2) Anna Shoemaker (Morris), 1823 (Reynolds, [496]).
Description: 29 x 23 inches, sight. Bust, head to left.
Date: *c.* 1810.
Owners: (1) Francis Bloodgood; (2) his daughter, Mrs. John Keyes Paige; (3) her daughter Miss Clara Antoinette Paige; (4) her nephew Alonzo W. Paige, Schenectady, N. Y.
Photograph: FARL 30685.
Reproduction: Reynolds, facing [496], as by Ezra Ames.
Exhibition: AIHA 1936, incorrectly as by Henry Inman.
Attribution: Reattributed to Ezra Ames by Miss Hope Mathewson (FARL), 1937.
Examined by IFC. [Illustrated p. 142]

[33] BLOODGOOD, MRS. FRANCIS, née Eliza Cobham (1769-1818) (dates supplied by the owner), married in 1792 (Reynolds, [496]).
Description: 30 x 24 inches. Bust, head slightly to right.
Date: *c.* 1810.
Owners: (1) Francis Bloodgood; (2) his daughter, Mrs. John Keyes Paige; (3) her daughter Miss Clara Antoinette Paige; (4) her nephew Alonzo W. Paige, Schenectady, N. Y.
Photograph: FARL 30689.
Examined by IFC.

[34] BOGART, HENRY I. (1729-1821). Lived in Albany; served in the Revolution as Assistant Deputy Quartermaster General under Colonel Morgan Lewis; was appointed Inspector of the Revenue of the Port of Albany in 1791, by George Washington; was also City Surveyor (information from Miss Eleanor H. Lovett).
Description: Bust, head to right.
Date: *c.* 1805.
Owners: (1) William H. Bogart, Aurora, N. Y., grandson of the sitter; (2) a niece of the sitter in Peoria, Ill.; (3) given to Miss Eleanor H. Lovett, 1951, New London, N. H., great-great-granddaughter of the sitter.
Photograph: The owner.
Attribution: Tentatively to Ezra Ames by Mrs. Haven Parker. The writers, judging from the photograph, accept the attribution.

[35] BOGART, JOHN (*c.* 1761-1853) (Reynolds, 619). [Patron]. Alderman (*Albany Directory*, 1813); skipper (Munsell, V, 1854, p. 226). A portrait painted for him is recorded in Account Book, May 8, 1812.
Unlocated.

[36] BRANT, JOSEPH, "THAYENDANEGEA" (1742-1807), Mohawk Chief; Colonel in the British Army *(CAB)*.
Description: 30½ x 24½ inches. Bust, head to left.
Date: A framed receipt at Fenimore House, Cooperstown, N. Y. (NYSHA), reads: "August 27th 1806 / Receivd of Mr Wm Caldwell / Thirty Dollars in full for / Painting a Portrait & frame / of Col. Brandt [sic] – / EZRA AMES."
Owners: Later owners (1) Miss Anne S. Van Cortlandt and her nieces Miss Catharine Van Cortlandt Mathews and Mrs. William V. Mason, Croton-on-Hudson, N. Y.; (2) after Miss Van Cortlandt's death in 1940, owned by the nieces; (3) Macbeth Gallery, New York City; (4) Otsego County Historical Society; (5) NYSHA, Cooperstown, N. Y., on loan at the NYSHA Museum at Ticonderoga, N. Y. See Marion Harland, *Some Colonial Homesteads and Their Stories*, New York and London, 1897, p. 187.
Reproduction: *Handbook of the Museum and Art Gallery of the NYSHA, Cooperstown*, 1942, p. 17.
Copy: By G[eorge] Catlin, listed in Numismatic and Antiquarian Society, *Descriptive Catalogue of A Loan Exhibition of Canadian Historical Portraits*, Montreal, 1887, p. 6, owned by Rev. l'Abbe Verreau.
[Illustrated p. 37]

[37] BRINCKERHOFF, MRS. JOHN, whose husband was a merchant (*Albany Directory*, 1826) and member of Common Council, Albany, 1807-1814 (Reynolds, 403 ff). A painting of his wife for John Brinckerhoff is recorded in Account Book, May 18, 1826.
Unlocated.

[38] BROWN, JACOB JENNINGS (1775-1828), Senior in Command, U. S. Army, 1821-1828 *(DAB)*.
Description: 28½ x 22¼ inches, sight. Bust, in uniform, head to right. Almost identical with No. 39.
Date: *c.* 1818, because the background is similar to that in the portrait of Mrs. Brown (No. 41) which is dated as probably 1818.
Owners: (1) Family of Mrs. Brown; (2) Munson-Williams-Proctor Institute, Utica, N. Y.
Photograph: Munson-Williams-Proctor Institute; print at FARL.
Reproduction: *Watertown* [N. Y.] *Daily Times*, January 28, 1939.
Attribution: The artist was unknown to the owner. Attributed to Ezra

Ames by Miss Hope Mathewson (FARL), 1940.
Examined by IFC.

[39] BROWN, JACOB JENNINGS (1775-1828).
Description: 29½ x 25½ inches, sight. Bust, in uniform, head to right. Almost identical with No. 38.
Date: *c.* 1818. Because the background is similar to that in the portrait of Mrs. Brown (No. 41) which is dated as probably 1818.
Owner: Old South Association, Boston, gift of Mrs. Marie Weston Chapman about 1880.
Photograph: FARL 31252.
Attribution: The artist was unknown to the owner. Attributed to Ezra Ames by Miss Hope Mathewson, (FARL), 1940.
Note: (a) Listed in the Historical Records Survey, *American Portraits Found in Massachusetts*, Boston, 1939, I, p. 56, as by an unknown artist; measurements there given as 27 x 21 inches. (b) A portrait of "Gen. Brown" listed and appraised in the Inventory, 1836, of the Ezra Ames estate, in a group of ten portraits at an "average – each 10.00," is doubtless the portrait painted by Ezra Ames listed as No. 16, "General Jacob Brown," [30 x 24 inches] in the handbill: *Catalogue Sale of Portraits*, 1842, in the Ezra Ames estate. It is here assumed that these entries refer to the portrait at the Old South Meeting House because the other portrait of General Brown (No. 38) was a family-owned portrait.
Examined by IFC and TB.

[40] BROWN, MRS. JACOB JENNINGS, née Pamela Williams (1785-1878), daughter of Captain Judah Williams; married Jacob Jennings Brown in 1802 (*Watertown*, [N. Y.], *Daily Times*, January 28, 1939).
Description: 29 x 23 inches, sight. Bust, head to left, with turban.
Date: Probably 1818. Either this portrait or No. 41 is referred to by the artist in Account Book, March 12, 1818, "To Painting a Portrait of his Lady," for "Majr General Brown."
Owners: (1) The family of Mrs. Brown; (2) Munson-Williams-Proctor Institute, Utica, N. Y. (founded by descendants of Mrs. Brown's family).
Photograph: Munson-Williams-Proctor Institute; print at FARL.
Attribution: The artist was unknown to the owner. Attributed to Ezra Ames by Miss Hope Mathewson (FARL), 1940.
Examined by IFC.

[41] BROWN, MRS. JACOB JENNINGS, née Pamela Williams (1785-1878).
Description: 30½ x 24 inches. Half-length, head to left.

Date: Probably 1818. Either this portrait or No. 40 is referred to by the artist in Account Book, March 12, 1818.

Owners: (1) Reverend G. F. Field, England; (2) M. Knoedler & Company, bought from Howard Young Galleries; (3) Mr. Harold T. Patterson, Atlanta, Georgia. (Mrs. Patterson is a great-great-granddaughter of the subject.)

Photograph: Print at FARL.

Exhibitions: M. H. de Young Memorial Museum, San Francisco, 1935, as by J. W. Jarvis, lent by Howard Young Galleries; Ferargil Galleries, N. Y., 1941, as by J. W. Jarvis.

Attribution: To Ezra Ames by William Sawitzky, 1940.

[Illustrated p. 168]

[42] BUELL, ELIAS (1737-1824), in 1820. Representative in the General Assembly of Vermont; moved to Albany in 1819; grandfather of Jesse Buell of Albany (Albert Welles, *History of the Buell Family*, New York, 1881, p. 63). Listed in the *Catalogue of Albany's Bicentennial Loan Exhibition at the Albany Academy, July 5 to July 24, 1886*, pp. 115,126, as follows: "Ezra Ames (deceased). / 76 Portrait of Elias Buel in 1820 ... [owned by] Jesse Buel."

Unlocated.

[43] BURNHAM, ELEAZER (born 1780), lawyer, residing in Aurora, N. Y.; twice a presidential elector. He married (1) Caroline Matilda Wood, (2) Urania Smith (E. B. Huntington, *A Genealogical Memoir of the Huntington Family*, Stamford, Conn., 1863, p. 149).

Description: 30 x 23 7/8 inches. Bust, head to right.

Date: 1826.

Inscription on back of canvas: "Eleazar [sic] Burnham / of Aurora / Ezra Ames of Albany / Painter. 1826."

Owners: (1) The sitter; (2) his nephew James Burnham Smith; (3) his son Luther L. Smith; (4) his nephew Mr. William C. Hook, Wichita, Kansas.

Photograph: The owner; print at FARL. [Illustrated p. 121]

[44] BURNHAM, MRS. ELEAZER, née Caroline Matilda Wood (died 1832), first wife of Eleazer Burnham (E. B. Huntington, *A Genealogical Memoir of the Huntington Family*, Stamford, Conn., 1863, p. 149).

Description: 29 7/8 x 23 7/8 inches. Half-length, head to left.

Date: 1830.

Inscription on back of canvas: "Caroline Matilda Burnham / of Aurora / Ezra Ames of Albany Painter / 1830."

Owners: (1) Eleazer Burnham; (2) his nephew James Burnham Smith;

(3) his son Luther L. Smith; (4) his nephew Mr. William C. Hook, Wichita, Kansas.
Photograph: The owner; print at FARL. [Illustrated p. 121]

[45] (?) CADY, DAVID (1755/56-1818), born in Stonington, Connecticut; son of Dr. Aaron Cady and Anna (Palmer) Cady (Cuyler Reynolds, *Hudson-Mohawk Genealogical and Family Memoirs*, New York, 1911, III, p. 1171).
Description: Bust, head to right. Almost identical with the portrait of AARON OGDEN, so-called, judging from a photograph of the latter portrait. See No. 226.
Date: Uncertain.
Owner: Mrs. John E. N. Hume, Schenectady, N. Y.
Photograph: FARL 30724.
Attribution: Tentatively to Ezra Ames by Miss Hope Mathewson (FARL), 1937; to Ezra Ames by Irwin F. Cortelyou, 1951. T. Bolton concurs, judging from a photograph.
Note: Mrs. de Lancey W. Watkins, aunt of the owner, thinks this portrait probably represents David Cady (FARL photomount).
Examined by IFC.

[46] CADY, MRS. DAVID, née Anna Schuler (1763-1851), married David Cady, November 4, 1784 (Cuyler Reynolds, *Hudson-Mohawk Genealogical and Family Memoirs*, New York, 1911, III, 1171).
Description: 29½ x 23 3/8 inches. Half-length, head to left.
Date: *c.* 1818.
Owners: (1) David Cady Smith, inherited by (2) Mrs. John Green, Schenectady, N. Y., a great-great-granddaughter of the sitter.
Attribution: The artist was unknown to the owner. Attributed to Ezra Ames by Irwin F. Cortelyou, 1951.
Examined by IFC.

[47] CALDWELL, JAMES. [Patron]. Merchant; elected a director of the Bank of Albany, 1792 (Reynolds, 381); personally financed the building of the First Presbyterian Meeting House at Caldwell (Fort George), N. Y. (Munsell, V, 1854, p. 26). Two portraits painted for him are recorded in Account Book, July 1805.
Unlocated.

[48] CALDWELL, JAMES. [Patron]. One of two portraits painted for him recorded in Account Book, July 1805. See No. 47.
Unlocated.

[49] CALDWELL, JAMES. [Patron]. A portrait painted for him is recorded in Account Book, July 27, 1819.
Unlocated.

[50] CAREY, MISS ELIZA. A painting entitled "Miss Eliza Carey" is listed and appraised at $25.00 in the Inventory, 1836, of the Ezra Ames estate.
Unlocated.

[51] CHESTER, JOHN (*c.* 1786-1829). Known only through an engraving by Rawdon, Clark and Company. See No. 567.

[52] CHESTER, JOHN (*c.* 1786-1829). Known only through an engraving by John Sartain. See No. 568.

[53] CLARKE, MRS. BEULAH ALLEN. Known only through an engraving by Peter Maverick. See No. 569.

[54] CLINTON, DeWITT (1769-1828), Mayor of New York City; Lieutenant Governor of New York State, 1811-1813; Governor of New York State, 1817-1822 and 1825-1828; elected president of The New-York Historical Society in 1817 *(DAB).*
Description: 28½ x 22½ inches. Bust, head to left.
Date: *c.* 1811.
Owner: Mrs. Arthur Iselin, Katonah, N. Y. (died 1953).
Photograph: FARL 625.
Attribution: Tentatively attributed to Ezra Ames by William Sawitzky, judging from a photograph, 1932. To Ezra Ames by Irwin F. Cortelyou after an examination of the picture, 1953. T. Bolton, judging from a photograph, accepts the attribution.
Examined by IFC.

[55] CLINTON, DeWITT (1769-1828).
Description: 51½ x 39¼ inches, sight. Half-length standing, head to left.
Date: 1818. Recorded in Account Book, March 8, 1818: "To Painting a Half length Portrait of Govnr Clinton (for the Corporation)," charged to Elisha Jenkins.
Owner: The City of Albany, on permanent loan at AIHA.
Photograph: AIHA; print at FARL.
Exhibition: AIHA 1946.
Note: This is one of the series of "Portraits of Seven Governors of New York" by Ezra Ames at AIHA.
Examined by IFC and TB. [Illustrated p. 141]

[56] CLINTON, DEWITT (1769-1828). Known only through an engraving by V. Balch. See No. 570.

[57] CLINTON, DeWITT (1769-1828). A portrait of "De W. Clinton (old)," is listed and appraised at $5.00 in the Inventory, 1836, of the Ezra Ames estate. Either this portrait or No. 58 may be the portrait painted by Ezra Ames, listed as No. 7, "De Witt Clinton [30 x 24 inches] in the handbill: *Catalogue Sale of Portraits*, 1842, in the Ezra Ames estate.
Unlocated.

[58] CLINTON, DeWITT (1769-1828). An "original" head of DeWitt Clinton is listed and appraised at $30.00 in the Inventory, 1836, of the Ezra Ames estate. Either this portrait or No. 57 may be the portrait painted by Ezra Ames, listed as No. 7, "De Witt Clinton [30 x 24 inches] in the handbill: *Catalogue Sale of Portraits*, 1842, in the Ezra Ames estate.
Unlocated.

[59] CLINTON, MRS. DeWITT, née Maria Franklin (died 1818), first wife of DeWitt Clinton; married February 13, 1796 *(DAB)*. A copy of a portrait painted of her for Joseph Delaplaine and charged to DeWitt Clinton is recorded in Account Book, July 31, 1818.
Unlocated.

[60] CLINTON, MRS. DeWITT, née Catherine Jones (1783-1855), second wife of DeWitt Clinton, married May 8, 1819. She was the daughter of Dr. Thomas Jones of New York City (DAB). Her mother was [Margaret Livingston Jones] the daughter of Philip Livingston (J. G. Wilson, *Memorial History of the City of New York*, 1893, III, footnote p. 401), whose portrait was also painted by Ezra Ames.
Description: 30 x 23 inches. Half-length, head to left.
Date: 1820. This is either the original or the replica of the portrait painted of her for DeWitt Clinton, both recorded in Account Book, January 28, 1820.
Owner: Presented in 1863 to the Long Island Historical Society by Philip Livingston Jones.
Photograph: FARL 20087.
Reproductions: J. G. Wilson, *Memorial History of the City of New York*, 1893, III, p. 401; Dorothie Bobbé, *DeWitt Clinton*, New York, 1933, facing p. 226.
Attribution: The artist was unknown to the owners. Attributed to Ezra Ames by Irwin F. Cortelyou, judging from a photograph. T. Bolton concurs, also judging from a photograph. [Illustrated p. 98]

[61] CLINTON, MRS. DeWITT, née Catherine Jones (1783-1855). A "Portrait of Mrs Clinton" and a "Coppy" of it charged to "Govn Clinton" are recorded in Account Book, January 28, 1820. This portrait is either the original or the replica of No. 60. Since only one of the two portraits (No. 60) has been located, it cannot be determined whether it or the unlocated portrait is the original.
Unlocated.

[62] CLINTON, FRANKLIN (1812-1842), Lieutenant, U. S. N.; son of DeWitt Clinton (Typescript compiled by Gertrude A. Barber, *Deaths Taken from The New York Evening Post*, XVIII, 1939). A portrait painted of "his son Franklin" for DeWitt Clinton is recorded in Account Book, September 5, 1818.
Unlocated.

[63] CLINTON, GEORGE (1739-1812), first Governor of New York State, 1777-1795, 1801-1804; Vice-President of the United States, 1804-1812 *(CAB)*.
History: This portrait was exhibited at the Society of Artists of the United States and the Pennsylvania Academy, Philadelphia, 1812; listed in the catalogue as No. 193 "George Clinton Esq late Vice-president of the United States"; purchased by the Pennsylvania Academy; and presumably destroyed at the time of the burning of the building in 1845. Mrs. Barbara S. Roberts, Registrar, The Pennsylvania Academy of the Fine Arts, in a letter to Dr. George Clinton Andrews, March 22, 1949, writes: "A partial search of later catalogues after 1845 shows no mention of the painting being in the collection of the Academy. It has been presumed, (although it is not specifically mentioned in any lists so far found of works destroyed in the fire) that it must have been lost in the fire of 1845."
Note: For details see pp. 63-67 herein.
Unlocated. Probably destroyed.

[64] CLINTON, GEORGE (1739-1812).
Description: 95 x 71 inches, sight. Full-length standing, head to right.*
Date: 1813.
Owner: Painted for the State of New York (Chapter 203, Laws of 1813 New York State); placed in Senate Chamber, State Capitol, Albany,

* The four bust portraits of George Clinton (Nos. 68,69,70, and 71) are very similar except that No. 71 has spandrels in all four corners, while the others have none. The three half-length standing portraits (Nos. 65,66, and 67) are similar to each other. The heads in all the portraits (Nos. 64-71) are very similar.

December 1813, where it remained until September 1882 when it was removed to the Executive Chamber of the Capitol.

Photograph: FARL 15380.

Reproductions: C. W. Bowen, *Centennial,* 1892, facing p. 34; *Art in America,* February 1950, facing p. 21; *American Collector,* August 1947, p. 6.

Exhibitions: Loan Exhibition of Portraits ... in Commemoration of the 150th Anniversary of the Constitution of the U. S., Corcoran Gallery of Art, Washington, D. C., Winter 1937-1938; AIHA 1946.

Note: For a discussion of this portrait see herein, pp. 74-75.

Copy: By Benjamin F. Landis at the Merchants Club, New York City, presented by Cornelius N. Bliss in 1924 (brought to the attention of the writers by Mr. William H. Borden).

Examined by IFC. [Illustrated p. 76]

[65] CLINTON, GEORGE (1739-1812).

Description: 53 x 41 inches. Half-length standing, head to right.*

Date: 1814.

Owners: Presented in 1858 to NYHS by George Clinton Tallmadge who presumably acquired the portrait from his grandfather Mathias B. Talmadge (whose family name is also thus spelled) which was recorded by Ames in his Account Book, May 1814: "Mathias B. Talmadge Esqr Dr To Painting a half length Portrait of the late Vice president George Clinton." George Clinton Tallmadge was a great-grandson of George Clinton.

Photograph: NYHS 6108c; print at FARL.

Reproduction: Donald A. Shelley, *Catalogue of American Portraits in the NYHS,* 1941, p. 56, and there incorrectly stated to be the portrait exhibited at the Pennsylvania Academy in 1812.

Note: For details concerning the history of this portrait see pp. 154, 157 herein.

Examined by IFC and TB. [Illustrated p. 146]

[66] CLINTON, GEORGE (1739-1812).

Description: 52 x 40 inches, sight. Half-length standing, head to right.*

Date: Uncertain.

Owner: The City of Albany, on permanent loan at AIHA.

Photograph: AIHA.

* The four bust portraits of George Clinton (Nos. 68,69,70, and 71) are very similar except that No. 71 has spandrels in all four corners, while the others have none. The three half-length standing portraits (Nos. 65,66, and 67) are similar to each other. The heads in all the portraits (Nos. 64-71) are very similar.

Reproduction: *Magazine of Art,* AIHA Edition, April 1948, cover.
Exhibition: AIHA 1946.
Note: This is one of the series of "Portraits of Seven Governors of New York," by Ezra Ames, at AIHA.
Examined by IFC and TB.

[67] CLINTON, GEORGE (1739-1812).
Description: 51 x 41 inches (FARL measurement). Half-length standing, head to right.*
Date: Uncertain.
Owners: (1) Ehrich Galleries; (2) purchased in 1916 by The Brook Club, New York City.
Photograph: FARL 385.
Reproduction: Ehrich Galleries, *One Hundred Early American Paintings*, New York, 1918, p. 11.
Examined by IFC.

[68] CLINTON, GEORGE (1739-1812).
Description: 30 x 24 inches. Bust, head to right.*
Date: 1818. Apparently the portrait, painted for Joseph Delaplaine's Gallery, recorded in Account Book, September 8, 1818.
Owners: (1) Joseph Delaplaine; (2) in 1825 Delaplaine's Gallery was sold to Peale's Museum, New York City, which failed and was sold in 1837; (3) Alexander M. White of Brooklyn, N. Y., who owned the portrait in 1889, and who is quoted by C. W. Bowen as saying: "This picture was bought by my brother at the sale of pictures at Peale's Museum many years ago." This was probably the Peale Sale of 1837 because the portrait is not listed in the Peale Museum Sale held in Philadelphia in 1854; (4) the Misses White; (5) bought from Miss Frances E. White, daughter of Alexander M. White, by Dr. George Clinton Andrews, New York City.
Photographs: (1) The owner; (2) FARL 41511 taken and presented by Irwin F. Cortelyou.
Reproductions: C. W. Bowen, *Centennial,* 1892, facing p. 34; Catalogue, *Exhibition of Early American Paintings*, Brooklyn Museum, 1917, facing p. 1.
Exhibitions: Loan Exhibition of Historical Portraits and Relics, Metropolitan Opera House, New York City, 1889, lent by Alexander

* The four bust portraits of George Clinton (Nos. 68,69,70, and 71) are very similar except that No. 71 has spandrels in all four corners, while the others have none. The three half-length standing portraits (Nos. 65,66, and 67) are similar to each other. The heads in all the portraits (Nos. 64-71) are very similar.

M. White, Brooklyn, N. Y., incorrectly attributed to Bass Otis; Exhibition of Early American Paintings, Brooklyn Museum, 1917, lent by the Misses White; Inaugural Exhibition, Museum of the City of New York, 1932, lent by Miss Frances E. White.
Examined by IFC and TB. [Illustrated p. 62]

[69] CLINTON, GEORGE (1739-1812).
Description: 31 x 25½ inches (measurement by Mr. Charles G. Loring, 1950). Bust, head to right.*
Date: Uncertain.
Owner:†Old South Association, Boston, presented by Mrs. Marie Weston Chapman about 1880.
Photograph: FARL 31255.
Bibliography: Listed in Historical Records Survey, *American Portraits Found in Massachusetts*, 1939, I, 83, as by Ezra Ames; measurements there given as 28 x 22 inches.
Examined by IFC and TB.

[70] CLINTON, GEORGE (1739-1812).
Description: 30 x 25 inches. Bust, head to right.*
Date: Uncertain.
Owners:†(1) Mr. Clinton Miller; sold in 1937 to (2) Mr. Stephen C. Clark; (3) on permanent loan at the NYSHA, Cooperstown, N. Y.
Photograph: M. Knoedler & Company; print at FARL.
Reproductions: (1) *Art in America*, April 1950, p. 94; (2) *Handbook of the Museum and Art Gallery of the NYSHA*, 1942, p. 16.
Exhibition: View of a New York State Community, NYSHA, Cooperstown, N. Y., 1939, lent by Mr. Stephen C. Clark.
Examined by IFC.

[71] CLINTON, GEORGE (1739-1812).
Description: 30½ x 24½ inches. Bust, head to right.*
Date: Uncertain.
Owners: †Mrs. John Tayler Cooper; (2) Mrs. Susan Cooper Krumbhaar;

* The four bust portraits of George Clinton (Nos. 68,69,70, and 71) are very similar except that No. 71 has spandrels in all four corners, while the others have none. The three half-length standing portraits (Nos. 65,66, and 67) are similar to each other. The heads in all the portraits (Nos. 64-71) are very similar.

† This is one of three portraits (Nos. 69,70, and 71) of which any one may be either of the two portraits listed in the Inventory, 1836, of the Ezra Ames estate: one, an "original" head, appraised at $30.00; and the other at $15.00. One of these is doubtless the portrait listed as No. 6, George Clinton, [30 x 24 inches] in the handbill: *Catalogue Sale of Portraits*, 1842, in the Ezra Ames estate.

(3) her husband Dr. Louis Krumbhaar; (4) presented by him to the Cazenovia Public Library; (5) sold by them to Mrs. Madeline Clinton Aherne, 1951; (6) Mr. Robert H. Palmiter, dealer, Bouckville, N. Y.
Photograph: Old Print Shop, New York City.
Exhibition: Listed in the *Catalogue of Albany's Bicentennial Loan Exhibition at the Albany Academy, July 5 to July 24, 1886*, pp. 114, 126, lent by Mrs. John Tayler Cooper.

[72] CLINTON, GEORGE WASHINGTON (1778-1818), lawyer, only son of Governor George Clinton and Cornelia (Tappen) Clinton (E. W. Spaulding, *His Excellency George Clinton*, New York, 1938, pp. 100-101, 267. Spaulding gives the date of death as 1813; however, the George Clinton Family Bible, examined by Dr. George Clinton Andrews, gives the date as 1818, and records his marriage to Anna Floyd in 1808).
Description: *c.* 30 x 25 inches, sight. Bust, head to right.
Date: *c.* 1813.
Owners: (1) Inherited from a relative by George Clinton Andrews; (2) bequeathed to his son, Dr. George Clinton Andrews, New York City, in 1940.
Photographs: (1) The owner; (2) FARL 41512, taken and presented by Irwin F. Cortelyou.
Attributions: Formerly to John Vanderlyn by Mr. Hermann Wunderlich. Attributed to Ezra Ames by Irwin F. Cortelyou and T. Bolton, 1950.
Note: A portrait of "[blank] Clinton, Jr" listed and appraised at $5.00 in the Inventory, 1836, of the Ezra Ames estate, is quite probably of George Washington Clinton, though it is barely possible that it is of his first cousin, George Clinton (1771-1809, son of James Clinton), who is recorded by Dorothie Bobbé (*DeWitt Clinton*, New York, 1933, index) and other writers as "George Clinton, Jr." However, a portrait painted by Ezra Ames is listed as No. 28, "George W. Clinton, Esq.," [30 x 24 inches] in the handbill: *Catalogue Sale of Portraits*, 1842, in the Ezra Ames estate, and the writers have reasoned that portraits with the same or like titles appearing in both the 1836 Inventory and the 1842 Sale are one and the same portraits. It is here assumed that these entries refer to the portrait of George Washington Clinton owned by Dr. George Clinton Andrews.
Examined by IFC and TB. [Illustrated p. 78]

[73] CLINTON, GEORGE WILLIAM (1807-1885), born in New York City, died in Albany; son of DeWitt Clinton; admitted to the bar in 1831; taken into partnership by John C. Spencer whose daughter he married. Moved to Buffalo; mayor, and from 1854-1877, judge of the Supreme Court of Buffalo; regent of the University of the State of

New York from 1856 until he died; was engaged in editing the State papers relating to George Clinton's public service, in the State Library in Albany (*New-York Daily Tribune*, September 8, 1885, p. 5, col. 5). Married Laura Catharine Spencer, May 1832 (E. M. Ruttenber, *History of the Town of New Windsor, Orange County, N. Y.*, Newburgh, N. Y., 1911, p. 141). A portrait painted of "his son George" for DeWitt Clinton is recorded in Account Book, September 5, 1818.
Unlocated.

[74] COOPER, CHARLES DeKAY (1769-1831), physician; born at Rhinebeck, N. Y.; moved to Albany, 1792; county judge; Secretary of State, 1817 (Jonathan Tenney, *New England in Albany*, Boston, 1883, p. 75).
Description: 29½ x 24 inches. Half-length, head to right.
Date: Uncertain.
Owner: Mrs. Weeks Stewart, Bayport, Long Island, N. Y., great-great-granddaughter of the sitter.
Photograph: FARL 32089.
Attribution: The artist was unknown to the owner. Attributed to Ezra Ames by Irwin F. Cortelyou, 1951. T. Bolton concurs, judging from a photograph.
Note: The artist records: "To Painting a Portrait of Doctr Cooper her Deceased Husband" for Mrs. Cooper in Account Book, December 28, 1834. The portrait owned by Mrs. Weeks Stewart is either an original, painted during Doctor Cooper's lifetime, or the replica recorded in the Account Book entry.
Examined by IFC.

[75] COOPER, CHARLES DeKAY (1769-1831). The artist records: "To Painting a Portrait of Doctr Cooper her Deceased Husband" for Mrs. Cooper in Account Book, December 28, 1834. This catalogue entry is made to list either the original portrait of Dr. Cooper or the replica painted after his death for Mrs. Cooper. See note to No. 74.
Unlocated.

[76] COOPER, MRS. CHARLES DeKAY, (Margaret Tayler), adopted daughter and relative of Lieutenant Governor John Tayler (J. D. Hammond, *History of Political Parties in the State of New-York*, Albany, 1842, I, 439-440).
Description: Bust, head to left.
Attribution: To Ezra Ames by Irwin F. Cortelyou, 1951, judging from a photograph.
Unlocated. The portrait is known only by a photograph owned by Mrs. Weeks Stewart, Bayport, L. I.

[77] CRANE, MRS. ELISHA, née Ruth Phelps (1753-*c.*1840), daughter of Benjamin Phelps and Ruth (Horton) Phelps; second wife of Elisha Crane; mother-in-law of John Meads (MS DAR genealogy compiled for Mrs. Joseph Larocque, Sr.).

Description: 29 3/8 x 25 3/8 inches. Half-length, head to left.

Date: 1818. "To Painting a Portrait of Mrs. Crane" for John Meads is recorded in Account Book, October 31, 1818.

Owners: (1) Orlando Meads; (2) his daughter Mrs. J. G. K. Duer; (3) her daughter Mrs. Joseph Larocque, Sr.; (4) her son Mr. Joseph Larocque, Jr., Washington, D. C., great-great-grandson of the sitter.

Photograph: By Irwin F. Cortelyou.

Attribution: The artist was unknown to the owner. Attributed to Ezra Ames by Irwin F. Cortelyou, 1951. T. Bolton concurs, judging from a photograph.

Examined by IFC.

[78] CROLIUS, CLARKSON (1773-1843), stoneware manufacturer in New York City, and politician (J. E. Stillwell, "Crolius Ware and its Makers," *NYHS Quarterly Bulletin,* July 1926, p. 61-62).

Description: 30 x 24 inches. Half-length, head to right.

Date: 1825.

Inscription on back of canvas: "Col Clarkson Crolius / when Speaker of the House of / Assembly of the State of New York / at 53 years of Age / Painted by Ezra Ames / Albany 1825."

Owner: Presented May 5, 1863, by Clarkson Crolius, Jr., son of the sitter, to NYHS.

Photograph: NYHS 6296; print at FARL.

Reproductions: Donald A. Shelley, *Catalogue of American Portraits in NYHS,* 1941, p. 67; Alan Burroughs, *Limners and Likenesses,* Cambridge, Mass., 1936, No. 78.

Note: Probably the portrait of Clarkson Crolius listed and appraised at $15.00 in the Inventory, 1836, of the Ezra Ames estate.

Examined by IFC and TB. [Illustrated p. 86]

[79] CUMMING, HOOPER (1787-1825), clergyman, pastor of the Second Presbyterian Church, Newark, N. J., and of the Third Presbyterian Church, Albany, N. Y. (Donald A. Shelley, *Catalogue of American Portraits in NYHS,* 1941, p. 68).

Description: 29 x 23 1/8 inches. Bust, head to right.

Date: *c.* 1818.

Owner: New Jersey Historical Society since the Civil War period.

Photograph: FARL 20327.

Exhibition: American Paintings from 1700-1900, Newark Museum, Newark, N. J., Winter 1930-1931.

Attributions: Formerly to Vanderlyn; to Ezra Ames by Irwin F. Cortelyou, 1951, judging from a photograph. T. Bolton concurs, also judging from a photograph.

[80] CUMMING, MRS. HOOPER, née Sophie Wright, AND HER DAUGHTER HARRIET, later Mrs. Edward A. Jee (Donald A. Shelley, *Catalogue of American Portraits in NYHS*, 1941, p. 68).
Description: Panel, 29¾ x 24 inches. Half-length, head to left, with child.
Date: *c.* 1818.
Owner: NYHS, bequest of Mrs. Julia C. Van Arsdale Jones, daughter of the sitter, 1896.
Photograph: NYHS 6195; print at FARL.
Reproduction: Donald A. Shelley, *Catalogue of American Portraits in NYHS*, 1941, p. 68.
Attributions: Formerly to Rembrandt Peale; to Ezra Ames by William Sawitzky, 1944.
Examined by IFC and TB.

[81] CUSHING, THOMAS HUMPHREY (1755-1822), served throughout the Revolutionary War and the War of 1812: commissioned Brigadier General in 1812; member of the Society of the Cincinnati (*National Cyclopedia of American Biography*, XII, 1904, p. 560).
Description: 29½ x 23¾ inches, sight. Bust, head to left. Cleaned in 1953.
Date: *c.* 1815.
Owners: (1) Miss Florence V. Bessac, Natchez, Miss.; (2) acquired from her in 1930 by Mr. Frederick Hill, Catskill, N. Y. (died 1952); (3) Estate of Frederick Hill; (4) purchased by Hirschl & Adler, New York City, 1953.
Photograph: FARL 30959 (before cleaning); reproduced herein from a photograph after cleaning.
Examined by IFC. [Illustrated p. 81]

[82] CUSHING, MRS. THOMAS HUMPHREY, née Margaret Eleanor Norwood; married first a Mr. McCrae (information at FARL from Mr. Frederick Hill).
Description: 29½ x 23¾ inches, sight. Bust, head to left. Cleaned in 1953.
Date: *c.* 1815.
Owners: (1) Miss Florence V. Bessac, Natchez, Miss.; (2) acquired from her in 1930 by Mr. Frederick Hill, Catskill, N. Y. (died 1952); (3) Estate of Frederick Hill; (4) purchased by Hirschl & Adler, New York City, 1953.

Photograph: FARL 30960.
Examined by IFC. [Illustrated p. 81]

[83] CUSHMAN, ISAAC (1759-1842). A portrait painted of his father for "Cushman Esq.," is recorded in Account Book, March 4, 1824. The patron is doubtless Hon. John P. Cushman (1784-1848), born in Pomfret, Connecticut, and later of Troy, N. Y. His father was Hon. Isaac Cushman of Pomfret, Connecticut (Henry Wyles Cushman, *A Historical and Biographical Genealogy of the Cushmans*, Boston, 1855, pp. 178, 318).
Unlocated.

[84] CUSHMAN, MRS. ISAAC, née Sarah Paine (died 1832). A portrait painted of his mother for "Cushman, Esq.," is recorded in Account Book, March 4, 1824. The patron is doubtless Hon. John P. Cushman (1784-1848), born in Pomfret, Connecticut, and later of Troy, N. Y. His mother was Sarah Paine Cushman, daughter of Seth Paine of Connecticut (Henry Wyles Cushman, *A Historical and Biographical Genealogy of the Cushmans*, Boston, 1855, pp. 178, 318).
Unlocated.

[85] CUSHMAN, JOHN P. (1784-1848). Known only through a lithograph. See No. 576.

[86] CUTTING, WILLIAM (1773-1820), lawyer, sheriff of New York County, 1807-1808; an associate of Robert Fulton in promoting steam navigation; married, in 1800, Gertrude, daughter of Walter and Cornelia (Schuyler) Livingston (Cuyler Reynolds, *Genealogical and Family History of Southern New York and the Hudson River Valley*, New York, 1914, II, 843).
Description: 28 x 24 inches. Bust, head to right.
Date: Uncertain.
Owners: (1) Mr. and Mrs. Bernard H. Cone; (2) Dr. and Mrs. Frederick G. Oppenheimer; (3) presented by them to Witte Memorial Museum, San Antonio, Texas, 1945.
Photograph: FARL 33297.
Exhibition: Museum of the City of New York, Winter 1939-1940, lent by Mr. and Mrs. Bernard H. Cone.
Attributions: Formerly attributed to Vanderlyn. Attributed to Ezra Ames by Irwin F. Cortelyou, 1951, judging from a photograph. T. Bolton concurs also judging from a photograph.

[87] CUYLER, JOHN C. [Patron]. Merchant (*Albany Directory*, 1813); Member of the Common Council, Albany, 1807 (Reynolds, 403). The

balance due on a portrait painted for him is recorded in Account Book, 1812.
Unlocated.

[88] DAVINSON, MR. A portrait painted of "her husband" for Mrs. Davinson is recorded in Account Book, October 19, 1824.
Unlocated.

[89] DAVIS, JAMES, AND SON. The painting of "his portrait & son" for James Davis is recorded in Account Book, September 15, 1817.
Unlocated.

[90] DE GRAFF, JOHN ISAAC (1783-1848), politician; banker; Mayor of Schenectady, 1832-1834, 1836, 1842, 1845; Representative from New York, U. S. Congress, 1827-1829, 1837-1839 *(BDAC)*. A portrait painted by Ezra Ames is listed as No. 26, "Hon. John I. De Graff" [30 x 24 inches] in the handbill: *Catalogue Sale of Portraits*, 1842, in the Ezra Ames estate.
Unlocated, unless No. 613 should prove to be by Ezra Ames.

[91] DELA VAN, MR. [Patron]. Possibly Henry W. Delavan (*c.* 1785-1836) the proprietor of a hardware store (*Albany Directory*, 1813) who died at Ballston, N. Y., September 29, 1836, aged 51 (Munsell, X, 1859, p. 262). A portrait painted for him is recorded in Account Book, February 1815.
Unlocated. However, see No. 358 and No. 365.

[92] DEWEY, TIMOTHY, merchant (*Albany Directory*, 1815). A portrait of "Mr Dewey" is listed and appraised at $15.00 in the Inventory, 1836, of the Ezra Ames estate. This is doubtless the portrait painted by Ezra Ames, listed as No. 32, "Timothy Dewey, Esq.," [30 x 24 inches] in the handbill: *Catalogue Sale of Portraits*, 1842, in the Ezra Ames estate.
Unlocated.

[93] De WITT, SIMEON (1756-1834), became geographer to the army during the Revolution; Surveyor-General of New York State from 1784 until his death *(DAB)*.
Description: Half-length standing, head to left.
Date: *c.* 1809-1810 (or possibly 1806, see Rutgers University, *Catalogue of Portraits*, New Brunswick, 1937, p. 10).
Owner: Rutgers University, New Brunswick, N. J.
Photograph: Rutgers University; print at FARL.
Reproduction: William S. Demarest, *History of Rutgers College*, New

Brunswick, 1924; Rutgers University, *Catalogue of Portraits*, New Brunswick, 1937, p. 14).
Exhibition: Early American Portraits, Newark Museum, 1947.
Note: Possibly the painting entitled "Simeon De Witt Esq" listed and appraised at $30.00 in the Inventory, 1836, of the Ezra Ames estate.
Examined by IFC.

[94] De WITT, SIMEON (1756-1834).
Description: 34¾ x 28 inches, oval. Half-length, head to right.
Date: *c.* 1810.
Owners: (1) Miss Sarah De Witt, descendant of sitter; (2) presented by her to the New York State Library, Albany.
Reproduction: Cuyler Reynolds, *Genealogical and Family History of Southern New York and the Hudson River Valley*, New York, 1914, III, facing p. 1239.
Attribution: To Ezra Ames by Dr. R. W. G. Vail.
Examined by IFC and TB.

[95] DIAMOND, THOMAS. [Patron]. A portrait painted for him is recorded in Account Book, May 3, 1794.
Unlocated.

[96] DIAMOND, MRS. [Patron]. A portrait painted for her is recorded in Account Book, October 27, 1806.
Unlocated.

[97] DICKERSON, MAHLON (1770-1853), Secretary of the Navy; Governor of New Jersey, 1815-1817; U. S. Senator for sixteen years (*National Cyclopaedia of American Biography*, 1894, V, 295).
Description: Half-length, head to right.
Date: Uncertain.
Owners: (1) Dietrich family of Albany, who sold it to (2) Clarence Mackay, New Haven, Conn; (3) Dora Lee Curtis, dealer, who sold it to (4) F. W. Pfeifer, Inc., New York City, who sold it in 1937.
Photograph: Print owned by Irwin F. Cortelyou, presented to her by Mrs. Dora Lee Curtis.
Attribution: Tentatively to Ezra Ames by Dora Lee Curtis. By Irwin F. Cortelyou and T. Bolton, 1951, judging from a photograph.
Unlocated.

[98] DOUGLASS, MRS. JAMES B., AND DAUGHTER. A portrait painted for "James B. Duglass" [obviously James B. Douglass (*Albany Directory*, 1823)] is recorded in Account Book, November 10, 1825: "To Painting his Lady's Portrait and Daughter[']s. / Picture

returned 1834." This is doubtless the portrait of "Mrs. Douglas & daughter" listed and appraised at $25.00 in the Inventory, 1836, of the Ezra Ames estate.
Unlocated.

[99] DRAPER, MR. [Patron]. A portrait painted for him is recorded in Account Book, March 27, 1792. The artist was then living in Worcester, Massachusetts.
Unlocated.

[100] DUNBAR, ROBERT, JR. (*c.* 1773-1837). [Patron]. For more than thirty years principal agent for the Patroon [Stephen Van Rensselaer III], died June 30, 1837, aged 64 (Reynolds, 523). Two portraits painted for him are recorded in Account Book, November 22, 1808.
Unlocated.

[101] DUNBAR, ROBERT, JR. (*c.* 1773-1837). [Patron]. One of two portraits painted for him. See No. 100.
Unlocated.

[102] DUNHAM, DAVID, a commission merchant of New York City (information at New Haven Colony Historical Society).
Description: Panel, 30¼ x 23¾ inches. Bust, head to left.
Date: *c.* 1825.
Owner: New Haven Colony Historical Society, New Haven, Conn.
Attributions: Formerly to Waldo and Jewett, and to Jarvis; to Ezra Ames by William Sawitzky, 1939. This portrait was brought to the attention of the writers by notes and a photograph in the late William Sawitzky's file on Ezra Ames lent to them by Mrs. Sawitzky.
Examined by IFC.

[103] DUSENBURY, MISS. A portrait of "Miss Dusenbury" is listed and appraised at $15.00 in the Inventory, 1836, of the Ezra Ames estate.
Unlocated.

[104] DWIGHT, THEODORE (1764-1846), lawyer, author, editor, poet. Lived in Albany, 1815-1817. Was identified with a group of writers known as the "Connecticut Wits." *(DAB).*
Description: 46 x 36 inches. Three-quarter-length seated, head to left. Small figure of "Pegasus" in the background.
Date: 1817. A portrait painted for him is recorded in Account Book, April 18, 1817.

Owner: Mr. C. K. Johnson, Hurley, N. Y. The portrait is said to have come from Madame Jumel's house in Saratoga Springs, N. Y.
Photograph: The owner.
Attribution: To Ezra Ames by Mr. Charles E. Baker, 1951, judging from a photograph.
Note: Identification of the sitter was made by Mr. Charles E. Baker, 1951. [Illustrated p. 90]

[105] DWIGHT, TIMOTHY (1752-1817), clergyman, grandson of Jonathan Edwards; president of Yale College from 1795 until his death *(CAB)*.
Description: 34¼ x 27¼. Half-length, head to left. Relined.
Date: *c.* 1805.
Owners: (1) Colonel William Jay; (2) his daughter, Mrs. Arthur Iselin, Katonah, N. Y. (died 1953).
Photograph: FARL 641.
Attributions: Formerly to John Trumbull. To Ezra Ames by Irwin F. Cortelyou, 1953. T. Bolton concurs, judging from a photograph.
Note: This may be the portrait of "Dr Dwight ... 'Kit-cat' size" listed and appraised at $20.00 in the Inventory, 1836, of the Ezra Ames estate, which in turn may be the portrait painted by Ezra Ames, listed as No. 36, "Rev. Dr. Dwight, 2 feet 8, by 3 feet," in the handbill: *Catalogue Sale of Portraits*, 1842, in the Ezra Ames estate. Though the measurements of the portrait owned by Mrs. Iselin are slightly smaller, it may have been reduced in size when it was relined.
Examined by IFC.

[106] DWIGHT, TIMOTHY (1752-1817). A portrait of "Timothy Dwight D. D. 3/4 size" is listed and appraised at $40.00 in the Inventory, 1836, of the Ezra Ames estate. This is doubtless the portrait painted by Ezra Ames, listed as No. 35, "Rev. Dr. Timothy Dwight, 3 feet 5, by 4 feet 5," in the handbill: *Catalogue Sale of Portraits*, 1842, in the Ezra Ames estate.
Unlocated.

[107] EGBERTS, MR. A portrait painted of and for him is recorded in Account Book, October 9, 1826.
Unlocated.

[108] ELLIS, MR. [Patron]. A portrait painted for him is recorded in Account Book, July 22, 1796.
Unlocated.

[109] EMES, HENRY (1783-1833), half-brother of Ezra Ames. A por-

trait of "Henry Emes" is listed and appraised at $25.00 in the Inventory, 1836, of the Ezra Ames estate.
Unlocated.

[110] EMES, JESSE (1739-1829), Captain in the American army during the Revolution; the father of Ezra Ames.
Description: 30½ x 24½ inches. Bust, head to left.
Date: *c.* 1790.
Owners: (1) Miss Mary L. Sutliff, Cohoes, N. Y., great-grandniece of Ezra Ames; (2) presented by her to AIHA.
Photograph: AIHA; print at FARL.
Exhibition: AIHA 1946.
Note: The sitter is said to be Jesse Emes, but looks so young as to raise a question.
Examined by IFC and TB. [Illustrated p. 2]

[111] EMES, JESSE (1739-1829).
Description: 30 x 23¾ inches. Bust, head to left.
Date: 1819.
Inscription on back of canvas: "J. Emes, AE.80 years / E. Ames, pt. 1819."
Owners: (1) Sally H. Hills, great-granddaughter of the subject; (2) her brother John Ames Hills; (3) bequeathed by him to AIHA.
Photograph: AIHA; print at FARL.
Reproduction: Mary L. Sutliff, *A Record of the Ancestors and the Descendants of Betsy Mulford Sutliff*, Albany, 1897, facing p. 26.
Exhibition: AIHA 1946.
Note: Probably the portrait listed with No. 112 as "Jesse Emes and lady," and appraised at $30.00 each in the Inventory, 1836, of the Ezra Ames estate.
Examined by IFC and TB. [Illustrated p. 97]

[112] EMES, MRS. JESSE, formerly Mrs. Fanny Parminter (Mary L. Sutliff, *A Record of the Ancestors and the Descendants of Betsy Mulford Sutliff*, Albany, 1897, p. 32); or Mrs. Parmature or Miss Palmateer; third wife of Jesse Emes, married January 28, 1819, at Petersham, Mass. (H. W. Reynolds, *Notices of Marriages & Deaths in Newspapers 1778-1820*, Poughkeepsie, 1930, Dutchess County Historical Society, IV, 41).
Description: 23 3/8 x 19 inches, oval mat. Bust, head to right.
Date: 1819.
Owner: Miss Edith S. Wade, Cohoes, N. Y., great-great-grandniece of Ezra Ames.
Photograph: AIHA; print at FARL.

Exhibition: AIHA 1946.
Note: Probably the portrait listed with No. 111 as "Jesse Emes and lady," and appraised at $30.00 each in the Inventory, 1836, of the Ezra Ames estate.
Examined by IFC and TB. [Illustrated p. 97]

[113] FAIRLEY, MAJOR. The "Painting & finishing the Drapery of Majr Fairleys Portrait," charged to Mrs. Fairley, is recorded in Account Book, June 19, 1794.
Unlocated.

[114] FERRIS, ISAAC (1798-1873), clergyman, born in New York City; pastorate at New Brunswick, 1821-1824, Second Church of Albany, 1824-1836, Market Street Church of New York City, 1836-1853; Chancellor of New York University, and Chancellor Emeritus from 1870 until his death (Reformed Dutch Church, Tercentenary Committee on Research and Publication, *Tercentenary Studies, 1928, Reformed Church in America,* 1928, pp. 235-236); organized the Third Reformed Protestant Dutch Church of Albany, 1836 (Munsell, X, 1859, p. 440). A portrait of "Mr. I. Ferris" is listed and appraised at $15.00 in the Inventory, 1836, of the Ezra Ames estate. This is doubtless the portrait painted by Ezra Ames, listed as No. 44, "Rev Dr. Isaac Ferris," [30 x 24 inches] in the handbill; *Catalogue Sale of Portraits,* 1842, in the Ezra Ames estate.
Unlocated.

[115] FONDEY FAMILY.
Description: 54 x 76 4/5 inches.
Date: 1803.
Inscription on the face of the painting:

John Fondey Junr	*AE 42*
Cornelia Fondey	*40*
Sarah Fondey	*19*
Isaac Fondey	*17*
Maria Fondey	*15*
William Fondey	*12*
Stephen Fondey	*8*

Drawn one fourth less than life / by Ezra Ames 1803. [On tombstone in background:] *Cornelia Fondey / obt 24 October 1797 / ae 21 days.*
Owner: Dr. Charles K. Winne, Jr., Albany, on permanent loan at AIHA.
Photograph: AIHA; print at FARL.
Exhibitions: AIHA 1934, 1946.
Examined by IFC and TB. [Illustrated p. 18]

[116] FOOT, MRS. EBENEZER, née Betsey Colt (1774-1847), wife of Ebenezer Foot (1773-1814), lawyer (Jonathan Tenney, *New England in Albany*, Boston, 1883, p. 84).
Description: 30 x 24 inches. Half-length, head to right.
Date: *c.* 1815-1820.
Owner: Mr. George Lindsley Burr, Dobbs Ferry, N. Y., great-great-grandson of the sitter.
Photograph: FARL 36723.
Attribution: The artist was unknown to the owner. Attributed to Ezra Ames by Miss Hope Mathewson (FARL), 1946.

[117] FORMAN, THE REVEREND. A portrait painted by Ezra Ames is listed as No. 45, "Rev. Dr. --- Forman" [30 x 24 inches] in the handbill: *Catalogue Sale of Portraits*, 1842, in the Ezra Ames estate.
Unlocated.

[118] FORSYTH, MR., a son of Dr. Russell Forsyth. Portraits painted of his two sons for "Dr. R[ussell] Forsyth" (1773-1856), physician, died October 30, 1856 (Munsell, VIII, 1857, p. 347), are recorded in Account Book, June 1830.
Unlocated.

[119] FORSYTH, MR., a son of Dr. Russell Forsyth. One of the two portraits recorded in Account Book, June 1830. See No. 118.
Unlocated.

[120] FOWLER, SAMUEL STEVENSON (1799-1850), vice-president and director of the Mechanics and Farmers' Bank; born in Albany, died in Rensselaer, N. Y.; married Julia Frances Gregory (MS genealogy owned by Mr. Marcus L. Blanchard).
Description: 29 x 23¼ inches. Bust, head to right.
Date: *c.* 1827.
Owners: (1) David B. Plum, grandson of the subject; (2) bequeathed to Lillian Blanchard; (3) now owned by her son Mr. Marcus L. Blanchard, Voorheesville, N. Y., great-great-grandson of the sitter.
Photograph: FARL 21364.
Attribution: The artist was unknown to the owner. Attributed to Ezra Ames by Irwin F. Cortelyou, 1951. T. Bolton concurs, judging from a photograph.
Examined by IFC. [Illustrated p. 197]

[121] GANSEVOORT, LEONARD. [Patron]. There were two cousins of this name: (1) Leonard Gansevoort (1751-1810) who lived at his

home, "White Hall," near Albany, and who was the brother of Peter Gansevoort (1749-1812); and (2) Leonard Gansevoort (1754-1834) who was the first judge of Albany County, 1794-1797 *(CAB)*. A portrait painted for "Leonard Gans[e]voort Esqr," is recorded in Account Book, August 18, 1802. From data presently available, it is impossible to determine to which of the cousins this entry refers.
Unlocated. However, this might possibly be No. 122 or conceivably No. 616.

[122] GANSEVOORT, LEONARD (1754-1834), cousin of Peter Gansevoort (1749-1812) and of Leonard Gansevoort (1751-1810) *(CAB)*.
Description: 29½ x 24½ inches, sight. Bust, head to left.
Date: Uncertain.
Owners: (1) Mrs. Herman V. Mynderse; (2) bequeathed to her niece Mrs. Van Rensselaer Ferguson, Ridgewood, N. J.
Photograph: FARL 30676.
Reproduction: Wood engraving by Goetze in *Harpers Magazine*, March 1881, p. 537, without attribution to an artist. Lawrence Park, in his *Gilbert Stuart*, New York, 1926, I, 335, states incorrectly that this engraving is after the portrait of Leonard Gansevoort (1751-1810), which he reproduces, III, 183, as by Stuart (see No. 616 herein), while William Sawitzky, in *Art in America*, June 1933, p. 84, states incorrectly that the engraving is after another portrait of the same Leonard Gansevoort (1751-1810) by Ezra Ames. Actually, it reproduces fairly closely the Ames portrait (No. 122) of his cousin, Leonard Gansevoort (1754-1834).

[123] GANSEVOORT, LEONARD (1754-1834), as a very old man.
Description: 29 x 24 inches. Bust, head to left.
Date: *c.* 1824.
Owners: (1) Mrs. Marcus T. Hun; (2) bequeathed by her to her daughter, Miss Mary V. Hun, Buffalo, N. Y.
Photograph: FARL 15433.
Exhibition: AIHA 1934, lent by Marcus T. Hun.

[124] GANSEVOORT, LEONARD (1751-1810), so-called, as an old man. However, the facial structure resembles the portraits of Leonard Gansevoort (1754-1834) by Ezra Ames, Nos. 122 and 123.
Description: 29½ x 23¼, sight. Bust, head to right.
Date: *c.* 1816.
Owners: Presented to AIHA by Mrs. J. Townsend Lansing.
Photograph: FARL 15665.
Exhibitions: AIHA 1934, lent by AIHA; AIHA 1946.
Examined by IFC and TB.

[125] GANSEVOORT, PETER (1749-1812), Revolutionary soldier, appointed Brigadier General of the U. S. Army, 1809 *(DAB)*.

Description: 29½ x 23½ inches, sight. Bust, in uniform, head to left. Copy after the portrait by Gilbert Stuart (reproduced: Lawrence Park, *Gilbert Stuart*, III, 184). The original Stuart is now owned by the family of Mrs. Joseph S. Frelinghuysen.

Date: 1821. Presumably the "Portrait of his father" painted for "Peter Gansevoort Esqr" recorded in Account Book, October 3, 1821.

Owners: (1) Mrs. Herman Melville; (2) her daughter Mrs. Henry B. Thomas; (3) her daughter Mrs. Walter B. Binnian, Cohasset, Massachusetts.

Photograph: By Irwin F. Cortelyou.

Note: A portrait of "Gen Gansvoort" listed and appraised in the Inventory, 1836, of the Ezra Ames estate, in a group of ten portraits at an "average – each 10.00," is doubtless the portrait painted by Ezra Ames listed as No. 14, "General Peter Gansevoort, from Stuart" [30 x 24 inches] in the handbill: *Catalogue Sale of Portraits*, 1842, in the Ezra Ames estate. It is here assumed that these entries refer to the portrait owned by Mrs. Walter B. Binnian.

Examined by IFC and TB.

[126] GANSEVOORT, MRS. PETER, née Catherine (Catrina or Catherina) Van Schaick (1752-1830), daughter of Wessel Van Schaick and Marie (Gerritse or Gerritsen) Van Schaick; married 1778 (Cuyler Reynolds, *Hudson-Mohawk Genealogical and Family Memoirs*, New York, 1911, I, 68; *DAB*).

Description: 29½ x 24½ inches. Half-length, head slightly to left.

Date: 1824. There is a receipted bill in the Catherine V. S. Gansevoort Estate Box, Manuscript Division, The New York Public Library, dated Albany, May 27th, 1824, to "Peter Gansevoort Esq / To E. Ames Dr / To Painting a Portrait . . . / $30.00," signed by Ezra Ames, June 3, [1824], inscribed by Peter Gansevoort on the back "1824. June 3d / Ezra Ames for / Portrait of my / mother, Cathe- / rine Gansevoort / Rect $30."

Owners: (1) Harmen and Peter Gansevoort, Jr.; (2) the Lansing family; (3) Roland Moore; (4) sold to Joseph S. Frelinghuysen, New York City; (5) sold to AIHA, 1950.

Photograph: M. Knoedler & Company, New York City; print at FARL.

Exhibition: Early American Paintings, Montclair Art Museum, Montclair, 1944.

Note: Mrs. Peter Gansevoort left a will dated June 30, 1829, now in the Manuscript Division of The New York Public Library, in which she stated in part: ". . . and to my sons Harmen and Peter their Executors and administrators and assigns I give and bequeath the Portrait of my deceased husband taken by Stewart and the Portraits of myself

and my brother in law Leonard Gansevoort deceased . . . ."
Examined by IFC. [Illustrated p. 98]

[127] GENET, EDMOND CHARLES (1763-1834), first Minister of the French Republic to the United States; married (1) Cornelia Tappen Clinton, daughter of Governor George Clinton, in 1794, (2) Martha Brandon Osgood, in 1814 *(DAB)*; known as "Citizen Genet."
Description: Panel, 29½ x 23½ inches. Bust, head to left.
Date: *c.* 1809-1810.
Owners: (1) George Clinton Genet, East Greenbush, N. Y., son of the sitter; (2) Mrs. George Clinton Genet; (3) presented by her to AIHA.
Photograph: FARL 15758.
Reproductions: *American Collector*, August 1947, p. 7; E. W. Spaulding, *His Excellency George Clinton*, 1938, facing p. 210.
Exhibitions: AIHA 1934, 1936.
Examined by IFC and TB. [Illustrated p. xvi]

[128] GERMAIN, MR. [Patron]. A portrait painted for him is recorded in Account Book, October 13, 1806.
Unlocated.

[129] GIBSON, MRS. ALEXANDER C., née Marcia Phebe Reynolds (1794-1856) wife of the Mayor of Schenectady who, at his wife's request, changed his name from Cruikshank to Gibson (note dated 5/18/31 by Marcus T. Reynolds at FARL).
Description: 30 x 23¾ inches. Half-length, head to left.
Date: 1824.
Inscription on back of canvas: "Marcia Phebe Reynolds, born at Minaville, married Alexander C. Gibson, Aug 1825. Died at Aurora, Illinois, 1856. Painted by Ames, 1824."
Owner: Formerly owned by Marcus T. Reynolds.
Photograph: FARL 15728.
Exhibition: AIHA 1934, lent by Marcus T. Reynolds.
Unlocated.

[130] GLEN, MR. [Patron]. An entry in the first Account Book dated February 22, 1794, reads: "of Mr. Glen for Portrait painting [£] 4 : 0 : 0." It is assumed that Ezra Ames received of Mr. Glen 4 pounds for painting a portrait for him.
Unlocated.

[131] GOLD, THOMAS RUGGLES (1764-1827), Representative from New York, 11th, 12th, and 14th U. S. Congress; member of State Senate,

1796-1802 *(BDAC)*. A portrait painted of "Thomas R. Gold" and for him is recorded in Account Book, 1821.
Unlocated.

[132] GOULD, PHARES (or Pharez), member of Assembly from Onondaga County, N. Y., 1838, 1839, 1840 (F. B. Hough, *The New York Civil List*, Albany, 1855, pp. 244, 246, 248, 298).
Description: 30 x 23¾ inches. Bust, head to right, wearing eyeglasses.
Date: Uncertain.
Owner: Brooklyn Museum, purchased in 1925.
Photograph: Brooklyn Museum.
Attribution: This portrait was brought to the attention of the writers by a photograph in the late William Sawitzky's file on Ezra Ames lent to them by Mrs. Sawitzky.
Examined by IFC.

[133] GOURLAY, JAMES. [Patron]. Merchant (*Albany Directory*, 1813); elected to the Common Council of Albany in 1810 (Reynolds, 408). A full-length portrait of a child painted for him is recorded in Account Book, March 17, 1815.
Unlocated.

[134] GOURLAY, MR., probably James Gourlay. [Patron]. A portrait painted for "Mr Gourlay" is recorded in Account Book, November 22, 1810.
Unlocated.

[135] GRIFFIN, EDWARD DORR (1770-1837), Congregational clergyman; president of Williams College *(DAB)*.
Description: 29½ x 23½ inches, sight. Bust, head to left.
Date: *c.* 1830.
Owner: Old South Association, Boston, presented by Mrs. Marie Weston Chapman about 1880.
Photograph: FARL 31251.
Attributions: Recorded at Old South Meeting House as a copy after Waldo and Jewett. Listed in the Historical Records Survey, *American Portraits Found in Massachusetts*, Boston, 1939, I, 183, as by an unknown artist. Attributed to Ezra Ames by Irwin F. Cortelyou, 1952, judging from a photograph. T. Bolton concurs, also judging from a photograph.
Note: This is doubtless the portrait painted by Ezra Ames, listed as No. 41, "Rev. Dr. Edward D. Griffin," [30 x 24 inches] in the handbill: *Catalogue Sale of Portraits*, 1842, in the Ezra Ames estate.

[136] HACKLEY, AARON. [Patron]. Possibly Aaron Hackley, Jr. (1783-1868), member, State Assembly, 1814, 1815, 1818; Representative from New York, U. S. Congress, 1819-1821 *(BDAC)*. A portrait painted for him is recorded in Account Book, May 31, 1816.
Unlocated.

[137] HACKLEY, MRS. AARON, possibly wife of Aaron Hackley, Jr., (1783-1868). A portrait painted of "his lady" for Aaron "Huckley" is recorded in Account Book, April 17, 1824. The name is spelled "Hackley" in Account Book, May 31, 1816. See No. 136.
Unlocated.

[138] HAMILTON, ALEXANDER (1757-1804). First Secretary of the Treasury.
Description: Oval, 30 x 25 inches. Bust, head and eyes to right.
Owners: (1) John Rogers Peters, New York City who willed it to his son (2) Lieutenant Colonel DeWitt Clinton Peters, M. D., who sold it in 1860 to (3) S. T. Williams, dealer, New York City, who sold it December 31, 1860 to (4) Joshua Marsden Van Cott, Brooklyn, who died in 1896 leaving it to his son (5) Dr. Joshua Marsden Van Cott, Brooklyn, who sold it December 24, 1928, to (6) Harry MacNeill Bland who sold it the same day to (7) Edward Small Moore, New York City, who bequeathed it to his wife (8) Mrs. Evelyn N. Moore, Lexington, Kentucky. (Information supplied by Mr. Harry MacNeill Bland).
Photograph: By Peter A. Juley & Son, New York City; print at FARL.
Note: A portrait of "Gen. Hamilton" listed and appraised in the Inventory, 1836, of the Ezra Ames estate, in a group of ten portraits at an "average – each 10.00," is doubtless the portrait painted by Ezra Ames, listed as No. 15, "General Alexander Hamilton," [30 x 24 inches] in the handbill: *Catalogue Sale of Portraits*, 1842, in the Ezra Ames estate. It is here assumed that these entries refer to the portrait owned by Mrs. Moore.

[139] HAMILTON, ALEXANDER (1757-1804).
Description: 30 x 25 inches. Bust, head to right.
Date: 1810.
Owner: Union College, Schenectady, N. Y. Listed as No. 103 in *Index to Portraits and Paintings at Union College*, June 1950. According to an article in *The Union Alumni Monthly*, January 1928, p. 71, the portrait was presented by General Alexander Hamilton, grandson of Alexander Hamilton, to Union College with a letter, dated December 8, 1875, to President Potter, stating that it was an "original portrait of my grandfather, Alexander Hamilton ... given me in 1833 by my late friend Mr. Winfield Scott Yates, formerly of Albany. Mr. Yates

informed me that he received this picture from his uncle, Gov. Joseph C. Yates, for whom it had been painted from life, shortly before my grandfather's death...." However, a portrait of "Genrl Hamilton" painted by Ames is recorded in Account Book, April 25, 1810, charged to Elijah Thomas and "delivered to Doctr C. C. Yates," father of Winfield Scott Yates (the nephew of Governor Yates); and because of the Yates connection it would seem that the portrait at Union College is the one mentioned in this entry.

Photograph: FARL 15479.

Reproduction: In color, *Fortune*, February 1951, p. 75.

Attributions: Unattributed as to artist in *Index to Portraits and Paintings at Union College*, June 1950, No. 103. Attributed to Ezra Ames by James H. Callender, 1931, and by William Sawitzky, 1932, judging from a photograph.

Note: For an account of this portrait see p. 157 herein.

Examined by IFC. [Illustrated p. 52]

[140] HAMILTON, ISAAC (*c.* 1779-1834). [Patron]. Alderman (Reynolds, 512); practiced law in Albany for more than thirty years; died at St. Mary's, Georgia, November 16, 1834, aged 55 (Munsell, X, 1859, p. 233). Two portraits painted for him are recorded in Account Book, July 21, 1815.

Unlocated.

[141] HAMILTON, ISAAC (*c.* 1779-1834). [Patron]. One of two portraits painted for him. See No. 140.

Unlocated.

[142] HANKINSON, JOHN, built "Monmouth" at Natchez, Mississippi, about 1812 or earlier (information at FARL from Miss Rachel A. Doan, 10/27/37).

Description: 30 x 23¾ inches. Bust, head to left.

Date: *c.* 1815. Painted in Albany.

Owners: (1) Florence V. Bessac, Natchez, Miss.; (2) acquired in 1930 by her cousin Miss Rachel A. Doane, Palenville, N. Y., great-grandniece of the sitter; (3) bequeathed to a relative Mr. Henry K. Doane, Holliston, Mass.

Photograph: FARL 30964.

[143] HANKINSON, MRS. JOHN, née Frances McCrae, daughter of Mrs. Thomas Humphrey Cushing by her first husband (information at FARL from Miss Rachel A. Doane, 10/27/37).

Description: 30 x 23¾ inches. Bust, head to right.

Date: *c.* 1815. Painted in Albany.

Owners: (1) Florence V. Bessac, Natchez, Miss.; (2) acquired in 1930 by her cousin Miss Rachel A. Doane, Palenville, N. Y.; (3) bequeathed to a relative Mr. Henry K. Doane, Holliston, Mass.
Photograph: FARL 30965.

[144] HANSEN, MISS. A portrait of "Miss Hansen" is listed and appraised at $5.00 in the Inventory, 1836, of the Ezra Ames estate.
Unlocated.

[145] HANSEN, ISAAC. [Patron]. Member of the Common Council, Albany, 1811, 1812, 1815 (Reynolds, 410, 411, 417). A portrait painted for him is recorded in Account Book, July 28, 1808.
Unlocated.

[146] HANSEN, ISAAC. [Patron]. A portrait painted for him is recorded in Account Book, June 16, 1810.
Unlocated.

[147] HILLHOUSE, THOMAS (1766-1834), born Montville, Conn.; married (1) Harriet Hosmer, 1797, (2) Anne Van Schaick Ten Broeck, 1812. One of the first settlers of Troy, N. Y.; retired to and died at Watervliet, N. Y. (Margaret P. Hillhouse, *Historical and Genealogical Collections Relating to the Descendants of Rev. James Hillhouse*, New York, 1924, pp. 283-284).
Description: 28½ x 23 inches. Bust, head to right.
Date: *c.* 1817.
Owners: Inherited by John T. E. Hillhouse, great-grandson of the sitter, who bequeathed it to his wife, Mrs. John T. E. Hillhouse, Haverford, Pa.
Photograph: The owner. [Illustrated p. 90]

[148] HOLLEY, MYRON (1779-1841), lawyer, abolitionist, treasurer of Erie Canal Commission, newspaper editor *(DAB, CAB)*.
Description: 29¾ x 23¾ inches. Bust, head to left.
Date: Uncertain.
Owner: NYHS, gift of Miss Sallie Holley, daughter of the sitter, 1892.
Photograph: NYHS; print at FARL.
Examined by IFC and TB.

[149] HUDSON, ROBERT (*c.* 1785-1825).
Description: 30 x 24 inches. Bust, head to left.
Date: *c.* 1820.
Inscription on back: (in substance) This is a portrait of Robert Hudson, Esqr. born in the City of Schenectady, N. Y., and died there in July

1825, aged about 40 years. This portrait was taken by Ames in Albany, N. Y.
Owner: Formerly owned by the late Mrs. Clarence Cary, a direct descendant of the sitter.
Photograph: Print at FARL.
Unlocated. [Illustrated p. 94]

[150] HUDSON, MRS. ROBERT, née Eliza ----.
Description: Panel, 30 x 24 inches. Half-length, head to left.
Date: *c.* 1820.
Inscription on back: "Portrait of Eliza Hudson, late wife of Robert Hudson of Schenectady, N. Y."
Owner: Formerly owned by the late Mrs. Clarence Cary, a direct descendant of the sitter.
Photograph: Print at FARL.
Unlocated. [Illustrated p. 94]

[151] HUMPHERY [*sic*], F. [possibly J. or G.] [Patron]. A balance due on a portrait for him is recorded in Account Book, January 13, 1819.
Unlocated.

[152] HUNTER, JAMES. The painting of his portrait for James Hunter is recorded in Account Book, October 9, 1826. There were two men of this name at this time in Albany: James Hunter (1796-1834), newspaper editor (Munsell, X, 1859, p. 227); and James Hunter, whitesmith (*Albany Directory*, 1826). It is impossible to determine which of the two men was the sitter for the portrait.
Unlocated.

[153] HURLBUT, JOSEPH (1799-1875), pastor of the Third Presbyterian Church, Albany, 1823-1824 (Henry Nicholas Dunning, *Lest We Forget the Lives and Labors of Those Who have served as Pastors of the Third Presbyterian Church of Albany, New York,* [1905] pp. 11-13). The "Painting his Portrait" for "Revd G. [possibly J.] Hurlbert," obviously Joseph Hurlbut, is recorded in Account Book, May 16, 1824. In Reynolds, 440, the name is spelled "Hulburt."
Unlocated.

[154] JACKSON, SAMUEL (1755-1845), born in England, died in Minaville, N. Y. (information at FARL from Mr. John Tuttle Jackson).
Description: 30¾ x 24¾ inches. Bust, head to left.
Date: *c.* 1805.
Owners: (1) Allan H. Jackson, Schenectady, N. Y., great-grandson of

the sitter; (2) his sister, Mrs. Harry Preston, Pittsfield, Mass.
Photograph: FARL 30663.
Attribution: The artist was unknown to the owner. Attributed to Ezra Ames by Irwin F. Cortelyou, 1951, judging from a photograph. T. Bolton concurs, also judging from a photograph.

[155] JAMES, JOHN (1789-1859), physician; born in Weybridge, Vermont; died in Alton, Illinois; settled in Albany as early as 1826 (*Albany Directory*); son of Daniel James and Mary (Emmes) James; married Mary Clark in 1833 (information from the owner, Mrs. Le Roy E. Fess).
Description: 29 x 24 inches. Bust, head to right.
Date: *c.* 1830.
Owners: (1) Dr. John James; (2) "in possession of" his sister Mrs. Daniel Pepoon; (3) his daughter Anna James Richmond; (4) her son George Richmond; (5) his widow Mabelle Jones Richmond; (6) their daughter Mrs. Le Roy E. Fess (Margaret Richmond), Clarence, N. Y., great-granddaughter of the sitter.
Photograph: The owner.
Attribution: The artist was unknown to the owner. The location of this portrait and its recent tentative attribution to Ezra Ames by Mrs. Haven Parker, were brought to the writers' attention by the owner in October, 1953. The writers accept the attribution, judging from a photograph. The attribution is documented by a note in the manuscript ledger of Dr. John James (page 70) at The New York State Library, Albany, examined by Irwin F. Cortelyou in 1950, which states that a charge of $5.50 for medicines received by Ezra Ames on December 16, 1826, September 3, 1831, and August 7, 1832, was "settled by his [Ames's] present of my picture in Possession of Mrs. Pepoon." Further documentation, submitted by the owner, is an undated entry in a fragment of the sitter's journal which reads: "I also promised her [Mrs. Pepoon] my picture now in the hands of Ames." An aunt of the owner states that another entry in the sitter's journal records a payment of $15.00 to Ezra Ames for a sitting.

[156] JAMES, KATHARINE BARBER (1834-1890), said to be portrait of Granddaughter of the artist; later the second wife of William Henry Prince. She was born December 6, 1834, daughter of the Reverend William James (1797-1868) and Marcia Lucretia (Ames) James, daughter of Ezra Ames. She is the Kitty Prince of the William James *Letters* (Mrs. Russel Hastings, "William James of Albany," *New York Genealogical and Biographical Record*, April 1924, pp. 108, 109).
Description: 29¾ x 24 inches. Child seated, nearly full length, head to right.

Date: Uncertain.
Owner: Miss Elizabeth S. Edwards, Albany, great-granddaughter of Ezra Ames.
Photograph: AIHA; print at FARL.
Exhibition: AIHA 1946.
Note: The owner believes the portrait to be of Katharine Barber James. However, the child looks too mature for a girl of one year. The portrait is certainly by Ezra Ames who died when Katharine Barber James was only a little over a year old.
Examined by IFC and TB. [Illustrated p. 128]

[157] JAMES, WILLIAM (1771-1832), of Albany; businessman, banker; the grandfather of William James the philosopher and of Henry James the novelist; married (1) 1796, Elizabeth Tillman, (2) 1798, Mary Ann Connolly, (3) 1803, Catharine Barber. His son William, by his first wife, married Ezra Ames's daughter Marcia Lucretia (Mrs. Russel Hastings, "William James of Albany," *New York Genealogical and Biographical Record,* April 1924, pp. 101-113).
Description: Panel, 36 x 28 inches. Half-length, head to left. Cleaned in 1951.
Date: 1822. A letter in the sitter's hand is inscribed "Wm James, E[sq.,] / Albany," and is dated 1822.
Owners: (1) French provincial collection; (2) Weltz (?), Paris, dealer; (3) Mrs. Cornelius J. Sullivan; (4) Union College, Schenectady, N. Y. A letter dated 5/22/51 from Mrs. E. C. S. Smith, Librarian, Union College, to IFC states: the picture was acquired from Mrs. Cornelius J. Sullivan, New York City, and "I get the impression ... its purchase was made possible through gifts from Mrs. Victor Morawetz, Henry James and other friends of the College. At no time in the correspondence was it attributed to anyone but Waldo and Jewett."
Photograph: FARL 41214.
Reproduction: *New York Times,* Rotogravure Section, April 20, 1930, as by Gilbert Stuart, in a "French provincial collection."
Attributions: Formerly to Waldo and Jewett, and to Gilbert Stuart. The location of the portrait and its attribution to Ezra Ames was found by the writers in the notes in the late William Sawitzky's file on Ezra Ames, lent to them by Mrs. Sawitzky.
Examined by IFC. [Illustrated p. 106]

[158] JAMES, MRS. WILLIAM, née Catharine Barber (1782-1859), third wife of William James (1771-1832) of Albany (Mrs. Russel Hastings, "William James of Albany," *New York Genealogical and Biographical Record,* April 1924, pp. 105-106).
Description: $29\frac{1}{2}$ x $23\frac{1}{2}$ inches. Half-length, head to right.

Date: 1822.

Owners: (1) Mrs. Alfred E. Schermerhorn, great-granddaughter of the sitter; (2) Mr. A. Coster Schermerhorn, Washington, D. C., on loan to Mrs. Reginald P. Rose, Syosset, Long Island, N. Y.

Photograph: FARL 21252.

Attributions: Formerly to Waldo; to Ezra Ames by Mrs. Reginald P. Rose, 1951. [Illustrated p. 106]

[159] JAMES, MRS. WILLIAM, née Marcia Lucretia Ames (1797/98-1886), daughter of Ezra Ames; married in 1824 to the Reverend William James (1797-1868), half brother of the father of Henry James the novelist and William James the philosopher (Mrs. Russel Hastings, "William James of Albany," *New York Genealogical and Biographical Record,* April 1924, pp. 104-113).

Description: $31\frac{1}{2}$ x $25\frac{1}{4}$ inches. Half-length, head slightly to left.

Date: *c.* 1827.

Owners: (1) Mrs. William James, the sitter, who willed it to her daughter (2) Mrs. Isaac Edwards, who willed it to her daughter (3) Miss Elizabeth S. Edwards, Albany.

Photograph: AIHA; print at FARL.

Exhibition: AIHA, 1946, lent by Miss Elizabeth S. Edwards.

Note: Probably the portrait listed as "Marcia L. Ames in black" and appraised at $25.00 in the Inventory, 1836, of the Ezra Ames estate.

Examined by IFC and TB.

[160] JAY, JOHN (1745-1829), Governor of New York, 1795-1801, statesman and diplomat, Chief Justice of the United States.

Description: 52 x 40 inches, sight. Half-length, head to right. Copy after the Gilbert Stuart original on loan at Metropolitan Museum.

Date: Uncertain.

Owner: The City of Albany, on permanent loan at AIHA.

Photograph: AIHA; print at FARL.

Exhibition: AIHA 1946.

Note: This is one of the series of "Portraits of Seven Governors of New York," by Ezra Ames, at AIHA.

Examined by IFC and TB. [Illustrated p. 141]

[161] JEFFERSON, THOMAS (1743-1846), third President of the United States, 1801-1809. A portrait of "Jefferson" is listed with other portraits described as "heads from Stuart" and is appraised at $30.00 in the Inventory, 1836, of the Ezra Ames estate. This is doubtless the portrait painted by Ezra Ames, listed as No. 3, "Head of Thomas Jefferson, copy from G. Stuart," [30 x 24 inches] in the handbill: *Catalogue Sale of Portraits,* 1842, in the Ezra Ames estate.

Unlocated.

[162] JEFFERSON, THOMAS (1743-1846). A portrait entitled "Small Jefferson framed" is listed and appraised at $10.00 in the Inventory, 1836, of the Ezra Ames estate.
Unlocated.

[163] JONES, HENRY (born *c.* 1790), studied law under Harmanus Bleecker (Munsell, I, 1850, p. 276).
Description: 47 x 35 inches. Half-length standing, head to right.
Date: 1810.
Inscription on back of canvas: "Henry Jones, Height 5 feet 6 inches Aged 20 Years / E. Ames pt 1810 S. N. York N. America."
Owner: NYHS.
Photograph: NYHS 8721c; print at FARL.
Reproduction: Donald A. Shelley, *Catalogue of American Portraits at NYHS,* 1941, p. 163.
Note: Henry T. Jones, counsellor (*Albany Directory,* 1815, 1816), was possibly the above.
Examined by IFC and TB. [Illustrated p. 54]

[164] JONES, DR. Possibly Dr. Thomas Jones the father of the second Mrs. DeWitt Clinton *(DAB)* and husband of Mrs. Thomas Jones, née Margaret Livingston, daughter of Philip Livingston (Florence Van Rensselaer, *The Livingston Family in America,* New York, 1949, p. 97). The "Balance due" on a portrait of "Dr. Jones" (crossed out) is recorded in the Inventory, 1836, of the Ezra Ames estate. The inference that this portrait is of Dr. Thomas Jones is based on the fact that Ames painted portraits of his wife and daughter.
Unlocated.

[165] JONES, MRS. THOMAS, née Margaret Livingston (1747-1830), daughter of Philip Livingston and Christina (Ten Broeck) Livingston; married Dr. Thomas Jones of New York City, 1776 (Florence Van Rensselaer, *The Livingston Family in America,* New York, 1949, p. 97); mother of Catherine Jones, the second Mrs. DeWitt Clinton (J. G. Wilson, *Memorial History of New York City,* 1893, III, 401).
Description: 30 x 24 inches. Half-length, head to left.
Date: *c.* 1820.
Owners: (1) Mrs. Richard Sands Tucker, granddaughter of the sitter; (2) her daughter, Mrs. F. J. Synge, London; (3) Samuel Auchmuty Tucker, New York City; (4) Mr. Richard D. Tucker, New York City.
Photograph: FARL 33183.
Attributions: Formerly to James Frothingham; to Ezra Ames in 1946 because of proof found by Mrs. S. A. Tucker, in a letter of the period.

[166] JONES, THOMAS P. A portrait of "T. P. Jones" is listed and appraised at $5.00 in the Inventory, 1836, of the Ezra Ames estate. This is doubtless the portrait painted by Ezra Ames, listed as No. 29, "Thomas P. Jones, Esq." [30 x 24 inches] in the handbill: *Catalogue Sale of Portraits*, 1842, in the Ezra Ames estate.
Unlocated.

[167] JORDAN, AMBROSE LATTING (1789-1865), lawyer, in Cooperstown, N. Y., 1813-1820; in Hudson, N. Y., 1820-1838; in New York City thereafter. Member of the State Assembly, State Senator, Attorney General of the State *(CAB;* date of birth in Catalogue, *A View of a New York State Community*, NYSHA, Cooperstown, N. Y., 1939, pp. 11-12).
Description: Panel, 29 7/8 x 23 3/8 inches. Bust, head to left.
Date: *c.* 1820-1825.
Owner: Mr. Stephen C. Clark, on permanent loan at NYSHA, Cooperstown, N. Y.
Photograph: NYSHA; print at FARL.
Reproduction: *Art In America*, April 1950, p. 97.
Exhibition: A View of a New York State Community, NYSHA, 1939, as by S. F. B. Morse. Lent by Mr. Stephen C. Clark.
Attributions: (1) To S. F. B. Morse; (2) tentatively to John Wesley Jarvis in *Art in America*, April 1950, p. 126; (3) to Ezra Ames by Irwin F. Cortelyou, 1951. T. Bolton concurs, judging from a photograph.
Note: A portrait of "A. Jordan" listed and appraised in the Inventory, 1836, of the Ezra Ames estate, in a group of ten portraits at an "average – each 10.00," is doubtless the portrait painted by Ezra Ames, listed as No. 27, "Hon. Ambrose L. Jordan," [30 x 24 inches] in the handbill: *Catalogue Sale of Portraits*, 1842, in the Ezra Ames estate. It is here assumed that these entries refer to the portrait at NYSHA.
Examined by IFC. [Illustrated p. 101]

[168] KANE, JOHN (1734-1808), came to America from Ireland in 1752; married Sybil Kent (1738-1806) in 1756; fled to Nova Scotia during the Revolution; returned to New York where his sons established the fur-trading firm known as Kane Brothers (Elizabeth D. Kane, *Story of John Kane of Dutchess County, N. Y.*, Philadelphia, privately printed, 1921, pp. 43, 75, 84).
Description: 36 x 28 inches. Half-length, head to left.
Date: *c.* 1804.
Owners: (1) John Kane; (2) his daughter Sybilla Adeline Kane Van Rensselaer; (2) her daughter Alida Van Rensselaer Carroll; (4) her daughter Cornelia Fitzhugh Conover; (5) Stephen H. P. Pell; (6) Mr. R.

Keith Kane, New York City.
Photograph: FARL 38357.
Examined by IFC and TB. [Illustrated p. 41]

[169] KENT, JAMES (1763-1847), jurist, chief justice of the Supreme Court of New York, 1804-1814, chancellor, 1814-1823 (DAB). Fifth president of The New-York Historical Society, 1828-1831.
Description: 36 x 28 inches. Half-length, head to right. The head is very similar to that in No. 170.
Date: *c.* 1812.
Owners: (1) Mrs. Isaac Edwards; (2) her daughter Miss Elizabeth S. Edwards and her son Mr. Henry Ames Edwards; (3) presented by them to AIHA.
Photograph: AIHA; print at FARL.
Exhibitions: Loan Exhibition at the Historical and Art Society, Albany, 1902, lent by Mrs. Isaac Edwards; AIHA 1946, lent by Miss Elizabeth S. Edwards.
Note: A portrait of "Chan Kent . . . 'Kit-cat size'" listed and appraised at $20.00 in the Inventory, 1836, of the Ezra Ames estate, is doubtless the portrait painted by Ezra Ames, listed as No. 19, "Chancellor James Kent, 2 feet 4, by 3 feet" in the handbill: *Catalogue Sale of Portraits*, 1842, in the Ezra Ames estate. It is here assumed that these entries refer to the portrait at AIHA.
Examined by IFC and TB. [Illustrated p. 75]

[170] KENT, JAMES (1763-1847).
Description: 30¾ x 24¾ inches. Bust, head to right. The head is very similar to that in No. 169.
Date: *c.* 1812.
Owner: Albany Academy for Girls.
Photograph: Albany Academy for Girls; print at FARL.
Reproduction: *New York History*, April 1941, facing p. 208.
Exhibition: AIHA 1946.

[171] KING, MRS. JAMES, née Ellen James (1800-1823), daughter of William James of Albany; married James King, lawyer (Mrs. Russel Hastings, "William James of Albany," *New York Genealogical and Biographical Record*, April 1924, p. 104-105, 110).
Description: 30 x 24 inches. Half-length, head to left.
Date: 1822.
Owners: (1) Mrs. Franklin Bartlett; (2) inherited by her daughter Mrs. Harry Horton Benkard, great-granddaughter of the sitter; (3) inherited by her daughter Mrs. Reginald P. Rose, Syosset, Long Island, N.Y.
Photograph: FARL 4951.

Reproductions: Mrs. Russel Hastings, "William James of Albany," *New York Genealogical and Biographical Record,* April 1924, facing p. 110; Brooklyn Museum, *Exhibition of Early American Paintings,* 1917, facing p. 2.

Exhibition: Exhibition of Early American Paintings, Brooklyn Museum, 1917, lent by Mrs. Franklin Bartlett. [Illustrated p. 106]

[172] KING, JOSHUA (1758-1839), born in Braintree, Massachusetts; died in Ridgefield, Connecticut; member of the Society of the Cincinnati. The entry for a portrait of "Genera[l] King" charged to William McHarg in Account Book, November 6, 1811, is probably incorrect as to the military title. Joshua King was promoted to lieutenant in 1779 and served to the close of the war. He was one of the guards of Major André. His daughter Sophia married William McHarg (*DAR Lineage Book,* Vol. 47, p. 265).

Unlocated.

[173] KING, MRS. JOSHUA, née Anne Ingersoll. Two portraits, one of "Genera[l] King," the other of his "Lady," charged to William McHarg are recorded in Account Book, November 6, 1811. See No. 172.

Unlocated.

[174] KNOWER, BENJAMIN (*c.* 1775-1839), hatter (*Albany Directory,* 1813); a founder, and president for many years of the Mechanics and Farmers' Bank, Albany; Treasurer of New York State, 1821-1824 (Jonathan Tenney, *New England in Albany,* Boston, 1883, p. 92).

Description: *c.* 30 x 24 inches. Bust, head to left. Almost identical with No. 175.

Date: Probably 1807. A bill, dated December 25, 1807, laid in the third Account Book, is receipted by Ezra Ames for "Painting a Portrait" and "- do - do - his Lady" for Benjamin Knower. The portrait not named was presumably of Benjamin Knower, either this one or No. 175.

Owner: Mechanics and Farmers' Bank, Albany.

Reproduction: Mechanics and Farmers' Bank, *Span of a Century, 1811-1911,* Albany.

Attribution: The artist was unknown to the owner. Attributed to Ezra Ames by Irwin F. Cortelyou and T. Bolton, 1951.

Examined by IFC and TB.

[175] KNOWER, BENJAMIN (*c.* 1775-1839).

Description: 31 x 25 inches. Bust, head to left. Almost identical with No. 174.

Date: Probably 1807. See No. 174.

Owners: (1) Mrs. Mary Penniman; (2) Count Jean de Suczannet, Victoria, British Columbia, Canada, in 1931.
Photograph: FARL 15561.
Attribution: To Ezra Ames by the late William Sawitzky according to notes in his file on Ezra Ames lent to the writers by Mrs. William Sawitzky.
Note: The identification of the sitter as Benjamin Knower instead of (as formerly) John Knower was made by Irwin F. Cortelyou and T. Bolton, 1951, because of the strong resemblance of the portrait to the portrait of Benjamin Knower owned by the Mechanics and Farmers' Bank.

[176] KNOWER, MRS. BENJAMIN (*c.* 1777-1833), "Sarah, wife of Benjamin Knower and mother-in-law of Governor Marcy, died aged 56" on February 19, 1833 (Munsell, IX, 1858, p. 263). A bill, dated December 25, 1807, laid in the third Account Book, is receipted by Ezra Ames for "Painting a Portrait," and "- do - do - his Lady" for Benjamin Knower.
Unlocated.

[177] LAGRANGE, JAMES (*c.* 1763-1827). [Patron]. Captain; died February 16, 1827, aged 64 (Munsell, IX, 1858, p. 147). Two portraits painted for him are recorded in Account Book, December 24, 1807.
Unlocated.

[178] LAGRANGE, JAMES (*c.* 1763-1827). [Patron]. One of two portraits painted for him. See No. 177.
Unlocated.

[179] LAMB, COL. A portrait painted by Ezra Ames is listed as No. 17, " Col. Lamb," [30 x 24 inches] in the handbill: *Catalogue Sale of Portraits*, 1842, in the Ezra Ames estate.
Unlocated.

[180] LANSING, GERRIT YATES (1783-1862), Representative from New York, U.S. Congress, 1831-1837; Regent of the University of the State of New York, 1829-1862; Chancellor of the Board, 1842; nephew of John Lansing, Jr. (*BDAC*).
Description: 29 x 23 inches. Half-length, head to right.
Date: 1830. Presumably the portrait painted of and for "Garret Y. Lansingh Esqr" recorded in Account Book, February 19, 1830.
Owners: (1) Gerrit Yates Lansing, grandson of the sitter; (2) his nephew Mr. Charles B. Lansing; (3) his son Mr. Gerrit Yates Lansing, Chagrin Falls, Ohio, great-great-grandson of the sitter.

Photograph: FARL 15390.
Attribution: William Sawitzky, judging from a photograph in 1932, was inclined to attribute this portrait to Ezra Ames. The entry in the Account Book confirms this tentative attribution.

[181] LANSING, JOHN, JR. (1754-1829), Chief Justice of the New York Supreme Court, 1798-1801, and Chancellor, 1801-1814 (*BDAC*).
Description: Bust, head to left.
Date: *c*. 1810.
Owners: (1) Mr. Lansing of Albany; (2) Thomas Addis Emmet in 1885.
Photograph: Print at FARL.
Attribution: Tentatively to Ezra Ames by Irwin F. Cortelyou and T. Bolton, 1953, judging from a very faded photograph.
Unlocated.

[182] LANSING, CHANCELLOR, Possibly John Lansing, Jr., (1754-1829). A portrait of "Chanr Lansingh" painted for "Judge Southerland" is recorded in Account Book, November 20, 1829. Chancellor John Lansing, Jr., was in Albany in 1829 before leaving for New York City where, after a few days, on December 12, he left his hotel and disappeared never to be heard of again (*BDAC*). The portrait could not have been of his nephew Gerrit Yates Lansing (1783-1862). The nephew was not appointed Chancellor until 1842 (*BDAC*).
Unlocated.

[183] LARNED, MRS., AND CHILD. A painting entitled "Mrs. Larned & child" is listed and appraised at $25.00 in the Inventory, 1836, of the Ezra Ames estate.
Unlocated.

[184] LE MAI, MRS. COL. Listed in the *Catalogue of Albany's Bicentennial Loan Exhibition at the Albany Academy, July 5 to July 24, 1886*, p. 117, as follows: "Ezra Ames (deceased). / 116 Portrait of Mrs. Col. Le Mai, daughter of Citizen Genet ... [owned by] Mrs. T. Kirby Van Zandt."
Unlocated.

[185] LEWIS, MRS. S. A portrait of "Mrs. S. Lewis" is listed and appraised at $5.00 in the Inventory, 1836, of the Ezra Ames estate.
Unlocated.

[186] LIVINGSTON, MAJOR, PICTURES. (1) Probably Major Henry Livingston, Jr. (1748-1828) of "Locust Grove" near Poughkeepsie, N.Y., brother of John Henry Livingston (1746-1825) of New York

City (William S. Thomas, "Henry Livingston," *Year Book, Dutchess County Historical Society*, 1919, pp. 32-45). In an undated section of the first Account Book, here assigned to April-May, 1793, the artist records the buying of oil and linen for Major Livingston's "pictures," and then the taking of them to New York City. It is here assumed that there were two pictures, companion portraits: one of Major Livingston, the other of his second wife-to-be whom he married in September of that year.
Unlocated.

[187] LIVINGSTON, MAJOR, PICTURES. (2) Probably Mrs. Henry Livingston, Jr., née Jean McLean Paterson who married Major Henry Livingston, Jr. (1748-1828), in September 1793 (William S. Thomas, "Henry Livingston," *Year Book, Dutchess County Historical Society*, 1919, p. 42). In an undated section of the first Account Book, here assigned to April-May, 1793, the artist records the buying of oil and linen for Major Livingston's "pictures" and then the taking of them to New York City. It is here assumed that there were two pictures, companion portraits: one of Major Livingston, the other of his second wife-to-be whom he married in September of that year.
Unlocated.

[188] LIVINGSTON, HENRY (1753-1823), son of Robert Livingston (1708-1790) and Maria (Thong) Livingston (Cuyler Reynolds, *Genealogical and Family History of Southern New York and the Hudson River Valley*, New York, 1914, III, 1310, there called Hendrick Livingston).
Date: *c.* 1823.
Owners: (1) Mrs. Geraldyn Redmond; (2) Mrs. William H. Osborn, New York City, and Tivoli, N.Y.
Reproduction: Edwin Brockholst Livingston, *The Livingstons of Livingston Manor*, 1910, facing p. 253, and there attributed to Ezra Ames; photostat at FARL.

[189] LIVINGSTON, JOHN HENRY (1746-1825), clergyman, Dutch Reformed Church (*DAB*); son of Henry Livingston (1714-1789), and brother of Major Henry Livingston, Jr. (1748-1828); pastor of the Collegiate Church, New York City; founded the Theological Seminary at New Brunswick, N.J. (J. Wilson Poucher, "Dutchess County Men of the Revolutionary Period," *Year Book, Dutchess County Historical Society*, XXIII, 1938, p. 48). A portrait of "Dr. Livingston" is listed and appraised at $15.00 in the Inventory, 1836, of the Ezra Ames estate. This is doubtless the portrait painted by

Ezra Ames, listed as No. 37, "Rev. Dr. John H. Livingston," [30 x 24 inches] in the handbill: *Catalogue Sale of Portraits*, 1842, in the Ezra Ames estate.
Unlocated.

[190] LIVINGSTON, JOHN HENRY (1746-1825). Isaac L. Kip, in a letter to Ezra Ames, dated New York, October 25th, 1817 (at NYHS), acknowledges receipt of a portrait of the "Rev. Dr. Livingston in good condition," and states "it has been viewed by many and the likeness approved it pleases me very well."
Unlocated.

[191] LIVINGSTON, DR., probably John Henry Livingston (1746-1825). A "Copy of a Portrait of Doctr Livingston" for Joseph Delaplaine is recorded in Account Book, October 14, 1818. The original was probably No. 190.
Unlocated.

[192] LIVINGSTON, MRS. PETER ROBERT, née Margaret Livingston (1738-1809), daughter of James Livingston and Maria (Kierstede) Livingston; married, 1758, Colonel Peter Robert Livingston, son of Robert Livingston (1708-1790) and Maria (Thong) Livingston (Cuyler Reynolds, *Genealogical and Family History of Southern New York and the Hudson River Valley*, New York, 1914, III, 1310-1311).
Description: 37 x 27½ inches, sight. Half-length, head to left.
Date: *c.* 1800.
Owner: Mrs. William Ten Broeck Mynderse, Scotia, N.Y., great-great-granddaughter of the sitter.
Photograph: FARL 30682.
Copy: There is a copy by F.R. Spencer owned by Gerald M. Livingston.
Examined by IFC.

[193] LIVINGSTON, ROBERT R. (1746-1813), Chancellor of New York State, 1777-1801; statesman and jurist (*DAB*).
Description: 36 x 28½ inches. Half-length, head to left. A copy after the portrait by Gilbert Stuart owned by Mr. John H. Livingston, Clermont, N.Y., 1926 (reproduced: Lawrence Park, *Gilbert Stuart*, 1926, III, 299).
Date: 1814-1815. A resolution recorded in the minutes of The Society for the Promotion of Useful Arts, now the AIHA, on March 10, 1814, requests its Committee of Fine Arts "to procure a copy of the best and most correct portrait of the late President of this Society, Robert R. Livingston"; in the subsequent minutes of February 28,

1815, a portrait of Robert R. Livingston is reported by the Committee of Fine Arts as "procured." Ames is not mentioned in these minutes but he had been elected chairman of the Committee of Fine Arts on March 2, 1814, which supports the assumption that he painted the copy procured; also, the copy is quite evidently the work of Ames.

Owner: AIHA.

Photograph: AIHA, and Peter A. Juley & Son, New York City; print at FARL.

Reproduction: *American Collector*, August 1947, p. 7.

Exhibition: "Parade of Patriots," Grand Central Art Galleries, New York City, May 21–June 5, 1942.

Examined by IFC and TB.

[194] LIVINGSTON, ROBERT R. (1746-1813). A portrait painted by Ezra Ames is listed as No. 59, "Chan. Robert R. Livingston, from Stuart," [30 x 24 inches] in the handbill: *Catalogue Sale of Portraits*, 1842, in the Ezra Ames estate.

Unlocated.

[195] LIVINGSTON, THOMAS. [Patron]. A portrait painted for him is recorded in Account Book, August 1810.

Unlocated.

[196] LOVETT, JOHN (1761-1818), lawyer, Representative from New York, U.S. Congress, 1813-1817(*BDAC*). A portrait of "Hon. John Lovett" is listed and appraised at $50.00 in the Inventory, 1836, of the Ezra Ames estate.

Unlocated.

[197] McGOURK, MRS. [Patron]. A portrait painted for her is recorded in Account Book, December 16, 1804.

Unlocated.

[198] MADISON, JAMES (1751-1836), fourth President of the United States. A portrait entitled "Head of Madison" is listed and appraised at $20.00 in the Inventory, 1836, of the Ezra Ames estate. This is doubtless the portrait painted by Ezra Ames listed as No. 4, "Head of James Madison, copy from G. Stuart," [30 x 24 inches] in the handbill: *Catalogue Sale of Portraits*, 1842, in the Ezra Ames estate.

Unlocated.

[198a] MADISON, MRS. JAMES, née Dolly Payne (1768-1849), widow of John Todd, Jr.; married James Madison in 1794 (*DAB*).

Description: 29 x 24 inches. Bust, head to left.
Date: *c*. 1810-1818.
Owners: (1) American Museum Collection; (2) purchased by Thomas J. Bryan, 1863; (3) presented to NYHS, 1867.
Photograph: NYHS.
Reproductions: C.W. Bowen, *Centennial Celebration of the Inauguration of George Washington*, 1892, facing p. 258, as by Rembrandt Peale; and Donald A. Shelley, *Catalogue of American Portraits in NYHS*, 1941, p. 207, as by Rembrandt Peale.
Attributions: Formerly to Rembrandt Peale; tentatively to Ezra Ames by Irwin F. Cortelyou, 1954. T. Bolton concurs. In the opinion of Mr. Charles Coleman Sellers, the portrait is not a typical Rembrandt Peale (letter to IFC, 4/25/54).
Note: This entry was inserted into the Catalogue too late for inclusion in the statistical table, p. 150, and the statistical summaries, p. 194.
Examined by IFC and TB.

[199] MALEY, JOHN (1743-1811), of Alsace, settled at Albany in 1768, and became a wealthy merchant (Marion H. Reynolds, *History and Descendants of John and Sarah Reynolds*, Brooklyn, 1924, p. 293); a director of the Bank of Albany, 1792 (Munsell, III, 1871, p. 94). Died November 1, 1811, aged 69 years (*Balance & State Journal*, I, n. s. November 5, 1811, p. 3.)
Description: 30 x 23¾ inches. Bust, head to right.
Date: 1812.
Inscription on back of canvas: "John Maley / Aged 69 years / E... Ames pt 1812" which shows that the portrait though probably started during the sitter's life was finished after his death.
Owners: (1) Marcus Tullius Reynolds, Albany; (2) bequeathed to Mr. Kenneth G. Reynolds, Loudonville, N.Y.
Photograph: FARL 15726.
Exhibition: AIHA 1934, lent by Marcus Tullius Reynolds.
Examined by IFC and TB.

[200] MALEY, MRS. JOHN, née Catharine Tremper (born 1748), daughter of Jacob W. Tremper of Kingston, N.Y. (Marion H. Reynolds, *History and Descendants of John and Sarah Reynolds*, Brooklyn, 1924, p. 293).
Description: 29¾ x 24 inches. Half-length, head to left.
Date: 1812.
Inscription on back of canvas: "Catharine Maley / Aged 64 years / pt 1812."
Owners: (1) Marcus Tullius Reynolds, Albany; (2) bequeathed to Mr. Kenneth G. Reynolds, Loudonville, N.Y.

Photograph: FARL 15727.
Exhibition: AIHA 1934, lent by Marcus Tullius Reynolds.
Examined by IFC and TB.

[201] MANCIUS, MR. An entry in Account Book, March 12, 1825, reads: "Mrs. Mancius D[ebto]r To Painting her Husbands Portrait."
Unlocated.

[202] MANCIUS, MRS. [Patron]. A copy of a portrait, probably meaning a replica, painted for her is recorded in Account Book, March 12, 1825.
Unlocated.

[203] MANDEVELL, MR., of Waterford. A portrait painted of him and for him is recorded in Account Book, October 1827. Possibly the name was "Mandeville." See No. 204.
Unlocated.

[204] MANDEVILLE, MRS. A portrait of "Mrs. Mandeville" is listed and appraised at $5.00 in the Inventory, 1836, of the Ezra Ames estate.
Unlocated.

[205] MARVIN, MRS. EMMA. A portrait of "Mrs Emma Marvin" is listed and appraised at $5.00 in the Inventory, 1836, of the Ezra Ames estate.
Unlocated.

[206] MATHER, ELIAS (1776-1843), son of Captain Elias Mather and Lucinda (Lee) Mather; married Cynthia Corning of Albany (information at FARL from the owner).
Description: 30 x 25 inches. Half-length, head to right. Rebacked.
Date: *c.* 1827.
Owner: Miss Gertrude Robinson Smith, New York City, great-granddaughter of the sitter.
Photograph: FARL 50616.
Attribution: The artist was unknown to the owner. Attributed to Ezra Ames by Irwin F. Cortelyou and T. Bolton, 1952, judging from a photograph.

[Illustrated p. 118]

[207] MEADS, JOHN (1777-1859), born in England (MS, DAR genealogy compiled for Mrs. Joseph Larocque, Sr.); formed a partnership in

cabinetmaking with William Alvord in 1827 in Albany (Reynolds, 466).

Description: 29 3/8 x 22 7/8 inches, sight. Bust, head to left.

Date: 1816. Doubtless one of "Two portraits" painted for John Meads recorded in Account Book, December 1816.

Owners: (1) Orlando Meads; (2) his daughter Mrs. J.G.K. Duer; (3) her daughter Mrs. Joseph Larocque, Sr.; (4) her son Joseph Larocque, Jr., Washington, D.C., great-great-grandson of the sitter.

Photograph: By Irwin F. Cortelyou.

Attribution: The artist was unknown to the owner. Attributed to Ezra Ames by Irwin F. Cortelyou, 1951. T. Bolton concurs, judging from a photograph.

Examined by IFC. [Illustrated p. 85]

[208] MEADS, MRS. JOHN, née Louisa Crane (born 1785), daughter of Elisha Crane and Ruth (Phelps) Crane; married John Meads, Albany, 1804 (MS DAR genealogy compiled for Mrs. Joseph Larocque, Sr.)

Description: 29¼ x 23 1/8 inches, sight. Half-length, head to right.

Date: 1816. Doubtless one of the "Two Portraits" painted for John Meads recorded in Account Book, December 1816.

Owners: (1) Orlando Meads; (2) his daughter Mrs. J.G.K. Duer; (3) her daughter Mrs. Joseph Larocque, Sr.; (4) her son Mr. Joseph Larocque, Jr., Washington, D.C., great-great-grandson of the sitter.

Photograph: By Irwin F. Cortelyou.

Exhibition: Doubtless the portrait listed in the *Catalogue of Albany's Bicentennial Loan Exhibition, Albany Academy, July 5 to July 24, 1886*, p. 118, as follows: " Ezra Ames (deceased) / Portrait of Mrs. Meads." No owner given.

Attribution: The artist was unknown to the owner. Attributed to Ezra Ames by Irwin F. Cortelyou, 1951. T. Bolton concurs, judging from a photograph.

Examined by IFC. [Illustrated pp. 85, 192]

[209] MEGS, MRS. A portrait painted of his mother for Dr. Megs is recorded in Account Book, May 10, 1824.

Unlocated.

[210] MELVILLE, MRS. ALLAN, née Maria Gansevoort (1791-1872), daughter of Peter Gansevoort and Catharine (Van Schaick) Gansevoort; married Allan Melville in 1914. Their son was Herman Melville the author of "Moby Dick." (Jay Leyda, *The Melville Log*, New York, 1951, I, xxvi, xxviii).

Description: 30 x 24 inches. Bust, head to left.
Date: Soon after her marriage in 1814, according to Mrs. Eleanor Melville Metcalf.
Owners: (1) Miss Helen Gansevoort Morewood; (2) sold by Knoedler & Company, 1939, to Dr. Henry Alexander Murray, Boston.
Photograph: FARL 32380.
Reproduction: Jay Leyda, *The Melville Log,* New York, 1951, II, plate II. [Illustrated p. 82]

[211] MELVILLE, MRS. ALLAN, née Maria Gansevoort (1791-1872).
Description: Panel 30 x 25 inches. Half-length, head to left.
Date: *c.* 1826.
Owners: (1) Thomas B. Clarke sale, 1919; (2) bought by E.E (?) Heckshe r for $700; (3) Thomas B. Clarke; (4) A.W. Mellon Educational and Charitable Trust, Washington, D.C.
Photograph: Print at FARL.
Reproductions: Catalogue of Thomas B. Clarke Sale, New York City, 1919 (24); Raymond M. Weaver, *Herman Melville, Mariner and Mystic,* New York, 1921, facing p. 64.
Exhibitions: Union League Club, New York City, 1921; Century Association, New York City, 1928; Philadelphia Museum, 1928. Exhibited in each case by Thomas B. Clarke.

[212] MILLS, MR. A portrait painted of the son of Mr. Mills for Mr. Mills is recorded in Account Book, October 16, 1827.
Unlocated.

[213] MITCHILL, SAMUEL LATHAM (1764-1831), scientist; Representative from New York, U.S. Congress, 1801-1804; Senator, U.S. Congress, 1804-1809, 1810-1813 (*BDAC*). A portrait of " Dr. Mitchill ... 'Kit-cat'" size is listed and appraised at $20.00 in the inventory, 1836, of the Ezra Ames estate. This is doubtless the portrait painted by Ezra Ames, listed as No. 23, "Hon. Samuel L. Mitchell, L.L.D.F.R.S.," [30 x 24 inches] in the handbill: *Catalogue Sale of Portraits,* 1842, in the Ezra Ames estate.
Unlocated.

[214] MORRIS, GOUVERNEUR (1752-1816), Member of the Continental Congress and of the Constitutional Convention; Minister to France, 1792-1794; Senator from New York, U.S. Congress, 1800-1803 (*DAB*). Vice-president, NYHS, 1810-1815, and its second president, 1816.

A portrait of "Gov. Morris ... 'Kit-cat' size" is listed and appraised at $20.00 in the Inventory, 1836, of the Ezra Ames estate.

This is doubtless the portrait painted by Ezra Ames, listed as No. 22, "Hon. Governeur [*sic*] Morris, 2 ft 4 by 3 ft" in the handbill: *Catalogue Sale of Portraits*, 1842, in the Ezra Ames estate. This was possibly a life portrait retained by the artist.
Unlocated.

[215] MORRIS, GOUVERNEUR (1752-1816).
Description: 35½ x 28 inches. Half-length, head to right. Almost identical with No. 216.
Date: 1817. Recorded in Account Book, June 21, 1817, as painted for Mrs. Morris. Probably a replica of either No. 214 or No. 216.
Owners: (1) The Morris Family; (2) Mr. Gouverneur Morris, great-grandson of the sitter, Coolidge P.O., New Mexico, on loan at Columbia University.
Photograph: Print at FARL.
Exhibitions: Loan Exhibition of Historical Portraits and Relics, Metropolitan Opera House, New York City, 1889, as by Thomas Sully, lent by the grandchildren of the sitter; George Washington Bicentennial Exhibition of Portraits, Corcoran Gallery of Art, Washington D.C., 1932, as by Thomas Sully, lent by the Morris family.
Attributions: To Thomas Sully in C.W. Bowen, *Centennial Celebration of the Inauguration of George Washington*, 1892, facing p. 160; and in E. Biddle and Mantle Fielding, *Life and Works of Thomas Sully*, Lancaster, 1921, No. 1279. To C.W. Peale, copy after Ames, in a note on FARL photomount. To Ezra Ames by William Sawitzky in *Catalogue, Descriptive and Critical of the Paintings and Miniatures in the Historical Society of Pennsylvania*, Philadelphia, 1942, p. 112.
Note: For details concerning the attribution and history of this portrait see pp. 159-163 herein.
Copy: There is a copy by Edward D. Marchant (at the State House, Philadelphia) either of this portrait or of No. 216.
Examined by IFC and TB.

[216] MORRIS, GOUVERNEUR (1752-1816).
Description: 36 x 28 inches. Half-length, head to right. Almost identical with No. 215.
Date: *c.* 1817, or earlier, possibly painted from life or possibly a replica of No. 214.
Owner: NYHS, presented by Stephen Van Rensselaer, November 11, 1817.
Photograph: NYHS: print at FARL.
Reproduction: Donald A. Shelley, *Catalogue of American Portraits in*

NYHS, p. 217.
Exhibition: 150th Anniversary of the Constitution of the U.S., Corcoran Gallery of Art, Washington, D.C., 1937-1938.
Note: For details concerning the history of this portrait see pp. 161-163 herein.
Copy: There is a copy by Edward D. Marchant (at the State House, Philadelphia) of this portrait or of No. 215.
Examined by IFC and TB. [Illustrated p. 160]

[217] MORRIS, GOUVERNEUR (1752-1816). A copy of a portrait of "Govn Morris" painted for Joseph Delaplaine is recorded in Account Book, October 14, 1818.
Unlocated.

[218] MOUNSEY, THOMAS. [Patron]. Tanner (*Albany Directory*, 1815). A portrait painted for him is recorded in Account Book, March 3, 1815.
Unlocated.

[219] MULFORD, EZEKIEL (1764-1811), tailor and farmer; husband of Sally Emes or Ames, sister of Ezra Ames. He was born at Easthampton, L.I.; married in 1791 at Staatsburg, N.Y.; moved to Watervliet Center, N.Y. (Mary L. Sutliff, *A Record of the Ancestors and Descendants of Betsy Mulford Sutliff*, Albany, 1897, p. 20).
Description: Bust, head to right.
Date: *c.* 1809-1810.
Owners: (1) Ezra Ames Mulford, Jr., grandson of the sitter, 1897; (2) said to have been bequeathed by him to his nephew [Orren], a son of his brother Delos W. Mulford (letter to IFC from Miss Mary L. Sutliff, 2/13/50).
Reproduction: Mary L. Sutliff, *A Record of the Ancestors and Descendants of Betsy Mulford Sutliff*, Albany, 1897, facing p. 15.
Unlocated.

[220] MULFORD, MRS. EZEKIEL, née Sally Emes or Ames (1773-1861), sister of Ezra Ames.
Description: 30½ x 24½ inches. Bust, head to right.
Date: *c.* 1804.
Owner: Miss Edith S. Wade, Cohoes, N.Y., great-great-grandniece of Ezra Ames.
Photograph: AIHA; print at FARL.
Reproduction: Mary L. Sutliff, *A Record of the Ancestors and Descendants of Betsy Mulford Sutliff*, Albany, 1897, facing p. 20.
Exhibition: AIHA 1946.
Examined by IFC and TB. [Illustrated p. 2]

[221] NEWMAN, HENRY (1780-1874), wool and leather merchant; a director of the Mechanics and Farmers' Bank, Albany (Catalogue, *Exhibition of American Portraits and Landscapes*, AIHA, June 2–September 20, 1936, No. 34, typewritten).
Description: 30 x 23¾ inches. Bust, head to left.
Date: 1810.
Inscription on back: "Henry Newman by Ezra Ames, 1810."
Owners: (1) Henry Newman; (2) John L. Newman; (3) Mr. Clarence E. Newman and Miss Evelyn Newman, grandchildren of the sitter; (4) Miss Evelyn Newman, Albany.
Photograph: FARL 16717.
Exhibitions: AIHA 1934, 1936, 1946.
Examined by IFC and TB. [Illustrated p. 57]

[222] NOTT, ELIPHALET (1773 1866), "in early life." Pastor of the First Presbyterian Church, Albany; president of Union College, Schenectady, N.Y., 1804-1866 (*DAB*). A portrait painted by Ezra Ames is listed as No. 40, "Rev. Dr. Eliphalet Nott in early life" [30 x 24 inches] in the handbill: *Catalogue Sale of Portraits*, 1842, in the Ezra Ames estate.
Unlocated.

[223] NOTT, ELIPHALET (1773-1866).
Description: 30x 24 inches. Bust, head to right. Restored and relined, at Museum of Fine Arts, Boston, 1931. Original of Nos. 224 and 225.
Date: 1820 or earlier; dated by the miniature copy, No. 486, which is dated by the engraving, No. 581.
Owners: Old South Association, Boston, presented by Mrs. Marie Weston Chapman about 1880; on permanent loan at Union College, Schenectady, N.Y., since 1931. Listed as No. 22 in *Index to Portraits and Paintings at Union College*, Union College, June 1950.
Photograph: Museum of Fine Arts, Boston; print at FARL.
Reproduction: *New York History*, April 1932, facing p. 168.
Note: A portrait of "Dr. Nott" listed as an "original" head and appraised at $30.00 in the Inventory, 1836, of the Ezra Ames estate is probably the portrait painted by Ezra Ames, listed as No. 38, "Rev. Dr. Eliphalet Nott," [30 x 24 inches] in the handbill: *Catalogue Sale of Portraits*, 1842, in the Ezra Ames estate. It is here assumed that both entries refer to the above portrait. For additional information see pp. 157-159 herein.
Examined by IFC. [Illustrated p. 156]

[224] NOTT, ELIPHALET (1773-1866).

Description: 29 x 23 7/8 inches. Bust, head to right. Replica of No. 223.
Date: Uncertain, but after its 1820 original, No. 223.
Owner: Union College, Schenectady, N.Y. Listed as No. 87 in *Index to Portraits and Paintings at Union College*, Union College, June 1950, where its authorship is questioned.
Note: A portrait of "Dr. Nott" listed and appraised at $15.00 in the Inventory, 1836, of the Ezra Ames estate, is probably the portrait painted by Ezra Ames listed as No. 39, " Rev. Dr. Eliphalet Nott (duplicate)," [30 x 24 inches], in the handbill: *Catalogue Sale of Portraits*, 1842, in the Ezra Ames estate. It is here assumed that these entries refer to the above-mentioned portrait. For additional discussion see p. 158 herein.
Examined by IFC.

[225] NOTT, ELIPHALET (1773-1866).
Description: 30 x 24 inches. Bust, head to right. Replica of No. 223.
Date: 1828. A portrait painted of Eliphalet Nott for Jesse W. Goodrich, E.H. Blatchford, and S.R. Wynkoop, members of the Class of 1829 at Union College, is recorded in Account Book, November 18, 1828.
Owner: Union College, Schenectady, N.Y. Listed as No. 84 in *Index to Portraits and Paintings at Union College*, Union College, June 1950.
Note: For additional information see pp. 158-159 herein.
Examined by IFC.

[226] OGDEN, AARON (1756-1839), so-called.
Description: Bust, head to right. Almost identical with the portrait of (?) DAVID CADY, No. 45.
Date: Uncertain.
Owner: Formerly owned by Mr. C.W. Lyon, dealer, New York City.
Note: This portrait was brought to the attention of the writers by notes on a photograph in the late William Sawitzky's file on Ezra Ames lent to them by Mrs. Sawitzky.
Unlocated.

[227] PADDOCK, PRISCILLA CLARK. According to family tradition she became the wife of Major Solomon Allen (1751-1821) (letter to IFC from Mr. J.W. Myer, Vice-Director, Museum of the City of New York, 2/13/51). However, see No. 5.
Description: 29¾ x 23¾ inches. Half length, head to left.
Date: *c.* 1800.

Owner: Museum of the City of New York, presented by Mrs. Frank Allen, 1932.
Photograph: FARL 18725.
Attribution: To Ezra Ames by the late William Sawitzky according to a note in his file on Ezra Ames lent to the writers by Mrs. William Sawitzky. The sitter was referred to in his notes as Jemima Paddock.
Examined by IFC and TB.

[228] PAIGE, JOHN KEYES (1788-1857), Clerk, New York State Supreme Court, 1823-1842; Mayor of Albany, April 1845–April 1846; married (1) 1817, Helen Maria Yates, daughter of Governor Joseph C. Yates, (2) 1833, Anna Maria Bloodgood, daughter of Francis Bloodgood; President of Canal Bank (Cuyler Reynolds, *Hudson-Mohawk Genealogical and Family Memoirs*, New York, 1911, II, 665-666; Reynolds, 566).
Description: 30 x 24 inches. Bust, head to left.
Date: 1826. Two portraits–"his portrait," presumably the above-mentioned, and "his Ladys Portrait" (No. 229)– are recorded for "John K. Page Esqr" in Account Book, October 1826.
Owners: (1) Joseph C.W. Paige; (2) his son Joseph Yates Paige; (3) Mrs. J. Lewi Donhauser, née Eliza Paige; (4) Dr. J. Lewi Donhauser, Loudonville, N.Y.
Photograph: FARL 15406.
Exhibition: AIHA 1946, lent by the estate of Eliza Paige Donhauser.
Attributions: Formerly to Francis Alexander; to Ezra Ames by Irwin F. Cortelyou and T. Bolton, 1950.
Examined by IFC and TB. [Illustrated p. 110]

[229] PAIGE, MRS. JOHN KEYES, née Helen Maria Yates (1797-1829), daughter of Governor Joseph C. Yates and Maria (Kane) Yates (Cuyler Reynolds, *Hudson-Mohawk Genealogical and Family Memoirs*, New York, 1911, II, p. 665; and information at FARL from Mrs. J. Lewi Donhauser, 1931).
Description: 30 x 24 inches. Bust, head to right.
Date: 1826. See No. 228.
Owners: (1) Joseph C.W. Paige; (2) his son Joseph Yates Paige; (3) Mrs. J. Lewi Donhauser, née Eliza Paige; (4) Dr. J. Lewi Donhauser, Loudonville, N.Y.
Photograph: FARL 15407.
Exhibition: AIHA 1946, lent by the estate of Eliza Paige Donhauser.
Attribution: The artist was unknown to the owner. Attributed to Ezra Ames by Miss Hope Mathewson (FARL), 1945.
Examined by IFC and TB. [Illustrated p. 110]

[230] PAIN, MRS. A portrait, "Kit Cat Size," painted of and for "Mrs Pain (Troy)" is recorded in Account Book, October 14, 1825.
Unlocated.

[231] PENNIMAN, MRS. OBADIAH, wife of Obadiah Penniman, bookseller (Jonathan Tenney, *New England in Albany*, Boston, 1883, p. 28). A portrait painted of "Mrs. Penniman" for Obadiah Penniman is recorded in Account Book, August 1811.
Unlocated.

[232] PENNIMAN, MR. S. A portrait painted of him and for him is recorded in Account Book, November 30, 1830.
Unlocated.

[233] PENNIMAN, MRS. S. Ames records the painting for Mr. S. Penniman of "his Ladys" portrait in Account Book, November 30, 1830.
Unlocated.

[234] PENNIMAN, SYLVANUS J. (*c.* 1781-1852), druggist in Albany, 1823-1832; in the oil business thereafter; died, aged 71, February 7, 1852 (Munsell, IV, 1853, pp. 349-351, biographical sketch). A portrait of him is listed and appraised at $5.00 in the Inventory, 1836, of the Ezra Ames estate. This is doubtless the portrait painted by Ezra Ames, listed as No. 33, "S.J. Penniman, Esq." [30 x 24 inches] in the handbill: *Catalogue Sale of Portraits*, 1842, in the Ezra Ames estate.
Unlocated.

[235] PHINNEY, ELIHU (1756-1813), Judge of Common Pleas, Otsego, N.Y. (*Albany Centinel*, November 29, 1799); Master, Otsego Lodge, No. 138, Cooperstown, N.Y.; Royal Arch Mason, Temple Chapter, No. 5, Albany (E.T. Reid, " Ezra Ames, Ne Plus Ultra," *The Royal Arch Mason*, March 1943, p. 10); established the *Otsego Herald* in April 1795 (Anna Chesebrough Wildey, *Genealogy of the Descendants of William Chesebrough of Boston, Rehoboth, Mass.*, New York, 1903, p. 343).
Description: 23¼ x 19¼ inches. Bust, head to right.
Date: Recorded in Account Book, December 23, 1799.
Owners: (1) Alexander S. Phinney; (2) Mrs. Alexander S. Phinney, Cooperstown, N.Y.
Photograph: NYSHA; print at FARL.
Attribution: The artist was unknown to the owner. Attributed to Ezra Ames by Irwin F. Cortelyou and T. Bolton, 1951, judging from a

photograph. The portrait was located with the help of Miss Janet R. MacFarlane, Curator, NYSHA.

[Illustrated p. 26]

[236] PLATT, C.Z., undoubtedly Charles Z. Platt. [Patron]. State Treasurer (*Albany Directory*, 1813) appointed February 10, 1813 (Reynolds, 412). A portrait painted for him is recorded in Account Book, October 3, 1810.
Unlocated.

[237] POMEROY, DR. [Patron]. A portrait painted for him is recorded in Account Book, October 29, 1810.
Unlocated.

[238] PORTER, GILES W. (1771-1859), of the firm of Giles W. and Ira Porter, merchant tailors (advertisement in *Albany Centinel*, February 22, 1799); elected director of the Mechanics and Farmers' Bank, 1812 (Mechanics and Farmers' Bank, *Span of a Century, 1811-1911;* and information from owner).
Description: 30 x 24 inches. Bust, head to left.
Date: *c.* 1816.
Owners: (1) Mrs. L.W. Stevens; a member of the Porter family; (2) given to Mrs. Rodney Procter, New York City, also a member of the Porter family.
Photograph: FARL 33575.
Note: The sitter cannot be Giles Porter (1723-1788) as stated by Mrs. L.W. Stevens in a letter to FARL, 1940, as the portrait is obviously by Ezra Ames and the dates of the first Giles are too early for Ames to have painted him. The present owner accepts the identity of the sitter to be Giles W. Porter (1771-1859).

[239] PORTER, IRA (died 1823). [Patron]. Merchant tailor; advertised in the *Albany Centinel*, February 22, 1799, and other issues, as of the firm of Giles W. and Ira Porter. Died at Ballston, N.Y., March 31, 1823 (Reynolds, p. 439). A portrait painted for him is recorded in Account Book, October 1813.
Unlocated.

[240] PORTER, IRA (died 1823). [Patron]. In the same Account Book entry of October 1813 which lists No. 239 above, Ira Porter is credited with "one portrait returned"—evidently a reference to a previous portrait painted for him by Ezra Ames.
Unlocated.

[241] POWERS, T. A portrait of "T. Powers" is listed and appraised at $5.00 in the Inventory, 1836, of the Ezra Ames estate.
Unlocated.

[242] PROUDFIT, MISS. A portrait of "Miss Proudfit" is listed and appraised at $5.00 in the Inventory, 1836, of the Ezra Ames estate.
Unlocated.

[243] PROVOST, GEORGE. Major in the British Army during the Revolution; became an American citizen after he married Anna Bogardus; their daughter married Samuel Dexter (letter at FARL from Mrs. Stanley McCormick 4/26/50).
Description: 31 x 24¾ inches. Bust, head to right. Relined.
Date: 1805. Two portraints painted for George Provost are mentioned in Account Book, October 29, 1805.
Owners: (1) Wirt Dexter, 1858; (2) Madame Samuel Dexter, 1890; (3) Mrs. Wirt Dexter, 1900; (4) Mrs. Stanley McCormick (Katharine Dexter) daughter of Wirt Dexter, Santa Barbara, California.
Photograph: FARL 39558.
Attribution: The artist was unknown to the owner. Attributed to Ezra Ames by Mrs. Thurman Rotan (FARL), 1950. [Illustrated p. 168]

[244] PROVOST, GEORGE. [Patron]. One of two portraits painted *for* George Provost mentioned in Account Book, October 29, 1805. The other has been identified as a portrait *of* George Provost. See No. 243.
Unlocated.

[245] RANDEL, JOHN, SR. A portrait painted by Ames of John Randel, Sr., brass founder (*Albany Directory*, 1818) for John Randel, Jr., surveyor (*Albany Directory*, 1818) is recorded in Account Book, April 5, 1813.
Unlocated.

[246] RANDEL, MRS. JOHN, SR., AND DAUGHTER. A portrait painted for John Randel [Jr.] of "his Mother & sister" is recorded in Account Book, September 9, 1812.
Unlocated.

[247] RATHBONE, child of Valentine W. Rathbone. A portrait painted by Ames for Valentine W. Rathbone, merchant (*Albany Directory*, 1813), of his child is recorded in Account Book, May 29, 1826.
Unlocated.

[248] REYNOLDS, MARCUS TULLIUS (1788-1864), son of Stephen Reynolds (1765-1833) and Lydia (Bartlett) Reynolds; Justice, New York Supreme Court; railroad president (Marion H. Reynolds, *The History and Descendants of John and Sarah Reynolds . . .* , Brooklyn, 1924, pp. 214-215).

Description: 30 x 23¾ inches. Bust, head to left.

Date: *c.* 1821.

Owners: (1) Marcus Tullius Reynolds, Albany, grandson of the sitter; (2) bequeathed to his nephew Mr. Kenneth G. Reynolds, Loudonville, N.Y., great-grandson of the sitter.

Photograph: FARL 15721.

Reproduction: Marion H. Reynolds, *The History and Descendants of John and Sarah Reynolds . . .* , Brooklyn, 1924, frontispiece.

Exhibitions: AIHA 1934, lent by Marcus Tullius Reynolds; AIHA 1946, lent by Mr. Kenneth G. Reynolds.

Examined by IFC and TB. [Illustrated p. 105]

[249] REYNOLDS, STEPHEN (1765-1833), physician of Schenectady, N.Y.; founder and president of the Washington Benevolent Society (Marion H. Reynolds, *The History and Descendants of John and Sarah Reynolds . . .* , Brooklyn, 1924, pp. 149-150).

Description: 29¾ x 24 inches. Bust, head to right.

Date: *c.* 1824.

Inscription on back of canvas: "Stephen Reynolds, M.D. Son of Stephen Reynolds and Rachel Denton. Born at Amenia City, Dutchess Co., N.Y., Sept. 1, 1765 (O.S.) [*sic*] Practised medicine at Minaville, N.Y., 1785-1832. Died at Amsterdam, N.Y., July 8, 1833. Portrait by Ames, c. 1824."

Owners: (1) Marcus Tullius Reynolds, Albany, great-grandson of the sitter; (2) bequesthed to his nephew Mr. Kenneth G. Reynolds, Loudonville, N.Y., great-great-grandson of the sitter.

Photograph: FARL 15724.

Reproduction: Marion H. Reynolds, *The History and Descendants of John and Sarah Reynolds . . .* , Brooklyn, 1924, facing p. 150.

Exhibitions: AIHA 1934, lent by Marcus Tullius Reynolds; AIHA 1946, lent by Mr. Kenneth G. Reynolds.

Examined by IFC and TB.

[250] REYNOLDS, MRS. STEPHEN, née Lydia Bartlett (1770-1843).

Description: 30 x 23½ inches. Bust, head to left.

Date: *c.* 1824.

Inscription on back of canvas: "Lydia Bartlett / born at Lebanon, Conn., Aug. 27, 1770, dau[ghter] of Nathaniel Bartlett and Mercy Otis / Married at Warrensburgh, Montgomery Co., N.Y. / Oct. 29,

1787, Stephen Reynolds of Minaville, Montgomery Co., N.Y. Died at Amsterdam, N.Y., Aug. 27, 1843. Portrait by Ames about 1824."
Owners: (1) Marcus Tullius Reynolds, Albany, great-grandson of the sitter; (2) bequeathed to his nephew Mr. Kenneth G. Reynolds, Loudonville, N.Y., great-great-grandson of the sitter.
Photograph: FARL 15725.
Reproduction: Marion H. Reynolds, *The History and Descendants of John and Sarah Reynolds* . . . , Brooklyn, 1924, facing p. 151.
Exhibitions: AIHA 1934, lent by Marcus Tullius Reynolds; AIHA 1946, lent by Mr. Kenneth G. Reynolds.
Examined by IFC and TB. [Illustrated p. 118]

[251] RICE, MRS. A portrait of "Mrs. Rice" is listed and appraised at $5.00 in the Inventory, 1836, of the Ezra Ames estate.
Unlocated.

[252] RICE, RANDEL. A "Portrait of Randel Rice, Deceased," painted for "Mr. Hatch (of Troy)," is recorded in Account Book, October 1827, and noted as " Returned."
Unlocated.

[253] RIVINGTON, MRS. A portrait of her for a Mrs. " Van Cleek," is recorded in Account Book, May 16, 1808.
Unlocated.

[254] RIVINGTON, JAMES (1724-1802), printer in London, and New York City; publisher of *The Royal Gazette* and the *Loyal Gazette* (*CAB*).
Description: 36¼ x 28¼ inches. Half length, head to left. This is a copy by Ames of a lost portrait by Stuart mentioned in the Inventory, 1836, of the Ezra Ames estate as "Portrait of Rivington by Stuart," which is doubtless the portrait listed as No. 60, "James Rivington, painted by G. Stuart, 2 feet 4 by 3 feet," in the handbill: *Catalogue Sale of Portraits*, 1842, in the Ezra Ames estate.
Date: 1806. The entry in Account Book, July 5, 1806, "Mr. Jas Rivington Dr" for a "Portrait & Frame" is here assumed to refer to this portrait.
Owner: NYHS, presented in 1858 by Dr. Samuel C. Ellis, grandson of Mrs. James Rivington and her first husband, Cornelius Van Horne.
Photograph: NYHS; print at FARL.
Reproduction: Donald A. Shelley, *Catalogue of American Portraits in NYHS*, 1941, p. 255.

Attribution: To Ezra Ames by Irwin F. Cortelyou and T. Bolton, 1951.
Note: For details concerning the attribution and history of this portrait see pp. 163-166 herein. The original portrait by Stuart is listed as No. 309 in the catalogue (copy at NYHS) of the 1866 sale of paintings owned by John Hunter of Pelham, N.Y.
Examined by IFC and TB. [Illustrated p. 165]

[255] ROBERTSON, WILLIAM. A portrait by Ezra Ames of "William Robertson" is listed without a number [30 x 24 inches] in the handbill: *Catalogue Sale of Portraits,* 1842, in the Ezra Ames estate.
Unlocated.

[256] ROCKWELL, MRS. SAMUEL, née Sarah Ann Spencer (1788-1863), born in Providence, R.I., died in Milledgeville, Georgia; married in Albany, N.Y., Samuel Rockwell of Greenbush, N.Y. (information at FARL from the owner).
Description: 29 x 24 inches. Repaired.
Date: 1818.
Inscription on back: "Sarah Ann Spencer Born / Nov. 2, 1788. / married Saml Rockwell Dec. 3rd 1808 / E. Ames pt. 1818."
Owners: (1) Charles Spencer Rockwell, great-grandson of the sitter; (2) his widow Mrs. Charles Spencer Rockwell, Savannah, Georgia.
Photograph: FARL 51245.
Note: Reported by Mrs. Thurman Rotan (FARL), 1953. Not examined by the writers.

[257] RODGERS, MRS., née Caroline Fairman. There are "2 portraits of Mrs. Rodgers (Caroline Fairman)" listed and appraised at $20.00 each, in the Inventory, 1836, of the Ezra Ames estate.
Unlocated.

[258] RODGERS, MRS., née Caroline Fairman. One of two portraits. See No. 257.
Unlocated.

[259] ROGERS, GEORGE (1814-1822), son of Judge Halsey Rogers and Deborah (Wing) Rogers (information at FARL from Mr. Walter Phelps Warren).
Description: 35 x 27 inches. Child, full-length standing, head to left.
Date: *c.* 1820.
Owner: Mrs. Thomas Vail, Troy, N.Y., grandniece of the sitter.
Photograph: FARL 21372.

Attribution: The artist was unknown to the owner. Attributed to Ezra Ames by Miss Hope Mathewson (FARL), 1936.

[260] ROMEYN, DIRCK (1744-1804), pastor Dutch Reformed Church, Schenectady, N.Y.; D.D., Queen's College now Rutgers University, 1789; a founder of Union College; appointed professor of theology by the General Synod of the Dutch Reformed Church, 1796 (*CAB*). A portrait painted of "Doctr Romeyn," presumably Dr. Dirck Romeyn, for "Doctr Romyne Beck" is recorded in Account Book, May 1814.
Unlocated.

[260a] ROOT, "GENERAL." Served in the War of 1812 (letter to IFC from Mr. William F. Whitehouse, 4/24/54).
Description: 28¾ x 23 inches. Bust, head to left.
Date: Uncertain.
Owner: Mr. William F. Whitehouse, Newport, R.I.
Photograph: FARL 10363.
Attribution: Formerly to Rembrandt Peale; to Ezra Ames by Miss Hope Mathewson (FARL), 1954.
Note: This entry was inserted into the Catalogue too late for inclusion in the statistical table, p. 150, and the statistical summaries, p. 194.

[261] RUGGLES, PHILO (1765-1829), lawyer; Surrogate of Dutchess County, 1813-1815; District Attorney of Dutchess County, 1819-1821; moved to New York City about 1826 (D.G. Brinton Thompson, *Ruggles of New York*, New York, 1946, pp. 17-20; *New York State Civil List for 1891*).
Description: 30 x 24 inches. Half-length, head to right.
Date: 1822.
Inscription on back: "Philo Ruggles, Aged 57. E. Ames pt 1822."
Owners: (1) Philo Ruggles; (2) Burnet Rathbone Ruggles, great-grandson of the sitter, to whom the portrait had descended in a straight line; (3) presented by him to Columbia University, New York City, in 1945.
Photograph: FARL 50791.
Examined by IFC and TB. [Illustrated p. 93]

[262] RUGGLES, MRS. PHILO, née Ellen Bulkley (1779-1865), daughter of Captain Joseph Bulkley and Ellen (Hubbell) Bulkley (D.G. Brinton Thompson, *Ruggles of New York*, New York, 1946, p. 18).
Description: 30 x 24 inches. Half-length, head to left.
Date: 1822.

Inscription on back: "Ellen Ruggles Aged 43 E. Ames pt 1822." Stencil on back: "Ellen Bulkeley [*sic*] / wife of Philo Ruggles."
Owners: (1) Philo Ruggles; (2) Burnet Rathbone Ruggles, great-grandson of the sitter, to whom it descended in a straight line; (3) presented by him to Columbia University, New York City, in 1945.
Photograph: FARL 50792.
Examined by IFC and TB. [Illustrated p. 93]

[263] RUSSELL, CALEB. [Patron]. Mason (*Albany Directory*, 1813). A portrait painted for him is recorded in Account Book, June 13, 1811.
Unlocated.

[264] SANGER, JUDGE. "Balance due" on a portrait of "Judge Sanger" is mentioned in the Inventory, 1836, of the Ezra Ames estate.
Unlocated.

[265] SCOVILLE, JOHN (1770-1816).
Description: 30 x 24 inches. Bust, head to left.
Date: *c*. 1810.
Inscription on a paper attached to the back of the portrait: "Portrait of John Scoville. Born Aug. 12, 1770. Died Aug. 17, 1816. Married Oct. 21, 1798. Ames, pinxt, Albany, N.Y."
Owners: (1) Mr. Frederick Betts; (2) inherited by his niece Mrs. Eliot Betts Hoadley, New York City; (3) her daughter Mrs. Ellery S. James, East Hampton, L.I.
Photograph: FARL 35157S.
Examined by IFC.

[266] SEDGWICK, THEODORE (1746-1813), judge of the Supreme Court of Massachusetts from 1802 until his death; father of Catharine Maria Sedgwick (*DAB*).
Description: 31½ x 25½ inches. Bust, head to left. Copy after the portrait by Gilbert Stuart reproduced in L. Park, *Gilbert Stuart*, 1926, IV, 456, now at the Museum of Fine Arts, Boston.
Date: Uncertain.
Owner: Old South Association, Boston, presented by Mrs. Marie Weston Chapman about 1880.
Photograph: FARL 31256.
Attributions: Listed in the Historical Records Survey, *American Portraits Found in Massachusetts*, 1939, II, 366, as a copy after Stuart by Horace Burdick. Attributed to Ezra Ames by Irwin F. Cortelyou and T. Bolton, 1951.

Note: A portrait of "Judge Sedgwick" is listed and appraised in the Inventory, 1836, of the Ezra Ames estate, in a group of ten portraits at an "average – each 10.00." This is doubtless the portrait painted by Ezra Ames, listed as No. 13, "Hon. Theodore Sedgwick, from Stuart" [30 x 24 inches] in the handbill: *Catalogue Sale of Portraits,* 1842, in the Ezra Ames estate. It is here assumed that these entries refer to the portrait at Old South Meeting House.
Examined by IFC and TB.

[267] SEDGWICK, THEODORE (1780-1839). [Patron]. Lawyer and writer; settled in Albany in 1803, where he formed a partnership with Harmanus Bleecker. His sister was Catharine Maria Sedgwick (*DAB*). A portrait painted for "T. Sedgewick, Esqr" is recorded in Account Book, July 13, 1809. Presumably the patron was Theodore Sedgwick (1780-1839), son of Theodore Sedgwick (1746-1813), judge of the Supreme Court of Massachusetts.
Unlocated.

[268] SEDGWICK, MR. [Patron]. A portrait painted for "Mr Sedgewick" is recorded in Account Book, March 18, 1813. Presumably this was Theodore Sedgwick (1780-1839).
Unlocated.

[269] SHAW, MISS. A portrait painted of his daughter for Henry Shaw is recorded in Account Book, September 3, 1831. The portrait was paid for in 1836 to Julius R. Ames, the artist's son and executor.
Unlocated.

[270] SHIPHERD, ZEBULON RUDD (1768-1841). [Patron]. Representative from New York, U.S. Congress, 1813-1815 (*BDAC*). Two portraits painted for "Zebulor Shepherd," obviously the abovementioned, are recorded in Account Book, April 17, 1805.
Unlocated.

[271] SHIPHERD, ZUBULON RUDD (1768-1841). [Patron]. One of two portraits painted for him. See No. 270.
Unlocated.

[272] SKINNER, DR. "Balance due" on a portrait of "Dr Skinner" is mentioned in the Inventory, 1836, of the Ezra Ames estate.
Unlocated.

[273] SMITH, EBENEZER. [Patron]. Merchant (*Albany Directory*, 1813). Two portraits painted for "E[b]enizer Smith" are recorded

in Account Book, November 1813.
Unlocated.

[274] SMITH, EBENEZER. [Patron]. One of two portraits painted for him. See No. 273.
Unlocated.

[275] SOLOMON, LEVI. A portrait painted of "her son Levy" for "Mrs Levy Solomans," probably Mrs. Solomon, widow of Levi Solomon (*Albany Directory*, 1823), is recorded in Account Book, February 6, 1829. A Levi Solomon established a tobacco factory at Albany in 1820 (Reynolds, 420).
Unlocated.

[276] SOLOMON, SAMUEL. A portrait painted of her son Samuel for "Mrs Levy Solomans," probably Mrs. Solomon, widow of Levi Solomon (*Albany Directory*, 1823), is recorded in Account Book, February 6, 1829. A Levi Solomon established a tobacco factory at Albany in 1820 (Reynolds, 420).
Unlocated.

[277] SOUTHWICK, SOLOMON (1773-1839), newspaper publisher; Postmaster of Albany (*DAB*); first president of the Mechanics and Farmers' Bank, Albany, 1811-1813 (Mechanics and Farmers' Bank, *Span of a Century, 1811-1911*, Albany).
Description: 30¾ x 24½ inches. Bust, head to right.
Date: Probably 1804. The portrait painted for Solomon Southwick recorded in Account Book, November 2, 1804, is probably this portrait.
Owner: Mechanics and Farmers' Bank, Albany.
Photograph: FARL 15439.
Reproduction: Mechanics and Farmers' Bank, *Span of a Century, 1811-1911*, Albany.
Exhibition: AIHA 1934.
Examined by IFC and TB.

[278] SOUTHWICK, SOLOMON (1773-1839). A charge against Solomon Southwick "To his Portrait for Delaplaine's N–Gallery" is recorded in Account Book, September 8, 1818.
Unlocated.

[279] SPAFFORD, HORATIO GATES, author of *Gazetteer of New York*, 1813; *Pocket Guide for Canals*, 1824; *New York Pocket Book*, 1825, etc. (S. Austin Allibone, *Critical Dictionary of English*

Literature and British and American Authors, 1870, II, p. 2189). A portrait of "H.G. Spafford ... 'Kit-cat size'" is listed and appraised at $20.00 in the Inventory, 1836, of the Ezra Ames estate.
Unlocated.

[280] SPENCER, MISS, daughter of Giles Spencer, trunk and bandbox maker (*Albany Directory*, 1816). A portrait painted of his daughter for Giles Spencer is recorded in Account Book, October 8, 1818.
Unlocated.

[281] SPENCER, MR. A portrait painted of "Judge Spencer['s] son," presumably one of the sons of Ambrose Spencer, for John Townsend who married Abby Spencer, daughter of Ambrose Spencer (Reynolds, [474]), is recorded in Account Book, March 19, 1822. Ambrose Spencer had three sons: (1) John Canfield Spencer (1788-1855), William Ambrose Spencer (1793-1854), and Theodore Spencer (1800-1870) (*CAB*).
Unlocated.

[282] SPENCER, MRS. A portrait of "Mrs. Spencer" is listed and appraised at $20.00 in the Inventory, 1836, of the Ezra Ames estate.
Unlocated.

[283] SPENCER ABBY (1790-1849), daughter of Ambrose Spencer and Laura (Canfield) Spencer; married John Townsend of Albany, July 7, 1810 (letter to IFC from Mrs. Edward L. Kernochan, 9/10/52).
Description: Three-quarter length, head to right. Body unfinished.
Date: *c.* 1810.
Photograph: Photostat at FARL, from photograph owned by Mrs. Edward L. Kernochan. Inscribed on back "Abby Spencer / wife of John Townsend / taken at the age of 20."
Attribution: To Ezra Ames by Irwin F. Cortelyou and T. Bolton, 1952, judging from the photograph.
Unlocated.

[284] SPENCER, AMBROSE (1765-1848), Chief Justice, New York State Supreme Court, 1819-1823; Mayor of Albany, 1824-1825; married, (1) 1784, Laura Canfield, who died, May 18, 1807; (2) December 12, 1807, Mary (Clinton) Norton, widow of Burrage Norton and sister of DeWitt Clinton; (3) 1809, her sister Catherine (Clinton) Norton, widow of Samuel Norton (*DAB; BDAC;* letter to IFC from Mrs. Edward L. Kernochan, 9/10/52).

Description: 36 x 27¼ inches. Half-length, head to right.
Date: 1811. A portrait for Ambrose Spencer, presumably of him, is recorded in Account Book, January 9, 1811, and is here assumed to be this portrait.
Owner: Mr. John De Witt Peltz, descendant of the sitter, New York City.
Photograph: FARL 17069.
Attribution: To Ezra Ames by William Sawitzky, 1942.
Examined by IFC and TB. [Illustrated p. 158]

[285] SPENCER, MRS. AMBROSE, née Mary Clinton (*c.* 1772-1808), who died September 4, 1808, at the age of 36 (Reynolds, 405); sister of DeWitt Clinton; widow of Burrage Norton (*DAB; BDAC*); later the second wife of Ambrose Spencer, married December 12, 1807 (H.W. Reynolds, *Notices of Marriages and Deaths* . . . , Poughkeepsie, N.Y., 1930, p. 97).
Description: 36 x 28 inches. Half-length, head to right.
Date: *c.* 1808.
Owners: (1) Mrs. John Townsend, stepdaughter of the sitter; (2) her daughter Mrs. Charles B. Lansing, Albany; (3) her son Gerrit Y. Lansing; (4) his nephew Mr. Charles B. Lansing, Chagrin Falls, Ohio.
Photograph: Photostat at FARL, from a photograph owned by Mrs. Edward L. Kernochan.
Exhibition: Doubtless either No. 226 or No. 227, both of which are listed as "Portrait of a sister of DeWitt Clinton . . . [owned by] Mrs. Charles B. Lansing," in the *Catalogue of Albany's Bicentennial Loan Exhibition at the Albany Academy, July 5 to July 24, 1886*, p. 123, artist unknown.
Note: Possibly the original of the "copy" (replica) painted for Alexander O. Spencer. See No. 286.

[286] SPENCER, MRS. [AMBROSE], probably Mary Clinton (Norton) Spencer (*c.* 1772-1808), the second wife of Judge Ambrose Spencer. The portrait is recorded in Account Book, 1822, as a "Copy of Judge Spencers Lady," and is charged to Alexander O. Spencer. He married Mary Norton, daughter of Mary Clinton (Norton) Spencer (letter to IFC from Mrs. Edward L. Kernochan, 8/3/52). Mary Clinton (Norton) Spencer is presumed, therefore, to be the sitter. This portrait is possibly a replica of No. 285.
Unlocated.

[287] SPENCER, MRS. AMBROSE, née Catherine Clinton (*c.* 1779-1837), who died August 20, 1837, at the age of 58 (Reynolds, 523);

sister of DeWitt Clinton; widow of Samuel Norton; later the third wife of Ambrose Spencer, married September 1809 (*DAB*).
Description: Panel, 29½ x 24 inches. Half-length, head to left.
Date: *c.* 1815.
Owners: (1) Mrs. John Townsend, stepdaughter of the sitter; (2) her daughter Mrs. Charles B. Lansing, Albany; (3) her granddaughter Mrs. Edward L. Kernochan, Colorado Springs, Colorado.
Photograph: Photostat at FARL, from a photograph owned by Mrs. Edward L. Kernochan.
Exhibition: Doubtless either No. 226 or No. 227, both of which are listed as "Portrait of a sister of DeWitt Clinton ... [owned by] Mrs. Charles B. Lansing," in the *Catalogue of Albany's Bicentennial Loan Exhibition at the Albany Academy, July 5 to July 24, 1886*, p. 123, artist unknown.

[288] SPENCER, GEORGE B. [Patron]. Merchant (*Albany Directory*, 1816). Son of Thomas Spencer and nephew of Spencer Stafford; partner in Staffords, Spencer & Company, Albany (Henry Marvin Benedict, *A Contribution to the Genealogy of the Stafford Family in America*, Albany, 1870, p. 11). Two portraits painted for him are recorded in Account Book, November 25, 1816.
Unlocated.

[289] SPENCER, GEORGE B. [Patron]. One of two portraits painted for him. See No. 288.
Unlocated.

[290] STAFFORD, SPENCER (1772-1844), merchant of Albany; a director of the Mechanics and Farmers' Bank; married (1) 1790, Dorothea Hallenbake, (2) 1807, Harriet Romeyn (Henry Marvin Benedict, *A Contribution to the Genealogy of the Stafford Family in America*, Albany, 1870, pp. 8-15).
Description: 29¾ x 23¾ inches. Bust, head to left.
Date: 1805, according to lithograph. See No. 582.
Owners: (1) Inherited by the sitter's son Samuel Spencer Stafford; (2) his daughter Mrs. W. Howard Gilder; (3) her daughter Miss Louise S. Gilder, New York City.
Photograph: FARL 18694.
Examined by IFC and TB. [Illustrated p. 45]

[291] STAFFORD, MRS. SPENCER, née Harriet Romeyn (1792-1849), the second wife of Spencer Stafford, married 1807 (information from the owner).
Description: 30 x 24 inches. Bust, head to right.
Date: 1807.

Inscription on back of canvas: "Harriet Stafford Daughter of Revd James V.C. Romeyn aged 15 years [the age possible added later] E. Ames pt 1807." Below the inscription is a brush sketch in black of Neptune seated on a turtle.
Owners: Inherited by the sitter's son, Samuel Spencer Stafford; (2) his daughter Mrs. W. Howard Gilder; (3)her daughter Miss Louise S. Gilder, New York City.
Photograph: FARL 18697.
Examined by IFC and TB. [Illustrated p. 45]

[292] STANSBURY, MRS. A portrait painted of his mother for the " Revd Arthur I (or J) Stansbary"—obviously the Arthur J. Stansbury (1781- *c.* 1845), clergyman (*CAB*), who was installed at the First Presbyterian Church, Albany, 1817 (Reynolds, 427)—is recorded in Account Book, December 28, 1818.
Unlocated.

[293] STANTON, GEORBE W., merchant (*Albany Directory*, 1821); vice-president of the Albany Exchange Bank, organized 1838 (Munsell, X, 1859, p. 286). A portrait painted of him and for him is recorded in Account Book, September 18, 1821.
Unlocated.

[294] STANTON, MRS. GEORGE W. A portrait painted of "his Lady" for George W. Stanton is recorded in Account Book, September 18, 1821.
Unlocated.

[295] STARR, MR. A portrait painted of his father for Chandler Starr, merchant (*Albany Directory*, 1826), is recorded in Account Book, October 9, 1826.
Unlocated.

[296] STEARNS, JOHN (1770-1848). [Patron]. Physician, born in Wilbraham, Massachusetts, died in New York City; moved to Albany in 1810, and to New York City in 1819; member of the State Senate, 1809-1813; first president of the New York Academy of Medicine (Jonathan Tenney, *New England in Albany*, Boston, 1883, p. 111). A portrait painted for him is recorded in Account Book, August 1813.
Unlocated.

[297] STEVENS, MRS., probably Mrs. John Cox Stevens, née Maria C. Livingston (born 1778), daughter of Robert C. Livingston, and cousin of Robert L. Livingston (born 1778) (Florence Van Rensse-

laer, *The Livingston Family in America*, New York, 1947, pp. 93, 117). A "Coppy" of a portrait of "Mrs. Stevens" painted for Robert L. Livingston is recorded in Account Book, December 5, 1814.
Unlocated.

[298] STEVENSON, JAMES. [Patron]. Receipt read over the telephone to Irwin F. Cortelyou by Miss Catharine Van Cortlandt Mathews, 4/1/51: "Mr. James Stevenson/To Painting a Portrait $25.00/To a Gilt Frame $21.00 / Received payment Albany, May 8, 1812 / E. Ames."
Unlocated.

[299] STEVENSON, JOHN (1734-1810), one of the first directors of the Bank of Albany (Reynolds, 381).
Description: 30 x 23¾ inches. Bust, head to right.
Date: Uncertain.
Owner: Mr. John De Witt Peltz, New York City, a descendant of the sitter.
Photograph: FARL 17065.
Examined by IFC and TB.

[300] STEVENSON, MRS. JOHN, née Magdalena Douw (1750-1817), daughter of Volckert Douw and Anna (de Peyster) Douw (information at FARL from Mr. John De Witt Peltz).
Description: 30 x 24 inches. Half-length, head to left. Similar to No. 301.
Date: Uncertain.
Owners: (1) Miss Anne S. Van Cortlandt, great-granddaughter of the sitter, and her nieces Miss Catharine Van Cortlandt Mathews and Mrs. William V. Mason; (2) after Miss Van Cortlandt's death in 1940, owned by the nieces, Croton-on-Hudson, N.Y.
Photograph: FARL 15589.
Examined by IFC.

[301] STEVENSON, MRS. JOHN, née Magdalena Douw (1750-1817).
Description: 29¾ x 23¾ inches. Half-length, head to left. Similar to No. 300.
Date: Uncertain.
Owner: Inherited by Mr. John De Witt Peltz, New York City, a descendant of the sitter.
Photograph: FARL 17066.
Examined by IFC and TB.

[302] STEWARD, GILBERT (born 1776, died some time before June 19, 1830), the name also spelled "Stewart," and "Stuart." Of

Orange County, N.Y., he established a grain business in Albany, returned to Orange County (G.A. Worth, *Random Recollections of Albany*, Albany, 1866, p. 47). In the firm of Charles Townsend and Gilbert Stewart (*Albany Register*, October 22, 1799). One of the first directors of the New York State Bank, Albany (Munsell, I, 1869, p. 293).
Description: 29¾ x 23½ inches. Bust, head to left.
Date: Uncertain.
Owners: (1) Inherited from the sitter's great-grandnephew Daniel Jackson Steward; (2) his daughter Miss Mary B. Steward, New York City.
Photograph: FARL 20674.
Attributions: To Jarvis by H.E. Dickson in his *John Wesley Jarvis*, New York, 1949, p. 366; to Ezra Ames by Irwin F. Cortelyou and T. Bolton, 1952.
Note: The artist records: "her Deceased Husbands Portrait" painted for Mrs. "Stuart" in Account Book, June 19, 1830. The portrait owned by Miss Mary B. Steward may be either the replica mentioned in the Account Book entry or an original portrait painted during the sitter's lifetime.
Examined by IFC and TB.

[302a] STEWARD, GILBERT (born 1776). This catalogue entry is made to list either the original portrait of Gilbert Steward or the replica painted after his death for Mrs. "Stuart," recorded in Account Book, June 19, 1830. See note to No. 302.
Unlocated.

[303] STEWARD, MRS. GILBERT, née Miss Smith (died some time after June 19, 1830, if she was the only wife of Gilbert Steward mentioned in the foregoing catalogue entry).
Description: 29½ x 23½ inches. Half-length, head to right.
Date: Uncertain. Possibly the portrait painted for "Mr. Gilbert Stewart" recorded in Account Book, May 8, 1812.
Owners: (1) Inherited by the sitter's great-grandnephew Daniel Jackson Steward; (2) his daughter Miss Mary B. Steward, New York City.
Photograph: FARL 20673.
Attributions: To Jarvis by H.E. Dickson in his *John Wesley Jarvis*, New York, 1949, p. 366; to Ezra Ames by Irwin F. Cortelyou and T. Bolton, 1952.
Examined by IFC and TB.

[304] STONE, WILLIAM LEETE (1792-1844), journalist and historian (*DAB*). A portrait of "Col. Stone" is listed and appraised at $5.00

in the Inventory, 1836, of the Ezra Ames estate. This is doubtless the portrait painted by Ezra Ames, listed as No. 30, "William L. Stone, Esq." [30 x 24 inches] in the handbill: *Catalogue Sale of Portraits*, 1842, in the Ezra Ames estate.
Unlocated.

[305] STRINGER, SAMUEL (1735-1817). [Patron]. Surgeon; born in Maryland; settled in Albany; Director of Hospitals and Chief Physician Northern Department, Continental Army, 1775-1777; Member of the Common Council, Albany, 1791, 1792; prominent in erecting first Masonic Lodge there (Reynolds, 380, 382, 427; and Francis B. Heitman, *Historical Register of Officers of the Continental Army during the War of the Revolution*, Washington, D.C., 1914, p. 525).
Unlocated.

[306] STRONG, JAMES. A portrait of "Mr Strong" is listed and appriased at $15.00 in the Inventory, 1836, of the Ezra Ames estate. This is doubtless the portrait painted by Ezra Ames, listed as No. 25, "Hon. James Strong, Esq.," [30 x 24 inches] in the handbill: *Catalogue Sale of Portraits*, 1842, in the Ezra Ames estate.
Unlocated.

[307] STRONG, THEODORE (1790-1869), mathematician; professor at Hamilton College, 1816-1826, and Rutgers College, 1827-1861; vice president of Rutgers College, 1839-1863 (*DAB*).
Description: 30 x 24 inches. Half-length, head to left.
Date: *c.* 1820.
Owners: (1) John C. Van Dyke, grandson of the sitter; (2) Theodore Strong, Jr., New Brunswick, N.J., great-grandson of the sitter.
Photograph: FARL 20833.
Attribution: To Ezra Ames by Miss Hope Mathewson (FARL), 1937.
Examined by IFC. [Illustrated p. 105]

[308] STUART, MRS. A portrait of Mrs. Stuart is listed and appraised at $5.00 in the Inventory, 1836, of the Ezra Ames estate.
Unlocated.

[309] SUTLIFF, MRS. HENRY, née Betsy Mulford (1792-1871), niece of Ezra Ames; daughter of Ezekiel Mulford and Sally (Emes) Mulford; married Henry Sutliff, 1815 (Mary L. Sutliff, *A Record of the Ancestors and the Descendants of Betsy Mulford Sutliff*, Albany, 1897, pp. 21, 33).
Description: Bust, head to left.

Date: *c.* 1810.

Owners: (1) Frank Beardsley Taylor, 1897, grandson of the sitter; (2) Mr. Walter H. Sutliff, Cleveland, Ohio, 1949, great-grandson of the sitter.

Reproduction: Mary L. Sutliff, *A Record of the Ancestors and the Descendants of Betsy Mulford Sutliff,* Albany, 1897, frontispiece.

[310] TALLMADGE, BENJAMIN (1754-1835), Colonel in the Continental Army; in charge of Major André during his imprisonment; Representative from Connecticut, U.S. Congress, 1801-1817 (*DAB; BDAC*) ; married (1) Mary Floyd, 1784, (2) Maria Hallett, 1808 (Arthur W. Talmadge, *The Talmadge, Tallmadge, and Talmage Genealogy,* New York, 1909, p. 88).

Description: *c.* 30 x 25 inches. Bust, head to right. Almost identical with the other portraits (Nos. 311 and 312) of Benjamin Tallmadge by Ezra Ames.*

Date: *c.* 1820-1826.

Owners: †(1) Mrs. John Bond Trevor, mother of the present owner; (2) Mr. John Bond Trevor, New York City, a great-great-grandson of the sitter.

Photograph: The owner; print at FARL.

Reproduction: Henry P. Johnston, *Memoir of Colonel Benjamin Tallmadge,* New York, 1904, facing p. 134, and there dated about 1820.

Examined by IFC and TB.

[311] TALLMADGE, BENJAMIN (1754-1835).

Description: 29 x 24 inches. Bust, head to right. Almost identical with the other portraits (Nos. 310 and 312) of Benjamin Tallmadge by Ezra Ames.*

Date: *c.* 1820-1826.

* "Copy of a Portrait of Col. Talmadge" and a "do — of his Lady" painted for "Cushman Esqr" of "Troy," N.Y., are recorded in Account Book, April 6, 1826. It is impossible to say to which of the three located portraits (Nos. 310-312) of Benjamin Tallmadge this entry refers; and whether or not it refers to the one located portrait (No. 313) of his wife. Presumably one of the listed portraits of Colonel Tallmadge and of Mrs. Tallmadge, respectively, is the original of which the others are replicas.

"Cushman Esqr" of "Troy" was doubtless John P. Cushman (1784-1848) of Troy. He married the eldest daughter of Benjamin Tallmadge (Henry Wyles Cushman, *A Historical and Biographical Genealogy of the Cushmans,* Boston, 1855, pp. 318-334; and *BDAC*). Ezra Ames also painted a portrait of John P. Cushman known only through the lithograph, No. 576.

†A portrait entitled "Gen Tallmadge" is listed and appraised at $5.00 in the Inventory, 1836, of the Ezra Ames estate and may be any one of the three portraits (Nos. 310-312) of Benjamin Tallmadge.

Owners: †(1) Estate of Elizabeth Delafield; (2) Litchfield Historical Society, Litchfield, Connecticut, since 1936.
Attribution: To Ezra Ames confirmed by Mr. James T. Flexner, 1952, by comparing the portrait with a photograph of No. 310.

[312] TALLMADGE, BENJAMIN (1754-1835).
Description: 29½ x 23 inches. Bust, head to right. Almost identical with the other portraits (Nos. 310 and 311) of Benjamin Tallmadge by Ezra Ames.*
Date: *c.* 1820-1826.
Owners: †(1) Mrs. Charles Peace Roy, Troy, N.Y.; (2) her daughter Mrs. Charles Lassell, Sandy Hook, Newtown, Connecticut.
Photograph: FARL 21327. [Illustrated p. 155]

[313] TALLMADGE, MRS. BENJAMIN, née Maria Hallett (died 1838), married Benjamin Tallmadge in 1808 (Arthur W. Talmadge, *The Talmadge, Tallmadge and Talmage Genealogy*, New York, 1909, pp. 87-88).
Description: 29½ x 23 inches. Half-length, head to left.
Date: *c.* 1820-1826.*
Owners: (1) Mrs. Charles Peace Roy, Troy, N.Y.; (2) her daughter Mrs. Charles Lassell, Sandy Hook, Newtown, Connecticut.
Photograph: FARL 21326. [Illustrated p. 155]

[314] TALLMADGE, MRS. BENJAMIN, née Maria Hallett. The original (presumably by Ezra Ames) or the "Copy" (replica) listed in the footnote.*
Unlocated.

[315] TALLMADGE, BENJAMIN (1792-1831), Lieutenant, U.S.N.; son of Colonel Benjamin Tallmadge (Arthur W. Talmadge, *The Talmadge,*

* "Copy of a Portrait of Col. Talmadge" and a "do – of his Lady" painted for "Cushman Esqr" of "Troy," N.Y., are recorded in Account Book, April 6, 1826. It is impossible to say to which of the three located portraits (Nos. 310-312) of Benjamin Tallmadge this entry refers; and whether or not it refers to the one located portrait (No. 313) of his wife. Presumably one of the listed portraits of Colonel Tallmadge and of Mrs. Tallmadge, respectively, is the original of which the others are replicas.

"Cushman Esqr" of "Troy" was doubtless John P. Cushman (1784-1848) of Troy. He married the eldest daughter of Benjamin Tallmadge (Henry Wyles Cushman, *A Historical and Biographical Genealogy of the Cushmans*, Boston, 1855, pp. 318-334; and *BDAC*). Ezra Ames also painted a portrait of John P. Cushman known only through the lithograph, No. 576.

†A portrait entitled "Gen Tallmadge" is listed and appraised at $5.00 in the Inventory, 1836, of the Ezra Ames estate and may be any one of the three portraits (Nos. 310-312) of Benjamin Tallmadge.

Tallmadge, and Talmage Genealogy, New York, 1909, p. 146).
Description: 30 x 25 inches. Bust, head to right.
Date: *c*. 1820-1826.
Owner: Mr. John Bond Trevor, New York City.
Photograph: The owner; print at FARL.
Examined by IFC and TB.

[316] TALLMADGE, MATTHIAS BURNETT (1774-1819), also spelled Mathias Burnet Talmadge; lawyer, studied under Chief Justice Spencer; Judge, U.S. District Court for New York (*CAB*).
Description: 36 x 28 inches. Half-length, head to left.
Date: *c*. 1815.
Owners: (1) The great-granddaughter of the sitter; (2) sold to Michael de Sherbinin, dealer, New York City; (3) Mabel Brady Garvan Collection, Yale University Art Gallery; on loan at the English Speaking Union, New York City.
Photograph: Yale University Art Gallery; print at FARL.
Reproduction: *Bulletin of the Associates in Fine Arts at Yale University*, June 1937, p. 25.
Note: This could not be the portrait charged to Matthias B. Tallmadge in Account Book, May 22, 1804, because the costume is that of 1810-1815.
Examined by IFC. [Illustrated p. 38]

[317] TALLMADGE, MATTHIAS B., obviously Matthias Burnett Tallmadge (1774-1819). [Patron]. A portrait painted for him is recorded in Account Book, May 22, 1804.
Unlocated.

[318] TALLMADGE, MRS. MATTHIAS BURNETT, née Elizabeth Clinton (1780-1825), daughter of George Clinton, Governor of New York State (Arthur W. Talmadge, *The Talmadge, Tallmadge, and Talmage Genealogy*, 1909, p. 130).
Description: 36 x 28 inches. Half-length, head to right.
Date: *c*. 1815.
Owners: (1) The great-granddaughter of the sitter; (2) sold to Michael de Sherbinin, dealer, New York City; (3) Mabel Brady Garvan Collection, Yale University Art Gallery, on loan at the English Speaking Union, New York City.
Photograph: Yale University Art Gallery; print at FARL.
Reproduction: *Bulletin of the Associates in Fine Arts at Yale University*, June 1937, p. 24.
Examined by IFC. [Illustrated p. 38]

[319] TAYLER, JOHN (1742-1829), became Lieutenant Governor of New York State in 1813 and served nine years; Acting Governor, 1817 (*National Cyclopaedia of American Biography*, XI, 1901, p. 349).
Description: 30½ x 24 inches. Bust, head to left. Relined. Very similar to No. 320.
Date: 1816.
Inscription on back of canvas (not visible in 1944 because of relining): "John Tayler Esqr. Born 4th July 1742 E. Ames pt 1816 –."
Owner: The Historical Society of the Tarrytowns; hanging at Philipse Castle Restoration, North Tarrytown, N.Y.
Photograph: FARL 32808.
Note: A portrait charged to John Tayler for Lynot Bloodgood, recorded in Account Book, August 28, 1816, may have been of John Tayler and if so, it is possibly the above-mentioned portrait. However, either this or No. 320 may be a replica of the other.
Examined by IFC and TB. [Illustrated p. 78]

[320] TAYLER, JOHN (1742-1829).
Description: 29¾ x 23¾ inches. Bust, head to left. Very similar to No. 319.
Date: Probably 1816. A portrait charged to John Tayler recorded in Account Book, August 14, 1816, may have been of John Tayler and if so, it is possibly this portrait, because this is a family portrait. However, either this or No. 319 may be a replica of the other.
Owners: (1) Mrs. John Tayler Cooper; (2) Mrs. Susan Cooper Krumbhaar; (3) her husband Louis Krumbhaar; (4) their son Dr. G. Douglas Krumbhaar; (5) sold by him, 1951, to Mr. Robert H. Palmiter, dealer, Bouckville, N.Y.
Exhibition: Listed in the *Catalogue of Albany's Bicentennial Loan Exhibition at the Albany Academy, July 5 to July 24, 1886,* lent by Mrs. John Tayler Cooper.
Examined by IFC.

[321] TAYLER, JOHN (1742-1829). [Patron]. A "Portrait for Delaplaine's Gallery" is charged to "Govnr Tayler" in Account Book, September 8, 1818. This was presumably a portrait of former Acting Governor John Tayler because Joseph Delaplaine of Philadelphia (*CAB*) was at that time collecting portraits for his Gallery of Distinguished Americans.
Unlocated.

[322] TAYLER, JOHN (1742-1829). "Govnr Taylors [*sic*] Portrait" is recorded without the name of a patron in Account Book, January 7, 1829.
Unlocated.

[323] TAYLER, JOHN (1742-1829). A portrait of "Gov Tayler" is listed and appraised at $20 in the Inventory, 1836, of the Ezra Ames estate. This is doubtless the portrait painted by Ezra Ames, listed as No. 12, "Hon John Taylor [*sic*] Lt. Gov.," [30 x 24 inches] in the handbill: *Catalogue Sale of Portraits*, 1842, in the Ezra Ames estate.
Unlocated.

[324] TEMPLE, MR. A "Portrait of his father" painted for "R[obert]. Temple Esqr (Rutland, Vermont)," is recorded in Account Book, 1821.
Unlocated.

[325] TEMPLE, ROBERT (1783-1834), lawyer; State Representative from Rutland County, Vermont, 1824-1826 (Leonard Deming, *Catalogue of the Principal Officers of Vermont as Connected with its Political History from 1778 to 1851*, Middlebury, Vt., 1851, p. 54).
Description: 30 x 24 inches. Half-length, head to left.
Date: 1816.
Inscription on stretcher: "R. S[probably T]emple; 1816, Ames of Albany."
Owners: (1) Presented by the sitter to his grandson who sold it in 1924 to (2) Ross H. Maynard, East Middlebury, Vt., who placed it in the (3) N. Acquavella Collection and Others, Sale, Anderson Galleries, N.Y., November 1926; sold to (4) John Levy, N.Y., for $325; sold to (5) M. Knoedler & Co., N.Y.
Photograph: Peter A. Juley; print at FARL.
Reproduction: Catalogue, N. Acquavella Collection and Others, Sale, New York, November 23-24, 1926, p. 17, with the name given as "R. Semple" obviously a mistake because the biography given in the catalogue fits in with the biography of Robert Temple. Furthermore: the name Semple does not appear in lists of the legislature at the period, whereas the name Robert Temple does, as noted above.
Unlocated.

[326] TEN BROECK, DIRCK (1765-1832). [Patron]. Son of Abraham Ten Broeck (1734-1810) (Emma Ten Broeck Runk, *The Ten Broeck Genealogy*, New York, 1897, pp. 59, 145); Member of the Common Council of Albany, 1793 (Reynolds, 384). A portrait painted for "Direct Ten Broek," obviously the above-mentioned, is recorded in Account Book, November 21, 1812.
Unlocated.

[327] TEN EYCK, HARMANUS (1749/50-1828), son of Jacob Hendrick

Ten Eyck and Annatje (Wendel [*sic*]) Ten Eyck of Albany; fire master and chimney viewer; married Margaret Bleecker, 1776 (*New York Genealogical and Biographical Record,* LXIII, July 1932, pp. 271, 281).

Description: 30 x 24¼ inches. Bust, head to right.

Date: *c.* 1807.

Owner: (1) Mrs. Burr Wendell, a descendant of the sitter; (2) her cousin Mrs. Arthur W. Butler, New York City.

Photograph: FARL 34914.

Examined by IFC and TB.

[328] TEN EYCK, HARMANUS (1749/50-1828). Listed in the *Catalogue of Albany's Bicentennial Loan Exhibition at the Albany Academy, July 5 to July 24, 1886,* pp. 114, 126, as follows: "Ezra Ames (deceased). / 68 Portrait of Harmanus Ten Eyck ... [owned by] J.H. Ten Eyck." The owner was probably Jacob H. Ten Eyck (1833-1898), the grandson of the sitter.

Unlocated, unless it is the portrait listed in entry No. 327. It might possibly be the portrait listed as No. 329, in which case it could not be No. 327.

[329] TEN EYCK, MR., probably Harmanus Ten Eyck (1749/50-1828). A copy of "his fathers portrait" painted for "J. Ten Eyck" is recorded in Account Book, July 24, 1829. Harmanus Ten Eyck had a son Jacob H. Ten Eyck (1781-1872), (*New York Genealogical and Biographical Record,* LXIII, July 1932, pp. 271, 281), who may have been the patron, "J. Ten Eyck."

Unlocated. Quite possibly the portrait listed in entry No. 328.

[330] THAYER, EUNICE. A portrait of "Eunice Thayer, unfin[ished]" is listed and appraised at $10.00 in the Inventory, 1836, of the Ezra Ames estate.

Unlocated.

[331] THOMPSON, SMITH (1768-1843), as a young man. Jurist, studied under James Kent; Secretary of the Navy, 1819-1823 (*DAB*). A portrait painted by Ezra Ames is listed as No. 20, "Judge Smith Thompson, in early life," [30 x 24 inches] in the handbill: *Catalogue Sale of Portraits,* 1842, in the Ezra Ames estate. Quite possibly the original or a replica of No. 332.

Unlocated.

[332] THOMPSON, SMITH (1768-1843). [Patron]. A portrait painted for him is recorded in Account Book, March 2, 1805. Quite possibly

the original or a replica of No. 331.
Unlocated.

[332a] THORN, JAMES VAN SLYCK (1788-1811), brother of Lieutenant Jonathan Thorn (No. 333); coxwain of the "Tonquin"; killed near Fort Astor, Oregon, by the Indians in June 1811 (Charles E. Thorn, *Heroic Life and Tragic Death of Lieutenant Jonathan Thorn, United States Navy*, New York, 1944, p. 23 [where the name is given as James Gilbert Thorn]; Florence Van Rensselaer, *The Livingston Family in America*, New York, 1949, p. 107).
Description: 34 x 26 inches. Half-length, head to left.
Date: Uncertain.
Owners: (1) Mrs. John French Ellis (Eliza Thorn); (2) her daughter Mrs. Theophilus Phillipse Hart; (3) her daughter Mrs. L. Casimir de Coppet; (4) her son Phillipse E.N. Greene; (5) his widow Mrs. Phillipse E.N. Greene, Rumson, N.J.
Photograph: By Irwin F. Cortelyou.
Attribution: The artist was unknown to the owner. Attributed to Ezra Ames by Irwin F. Cortelyou, 1953. T. Bolton concurs, judging from a photograph.
Examined by IFC.

[333] THORN, JONATHAN (1779-1811), Lieutenant, U.S.N.; born in Schenectady, N.Y.; son of Samuel [Gilbert] Thorn; was made Commandant of the New York Navy Yard in 1806; was furloughed from the Navy to command the "Tonquin," fitted out by John Jacob Astor to establish Fort Astor, later Astoria, Oregon, a fur trading post on the Columbia River. He was killed near there by the Indians in June 1811 (Thorn, Charles E., *Heroic Life and Tragic Death of Lieutenant Jonathan Thorn, United States Navy*, New York, 1944, pp. 3, 7, 16-23).
Description: 30¾ x 24½ inches. Bust, head to left. Almost identical with No. 333a except for the shape of the canvas, and is said to be the original of No. 333a.
Date: Either this portrait or No. 333a is doubtless the one referred to by the artist in Account Book, May 1806, as of "Leut Thorne Esqr."
Owners: (1) Mrs. John French Ellis (Eliza Thorn); (2) her daughter Mrs. Theophilus Phillipse Hart; (3) her daughter Mrs. L. Casimir de Coppet; (4) her son Phillipse E.N. Greene; (5) his son Phillipse E.N. Greene, Jr., Rumson, N.J.
Reproduction: Either this portrait or No. 333a in Thorn, *Heroic Life*, frontispiece.
Attribution: The artist was unknown to the owner. Attributed to Ezra Ames by Irwin F. Cortelyou, 1953.

Note: The portrait of Lt. Thorn mentioned in Account Book is stated herein page 44 as unidentified. Both portraits (Nos. 333 and 333a), either one of which may be the one listed in Account Book, were located after the text was in type.
Examined by IFC.

[333a] THORN, JONATHAN (1779-1811).
Description: 30 x 23½ inches, in oval frame. Bust, head to left. Almost identical with No. 333 except for the shape of the canvas, and is said by the owner to be a replica of No. 333.
Date: Either this portrait or No. 333 is doubtless the one referred to by the artist in Account Book, May 1806, as of "Leut Thorne Esqr."
Owners: (1) Mrs. John French Ellis (Eliza Thorn); (2) her daughter Mrs. Theophilus Phillipse Hart; (3) her daughter Mrs. L. Casimir de Coppet; (4) her son Phillipse E.N. Greene; (5) his widow Mrs. Phillipse E.N. Greene, Rumson, N.J.
Photograph: By Irwin F. Cortelyou.
Reproduction: Either this portrait or No. 333 in Thorn, *Heroic Life*, frontispiece.
Attribution: The artist was unknown to the owner. Attributed to Ezra Ames by Irwin F. Cortelyou, 1953. T. Bolton concurs, judging from a photograph.
Note: The portrait of Lt. Thorn mentioned in Account Book is stated herein page 44 as unidentified. Both portraits (Nos. 333 and 333a), either one of which may be the one listed in Account Book, were located after the text was in type.
Examined by IFC.

[334] THORP, AARON, partner in Thorp & Sprague, stage proprietors (*Albany Directory*, 1828).
Description: 30 x 24 inches. Half-length, head to right. Restored, 1942.
Date: 1826. Three portraits painted for Aaron Thorp, (1) of himself, (2) of his wife, and (3) of their "Child" [Frances Mary Thorp], are recorded in Account Book, May 1826.
Owners: (1) Miss Frances K. Van Vechten, Castleton-on-Hudson, N.Y., niece of the sitter; (2) inherited by her cousins, Mrs. H.B. Robie and Miss Eleanor B. Weir, New York City; (3) Miss Eleanor B. Weir.
Photograph: FARL 30368.
Attribution: At the time the portrait was photographed in 1937 the artist was unknown to the owner. Attributed to Ezra Ames by William Sawitzky, 1942, judging from a photograph. Attribution confirmed by entry in Account Book, May 1826.
Examined by IFC and TB. [Illustrated p. 117]

[335] THORP, MRS. AARON, née Mary Dunn (information at FARL from Miss Frances K. Van Vechten, 1937).
Description: 30 x 24 inches. Half-length, head to left. Restored, 1942.
Date: 1826.
Owners: (1) Miss Frances K. Van Vechten, Castleton-on-Hudson, N.Y., niece of the sitter; (2) inherited by her cousins, Mrs. H.B. Robie and Miss Eleanor B. Weir, New York City; (3) Miss Eleanor B. Weir.
Photograph: FARL 30369.
Attribution: At the time the portrait was photographed in 1937 the artist was unknown to the owner. Attributed to Ezra Ames by William Sawitzky, 1942, judging from a photograph. Attribution confirmed by entry in Account Book, May 1826.
Examined by IFC and TB. [Illustrated p. 117]

[336] THORP, FRANCES MARY, daughter of Aaron Thorp and Mary (Dunn) Thorp.
Description: 30 x 24 inches. Half-length, standing, head to right.
Date: 1826.
Owners: (1) Miss Frances K. Van Vechten, Castleton-on-Hudson, N.Y., cousin of the sitter; (2) inherited by her cousins, Mrs. H.B. Robie and Miss Eleanor B. Weir, New York City; (3) Miss Eleanor B. Weir.
Photograph: FARL 30370.
Attribution: To Ezra Ames by Miss Hope Mathewson (FARL), 1937. Attribution confirmed by entry in Account Book, May 1826.
Examined by IFC and TB.

[337] THROOP, ENOS THOMPSON (1784-1874), Lieutenant Governor of New York State, 1828; Governor, 1830-1832 (*DAB*).
Description: 51½ x 39½ inches, sight. Half-length standing, head to left.
Date: *c*. 1829–.
Owner: The City of Albany, on permanent loan at AIHA.
Photograph: AIHA; print at FARL.
Exhibition: AIHA 1946.
Note: This is one of the series of "Portraits of Seven Governors of New York," by Ezra Ames, at AIHA.
Examined by IFC and TB. [Illustrated p. 131]

[338] THROOP, ENOS THOMPSON (1784-1874). A portrait painted by Ezra Ames is listed as No. 9, "Enos T. Throop," [30 x 24 inches] in the handbill: *Catalogue Sale of Portraits*, 1842, in the Ezra Ames estate.
Unlocated.

[339] TIBBITS, GEORGE (1763-1849). Representative from New York, U.S. Congress, 1803-1805; Mayor of Troy, N.Y., 1830-1836 (*BDAC*).
Description: 29½ x 23¾ inches, sight. Bust, head to left.
Date: *c.* 1833.
Owners: (1) Reverend John Knox Tibbits, Hoosick, N.Y., (hanging in the house of his sister Miss Sarah Bleecker Tibbits, Troy, N.Y., 1936); presented by him to his son (2) George Dudley Tibbits, Washington, D.C., 1950.
Photograph: FARL 21308. [Illustrated p. 122]

[340] TIBBITS, MRS. GEORGE, née Sarah Noyes (1767-1846), married 1789 (information at FARL from Miss Sarah Bleecker Tibbits, Troy, N.Y., 1936).
Description: 29½ x 23½ inches, sight. Half-length, head to right.
Date: *c.* 1833.
Owners: Same as for No. 339.
Photograph: FARL 21309. [Illustrated p. 122]

[341] TOMPKINS, DANIEL D. (1774-1825), fourth Governor of New York State, 1807-1817; Vice-President of the United States, 1817-1825 (*DAB*).
Description: 52 x 41¼ inches, sight. Half-length standing, head to left. Rather similar to No. 342.
Date: *c.* 1815–.
Owner: The City of Albany, on permanent loan at AIHA.
Photograph: AIHA; print at FARL.
Exhibition: AIHA 1946.
Note: This is one of the series of "Portraits of Seven Governors of New York," by Ezra Ames, at AIHA.
Examined by IFC and TB. [Illustrated p. 141]

[342] TOMPKINS, DANIEL D. (1774-1825).
Description: 52½ x 40½, sight. Half-length standing, head to left. Rather similar to No. 341.
Date: *c.* 1815–.
Owner: Columbia University, New York City.
Photograph: FARL 50802.
Reproduction: Cuyler Reynolds, *Genealogical and Family History of Southern New York and the Hudson River Valley*, New York, 1914, II, facing p. 876.
Attribution: The artist was unknown to the owner. Attributed to Ezra Ames by Irwin F. Cortelyou and T. Bolton, 1952.
Examined by TB.

[343] TOMPKINS, DANIEL D. (1774-1825).
Description: 30 x 23¾ inches. Bust, head to right.
Date: Uncertain.
Owner: Dr. Haven Emerson, New York City, a descendant of the sitter.
Photograph: FARL 34985s.
Attributions: Formerly to James Frothingham by Mrs. Laurence B. Barretto (FARL); to Ezra Ames by Irwin F. Cortelyou and T. Bolton, 1952, judging from a photograph.

[343a] TOMPKINS, DANIEL D. (1774-1825).
Description: 30 5/8 x 24 5/8 inches. Bust, head to left. Retouched and varnished in 1945 and 1947.
Date: Uncertain.
Owners: Accessioned June 12, 1946 at the Staten Island Institute of Arts and Sciences, St. George, Staten Island, N.Y. It had belonged to the Institute for many years before that date.
Photograph: Staten Island Institute of Arts and Sciences.
Attribution: The artist was unknown to the owner. Attributed to Ezra Ames by Charles E. Baker, 1953, judging from a photograph.
Examined by IFC.

[344] TOMPKINS, MRS. DANIEL D., née Hannah Minthorne (1781-1829), daughter of Mangle Minthorne; married Daniel D. Tompkins in 1798 (Robert A. and Clare F. Tompkins, *The Tomkins-Tompkins Genealogy*, 1942, p. 74).
Description: 53 x 41 inches. Three-quarter length, head to right.
Date: *c.* 1809.
Owner: Gift to NYHS from the family of Mrs. Daniel D. Tompkins, 1951.
Photograph: NYHS 1932-c.
Attribution: The artist was unknown to the owner. Attributed to Ezra Ames by Irwin F. Cortelyou, 1952. T. Bolton concurs.
Examined by IFC and TB. [Illustrated p. 47]

[345] TOMPKINS, SARAH ANN (1805-1845), as a child; daughter of Governor Daniel D. Tompkins; married Archibald Gordon (Robert A. and Clare F. Tompkins, *The Tomkins-Tompkins Genealogy*, 1942, p. 160).
Description: 31½ x 25 inches. Full-length, seated, with doll.
Date: 1809. The sitter is similar to her portrait in the Tompkins family group portrait (No. 346) which is dated 1809.
Owners: (1) Mrs. Edith G. Halpert; New York City; (2) sold to Shelburne Museum, Shelburne, Vermont.
Photograph: Downtown Gallery; print at FARL.

Attribution: To Ezra Ames by Irwin F. Cortelyou, 1951, judging from a photograph. T. Bolton concurs, also judging from a photograph.
Note: The identification of the sitter was made by Irwin F. Cortelyou from the Tompkins family group picture by Ezra Ames (No. 346).

[346] TOMPKINS CHILDREN. The children of Governor Daniel D. Tompkins, a group portrait including likenesses of the following: Arietta, aged 10; Griffen, aged 8; Hannah, aged 6; Sarah Ann, aged 4; Minthorne, aged 3 (inscription on the back of the canvas).
Description: 39 5/8 x 51½ inches, sight. Oblong canvas.
Date: 1809.
Inscription on back: "E. Ames, Pt. 1809"; and names and ages of children as given above.
Owners: (1) Mrs. Willard Tompkins, presented by her to (2) Staten Island Institute of Arts and Sciences, St. George, Staten Island, N.Y., 1944.
Photograph: FARL 40519, taken and presented by Irwin F. Cortelyou.
Examined by IFC. [Illustrated p. 46]

[347] TOWNSEND, ABSALOM (1786-1861), son of Absalom Townsend and Helena (De Kay) Townsend; married Elizabeth Lansing (notes of Major Merle-Smith); junior counsellor (*Albany Directory*, 1815).
Description: 30 x 24 inches. Bust, head to left.
Date: 1816. The portrait painted for Absalom Townsend recorded in Account Book, March 13, 1816, is presumably this portrait.
Owners: (1) Inherited by Major Van Santvoord Merle-Smith, Oyster Bay, L.I., great-grandson of the sitter; (2) bequeathed to Mrs. Van Santvoord Merle-Smith.
Photograph: FARL 20165.
Attribution: The artist was unknown to the owner. Attributed to Ezra Ames by Miss Hope Mathewson (FARL), 1935.
Examined by IFC and TB. [Illustrated p. 152]

[348] TOWNSEND, MRS. ABSALOM, née Helena De Kay (1746-1814), mother of Absalom Townsend (1786-1861); daughter of Colonel Thomas De Kay (letter at FARL from Mrs. Eben Erskin Olcott, New York City, 1/13/33).
Description: 29¼ x 23 1/8 inches. Bust, head to left.
Date: *c*. 1813.
Owners: Inherited by (1) Mrs. Eben Erskin Olcott, New York City, great-granddaughter of the sitter; (2) bequeathed to her daughter Miss Katharine Olcott, Pleasantville, N.Y.
Photograph: FARL 18608.
Attribution: The artist was unknown to the owner. Attributed to Ezra

Mrs. Chas. Townsend Olcott, Wilton, Conn. 1971

Ames by Irwin F. Cortelyou, 1951, judging from a photograph. T. Bolton concurs, also judging from a photograph.

[349] TOWNSEND, CAPTAIN SOLOMON. [Patron]. Possibly Solomon D. Townsend, merchant (*Albany Directory*, 1815) who died April 25, 1834 (Munsell, IX, 1858, p. 282). The balance due on a portrait painted for him is recorded in Account Book, November 7, 1808.
Unlocated.

[350] TROTTER, JOHN, merchant (*Albany Directory*, 1823). A portrait painted of him and for him is recorded in Account Book, June 20, 1829.
Unlocated.

[351] TROTTER, son of John Trotter. A portrait painted of his son for John Trotter is recorded in Account Book, June 20, 1829.
Unlocated.

[352] TROTTER, MATHEW (died 1830). [Patron]. Lieutenant and Quartermaster during the Revolution; General; river captain; merchant (Reynolds, pp. 401–, 488; and Berthold Fernow, *Documents Relative to the Colonial History of the State of New York*, XV, 1887, pp. 258, 260, 539). A portrait painted for him is recorded in Account Book, December 13, 1811.
Unlocated.

[353] TULLY, WILLIAM, JR., (1785-1859), physician; president, Vermont Academy of Medicine; moved to Albany in 1826, and was an associate of Dr. Alden March; moved to New Haven in 1829 (*CAB*).
Description: 30¼ x 23¾ inches. Bust, head to right.
Date: 1826.
Owner: Presented to Yale University in 1906 by Miss Elizabeth Tully, a daughter of the sitter.
Photograph: Yale University Art Gallery.
Examined by IFC and TB. [Illustrated p. 113]

[354] UNIDENTIFIED MAN. A "Portrait of a Youth" by [Ezra] Ames is listed as No. 327 in the catalogue *First Annual Exhibition of the Society of Artists of the United States, Philadelphia,* 1811, p. 16. This might have been the portrait of Henry Jones (No. 163 herein) now at NYHS. If not, the portrait is still:
Unlocated.

[355] UNIDENTIFIED MAN. A "portrait of a Gentleman" by [Ezra] Ames is listed as No. 24 in the catalogue *Second Annual Exhibition*

of the Society of Artists of the United States and the Pennsylvania Academy, 1812, p. 17.
Unlocated.

[356] UNIDENTIFIED MAN.
Description: 30 x 23 inches, sight. Bust, head to left.
Date: *c*. 1805.
Owner: Purchased in Philadelphia by Mr. and Mrs. Harry A. Jeffcott, Middletown, Delaware.
Photograph: Print at FARL.
Attribution: To Ezra Ames by Miss Hope Mathewson (FARL), 1952.

[357] UNIDENTIFIED MAN. Lived in Albany, probably a member of the McHarg or Ten Broeck families (information at FARL from Mrs. W. Harman Brown, 10/11/39).
Description: 30 x 24 inches. Bust, head to left.
Date: *c*. 1805.
Owners: (1) Mrs. Ten Broeck, Albany, who had no direct heirs; (2) Mr. and Mrs. W. Harman Brown (the latter a connection by marriage of Mrs. Ten Broeck), Flushing, N.Y.; (3) sold after Mrs. Brown's death and acquired from an intermediary dealer by Penrose and Edgette, Inc., dealers, New York City; (4) sold to Mrs. J. Amory Haskell, New York City and Red Bank, N.J.; (5) sold at Mrs. J. Amory Haskell Sale, Parke-Bernet Galleries, New York City, April 26-29, 1944, p. 188 in catalogue.
Photograph: FARL 32794.
Attribution: To Ezra Ames by Irwin F. Cortelyou and T. Bolton, 1952, judging from a photograph.
Unlocated.

[358] UNIDENTIFIED MAN. Lived in Albany, probably a member of the McHarg, Ten Broeck, or Delavan families (information at FARL from Mr. and Mrs. W. Harman Brown, 10/11/39).
Description: 30 x 24 inches. Bust, head to right.
Date: *c*. 1815.
Owners: Same as for No. 357.
Photograph: FARL 32795.
Attribution: To Ezra Ames by Miss Hope Mathewson (FARL), 1939.
Note: If the sitter is a Delavan, this portrait, or the portrait listed below as "Unidentified Woman, Called 'Lady in Red Shawl'" (No. 365) could be the portrait painted for "Mr Dela Van" recorded in Account Book, February 1815 (No, 91 herein).
Unlocated.

[359] UNIDENTIFIED MAN. Lived in Albany, probably a member of the McHarg or Ten Broeck families (information at FARL from Mrs. W. Harman Brown, 10/11/39).
Description: 30 x 24 inches. Bust, head to left.
Date: *c*. 1810. The head and costume are similar to the head and costume in No. 163, which is dated 1810.
Inscription on back of canvas: "Hariette D. McHarg," probably a former owner.
Owners: (1) Probably Hariette D. McHarg; (2) Mrs. Ten Broeck, Albany, who had no direct heirs; (3) Mr. and Mrs. W. Harman Brown (the latter a connection by marriage of Mrs. Ten Broeck), Flushing, N.Y.; (4) sold after Mrs. Brown's death and acquired from an intermediary dealer by Penrose and Edgette, Inc., dealers, New York City; (5) sold to Mrs. J. Amory Haskell, New York City and Red Bank, N.J.; (6) sold at Mrs. J. Amory Haskell Sale, Parke-Bernet Galleries, New York City, May 17-20, 1944, p. 188 in catalogue; (7) bought back by Miss Helena Penrose, dealer, New York City.
Photograph: FARL 32793.
Attribution: To Ezra Ames by Miss Hope Mathewson (FARL), 1939,
Examined by IFC.

[360] UNIDENTIFIED MAN.
Description: 35½ x 28 inches, sight. Half-length, head to right.
Date: Uncertain.
Owner: The Old South Association, Boston, presented by Mrs. Marie Weston Chapman about 1880.
Photograph: FARL 31248.
Attribution: To Ezra Ames by Miss Hope Mathewson (FARL), 1941.
Note: Said to be a copy after an original by Henry Inman (letters to IFC from Mr. Charles G. Loring, 1/29/51). Listed in the Massachusetts Historical Records Survey, *American Portraits Found in Massachusetts*, Boston, 1939, II, 492, as by an unknown artist, with the measurements there given incorrectly as 30 x 25 inches. The writers think that it is more likely a copy after a portrait by Stuart than a copy after a portrait by Inman.
Examined by IFC and TB.

[361] UNIDENTIFIED MAN. Formerly called "John Jay."
Description: 36 x 28 inches. Half-length, head to right.
Date: *c*. 1810.
Owners: (1) Mrs. Frank Sullivan Smith who willed it to (2) the New York Genealogical and Biographical Society, 1924, as of "John Jay, said to have been painted in England by an artist named Hughes."

Photograph: FARL 39708 from a photograph.
Attribution: To Ezra Ames by Michael de Sherbinin, in " Ezra Ames' (1768-1836) 'Portrait of a Gentleman,' Who is it?" in *The New York Genealogical and Biographical Record*, LXXII, 1941, p. 32, with a reproduction of the portrait. It is there stated that William Sawitzky "fully concurs" in this attribution.
Examined by IFC.

[362] UNIDENTIFIED MAN. Formerly called "Gilbert Stuart."
Description: 30 x 24 inches. Bust, head to left.
Date: *c*. 1810.
Owners: (1) F. Bulkeley Smith, Worcester, Mass.; (2) bought for $500.00 by G.S. Parker at F. Bulkeley Smith sale, New York City, April 22-23, 1920 (*American Art Annual*, 1920, XVII, 298).
Identity of sitter: The late Charles Henry Hart considered this to be a portrait of Gilbert Stuart by James Frothingham painted about 1810, that is, when Stuart was about fifty-five years old (Catalogue, F.B. Smith Sale, Plaza Hotel, New York City, 1920). However, a portrait of Stuart painted by C.W. Peale about 1795 when Stuart was about forty years old, owned by NYHS, shows him as an older man than the sitter in this portrait.
Photograph: FARL 40125.
Attributions: Formerly to James Frothingham by C.H. Hart; to Ezra Ames by Irwin F. Cortelyou and T. Bolton, 1951, judging from a photograph.
Unlocated.

[363] UNIDENTIFIED MOTHER AND CHILD. A painting by Ezra Ames is listed as No. 46, " Group. Likeness of a mother and child," [30 x 24 inches] in the handbill: *Catalogue Sale of Portraits*, 1842, in the Ezra Ames estate.
Unlocated.

[364] UNIDENTIFIED WOMAN.
Description: 30 x 24 inches. Half-length, head to right. Relined.
Date: *c*. 1815.
Attribution: To Ezra Ames by William Sawitzky. This portrait was brought to the attention of the writers by a photograph (with information given above except for the date) found in the late William Sawtizky's file on Ezra Ames lent to them by Mrs. William Sawitzky.
Unlocated.

[365] UNIDENTIFIED WOMAN. Called "Lady in Red Shawl." Lived in Albany, probably a member of the McHarg or Ten Broeck families

(information at FARL from Mrs. W. Harman Brown, 10/11/39). She might be a Mrs. Delavan, wife of "Unidentified Man" (No. 358) (FARL photomount, 1939).

Description: 30 x 23¾ inches. Half-length, head to left.

Date: *c*. 1815.

Owners: (1) Mrs. Ten Broeck, Albany, who had no direct heirs; (2) Mr. and Mrs. W. Harman Brown (the latter a connection by marriage of Mrs. Ten Broeck), Flushing, N.Y.; (3) sold after Mrs. Brown's death and acquired from an intermediary dealer by Penrose and Edgette, Inc., dealers, New York City; (4) sold to Mrs. J. Amory Haskell, New York City and Red Bank, N.J.; (5) sold at Mrs. J. Amory Haskell Sale, Parke-Bernet Galleries, New York, May 17-20, 1944, p. 187 in catalogue.

Photograph: FARL 32792.

Attribution: To Ezra Ames by Miss Hope Mathewson (FARL), 1939.

Unlocated.

[366] UNIDENTIFIED WOMAN. So-called portrait of "Maria Van Schaick."

Description: 30 x 24 inches. Half-length, head to left.

Date: Uncertain.

Owners: (1) James S. Wade; (2) his daughter Miss Edith S. Wade, Cohoes, N.Y.

Photograph: AIHA; print at FARL.

Exhibition: AIHA 1946.

Note: The sitter has been called Maria Van Schaick by the owner because of a resemblance to the Maria Van Schaick portrait owned by AIHA. The resemblance does not seem sufficient evidence to the writers for the identification.

Examined by IFC and TB.

[367 to 376] UNIDENTIFIED WOMEN. Ten portraits by Ezra Ames, each entitled "Portrait of a lady" [30 x 24 inches] are listed as Nos. 47 through 56 in the handbill: *Catalogue Sale of Portraits*, 1842, in the Ezra Ames estate.

Unlocated.

[377] VAN BUREN, MARTIN (1782-1862), as a young man. Lawyer; Governor of New York State, 1828-1829; Vice-President of the United States, 1833-1837; eighth President of the United States, 1837-1841 (*Century Cyclopedia of Names*, 1911).

Description: 30 x 24 inches. Bust, head to right.

Date: Uncertain.

Owner: New Haven Colony Historical Society, presented in 1885 by

Miss M.R. Hogeboom, a kinswoman of the sitter.
Attribution: The location of the portrait and its attribution to Ezra Ames was found by the writers in the notes in the late William Sawitzky's file on Ezra Ames, lent to them by Mrs. William Sawitzky.
Examined by IFC.

[378] VAN BUREN, MARTIN (1782-1862).
Description: 52¾ x 41 inches. Half-length standing, head to right. The head is similar to that in No. 379.
Date: *c.* 1828–.
Owner: The City of Albany, on permanent loan at AIHA.
Photograph: AIHA; print at FARL.
Reproductions: *Magazine of Art,* AIHA Edition, December 1946; *American Collector,* August 1947, p. 6.
Exhibitions: View of a New York State Community, NYSHA, Cooperstown, N.Y., 1939; AIHA 1946.
Note: This is one of the series of "Portraits of Seven Governors of New York," by Ezra Ames, at AIHA.
Examined by IFC and TB. [Illustrated p. 131]

[379] VAN BUREN, MARTIN (1782-1862).
Description: 29¾ x 23½ inches. Bust, head to right. The head is similar to that in No. 378.
Date: Uncertain.
Owner: Old South Association, Boston, presented by Mrs. Marie Weston Chapman about 1880.
Photograph: FARL 31254.
Attribution: The artist was unknown to the owner. Attributed tentatively to Ezra Ames by Miss Hope Mathewson (FARL), 1947; to Ezra Ames by Irwin F. Cortelyou and T. Bolton in 1951.
Note: This is possibly the portrait painted by Ezra Ames, listed as No. 5, "Head of Martin Van Buren," [30 x 24 inches] in the handbill: *Catalogue Sale of Portraits,* 1842, in the Ezra Ames estate; which is presumably one of the two portraits of Martin Van Buren listed and each appraised at $30.00, one an "original head," in the Inventory, 1836, of the Ezra Ames estate.
Examined by IFC and TB.

[380] VAN BUREN, MARTIN (1782-1862). Two portraits of Martin Van Buren are listed in the Inventory, 1836, of the Ezra Ames estate, each appraised at $30.00; one an "original" head. One is presumably No. 379. The other is:
Unlocated.

[381] VAN CORTLANDT, PHILIP (1749-1831), eldest son of Pierre Van Cortlandt I (1721-1814) and Joanna (Livingston) Van Cortlandt; Revolutionary officer; Member of Congress, 1793-1809 (*BDAC*); and Florence Van Rensselaer, *The Livingston Family in America*, New York, 1949, p. 89).

Description: 36 x 29 inches. Half-length, head to right.

Date: *c*. 1809-1810.

Owners: (1) Philip Van Cortlandt Van Wyck, nephew and adopted son of the sitter, 1870; (2) his daughter Ann Van Rensselaer Van Wyck Wells, 1919; (3) his son-in-law Schuyler Van Cortlandt Hamilton, Croton-on-Hudson, N.Y., 1939; (4) Parke-Bernet Galleries, sale, April 18, 1940 (sold for $475.00); (5) presented to Metropolitan Museum by Christian A. Zabriskie, on loan at New York Tax Court, 70 East 45th Street, New York City.

Photograph: Metropolitan Museum; print at FARL.

Reproduction: *Bulletin of The Metropolitan Museum of Art*, July, 1940, p. 149.

Attribution: To Ezra Ames by the late William Sawitzky according to a note in his file on Ezra Ames lent to the writers by Mrs. Sawitzky.

Examined by IFC. [Illustrated p. xvi]

[382] VAN CORTLANDT, MRS. PIERRE I, née Joanna Livingston (1722-1808), daughter of Gilbert Livingston and Cornelia (Beekman) Livingston; married Pierre Van Cortlandt I (1721-1814), in 1748 (Florence Van Rensselaer, *The Livingston Family in America*, New York, 1949, p. 89).

Description: 30 x 25 inches. Bust, profile, head to right.

Date: *c*. 1792, if painted from life. However, see note below.

Owners: (1) Miss Anne S. Van Cortlandt, Croton-on-Hudson, N.Y., great-granddaughter of the sitter, and her nieces Miss Catharine Van Cortlandt Mathews and Mrs. William V. Mason; (2) after Miss Van Cortlandt's death in 1940, owned by the nieces, Croton-on-Hudson, N.Y.

Photograph: FARL 15590.

Note: Probably painted from a wax miniature profile of the sitter by an unknown artist, at the Museum of the City of New York.

Examined by IFC.

[383] VAN CORTLANDT, PIERRE II (1762-1848), son of Pierre Van Cortlandt I (1721-1814) and Joanna (Livingston) Van Cortlandt; Major General in the Militia; married (1) 1801, Catharine, daughter of Governor George Clinton and widow of Captain John Taylor of the British Army; (2) 1813, Anne, daughter of John Stevenson and Magdalena (Douw) Stevenson (*CAB*: and Florence Van Rensselaer,

The Livingston Family in America, New York, 1949, pp. 89, 106).
Description: 31 x 25 inches. Bust, head to right.
Date: *c.* 1815. Because his second wife's portrait is dated 1815, by a a signed receipt, this portrait may have been painted as a companion to it during the same year.
Owners: (1) Miss Anne S. Van Cortlandt, Croton-on-Hudson, N.Y., granddaughter of the sitter, and her nieces Miss Catharine Van Cortlandt Mathews and Mrs. William V. Mason; (2) after Miss Van Cortlandt's death in 1940, owned by the nieces, Croton-on-Hudson, N.Y.
Photograph: FARL 15586.
Examined by IFC. [Illustrated p. 82]

[384] VAN CORTLANDT, MRS. PIERRE II, née Catharine Clinton (1770-1811), daughter of Governor George Clinton; widow of Captain John Taylor of the British Army; later the first wife of Pierre Van Cortlandt II, married 1801 (*CAB;* Florence Van Rensselaer, *The Livingston Family in America,* New York, 1949, p. 106).
Description: 30 x 24 inches. Half-length, profile, head to right.
Date: *c.* 1811.
Owners: (1) Miss Anne S. Van Cortlandt and her nieces Miss Catharine Van Cortlandt Mathews and Mrs. William V. Mason, Croton-on-Hudson, N.Y.; (2) after Miss Van Cortlandt's death in 1940, owned by the nieces; (3) sold at the Mrs. Nelson Williams and Other Collections Sale, Parke-Bernet Galleries, New York City, March 7, 1942, for $125 to Joseph B. Brenauer; (4) bequeathed by him to the Museum of the City of New York, 1946.
Photograph: FARL 15591.
Reproduction: Catalogue, Mrs. Nelson Williams and Other Collections Sale, Parke-Bernet Galleries, New York City, March 7, 1942, p. 14.
Note: According to family tradition the portrait was started just before she died, and finished after her death, with the second wife-to-be sitting as a model.
Examined by IFC and TB.

[385] VAN CORTLANDT, MRS. PIERRE II, née Anne Stevenson (1774-1821), the second wife of Pierre Van Cortlandt II, married 1813. (*CAB;* Catalogue, Mrs. Nelson Williams and Other Collections Sale, Parke-Bernet Galleries, March 7, 1942, pp. 14, 15).
Description: 36 x 28 inches. Half-length, head to right.
Date: 1815. A receipt in the possession of the owners, dated September 18, 1815, made out to Pierre Van Cortlandt for a portrait of his "Lady" ($35) and a burnished gilt frame ($25) undoubtedly refers to this portrait.

Owners: (1) Miss Anne S. Van Cortlandt, Croton-on-Hudson, N.Y., granddaughter of the sitter, and her nieces, Miss Catharine Van Cortlandt Mathews and Mrs. William V. Mason; (2) after Miss Van Cortlandt's death in 1940, owned by the nieces, Croton-on-Hudson, N.Y.

Photograph: FARL 15582.

Reproduction: Either this portrait or the replica listed in No. 386 is reproduced in H.D. Eberlein, *Manors and Historic Homes of the Hudson River Valley*, Philadelphia and London, 1924, p. 124.

Examined by IFC.

[386] VAN CORTLANDT, MRS. PIERRE II, née Anne Stevenson (1774-1821).

Description: 36 x 28 inches. Half-length, head to right. Replica of No. 385.

Date: 1815. Since the original of which this is a replica is dated 1815, it may be assumed that it was painted during the same year.

Owners: (1) Originally painted for another member of the Van Cortlandt family; (2) Miss Anne S. Van Cortlandt, granddaughter of the sitter, Croton-on-Hudson, N.Y., and her nieces Miss Catharine Van Cortlandt Mathews and Mrs. William V. Mason; (3) after Miss Van Cortlandt's death in 1940, owned by the nieces; (4) sold at the Mrs. Nelson Williams and Other Collections Sale, Parke-Bernet Galleries, New York City, March 7, 1942, for $400.

Reproduction: Catalogue, Mrs. Nelson Williams and Other Collections Sale, Parke-Bernet Galleries, New York City, March 7, 1942, p. 15.

Unlocated.

[387] VANDER HEYDEN, JACOB (*Albany Directory*, 1813-1817). [Patron]. A portrait painted for "Jacob Vanderhyden," obviously the above-mentioned, is recorded in Account Book, June 1805.

Unlocated.

[388] VAN INGEN, MR. A "portrait of his son" painted for James Van Ingen is recorded in Account Book, September 13, 1817. James Van Ingen was a clerk in the Bank of Albany from 1792 until he became Clerk of the House of Assembly (Munsell, I, 1869, p. 291); died February 22, 1843, aged 76 (Munsell, X, 1859, p. 337). He was one of the owners of the steamboats *Hope* and *Perseverance* for which Ames made symbolic paintings, No. 521 and No. 526 (John H. Morrison, *History of American Steam Navigation*, New York, 1903, p. 44).

Unlocated.

[389] VAN KLEECK, LAWRENCE L. [Patron]. Collector of the revenue (*Albany Directory,* 1816-1818), also spelled Van Kleek; elected city and county clerk of Albany, 1826 (Reynolds, p. 463). A portrait painted for "Lawrence Van Cleek," obviously the above-mentioned, is recorded in Account Book, January 31, 1811.
Unlocated.

[390] VAN NESS, WILLIAM W. (1776-1823) Judge, New York Supreme Court (*CAB*). A portrait of "Judge Van Ness... Kit-cat size" is listed and appraised at $20.00 in the Inventory, 1836, of the Ezra Ames estate. This is doubtless the portrait painted by Ezra Ames, listed as No. 21, "Judge Wm. W. Van Ness, 2 ft 4 by 3 ft" in the handbill: *Catalogue Sale of Portraits,* 1842, in the Ezra Ames estate.
Unlocated.

[391] VAN RENSSELAER, MISS. A portrait painted of her for Lawrence L. Van Kleeck, "collector of the revenue" (*Albany Directory,* 1818) is recorded in Account Book, April 1, 1812.
Unlocated.

[392] VAN RENSSELAER, JOHN S., county judge confirmed, 1824 (Reynolds, 441). A portrait painted of him and for him is recorded in Account Book, August 21, 1829.
Unlocated.

[393] VAN RENSSELAER, MRS. JOHN S. A portrait painted of her for John S. Van Rensselaer is recorded in Account Book, August 21, 1829.
Unlocated.

[394] VAN RENSSELAER, SOLOMON (1774-1852), Adjutant General, New York Militia; Representative from New York, U.S. Congress, 1819-1822; resigned to become Postmaster of Albany; married Harriet, daughter of Philip Van Rensselaer (*CAB, BDAC*).
Description: 29¾ x 23¾ inches. Bust, head to left.
Date: 1819. Presumably the portrait painted of and for Solomon Van Rensselaer recorded in Account Book, December 6, 1819.
Owners: (1) Mrs. Edward W. Rankin; (2) her son and daughter, Miss Emily W. Rankin and Mr. Edward E. Rankin, descendants of Philip Van Rensselaer. The portrait has remained in the same house in Albany ever since it was painted.
Photograph: FARL 15391.
Exhibitions: AIHA 1934, and 1946, lent by Mrs. Edward W. Rankin.

Note: For details see pp. 166-167 herein.
Examined by IFC. [Illustrated p. 86]

[395] VAN RENSSELAER, SOLOMON (1774-1852). A portrait painted for Joseph Delaplaine of "Genl Sol Van Rensselare" is recorded in Account Book, September 8, 1818. In *A Legacy of Historical Gleanings*, I, 400-401, by Mrs. Catharina Van Rensselaer Bonney, a daughter of Solomon Van Rensselaer, there is a letter from Joseph Delaplaine, Philadelphia, February 28, 1822, to Solomon Van Rensselaer in which Delaplaine states: "It gives me pleasure to mention, that *your portrait* in my Gallery is recognized by all who know you." The portrait was purchased, with a number of others in the Gallery, by P.T. Barnum, and was destroyed when Barnum's Museum, New York City, burned down in 1865.
Note: For details see pp. 166-167 herein.
Destroyed.

[396] VAN RENSSELAER, STEPHEN III (1764-1839), as a young man. Patroon; Major General in State Militia; Lieutenant Governor of New York State, 1795-1801; Representative from New York, U.S. Congress, 1822-1829, succeeding Solomon Van Rensselaer (*DAB*).

A portrait of "St. Van Rensselaer (copy)" is listed and appraised in the Inventory, 1836, of the Ezra Ames estate, in a group of ten portraits at an "average—each 10.00." This is doubtless the portrait painted by Ezra Ames, listed as No. 11, "Hon. Stephen Van Rensselaer, in early life," [30 x 24 inches] in the handbill: *Catalogue Sale of Portraits*, 1842, in the Ezra Ames estate. Since Ezra Ames also made a copy in miniature (No. 503 herein) of a portrait in oil of Stephen Van Rensselaer, as a young man, by Gilbert Stuart (reproduced: Lawrence Park, *Gilbert Stuart*, New York, 1926, IV, 540), presumably this unlocated copy in oil by Ezra Ames was likewise after the portrait by Stuart.
Unlocated.

[397] VAN RENSSELAER, STEPHEN III (1764-1839). [Patron]. He is charged by Ames "To a Portrait for J. Delaplain[e], Philadelphia" in Account Book, October 14, 1818, This was obviously a portrait *of* Stephen Van Rensselaer because Joseph Delaplaine of Philadelphia (*CAB*) was at that time collecting portraits for his Gallery of Distinguished Americans.
Unlocated.

[398] VAN RENSSELAER, STEPHEN III (1764-1839).
Description: 26 x 22¾ inches, rectangular canvas framed as oval.

Bust, head to left.

Date: Probably the portrait recorded in Account Book, April 24, 1819, painted for Stephen Van Rensselaer and "Delivered to your son S – V – R Junr." This conclusion supersedes the alternatives given herein, p. 170.

Owners: (1) Mrs. Howard Townsend, née Justine Van Rensselaer, daughter of Stephen Van Rensselaer IV, [Jr]; (2) her son Dr. Howard Townsend, Poughkeepsie, N.Y.; (3) Albert Duveen, New York City; (4) Macbeth Gallery, New York City; (5) NYSHA, Cooperstown, N.Y.

Photograph: Macbeth Gallery; print at FARL.

Reproduction: *Handbook of the Museum and Art Gallery of the NYSHA*, 1942, p. 19.

Examined by IFC. [Illustrated p. 86]

[399] VAN RENSSELAER, GENERAL S., probably Stephen Van Rensselaer III (1764-1839). On June 3, 1825, Ezra Ames recorded in his Account Book the painting of a "Copy of General S. Van Rensselaer's portrait," and charged it to "Genl Dunbar." General Robert Dunbar, at the time of his death in 1837, had been principal agent of the Patroon [Stephen Van Rensselaer III] for more than thirty years. (Reynolds, p. 523).

Unlocated.

[400] VAN RENSSELAER, STEPHEN. Presumably Stephen Van Rensselaer III (1764-1839). Listed in the *Catalogue of Albany's Bicentennial Loan Exhibition at the Albany Academy, July 5 to July 24, 1886*, p. 115, as follows: "Ezra Ames (deceased). / 77 Portrait of Stephen Van Rensselaer ... [owned by] Mrs. C.G. Van Rensselaer." The exhibitor was probably Catherine Westerlo (Bleecker) Van Rensselaer. She was the widow of Cornelius Glen Van Rensselaer (1801-1871) (Kiliaen Van Rensselaer, *The Van Rensselaer Manor* .... (Col. Lords), Baltimore, 1929, p. 66).

Unlocated. However, this might be the portrait of Stephen Van Rensselaer III, said to be by Samuel F.B. Morse, which Mrs. Theodore Strong of New Brunswick, N.J., inherited from her aunt Miss Katherine Westerlo Van Rensselaer who was the daughter of Mrs. C.G. Van Rensselaer.

[401] VAN RENSSELAER, STEPHEN III (1764-1839), as an old man.

Description: 30 x 24 inches. Bust, head to right. Head very similar to Nos. 402 and 402a.

Date: Uncertain.

Owner: Old South Association, Boston, the gift of Mrs. Marie Weston Chapman about 1880.

Photograph: FARL 31257.
Attribution: Listed in Massachusetts Historical Records Survey, *American Portraits Found in Massachusetts*, 1939, II, 421, as by an unknown artist; with measurements given, incorrectly, as 24 x 18 inches. Attributed to Ezra Ames by Irwin F. Cortelyou and T. Bolton, 1952.
Note: A portrait of "St. Van Rensselaer," listed and appraised at $20.00 in the Inventory, 1836, of the Ezra Ames estate, is doubtless the portrait painted by Ezra Ames listed as No. 10, "Hon. Stephen Van Rensselaer, Lt. Gov." [30 x 24 inches] in the handbill: *Catalogue Sale of Portraits*, 1842, in the Ezra Ames estate. It is here assumed that these entries refer to the portrait owned by Old South Association since several portraits of other sitters by Ezra Ames owned by Old South Association apparently came from the sale in 1842.
Examined by IFC and TB.

[402] VAN RENSSELAER, STEPHEN III (1764-1839), as an old man.
Description: 30 x 25 inches. Bust, head to right. Head very similar to Nos. 401 and 402a.
Date: Uncertain.
Owners: (1) William Bayard Van Rensselaer, grandson of the sitter; (2) Mrs. William Bayard Van Rensselaer, née Louisa Greenough Lane, who willed it to (3) Mr. Stephen Van Rensselaer Crosby, Boston, great-grandson of the sitter.
Photograph: FARL 15385.
Attribution: To Ezra Ames by William Sawitzky. This portrait was brought to the attention of the writers by notes found in the late William Sawitzky's file on Ezra Ames lent to them by Mrs. Sawitzky.

[402a] VAN RENSSELAER, STEPHEN III (1764-1839), as an old man.
Description: Bust, head to right. Head very similar to Nos. 401 and 402.
Date: Uncertain.
Owner: (1) Mrs. Charles Alden; (2) Mrs. James Carroll Frazer, Washington, D.C., deceased.
Photograph: Print at FARL.
Attribution: To Ezra Ames by Irwin F. Cortelyou, 1953, judging from a photograph. T. Bolton concurs, also judging from a photograph.
Unlocated.

[403] VAN SCHAICK, MARIA (1782-1865), daughter of John Gerritsen [or Gerritse] Van Schaick and Anna (Van Schaick) Van Schaick; 2d wife of Gerrit B. Peebles, married 1818 (Cuyler Reynolds, *Hudson-*

Mohawk Genealogical and Family Memoirs, New York, 1911, III, 994; letter to IFC from Mr. George S. Van Schaick, 5/2/52).
Description: 31 x 24 inches. Half-length, head to left. Cleaned, 1949.
Date: Possibly the portrait recorded in Account Book, August 10, 1808, for Mr. John Van Schaick.
Owner: Presented to AIHA in 1915 by Mrs. Abraham Lansing.
Photograph: FARL 15666.
Reproductions: *N.Y. Times Magazine*, September 5, 1926; Alan Burroughs, *Limners and Likenesses*, Cambridge, Mass., 1936, No. 79.
Exhibitions: AIHA 1934, 1946.
Examined by IFC and TB.

[404] VAN SCHOONHOVEN, GUERT, of Schaghticoke, N.Y. (letter to IFC from Miss Frances H. Dwight, 3/10/51).
Description: 30 x 24 inches. Bust, head to right.
Date: 1821. Since it is a companion portrait to that of his wife (No. 405), this portrait was presumably painted during the same year.
Owners: (1) Miss Lucy Kirkland who bequeathed it to a distant cousin, (2) who was the mother of the present owners, (3) the Misses Laura and Frances H. Dwight, Boston.
Photograph: FARL 41513. The negative, made by the late Edward Crosby Doughty, Williamstown, Mass., was presented by him to Irwin F. Cortelyou who deposited it at FARL.
Attribution: To Ezra Ames by William Sawitzky. This portrait was brought to the attention of the writers by notes found in the late William Sawitzky's file on Ezra Ames lent to them by Mrs. Sawitzky.

[405] VAN SCHOONHOVEN, MRS. GUERT (born 1771), née Mary Frances Davis, daughter of Richard Davis of Poughkeepsie, N.Y. (letter to IFC from Mrs. Joseph Jenkins, 5/1/51).
Description: 30 x 24 inches. Half-length, head slightly to left.
Date: 1821. Presumably the "Portrait of his Lady" painted for "Guint Van Schoonhovn," recorded in Account Book, April 3, 1821.
Owners: (1) Miss Lucy Kirkland who bequeathed it to a distant cousin, (2) who was the mother of the present owners, (3) the Misses Laura and Frances H. Dwight, Boston, relatives of the sitter.
Photograph: FARL 41514. The negative, made by the late Edward Crosby Doughty, Williamstown, Mass., was presented by him to Irwin F. Cortelyou who deposited it at FARL.
Attribution: To Ezra Ames by William Sawitzky. This portrait was brought to the attention of the writers by notes found in the late William Sawitzky's file on Ezra Ames lent to them by Mrs. Sawitzky.

[406] VAN VECHTEN, ABRAHAM (1762-1837), lawyer, studied with

John Lansing; appointed Attorney General of New York State, 1810 and 1813, and held many other State offices (record at M. Knoedler & Co., 10/18/51; and Stephen C. Hutchins, *Civil List . . . of the Colony and State of New York*, Albany, 1880, passim).
Description: 29 7/8 x 23¾ inches. Bust, head to left.
Date: *c.* 1815.
Owners: (1) Schuyler Van Vechten Hoffman; (2) Winsor White, Mamaroneck, N.Y.; (3) M. Knoedler & Co., New York City.
Photograph: M. Knoedler & Co.
Examined by IFC.

[407] VAN WIE, GERRIT W., (*c.* 1769-1842). [Patron]. Innkeeper (*Albany Directory*, 1813); died June 3, 1842, aged 73 (Munsell, X, 1859, p. 330). A portrait painted for "Garret Van Wie," obviously the above-mentioned, is recorded in Account Book, August 13, 1808.
Unlocated.

[408]•VARNUM, JOSEPH BRADLEY (1750/51-1821), Speaker of the House of Representatives, 1807-1811; Senator from Massachusetts, 1811-1817; Major General of the Massachusetts Volunteer Militia, 1805-1821 (*BDAC*).
Description: Panel, 30 x 24½ inches. Bust, head to left.
Date: *c.* 1819.
Owners: Descended in the family to Mrs. Edward de Rose, great-granddaughter of the sitter. Mrs. de Rose died, 1944.
Photograph: FARL 34386.
Attribution: The artist was unknown to the owner. Attributed to Ezra Ames by Miss Hope Mathewson (FARL), 1946.
Note: A portrait by Charles Loring Elliott of the sitter, also once owned by Mrs. Edward de Rose, is probably based on this portrait.
Unlocated.

[409] VOORHEES, MRS. SAMUEL, née Betsey Reynolds (1790-1858), daughter of Dr. Stephen and Lydia (Bartlett) Reynolds; born Minaville, N.Y.; married, 1811, Dr. Samuel Voorhees (Marion H. Reynolds, *History and Descendants of John and Sarah Reynolds*, Brooklyn, 1924, pp. 150, 217). She was noted for her needlework. Her letter to Lafayette, September 4, 1828, presenting examples of her skill, and the reply from Lafayette, November 12, 1828, are published in the *Saturday Globe*, Utica, N.Y., February 27, 1904.
Description: 30 x 23 inches. Half-length, head to left.
Date: *c.* 1813.
Owners: (1) Marcus T. Reynolds, Albany; (2) bequeathed to his nephew, Mr. Kenneth G. Reynolds, Loudonville, N.Y.

Photograph: FARL 15729.
Exhibition: AIHA 1934, lent by Marcus T. Reynolds.
Examined by IFC and TB.

[410] VOORHEES, MRS. SAMUEL, née Betsey Reynolds (1790-1858).
Description: This is a duplicate of No. 409 (letter, to IFC, 1/19/51, from Mrs. Frank G. Miller, Amsterdam, N.Y., chairman of the House Committee of Montgomery County Historical Society, Fort Johnson, N.Y.).
Owners: (1) Mrs. Frank Wilde, granddaughter of the sitter; (2) bequeathed by her to Montgomery County Historical Society, Fort Johnson, N.Y.

[411] WADE, MRS. JAMES, née Sally Mulford (1794-1834), niece of Ezra Ames and daughter of Ezekiel Mulford and Sally (Emes) Mulford.
Description: 28 x 20½ inches. Half-length, head to left.
Date: *c*. 1813, the time of her marriage.
Owners: (1) James S. Wade, 1897; (2) Miss Edith S. Wade, Cohoes, N.Y.
Photograph: AIHA; print at FARL.
Reproduction: Mary L. Sutliff, *A Record of the Ancestors and the Descendants of Betsy Mulford Sutliff*, Albany, 1897, facing p. 8.
Exhibition: AIHA 1946.
Examined by IFC and TB.

[412] WALKER, WILLARD, merchant (*Albany Directory*, 1820-1823); Member of the Common Council, 1824 (Reynolds, 451). A portrait painted of him and for him is recorded in Account Book, June 19, 1830.
Unlocated.

[413] WALKER, MRS. WILLARD. The painting of "his Ladys" portrait for Willard Walker is recorded in Account Book, June 19, 1830.
Unlocated.

[414] WALSH, ANN (1800-1811), daughter of Dudley Walsh (1761-1816), president of the Bank of Albany (Reynolds, 418).
Description: 29¾ x 25¾ inches. Child, half-length standing, head to right.
Date: 1807.
Owner: Inherited by Mr. John De Witt Peltz, New York City, a descendant of the sitter's family.
Photograph: FARL 17067.
Examined by IFC and TB. [Illustrated p. 48]

[415] WALSH, DUDLEY. [Patron]. In the Catalogue, Mrs. Nelson Williams and Other Collections Sale, Parke-Bernet Galleries, N.Y., March 7, 1942, p. 15, there is a mention of "a receipted bill, dated Albany, Jan. 5th, 1813, for payment of the sum of $66 for painting a portrait, addressed to Mr. Dudley Walsh and signed EZRA AMES."
Unlocated.

[416] WALTON, JONATHAN (died 1839), born in Philadelphia; portrait painted in Schenectady, N.Y.; buried in St. George's churchyard, Schenectady (information at FARL from Miss Helen de Lancey Watkins).
Description: 30 x 24 inches. Bust, head to left.
Date: *c.* 1830-1835.
Owner: Miss Helen de Lancey Watkins, Schenectady, N.Y., great-great-granddaughter of the sitter.
Photograph: FARL 30375.
Attributions: Henry Inman had been suggested to the owner as the artist who painted this portrait. Attributed to Ezra Ames by Irwin F. Cortelyou, 1951. T. Bolton concurs, judging from a photograph.
Examined by IFC.

[417] WALTON, MRS. JONATHAN, née Margaret Ann Thatcher (died 1843), came from Philadelphia; portrait painted in Schenectady, N.Y.; buried in St. George's churchyard, Schenectady (information at FARL from Miss Helen de Lancey Watkins).
Description: 29½ x 24 inches. Half-length, head to right.
Date: *c.* 1830-1835.
Owner: Miss Helen de Lancey Watkins, Schenectady, N.Y., great- great-granddaughter of the sitter.
Photograph: FARL 30374.
Attributions: Henry Inman had been suggested to owner as the artist who painted this portrait. Attributed to Ezra Ames by Irwin F. Cortelyou, 1951. T. Bolton concurs, judging from a photograph.
Examined by IFC. [Illustrated p. 134]

[418] WARFORD, JOSEPH. [Patron]. A portrait painted for him is recorded in Account Book, May 4, 1810.
Unlocated.

[419] WASHINGTON, GEORGE (1732-1799). First President of the United States.
Description: 94 x 70 inches. Full-length standing, head to left. Probably based on the Heath engraving of one of the "Lansdowne" type portraits of Washington by Gilbert Stuart. The engraving is re-

produced: *Art in America*, February 1950, facing p. 21.
Date: 1813.
Owner: The State of New York; in the Executive Chamber, New York State Capitol, Albany. The resolution authorizing the painting of the portrait passed the House of Assembly, April 13, 1813, See: *New York State Laws*, Albany, Southwick, 1813, chapter 203, section XXXVIII, 335.
Photograph: FARL 15383.
Note: For a discussion of this portrait see pp. 73-74, 77, herein.
Examined by IFC. [Illustrated p. 76]

[420] WASHINGTON, GEORGE (1732-1799).
Description: 30 x 23¾ inches. Bust, head to left. Copy after one of the "Athenaeum" type portraits of Washington by Gilbert Stuart.
Date: 1826.
Inscription on back: "E. Ames Pt 1826."
Owner: AIHA.
Photograph: FARL 15732.
Exhibitions: Albany Gallery of Fine Arts, 1840; AIHA 1934, 1946.
Note: Presumably the portrait listed as "Washington (finished)" and appraised at $30.00 in the Inventory, 1836, of the Ezra Ames estate, which is doubtless the portrait painted by Ezra Ames listed as No. 1, "George Washington, copy from G. Stuart," [30 x 24 inches] in the handbill: *Catalogue Sale of Portraits*, 1842, in the Ezra Ames estate.
Examined by IFC and TB.

[421] WASHINGTON, GEORGE (1732-1799). A portrait entitled "Sm[all] Washington" is listed and appraised at $2.00 in the Inventory, 1836, of the Ezra Ames estate.
Unlocated.

[422] WATKINS, MR. A portrait painted by Ezra Ames is listed as No. 34, "___Watkins, Esq." [30 x 24 inches] in the handbill: *Catalogue Sale of Portraits*, 1842, in the Ezra Ames estate.
Unlocated.

[423] WATSON, MISS, daughter of Elkanah Watson. Probably Mary Lucia Watson (1797-1853), who married General Aaron Ward (William R. Deane, *A Biographical Sketch of Elkanah Watson ... with a Brief Genealogy of the Watson Family*, Albany, 1864, pp. 14-16). A portrait painted for Elkanah Watson of his daughter is recorded in Account Book, January 10, 1818.
Unlocated.

[424] WATSON, ELKANAH (1758-1842), merchant, canal promoter, agriculturalist (*DAB*).
Description: 59 x 47½ inches. Half-length standing, head to left. Copy after the portrait by John Singleton Copley which is owned by the Trustees of Thomson Hall, Princeton, N.J., on permanent loan at the Princeton University Museum.
Date: *c.* 1809-1810.
Owners: (1) Ezra Ames, (2) AIHA, presented by the artist's family in the 1840's.
Photographs: FARL 15713; and AIHA.
Reproduction: *The New York Times Magazine*, September 5, 1926, p. 16.
Exhibitions: Albany Gallery of Fine Arts about 1840; AIHA 1934, 1946.
Note: A portrait of "Elkanah Watson 3/4 size" listed and appraised at $40.00 in the Inventory, 1836, of the Ezra Ames estate is doubtless the portrait painted by Ezra Ames, listed as No. 58, "Elkanah Watson, Esq. copy from Copely [*sic*], 4 feet by 5," in the handbill: *Catalogue Sale of Portraits*, 1842, in the Ezra Ames estate. It is here assumed that these entries refer to the portrait at AIHA.
Examined by IFC and TB. [Illustrated p. 139]

[425] WATSON, ELKANAH (1758-1842). A portrait painted of him and for him is recorded in Account Book, September 15, 1818.
Note: Presumably the original upon which the engraving by V. Balch (No. 585) was based.
Unlocated.

[426] WEEKS, MRS. A portrait painted by Ezra Ames for John Randel [Jr.] of "his sister, Mrs. Weeks," is recorded in Account Book, September 9, 1812.
Unlocated.

[427] WEGDON, MR. [Patron]. A portrait painted for him is recorded in Account Book, March 4, 1812.
Unlocated.

[428] WELCH, BARTHOLOMEW T. (1794-1870), pastor, Baptist Church, Albany (Jonathan Tenney, *New England in Albany*, Boston, 1883, p. 119). A portrait of "Rev. B.T. Welch ... Kit-cat size" is listed and appraised at $20.00 in the Inventory, 1836, of the Ezra Ames estate. This is doubtless the portrait painted by Ezra Ames, listed as No. 43, "Rev. Dr. B.T. Welch, 2 feet 8 by 3 feet," in the handbill: *Catalogue Sale of Portraits*, 1842, in the Ezra Ames estate.
Unlocated.

[429] WELCH, BARTHOLOMEW T. (1794-1870). A portrait of "B.T. Welch" is listed and appraised at $30.00 in the Inventory, 1836, of the Ezra Ames estate.
Unlocated.

[430] WELLS, MR. I.M. [Patron]. The balance due on a portrait painted for him is recorded in Account Book, May 14, 1813.
Unlocated.

[431] WENTWORTH, THOMAS H. "Balance due" on a portrait of "Wentworth" is recorded in the Inventory, 1836, of the Ezra Ames estate. This is doubtless the portrait painted by Ezra Ames listed as No. 31, "Thomas H. Wentworth, Esq." [30 x 24 inches] in the handbill: *Catalogue Sale of Portraits*, 1842, in the Ezra Ames estate.
Unlocated.

[432] WHIPPLE, BARNUM (*c*. 1780-1857), skipper (*Albany Directory*, 1821), and Harbor Master of Albany (Reynolds, 527); for 60 years a resident of Albany; died at Staten Island, February 28, 1857, aged 77 years (Reynolds, 623). A portrait painted of and for "Barnum Whiple" is recorded in Account Book, April 9, 1822.
Unlocated.

[433] WHIPPLE, MRS. BARNUM. A portrait of "Mrs. B. Whipple" is listed and appraised at $5.00 in the Inventory, 1836, of the Ezra Ames estate.
Unlocated.

[434] WHITNEY, ELI (1765-1825), so-called.
Description: Bust, head to left.
Date: *c*. 1804.
Owner: Hopkins Grammar School, New Haven, Conn.
Photograph: Yale University Art Gallery.
Attribution: This portrait was brought to the attention of the writers by a note on the back of a photograph in the late William Sawitzky's file on Ezra Ames lent to them by Mrs. Sawitzky.

[435] WILKIN, JAMES WHITNEY (1762-1845), lawyer, practiced in Goshen, N.Y.; Major General in State Militia; State Senator, 1801-1804 and 1811-1814; Representative from New York, U.S. Congress, 1815-1819 (Franklin B. Hough, *The New York Civil List*, Albany 1855, p. 193).
Description: Half-length, head to right.

Date: *c*. 1822.
Owner: Mrs. Edson C. Price in 1933, Albany, a great-granddaughter of the sitter.
Attribution: This portrait was brought to the attention of the writers by notes and a photograph in the late William Sawitzky's file on Ezra Ames lent to them by Mrs. Sawitzky.

[436] WILKINSON, WILLIAM, of Providence. A portrait painted of him and for him, delivered to Mr. Mather, is recorded in Account Book, October 17, 1821.
Unlocated.

[437] WILLIAMS, COLONEL. A portrait of "____Williams" is listed and appraised in the Inventory, 1836, of the Ezra Ames estate, in a group of ten portraits at an "average each $10.00." This is doubtless the portrait painted by Ezra Ames, listed as No. 18, "Col. _____Williams," [30 x 24 inches] in the handbill: *Catalogue Sale of Portraits*, 1842, in the Ezra Ames estate.
Unlocated.

[438] WILLIAMS, MR. D. A portrait, "Kit Cat Size," painted of and for "Mr. D. Williams," is recorded in Account Book, October 14, 1825.
Unlocated.

[439] WILLIAMS, MRS. D., AND CHILD. A portrait painted of his "Lady & Child" for "Mr. D. Williams" is recorded in Account Book, October 14, 1825.
Unlocated.

[440] WOODRUFF, HUNLOKE (*c*. 1754-1811), physician, Member of the Common Council, Albany; trustee of the Albany Library; died July 4, 1811, aged 57 (Reynolds, pp. 381, 386, 410).
Date: Two portraits painted for "Doctr H. Woodroof" are recorded in Account Book, November 1, 1808, and July 1809. One of these was presumably the portrait mentioned in the following quotation.
Owner: "An excellent likeness of him, painted by an Albany artist, Mr. Ames, is in the possession of his family" (Munsell, IX, 1858, p. 92, a biographical notice about Dr. Hunloke Woodruff).
Unlocated.

[441] WOODRUFF, HUNLOKE (*c*. 1754-1811). [Patron]. This is one of two portraits painted for "Doctr H. Woodroof," obviously the above-mentioned patron, recorded in Account Book, November 1, 1808, and July 1809. One of these was presumably No. 440.
Unlocated.

[442] WYNKOOP, MISS. A portrait of "Miss Wynkoop" is listed and appraised at $15.00 in the Inventory, 1836, of the Ezra Ames estate.
Unlocated.

[443] YATES, ANDREW (1773-1844), Congregational clergyman, East Hartford, Conn., 1801-1814; professor, Union College, 1797-1801, 1814-1825. (*CAB*).
Description: 30 x 24 inches. Bust, head to right.
Date: *c.* 1823.
Owners: (1) John de Lancey Watkins, Schenectady, N.Y., great-great-grandson of the sitter; (2) Robert W. Leavitt, nephew of the former owner, Lake George Village, N.Y.
Photograph: FARL 30714.
Attribution: Tentatively to Ezra Ames by Miss Hope Mathewson (FARL), 1937; to Ezra Ames by Irwin F. Cortelyou, 1951, judging from a photograph. T. Bolton concurs, also judging from a photograph.

[444] YATES, ANDREW (1773-1844). A portrait of "Rev. A. Yates" listed and appraised in the Inventory, 1836, of the Ezra Ames estate, in a group of ten portraits at an "average—each 10.00" is doubtless the portrait painted by Ezra Ames, listed as No. 42, " Rev. Dr. Andrew Yates," [30 x 24 inches] in the handbill: *Catalogue Sale of Portraits*, 1842, in the Ezra Ames estate.
Unlocated, unless this proves to be the same as No. 443.

[445] YATES, DR. C., probably Dr. Christopher C. Yates (*c.* 1778-1848), physician; of Albany and New York City (Sylvester D. Willard, *Annals of the Medical Society of the County of Albany*, 1806-1851 . . . , Albany, 1864, pp. 289, 290). A portrait of "Dr. C. Yates" is listed and apparised in the Inventory, 1836, of the Ezra Ames estate, in a group of ten portraits at an "average—each 10.00."
Unlocated.

[446] YATES, JOHN W[ATERS] (1769-1828), cashier, New York State Bank, Albany; died March 28, 1828, aged 58 (Gorham A. Worth, *Random Recollections of Albany*, Albany, 1866, p. 66). A portrait of "John W. Yates Esq (nearly whole length)" is listed and appraised at $50.00 in the Inventory, 1836, of the Ezra Ames estate.
Unlocated.

[447] YATES, JOHN W[ATERS]. (1769-1828). A portrait painted by Ezra Ames is listed as No. 24, "Hon. John W. Yates," [30 x 24

inches] in the handbill: *Catalogue Sale of Portraits*, 1842, in the Ezra Ames estate.
Unlocated.

[447a] YATES, JOHN WATERS (1769-1828).
Description: Panel, 30 x 23½ inches. Bust, head to right.
Date: *c*. 1815.
Owners: (1) Has always been owned in the family of the sitter; (2) a descendant, Mr. H. Hobart Porter; (3) inherited in 1947 by his daughters, Mrs. Robert L. Hamill, Mrs. Harold E.B. Pardee, Mrs. J. Horton Ijams, all of New York City, great-great-granddaughters of the sitter.
Photograph: FARL 37354.
Attributions: Formerly to John Vanderlyn; to Ezra Ames by Miss Hope Mathewson (FARL), 1953.

[448] YATES, JOSEPH CHRISTOPHER (1768-1837), lawyer, Mayor of Schenectady, N.Y., 1798-1808; Governor of New York State, 1823, 1824 (The New York Red Book, Albany, 1950, p. 661).
Description: 52½ x 41 inches, sight. Half-length standing, head and eyes to left. Head similar to Nos. 449 and 450.
Date: *c*. 1823–.
Owner: City of Albany, on permanent loan at AIHA.
Photograph: AIHA; print at FARL.
Exhibition: AIHA 1946.
Note: This is one of the series of "Portraits of Seven Governors of New York," by Ezra Ames, at AIHA.
Examined by IFC and TB. [Illustrated p. 141]

[449] YATES, JOSEPH CHRISTOPHER (1768-1837).
Description: 30 x 24 inches. Bust, head and eyes to left. Very similar to No. 450.
Date: Uncertain.
Owners: (1) Joseph C.W. Paige; (2) inherited by his son Joseph Yates Paige; (3) inherited by his daughter Mrs. J. Lewi Donhauser; (4) Dr. J. Lewi Donhauser, Loudonville, N.Y.
Photograph: FARL 15405.
Exhibition: AIHA 1936, lent by Mrs. J. Lewi Donhauser.
Attributions: Formerly to John Vanderlyn. William Sawitzky was "inclined" to attribute it to Ezra Ames, 1932, judging from a photograph. Attributed to Ezra Ames by Irwin F. Cortelyou and T. Bolton, 1950.
Examined by IFC and TB.

[450] YATES, JOSEPH CHRISTOPHER (1768-1837).
Description: 30 x 24 inches, in oval frame. Bust, head and eyes to left. Very similar to No. 449.
Date: *c.* 1825.
Owner: Miss Helen de Lancey Watkins, Schenectady, N.Y., great-great-great-granddaughter of the sitter.
Photograph: FARL 30372.
Attribution: The artist was unknown to the owner. Attributed to Ezra Ames by Irwin F. Cortelyou, 1951. T. Bolton concurs, judging from a photograph.
Examined by IFC.

[451] YATES, JOSEPH CHRISTOPHER (1768-1837). A portrait of "Gov. Yates," listed and appraised in the Inventory, 1836, of the Ezra Ames estate in a group of ten portraits at an "average—each 10.00," is doubtless the portrait painted by Ezra Ames, listed as No. 8, "Joseph C. Yates," [30 x 24 inches] in the handbill: *Catalogue Sale of Portraits*, 1842, in the Ezra Ames estate.
Unlocated.

[452] YATES, MRS. JOSEPH CHRISTOPHER, née Ann Elizabeth de Lancey (born 1770), third wife of Governor Joseph C. Yates (information at FARL from Miss Helen de Lancey Watkins).
Description: 30 x 24 inches. Half-length, head to right.
Date: *c.* 1825.
Owner: Miss Helen de Lancey Watkins, Schenectady, N.Y., great-great-great-granddaughter of the sitter.
Photograph: FARL 30373.
Attribution: The artist was unknown to the owner. Attributed to Ezra Ames by Irwin F. Cortelyou, 1951. T. Bolton concurs, judging from a photograph.
Examined by IFC.

XII

PORTRAITS IN MINIATURE

THE WORD MINIATURE is here used to mean a small portrait painted on ivory or on paper. Sixty-one miniatures are listed in this catalogue as by Ezra Ames. Of these sixty-one, thirty-five have not been located but are known through the artist's record of them in his Account Books or, in two cases, through other records. The remaining twenty-six are located and have been studied by the authors.

Twenty-two of the located miniatures, along with some others thought to be by Ezra's son, or possibly by him, have histories of continuous ownership within the family through direct descent from the artist or his sister, Sally Emes Mulford. These records of ownership, when accompanied by a family belief that any given miniature had been painted by Ezra himself, are the chief reasons for the writers' acceptance of most of them. No miniature signed on the face by Ezra Ames has been found. This fact, and the great variety in size, shape, technique, and color among the family-inherited miniatures have made all questions of attribution difficult and in some cases uncertain.

Of the twenty-two accepted miniatures in the above-mentioned group there are fourteen, including three self-portraits, of identified members of the artist's or his sister's family and five others which, though unidentified as to sitters, may also be family portraits, leaving only three of the family-inherited miniatures known to be of sitters outside the two families. A discussion of a number of the family portraits, with illustrations, will be found on pages 136–137 and 138.

The only miniatures in the family collections not definitely assigned by the owners to Ezra Ames were several whose owner (Miss Elizabeth Seelye Edwards, Ezra's great-granddaughter) expressed uncertainty whether they had been painted by that artist or by his son, Julius Rubens Ames (1801–1850). The writers accepted as by Ezra Ames those miniatures in her collection which, judged by the costumes and the ages of the sitters, were painted too early to be attributed to Julius Ames. Miniatures in this collection, painted after about 1820 when both artists were active, were assigned to one or the other artist according to whether their technique and color resembled or differed from Ezra's earlier miniatures. A study of the only miniature known to carry an inscription that "J.[ulius] R. Ames pinx^{t}" was also an aid, as well as the miniature of Jesse Hawley inscribed on the wood backing as by Ezra Ames. Five were judged to be by Julius Ames, and three were left as open questions and are listed as such in Section XVI.

The accepted family-inherited miniatures and the one of Jesse Hawley were used for comparison in rejecting a number of miniatures not in these family collections but heretofore attributed to Ezra Ames. These are listed in Section XV. Only four miniatures outside these collections have been accepted as the work of Ezra Ames.

Of the twenty-six located miniatures, nineteen are on ivory and seven are on paper. Three of the twenty-six show accessories in their backgrounds. Among those painted on ivory, four have blue hatched backgrounds, two have pinkish to warm-brown backgrounds, two have tan and another two have sky backgrounds, and one each has a dark-gray, brownish-gray, dark-green, or shaded yellow-brown background. With one exception, the miniatures on paper have unpainted backgrounds. The costumes, whether painted on paper or on ivory, are mostly black for the men, with a few in dark-blue, one in dark-gray, and one in dark-brown. The costumes in the miniatures of women are evenly divided between black and white.

Each of the miniatures listed here is accepted by the writers as by Ezra Ames, whether or not a notation to that effect appears in the entry.

[453] AMES, ANGELO (1803-1886), as a boy. Younger son of Ezra Ames.
Description: Oval, ivory 2½ x 2¾ inches. Bust, head to left.
Date: *c*. 1818.
Owner: Miss Elizabeth S. Edwards, Albany. See note below.
Photograph: By Irwin F. Cortelyou.
Exhibition: Loan Exhibition at Historical and Art Society, Albany, 1902 (41), lent by Mrs. Isaac Edwards.
Note: The sixteen miniatures which now belong or until recently belonged to Miss Elizabeth Seelye Edwards (Nos. 453-457, 459, 469, 484, 486, 495-500, and 503) have the following ownership history which is not given in full in the other above-mentioned catalogue entries: (1) Angelo Ames, son of the artist; (2) Mrs. Isaac Edwards, granddaughter of the artist; (3) Miss Elizabeth Seelye Edwards and Mr. Henry Ames Edwards, great-grandchildren of the artist; (4) after the death of Mr. Edwards early in 1951, they passed to Miss Elizabeth Seelye Edwards, Albany, N.Y.; (5) eight (Nos. 454, 484, 496-500, and 503) were presented in July 1951 by Miss Edwards to the Albany Institute of History and Art; the others remain in her possession. Half of these sixteen are self-portraits or portraits of members of the artist's immediate family; five are unidentified as to sitter. In the collection of Miss Edwards were also miniatures painted by the artist's son, Julius Rubens Ames. In several instances the owner did not know which were painted by Ezra and which by Julius. The writers' attributions are discussed and explained in the introduction to this section of the Catalogue – "Portraits in Miniature."
Examined by IFC and TB. [Illustrated p. 127]

[454] AMES, ANGELO (1803-1886), in uniform.
Description: Rectangle, ivory 3½ x 2 7/8 inches. Bust, head straight forward.
Date: *c*. 1827.
Owner: Presented by Miss Elizabeth S. Edwards, Albany, to AIHA in 1951. See note to No. 453.
Photograph: By Irwin F. Cortelyou.
Exhibition: Loan Exhibition at Historical and Art Society, Albany, 1902 as (42) "Angelo Ames in uniform," lent by Mrs. Isaac Edwards.
Examined by IFC and TB. [Illustrated p. 127]

[455] AMES, EZRA (1768-1836), with a paint brush in his hand.
Description: Oval, ivory 2¾ x 2 inches, in locket. Bust, head to right.
Date: *c*. 1790.
Owner: Miss Elizabeth S. Edwards, Albany. See note to No. 453.
Photograph: By Irwin F. Cortelyou.

Attribution: To Ezra Ames by Irwin F. Cortelyou and T. Bolton, 1950, who jointly identified the sitter.
Examined by IFC and TB. [Illustrated p. 8]

[456] AMES, EZRA (1768-1836).
Description: Oval, ivory 2 x 1 5/8 inches, in locket. Bust, head to right.
Date: *c*. 1800.
Owner: Miss Elizabeth S. Edwards, Albany. See note to No. 453.
Photograph: By Irwin F. Cortelyou.
Exhibition: Loan Exhibition at Historical and Art Society, Albany, 1902 (38), lent by Mrs. Isaac Edwards.
Attribution: To Ezra Ames by Irwin F. Cortelyou and T. Bolton, 1950, who jointly identified the sitter.
Note: Probably based on the self-portrait in oil, No. 8.
Examined by IFC and TB. [Illustrated p. 8]

[457] AMES, EZRA (1768-1836).
Description: Rectangle, ivory 3½ x 3 inches. Bust, head to right.
Date: *c*. 1810.
Owner: Miss Elizabeth S. Edwards, Albany. See note to No. 453.
Photograph: By Irwin F. Cortelyou.
Note: Probably a copy by Ezra Ames of the self-portrait in oil, No. 9.
Examined by IFC and TB. [Illustrated p. 127]

[458] AMES, EZRA (1768-1836).
Description: Oval, ivory 3 1/8 x 2½ inches. Bust, head to right.
Date: *c*. 1818.
Owners: (1) Presented to Miss Lydia Cary, Albany, by the artist; (2) Miss Elisabeth Luther Cary, New York City, in 1927.
Photograph: FARL 9536.
Exhibition: Exhibition of Miniatures, Metropolitan Museum, 1927, lent by Miss Elisabeth Luther Cary.
Unlocated.

[459] AMES, MRS. EZRA, née Zipporah Wood (1775-1836), wife of the artist.
Description: Oval, ivory 3 x 2½ inches. Bust, head to right.
Date: *c*. 1820.
Owner: Miss Elizabeth S. Edwards, Albany. See note to No. 453.
Photograph: By Irwin F. Cortelyou.
Exhibition: Loan Exhibition at Historical and Art Society, Albany, 1902 (43), lent by Mrs. Isaac Edwards.
Examined by IFC and TB. [Illustrated p. 137]

[460] AMES, MARCIA LUCRETIA (1797/98-1886), daughter of Ezra Ames; married in 1824 to the Reverend William James (1797-1868), half brother of the father of Henry James the novelist and William James the philosopher (Mrs. Russel Hastings, "William James of Albany," *New York Genealogical and Biographical Record*, April 1924, pp. 104-113).
Description: Rectangle, ivory 3¼ x 2¾ inches. Half-length, head to left.
Date: *c*. 1820.
Inscription on back of frame in pencil: "Mrs. James by Ezra Ames."
Owner: Miss Gladys Ladu, Schenectady, N.Y.
Photograph: AIHA; print at FARL.
Exhibition: AIHA 1946.
Examined by IFC. [Illustrated p. 137]

[461] BULKEY, MR. [Patron]. A miniature painted for him is recorded in Account Book, February 14, 1805.
Unlocated.

[462] CLINTON, GEORGE (1739-1812), first Governor of New York State, 1777-1795, 1801-1804; Vice-President of the United States, 1804-1812 (*CAB*). The following entry is recorded in Account Book, March 28, 1794:

"for Mrs [George] Clinton miniatr 2: 0: 0
for his Excel[l]encys Do 2: 0: 0"

From this one may infer that the artist painted two miniatures: one of George Clinton and the other of his wife.
Unlocated.

[463] CLINTON, MRS. GEORGE, née Cornelia Tappen (1744-1800) married in 1770 (E.W. Spaulding, *His Excellency George Clinton*, 1938, p. 30, 240). See No. 462 for reference to miniature painted of her in 1794.
Unlocated.

[464] D., A. [Patron]. A miniature painted for "A.D." is recorded in Account Book, September 14, 1792. The artist was then living in Worcester, Massachusetts.
Unlocated.

[465] DEWETT, MR. M. [Patron]. The entry "for Mr. M. Dewetts m[iniatur]e" recorded in Account Book, April 1, 1794, may or may not be of him as well as for him.
Unlocated.

[466] DIXON, POLLY. [Patron]. A miniature painted for her is recorded in Account Book, December 4, 1790. The artist was then living in Worcester, Massachusetts.
Unlocated.

[467] DOLE, JOHN M. [Patron]. A miniature painted for him is recorded in Account Book, July 30, 1798.
Unlocated.

[468] ELLIS, MR. [Patron]. A miniature painted for him is recorded in Account Book, July 22, 1796.
Unlocated.

[469] EMES, HENRY (1783-1833), half brother of Ezra Ames.
Description: Rectangle, ivory 3½ x 2¾ inches. Bust, head to left.
Date: *c.* 1832.
Owner: Miss Elizabeth S. Edwards, Albany. See note to No. 453.
Photograph: By Irwin F. Cortelyou.
Exhibition: Loan Exhibition at Historical and Art Society, Albany, 1902, as (44) "Harry Emes," lent by Mrs. Isaac Edwards.
Examined by IFC and TB. [Illustrated p. 127]

[470] FOLLET, FRANCIS. [Patron]. Real estate broker in Albany (*Albany Centinel*, March 19, 1799, and other issues). A miniature painted for him is recorded in Account Book, March 26, 1795.
Unlocated.

[471] FONDEY, JOHN, JR. (born *c.* 1761).
Description: Oval, ivory 3½ x 2¼ inches. Bust, head to right.
Date: *c.* 1803. Since it greatly resembles the head of John Fondey, Jr., in the oil painting (No. 115) of the Fondey Family, dated 1803, this miniature was presumably copied from the large picture before it left the studio.
Owner: AIHA.
Photograph: FARL 15765.
Examined by IFC and TB.

[472] FULLERTON, SAMUEL. [Patron]. Of Worcester, Massachusetts (U.S. *Census*, 1790, p. 245). Presumably the patron whose name is spelled "Sam[u]el Fallington," for whom Ames recorded the painting of a miniature in Account Book, January 29, 1791.
Unlocated.

[473] HARRIS, MR. [Patron]. A miniature painted for him is re-

corded in Account Book, April 21, 1792. The artist was then living in Worcester, Massachusetts.
Unlocated.

[474] HARRIS, STEPHEN. A miniature painted of him and for him is recorded in Account Book, January 17, 1793. The artist was then living in Worcester, Massachusetts.
Unlocated.

[475] HAWKINS, MRS. SAMUEL. [Patron]. A miniature painted for her is recorded in Account Book, August 8, 1795.
Unlocated.

[476] HAWLEY, JESSE (1773-1842), Member, New York Assembly from Genesee County, 1820-1821 (Donald A. Shelley, *Catalogue of American Portraits in NYHS*, 1941, p. 130).
Description: Rectangle, ivory 3½ x 3 3/8 inches. Bust, head to left.
Date: *c.* 1825.
Inscription on wood backing: "Jesse Hawley / Author of the Essays in the Ontario Messenger / Signed Hercules, on Canal Navign pubd in 1807 / painted by Ames."
Owner: NYHS, gift of Jesse Hawley.
Photograph: NYHS; print at FARL.
Reproductions: Donald A. Shelley, *Catalogue of American Portraits in NYHS*, 1941, p. 130; H.B. Wehle, *American Miniatures*, Garden City, 1927, facing p. 62.
Exhibition: Exhibition of Miniatures, Metropolitan Museum, 1927.
Examined by IFC and TB. [Illustrated p. 109]

[477] HAYKE, JOHN. [Patron]. A miniature painted for him is recorded in Account Book, February 25, 1794.
Unlocated.

[478] HENRY, MRS. WILLIAM, née Ann Alexander, mother of Joseph Henry (1797-1878) the physicist and first director of the Smithsonian Institution (*DAB*).
Description: Rectangle, watercolor on paper painted in oval 5 3/16 x 4 5/16. Head straight forward, white lace cap with black ribbons.
Date: Uncertain.
Owner: Henry H. Leake, Albany, N.Y. On loan at the Albany County Historical Society; now on exhibition at the Ten Broeck Mansion, Albany.
Attribution: Tentatively to Ezra Ames by Irwin F. Cortelyou, 1951.
Examined by IFC.

[479] HILLS, MRS. JOHN, née Huldah Mulford (1806-1878), daughter of Ezekiel Mulford and Sally (Emes) Mulford; niece of Ezra Ames; married 1829 (reference: see Mary L. Sutliff below, p. 26).
Description: Watercolor on paper, painted in oval. Bust, head to right.
Date: *c.* 1828.
Owners: (1) Miss Sally Huldah Hills, daughter of the sitter, in 1897, (2) Miss Gladys Ladu, great-great-granddaughter of the sitter, Schenectady, N.Y.
Reproduction: Mary L. Sutliff, *A Record of the Ancestors and the Descendants of Betsy Mulford Sutliff,* Albany, 1897, facing p. 7.

[480] HILLS, MRS. JOHN, née Huldah Mulford (1806-1878).
Description: Rectangle, watercolor on paper 5¾ x 4¼ inches. Bust, with cap.
Date: *c.* 1831.
Inscription on back of frame written in ink: "Huldah Mulford Hills – by Ezra Ames."
Owner: Miss Gladys Ladu, Schenectady, N.Y., great-great-granddaughter of the sitter.
Photograph: AIHA; print at FARL.
Exhibition: AIHA 1946.
Examined by IFC. [Illustrated p. 136]

[481] HODGE, JAMES. [Patron]. Stone cutter (*Albany Directory,* 1813); one of the founders of the Mechanics' Society (MS Register of the Society at the New York State Library); his advertisement appears in the *Albany Gazette,* February 5, 1810, and in other issues. A miniature painted for him is recorded in Account Book, July 20, 1804.
Unlocated.

[482] HOOKER, JOHN. [Patron]. A miniature painted for him is recorded in Account Book, March 3, 1794.
Unlocated.

[483] LANTON, DR. WILLIAM. [Patron]. A miniature painted for him is recorded in Account Book, October 17, 1792. The correct surname may be Lawton. The artist was then living in Worcester, Massachusetts.
Unlocated.

[484] LIVINGSTON, ROBERT R. (1746-1813), Chancellor of New York State, 1777-1801; statesman and jurist (*DAB*).
Description: Rectangle, ivory 5 1/8 x 3¼ inches. Bust, head to left. Based on the oil portrait by Gilbert Stuart owned by Mr. John H.

Livingston, Clermont, N.Y., 1926 (reproduced: Lawrence Park, *Gilbert Stuart*, 1926, III, 299).
Date: *c.* 1814.
Owner: Presented by Miss Elizabeth S. Edwards, Albany, to AIHA in 1951. See note to No. 453.
Photograph: AIHA; print at FARL.
Examined by IFC.

[485] MULFORD, EZRA AMES (1804-1861), as a boy. Physician, son of Ezekiel and Sally (Emes) Mulford and nephew of Ezra Ames; studied medicine with his brother-in-law, Dr. James Wade (Mary L. Sutliff, *A Record of the Ancestors and the Descendants of Betsy Mulford Sutliff*, Albany, 1897, pp. 21, 24).
Description: Rectangle, black and sepia watercolor on paper 4 3/8 x 4 1/8 inches. Bust, head to left.
Date: *c.* 1819.
Owner: Miss Edith S. Wade, Cohoes, N.Y.
Photograph: AIHA; print at FARL.
Exhibition: AIHA 1946.
Examined by IFC and TB.

[486] NOTT, ELIPHALET (1773-1866), pastor of the First Presbyterian Church, Albany; president of Union College, Schenectady, N.Y., 1804-1866 (*DAB*).
Description: Rectangle, ivory 3¾ x 2¾. Bust, head slightly to right.
Date: 1820 (see inscription on third state of engraving, No. 581).
Owner: Miss Elizabeth S. Edwards, Albany. See note to No. 453.
Photograph: AIHA; print at FARL.
Exhibition: Loan Exhibition at Historical and Art Society, Albany, 1902 (46), lent by Mrs. Isaac Edwards.
Note: The above is probably a copy by Ezra Ames from the oil portrait (No. 223) painted in or before 1820.
Examined by IFC and TB.

[487] PHILLIPS. [Patron]. Possibly Jonathan Phillips of Worcester, Massachusetts (U.S. *Census*, 1790, p. 244). A miniature painted for this patron is recorded in Account Book, September 1791. The artist was then living in Worcester.
Unlocated.

[488] ROGERS, JAMES. [Patron]. A miniature painted for him is recorded in Account Book, 1797.
Unlocated.

[489] SANFORD, MR. A miniature painted of him and for him is recorded in Account Book, July 13, 1792. The artist was then living in Worcester, Massachusetts.
Unlocated.

[490] SEYMORE. [Patron]. A miniature painted for this patron is recorded in Account Book, December 4, 1790. The artist was then living in Worcester, Massachusetts.
Unlocated.

[491] SHARLIFF, HEZEKIAH. [Patron]. A miniature painted for "Mr Hez[eki]ah Sharliff" is recorded in Account Book, February 26, 1796.
Unlocated.

[492] SPALDING, MR. [Patron]. A miniature painted for him is recorded in Account Book, March 26, 1794.
Unlocated.

[493] THOMPSON, SMITH (1768-1843). [Patron]. A miniature painted for him is recorded in Account Book, March 2, 1805.
Unlocated.

[494] TREAT, DR. D. A miniature painted of him and for him is recorded in Account Book, January 1794.
Unlocated.

[495] UNIDENTIFIED GIRL OF THE AMES FAMILY.
Description: Oval, ivory 1¼ x 7/8 inches, in locket. Bust, head to right. Light hair, long curls, brown eyes.
Date: *c.* 1790.
Owner: Miss Elizabeth S. Edwards, Albany. See note to No. 453.
Photograph: By Irwin F. Cortelyou.
Attribution: To Ezra Ames by Irwin F. Cortelyou and T. Bolton, 1950.
Examined by IFC and TB.

[496] UNIDENTIFIED MAN.
Description: Oval, ivory 2 7/8 x 2¼ inches. Bust, head to left. Brown hair brushed forward, blue eyes; blue figured vest and blue coat.
Date: Uncertain.
Owner: Presented by Miss Elizabeth S. Edwards, Albany, to AIHA in 1951. See note to No. 453.
Photograph: By Irwin F. Cortelyou.
Attribution: To Ezra Ames by Irwin F. Cortelyou and T. Bolton, 1950.
Examined by IFC and TB.

[497] UNIDENTIFIED MAN (unfinished).
Description: Oval, ivory 2 5/16 x 1¾ inches. Bust, head to left. Blue eyes, white stock, background partly crosshatched in blue; coat and hair unfinished.
Date: Uncertain.
Owner: Presented by Miss Elizabeth S. Edwards, Albany, to AIHA in 1951. See note to No. 453.
Attribution: To Ezra Ames by Irwin F. Cortelyou and Robert G. Wheeler, 1951.
Examined by IFC.

[498] UNIDENTIFIED MAN (unfinished).
Description: Oval, ivory 3¼ x 2½ inches. Bust, head to left. Damaged with a moist thumbprint.
Date: Uncertain.
Owner: Presented by Miss Elizabeth S. Edwards, Albany, to AIHA in 1951. See note to No. 453.
Attribution: To Ezra Ames by Irwin F. Cortelyou and T. Bolton, 1950.
Examined by IFC and TB.

[499] UNIDENTIFIED WOMAN.
Description: Rectangle, water color on paper 3 3/16 x 3¼. Bust, head slightly to left, with cap.
Date: Uncertain.
Owner: Presented by Miss Elizabeth S. Edwards, Albany, to AIHA in 1951. See note to No. 453.
Attribution: Tentatively to Ezra Ames by Irwin F. Cortelyou, 1951.
Examined by IFC.

[500] UNIDENTIFIED WOMAN (unfinished).
Description: Oval, ivory 2¾ x 2¼ inches. Bust, head slightly to right. Dark hair parted in center, ringlets.
Date: Uncertain.
Owner: Presented by Miss Elizabeth S. Edwards, Albany, to AIHA in 1951. See note to No. 453.
Attribution: To Ezra Ames by Irwin F. Cortelyou and T. Bolton, 1950.
Examined by IFC and TB.

[501] UNIDENTIFIED WOMAN.
Listed in the *Catalogue of Albany's Bicentennial Loan Exhibition at the Albany Academy, July 5 to July 24, 1886*, pp. 122, 126, as follows: "Ezra Ames (deceased). / 212 Portrait of a lady (water-color) . . . [owned by] Cantine Tremper."
Unlocated.

[502] VAN CORTLANDT, MRS. PIERRE II, née Catharine Clinton (1770-1811), daughter of Governor George Clinton; widow of Captain John Taylor of the British Army; later the first wife of Pierre Van Cortlandt II, married 1801 (*CAB;* Florence Van Rensselaer, *The Livingston Family in America,* New York, 1949, p. 106).

Description: Oval, ivory 3½ x 2½ inches. Bust, profile, head to right.

Date: *c.* 1811.

Owners: (1) Miss Anne S. Van Cortlandt, granddaughter of the sitter, and her nieces Miss Catharine Van Cortlandt Mathews and Mrs. William V. Mason, Croton-on-Hudson, N.Y.; (2) after the death of Miss Van Cortlandt in 1940, owned by her nieces; (3) purchased by Joseph B. Brenauer for $145 at Van Cortlandt Sale, 1941; (4) bequeathed by him to the Museum of the City of New York, 1946.

Photograph: FARL 35083s.

Reproduction: Catalogue, Van Cortlandt and Other Collections Sale; Parke-Bernet Galleries, New York City, February 6-8, 1941, p. 94.

Note: The above is probably based on the head in the half-length portrait, No. 384.

Examined by IFC and TB.

[503] VAN RENSSELAER, STEPHEN III (1764-1839), as a young man.

Description: Oval, ivory 2 7/8 x 2 3/8 inches. Bust, head to left. Copy after a portrait in oil by Gilbert Stuart (reproduced: Lawrence Park, *Gilbert Stuart,* New York, 1926, IV, 540).

Date: *c.* 1814.

Owner: Presented by Miss Elizabeth S. Edwards, Albany, to AIHA in 1951. See note to No. 453.

Photograph: By Irwin F. Cortelyou.

Attribution: To Ezra Ames by Irwin F. Cortelyou and T. Bolton, 1950.

Note: Identification of sitter was made by Irwin F. Cortelyou, 1950.

Examined by IFC and TB.

[504] WADE, EZEKIEL MULFORD (1814-1886), as a child. Grandnephew of Ezra Ames; son of Dr. James Wade and Sally (Mulford) Wade (Mary L. Sutliff, *A Record of the Ancestors and the Descendants of Betsy Mulford Sutliff,* Albany, 1897, p. 22.)

Description: Oval, sepia watercolor on paper 3 x 2 1/8 inches. Bust, head to left.

Date: *c.* 1822.

Owner: Miss Edith S. Wade, Cohoes, N.Y., granddaughter of the sitter.

Photograph: AIHA; print at FARL.

Exhibition: AIHA 1946.

Examined by IFC and TB.

[505] WADE, JAMES (1789-1868), physician, married Sally Mulford, niece of Ezra Ames, 1813, the daughter of Ezekiel Mulford and Sally (Emes) Mulford (Mary L. Sutliff, *A Record of the Ancestors and the Descendants of Betsy Mulford Sutliff,* Albany, 1897, pp. 21-22).
Description: Rectangle, sepia watercolor on paper 4½ x 3½ inches, painted in an oval. Half-length, head to right.
Date: *c.* 1822.
Owner: Miss Edith S. Wade, Cohoes, N.Y., great-granddaughter of the sitter.
Photograph: AIHA; print at FARL.
Exhibition: AIHA 1946.
Examined by IFC and TB. [Illustrated p. 136]

[506] WHEELER, JOSEPH. [Patron]. "Reg. of Prob." (*Massachusetts Spy*, April 7, 1790); of Worcester, Massachusetts (*U.S. Census*, 1790, p. 245). A miniature painted for him is recorded in Account Book, December 4, 1790.
Unlocated.

[507] WHEELER, JOSEPH. [Patron]. A miniature painted for him with a locket and setting is recorded in Account Book, October 1791. That portion of this entry in the Account Book which records a miniature possibly refers to payment for the miniature No. 506.
Unlocated.

[508] WHEELER, THEOPHILUS. [Patron]. Of Worcester, Massachusetts (*U.S. Census, 1790*, p. 245). Doubtless the patron whose name is spelled "Theopelous Whealer," for whom Ames recorded the painting of a miniature in Account Book, December 4, 1790.
Unlocated.

[509] WILLARD, LEVI. [Patron]. His payment for a miniature is recorded in Account Book, May 1, 1794.
Unlocated.

[510] YATES, MRS. [Patron]. Two miniatures painted for "Mrs. Ya[tes]" are recorded in Account Book, February 10, 1794.
Unlocated.

[511] YATES, MRS. [Patron]. One of two miniatures painted for her in 1794. See No. 510.
Unlocated.

[512] YATES, MISS CORN[ELIA]. [Patron]. Quite possibly Cornelia (*c.* 1775-1837), the daughter of Pieter Yates (of Albany ?), who married Willem Teller, son of Jacobus Teller. She died January 12, 1837, in her sixty-second year (Jonathan Pearson, *Contributions for the Genealogies of the Descendants of the First Settlers of the Patent and City of Schenectady from 1662 to 1800*, Albany, 1873, p. 190). Two miniatures painted for "Miss Corn[elia] Yates" are recorded in Account Book, April 24, 1794.
Unlocated.

[513] YATES, MISS CORN[ELIA]. [Patron]. One of two miniatures painted for her in 1794. See No. 512.
Unlocated.

XIII

LANDSCAPES, FIGURE COMPOSITIONS, STILL LIFE, AND DRAWINGS

THIS SECTION includes paintings and drawings in various media, both located and known only through a pictorial or documentary record. The fact that a picture is listed here indicates that the writers accept it as by Ezra Ames, whether or not a note to that effect appears in the entry.

[514] ADAM AND EVE. A painting entitled "Adam & Eve" is listed and appraised at $5.00 in the Inventory, 1836, of the Ezra Ames estate.
Unlocated.

[515] ALLEGORICAL PAINTING. An allegorical painting for "T[emple] Lodge &c," charged to William Barclay, accountant (*Albany Directory*, 1815), is recorded in Account Book, March 1, 1819.
Unlocated.

[516] ALLEGORY OF FAITH AND DEATH. A painting entitled "Allegory of Faith & Death" is listed and appraised at $10.00 in the Inventory, 1836, of the Ezra Ames estate.
Unlocated.

[517] ALLEGORY OF PROVIDENCE. A painting entitled " Allegory of Providence" is listed and appraised at $10.00 in the Inventory, 1836, of the Ezra Ames estate.
Unlocated.

[518] AMES, FISHER (1758-1808), orator and statesman (*DAB*).
Description: Pencil drawing on tan paper, 5 1/8 x 4 7/8 inches. Half-length, head to left. A copy, probably from an engraving, after the portrait by Gilbert Stuart.
Date: Uncertain.
Inscription: Bears title below figure: "Fisher Ames."
Owner: Presented to AIHA in 1941 by Miss Elizabeth S. Edwards and Henry Ames Edwards, Albany, great-grandchildren of Ezra Ames.
Examined by IFC and TB.

[519] APPLE AND A PEAR. A painting of "an Apple & a Pear" charged to "His Excellency Govr [DeWitt] Clinton" is recorded in Account Book, December 1821.
Unlocated.

[520] ASSAULT OF THE ISLE OF [?]. A painting entitled "the asalt of the Ile of [?]" charged to James Caldwell is recorded in Account Book, July 3, 1810.
Unlocated.

[521] BEAVER ASSIDUITY FOR STEAMBOAT. A painting entitled "the Beaver Assiduity for steamboat" charged to James Van Ingen is recorded in Account Book, April 24, 1811. This probably was a painting for the steamboat *Perseverance*. The *Perseverance* was launched in the Hudson River in 1811 (Reynolds, 410). It might possibly be the painting of the coat of arms of the City of Albany at AIHA, which shows a beaver at work and the motto "Assiduity." For further details see pp. 59-60 herein.
Unlocated.

[522] DIANA. A painting entitled "Diana" is listed and appraised at $10.00 in the Inventory, 1836, of the Ezra Ames estate.
Unlocated.

[523] EAGLE. A painting entitled "Portrait of an Eagle" is listed and appraised at $6.00 in the Inventory, 1836, of the Ezra Ames estate.
Unlocated.

[524] ECLIPSE OF THE SUN. "It [the eclipse] was captured by Ezra Ames and Simeon De Witt. The former made a painting of it, and the latter described it. . . . Mr. De Witt in describing the painting says: 'The edge of the Moon was strongly illuminated, and had the brilliancy of polished silver. No common colors could express this; I therefore directed it to be attempted by a raised silver rim.'" (G.A. Worth, *Random Recollections of Albany*, Albany, 1868, p. 41). In 1806 Simeon De Witt presented his [Ezra Ames's] painting "Eclipse of the Sun" to the American Philosophical Society in Philadelphia. This canvas is now lost. (R.G. Wheeler, *American Collector*, August 1947, p. 7).
Unlocated.

[525] FAMILY GROUP.
Description: Brush drawing in outline on paper, 20 x 16 inches.

Date: Uncertain.
Owner: Presented to AIHA in 1941 by Miss Elizabeth S. Edwards and Mr. Henry Ames Edwards, Albany, great-grandchildren of Ezra Ames.
Examined by IFC and TB.

[526] FIGURE OF HOPE FOR STEAMBOAT. A painting entitled "figure of Hope for steamboat" charged to James Van Ingen is recorded in Account Book, March 20, 1811. This was undoubtedly painted for the steamboat *Hope*. The *Hope* was launched in the Hudson River, March 19, 1811 (Reynolds, 409).For further details see pp. 59-60 herein.
Unlocated.

[527] FISH. A painting entitled "Fish" charged to "Govnr [DeWitt] Clinton" is recorded in Account Book, October 10, 1818.
Unlocated.

[528] FISH: LAKE HERRING. A "Portrait of a Lake Herring" charged to "Govnr [DeWitt] Clinton" is recorded in Account Book, March 25, 1818.
Unlocated.

[529] FISH: PIKE. A painting of a "Pike–fish" charged to " Govnr [DeWitt] Clinton" is recorded in Account Book, December 23, 1820.
Unlocated.

[530] FISH: SILVER LAKE WHITE FISH. A painting of a "Silver Lake White Fish" charged to "Govenr [Dewitt] Clinton" is recorded in Account Book, April 23, 1822.
Unlocated.

[531] FISH: WHITE LAKE FISH. A "Portrait of a White Lake Fish" charged to "Govnr [DeWitt] Clinton" is recorded in Account Book, March 8, 1818.
Unlocated.

[532] FRUIT PIECE. A painting entitled "Fruit Piece" is listed and appraised at $20.00 in the Inventory, 1836, of the Ezra Ames estate.
Unlocated.

[533] HAMILTON, ALEXANDER (1757-1804). A portrait drawing of Alexander Hamilton is mentioned in a letter at the NYHS from Williams & Whiting to Ezra Ames, dated at New York January 11, 1810: "We have been waiting . . . to hear from you on the Subject of Genl Hamilton's Portrait – We have now got the work in press,

& should have the engraving in hand also – Please to inform us ... whether we may expect this drawing prepared ...." The engraving by Leney after this drawing is No. 577 herein. For further details see pp. 49-50 herein.
Unlocated.

[534] HOLY FAMILY.
Description: Canvas, 30 x 24 inches.
Date: Uncertain.
Owner: Miss Elizabeth S. Edwards, Albany, great-granddaughter of Ezra Ames.
Photograph: AIHA; print at FARL.
Exhibition: AIHA, 1946, lent by Miss Elizabeth S. Edwards.
Examined by IFC and TB.

[535] A VIEW OF LAKE GEORGE & CALDWELL VILLAGE TAKEN FROM THE WEST SIDE OF THE FORT [WITHOUT FORT].
Description: Panel, oblong, 28 x 36 inches. The fort which appeared originally in the foreground has been painted out. The perspective lines may still be seen under the overpainting. Ezra Ames was no doubt referring to this overpainting in his Account Book entry of August 26, 1822: "To altering a paint[in]g of Lake Georg[e] $2.00" for James Caldwell. Similar to No. 536 except that in the latter picture the fort still appears in the foreground.
Date: *c*. 1812. Since this was painted at the site it is presumably the original of the two landscapes of Lake George (Nos. 536, 537) entered in Account Book in 1812.
Inscription: (a) On the front along the lower margin, the title given above; (b) on the back, "Wm Caldwell / A[l]bany / Taken by Ezra Ames / from Fort George / By request / of my Father who took him / to the Lake to make this view."
Owners: (1) James Caldwell; (2) his son William Caldwell; (3) Miss Anne S. Van Cortlandt and her nieces Miss Catharine Van Cortlandt Mathews and Mrs. William V. Mason; (4) after Miss Van Cortlandt's death in 1940, owned by her nieces, Croton-on-Hudson, N.Y.
Photograph: FARL 34718.
Note: For further discussion see pp. 67-69 herein.
Examined by IFC. [Illustrated p. 69]

[536] LANDSCAPE: PERSPECTIVE PAINTING OF LAKE GEORGE [WITH THE FORT].
Description: Panel, oblong, 27 x 35 1/8 inches. Similar to No. 535 except that in the latter picture the fort has been painted out.
Date: 1812. A "Perspective painting of Lake George" charged to

John Tayler is recorded in Account Book, September 1812.
Owners: (1) John Tayler, remaining on the walls of his home "Norman Vale," near Albany, until acquired by the present owner, (2) Mrs. Weeks Stewart, Bayport, Long Island, N.Y.
Photograph: FARL, taken and presented by Irwin F. Cortelyou.
Attribution: Located and attributed to Ezra Ames by Irwin F. Cortelyou, 1951. T. Bolton concurs in the attribution, judging from a photograph.
Note: For further discussion see pp. 67-69.
Examined by IFC. [Illustrated p. 68]

[537] LANDSCAPE: VIEW OF LAKE GEORGE. A painting entitled "View of Lake George" charged to James Kane is recorded in Account Book, March 13, 1812.
Unlocated.

[538] LANDSCAPE: ROMANTIC LANDSCAPE, also called THE LADY OF THE LAKE, and ALLEGORICAL LANDSCAPE.
Description: Canvas, 34¼ x 45½ inches.
Date: Uncertain.
Owner: Presented to AIHA in 1943 by Miss Elizabeth S. Edwards and Mr. Henry Ames Edwards, Albany, great-grandchildren of Ezra Ames.
Photograph: AIHA; print at FARL.
Exhibitions: Chicago Art Institute, Chicago, 1945; Whitney Museum of American Art, New York City, 1945, measurements as given above; AIHA 1946.
Note: A painting entitled "Voyage of Life" listed and appraised at $20.00 in the Inventory, 1836, of the Ezra Ames estate, may be the above painting. For further discussion see pp. 69-71 herein.
Examined by IFC and TB. [Illustrated p. 70]

[539] LAST SUPPER. A painting entitled "The Last Supper (original)" is listed and appraised at $50.00 in the Inventory, 1836, of the Ezra Ames estate. This is doubtless the picture painted by Ezra Ames, listed as No. 64, "The Last Supper, (original,) 3 feet 5 by 4 feet 5," in the handbill: *Catalogue Sale of Portraits*, 1842, in the Ezra Ames estate.
Unlocated.

[540] LION. A painting of a "Lion" is recorded in Account Book, December 22, 1800. The name of the patron is not noted.
Unlocated.

[541] LION AND LADY. A painting entitled "Lion & Lady" is

listed and appraised at $5.00 in the Inventory, 1836, of the Ezra Ames estate.
Unlocated.

[542] LUCRETIA. A painting of "Lucretia" is one of three "paintings on Glass... each 4.00" listed in the Inventory, 1836, of the Ezra Ames estate.
Unlocated.

[543] MADONNA AND CHILD.
Description: Canvas. Composition based on that of Raphael's "MADONNA OF THE CHAIR."
Date: Uncertain.
Owner: Miss Elizabeth S. Edwards, Albany, great-granddaughter of Ezra Ames; on loan at AIHA since 1951.
Photograph: By Irwin F. Cortelyou.
Note: Possibly the portrait listed as "Madonna and infant," and appraised at $40.00 in the Inventory, 1836, of the Ezra Ames estate.
Examined by IFC and TB.

[544] MAGDALEN. A painting entitled "Magdalen" is listed and appraised at $30.00 in the Inventory, 1836, of the Ezra Ames estate.
Unlocated.

[545] MOURNING BRIDE. A painting entitled "Mourning bride" is listed and appraised at $15.00 in the Inventory, 1836, of the Ezra Ames estate.
Unlocated.

[546] MURDER OF THE PRINCES IN THE TOWER.
Description: Drawing in pencil on paper, 8½ x 6 7/8 inches. Unfinished.
Date: Uncertain.
Owner: Presented to AIHA in 1941 by Miss Elizabeth S. Edwards and Mr. Henry Ames Edwards, Albany, great-grandchildren of Ezra Ames.
Examined by IFC.

[547] MURDER OF THE PRINCES IN THE TOWER. A painting with this title is listed and appraised at $50.00 in the Inventory, 1836, of the Ezra Ames estate. This is doubtless the picture painted by Ezra Ames listed as No. 62, "Murder of the Princes in the Tower, 4 feet 9 by 7 feet 3," in the handbill: *Catalogue Sale of Portraits*, 1842, in the Ezra Ames estate.
Unlocated.

[548] MUSIDORA. A painting entitled "Musidora" is listed and appraised at $20.00 in the Inventory, 1836, of the Ezra Ames estate.
Unlocated.

[549] OWL. A painting entitled "[Portrait of an] Owl" is listed and appraised at $3.00 in the Inventory, 1836, of the Ezra Ames estate.
Unlocated.

[550] OX. A painting entitled "[Portrait of an] Ox" is listed and appraised at $3.00 in the Inventory, 1836, of the Ezra Ames estate.
Unlocated.

[551] PAUL AND VIRGINIA. A painting entitled "Paul & Virginia" is listed and appraised at $30.00 in the Inventory, 1836, of the Ezra Ames estate.
Unlocated.

[552] ROMAN CHARITY. A painting entitled "Roman Charity" is listed and appraised at $15.00 in the Inventory, 1836, of the Ezra Ames estate.
Unlocated.

[553] SAMSON AND THE PHILISTINES. A painting by Ezra Ames is listed as No. 65, "Sampson [*sic*] and the Philistines, 3 feet by 4 feet 5" in the handbill: *Catalogue Sale of Portraits*, 1842, in the Ezra Ames estate. This is doubtless the picture entitled " Binding of Samson" listed and appraised at $25.00 in the Inventory, 1836, of the Ezra Ames estate.
Unlocated.

[554] SHAKESPEARE'S TEMPEST. CAVE SCENE.
Description: Canvas, 18½ x 25 inches.
Date: Uncertain.
Owner: Miss Elizabeth S. Edwards, Albany, great-granddaughter of Ezra Ames; on loan at AIHA since 1951.
Photograph: AIHA; print at FARL.
Exhibition: AIHA 1946, lent by Miss Elizabeth S. Edwards.
Note: Listed as "small Scene from the Tempest (cave)," in the Inventory, 1836, of the Ezra Ames estate.
Examined by IFC and TB.

[555] SHAKESPEARE'S TEMPEST. SHIPWRECK SCENE. A painting entitled "Scene from the Tempest (shipwreck)" is listed and appraised at $50.00 in the Inventory, 1836, of the Ezra Ames estate.

This is doubtless the picture painted by Ezra Ames, listed as No. 63, "Shipwreck scene from the Tempest, 4 feet by 5," in the handbill: *Catalogue Sale of Portraits*, 1842, in the Ezra Ames estate.
Unlocated.

[556] STUDENT. A painting entitled "Student" is one of three "paintings on Glass ... each 4.00" listed in the Inventory, 1836, of the Ezra Ames estate.
Unlocated.

[557] UNIDENTIFIED GIRL.
Description: Drawing in pen and ink on paper, 8 x 5 1/8 inches. Half-length, head to right.
Date: Uncertain.
Owner: Presented to AIHA in 1941 by Miss Elizabeth S. Edwards and Mr. Henry Ames Edwards, Albany, great-grandchildren of Ezra Ames.
Examined by IFC.

[558] UNIDENTIFIED SITTERS: "FIVE HEADS." A painting entitled "Five Heads" is listed and appraised at $15.00 in the Inventory, 1836, of the Ezra Ames estate. This is possibly one of the two pictures painted by Ezra Ames listed as Nos. 66 and 67, "Groups of Heads," [30 x 24 inches] in the handbill: *Catalogue Sale of Portraits*, 1842, in the Ezra Ames estate.
Unlocated.

[559] UNIDENTIFIED SITTERS: GROUPS OF HEADS. One of two pictures of that title mentioned in entry No. 558.
Unlocated.

[560] UNIDENTIFIED SITTERS. GROUP OF THREE CHILDREN. A painting entitled "Groupe of 3 children" is listed and appraised at $10.00 in the Inventory, 1836, of the Ezra Ames estate.
Unlocated.

[561] UNIDENTIFIED WOMAN. A painting of a "Lady" is one of three "paintings on Glass ... each 4.00" listed in the Inventory, 1836, of the Ezra Ames estate.
Unlocated.

[562] VENUS. A painting entitled "Venus" is listed and appraised at $40.00 in the Inventory, 1836, of the Ezra Ames estate.
Unlocated.

[563] VENUS AND CUPID. A painting entitled "Venus and cupid" is listed and appraised at $40.00 in the Inventory, 1836, of the Ezra Ames estate. This is doubtless the picture painted by Ezra Ames, listed as No. 68, "Venus and Cupid, 2 feet 4 by 3 feet," in the handbill: *Catalogue Sale of Portraits*, 1842, in the Ezra Ames estate.
Unlocated.

XIV

PRINTS AFTER PORTRAITS BY EZRA AMES

GENERALLY a lithograph, an engraving, or an etching of a portrait was not made directly from the portrait, but was based on a drawing made of the portrait. For this reason it is generally difficult to state with certainty, when replicas or near-replicas exist, on which portrait a print is based.

D. M. Stauffer, *American Engravers Upon Copper and Steel*, New York, 1907, 2 vols., and Mantle Fielding, *Supplement*, 1917, are referred to respectively as: Stauffer; and Stauffer, *Supplement*.

In the research for the portraits and miniatures (Nos. 1–513), the writers came across certain prints after portraits by Ezra Ames which are listed below. No extensive search was made solely to find such prints.

[564] ALLEN, SOLOMON (1751-1821).
Engraving: By B. Tanner and W.R. Jones.
Description: Stipple, rectangle 3 7/8 x 3¼ inches. Half-length, head to right.
Inscription: "Painted by E. Ames. – Engraved by B. Tanner & W.R. Jones. / Revd Solomon Allen. / AET: 70." (Stauffer, No. 1507. See also Stauffer No. 3081.)
Note: The portrait after which this was engraved is probably No. 5. However since no copy of this engraving has been located, comparison with the extant portrait has not been possible.

[565] AMES, EZRA (1768-1836).
Engraving: By H.B. Hall's Sons.
Description: Line, vignette, 4 x 3½ inches. Bust, head to right.
Inscription: "Ezra Ames [facsimile of signature] / Engd by H.B. Hall's Sons, New York."
Publication: George Rogers Howell and Jonathan Tenney, *Bi-Centennial History of Albany*, New York, 1886, facing p. 739.
Reproduction: William Dunlap, *The Arts of Design in the United States*, Boston, 1918, III, facing p. 24.
Note: Probably based on the miniature dated about 1810, No. 457.

[566] BLATCHFORD, SAMUEL (1767-1828).
Engraving: By William D. Smith.
Description: Line, rectangle 12 13/16 x 10¼ inches. Half-length, head to left.
Inscription: "Painted by Ames. – Engd by Wm. D. Smith. / Samuel Blatchford, D.D." (Stauffer, *Supplement,* No. 1465.)
Note: This engraving may have been made after the unlocated portrait No. 27. However, since no copy of this engraving has been located, comparison with the extant reproduction of the portrait has not been possible.

[567] CHESTER, JOHN (*c.* 1786-1829), pastor of the Second Presbyterian Church, Albany, died January 12, 1829, at Philadelphia, aged 43 years (Reynolds, 445).
Engraving: By Rawdon, Clark & Co., dated 1819.
Description: Line engraving, rectangle, 3½ x 3 inches. Bust, head to left.
Inscription: "Rev. John Chester D. D. / Drawn & engraved by Rawdon, Clark & Co." (Stauffer, No. 2642.)
Note: A copy of this engraving is at FARL.

[568] CHESTER, JOHN (*c.* 1786-1829).
Engraving: By John Sartain.
Description: Mezzotint, rectangle 4 1/8 x 3½ inches exclusive of inscription. Half-length, head to right.
Inscription: "ENGRAVED BY JOHN SARTAIN FROM A PICTURE BY AMES / REV. JOHN CHESTER. D. D."
Note: A copy of this engraving is at FARL.

[569] CLARKE, MRS. BEULAH ALLEN.
Engraving: By Peter Maverick.
Description: Stipple, rectangle 4½ x 3½ inches.
Inscription: "Painted by Ames – Engrd by Peter Maverick. / Mrs Beulah Allen Clarke. / Utica, N.Y." (Stauffer, *Supplement,* No. 1024. A footnote states: "This is S[tauffer] 2193, and is published in '*Sermon on Death of Mrs. B.A. Clarke,* N.Y., 1827.")
Note: A copy of this engraving has not been located.

[570] CLINTON, DeWITT (1769-1828).
Engraving: By V[istus] Balch (who is first listed as an engraver in Albany in 1820 – Ms. Dictionary of Artists in America at NYHS).
Description: Line, rectangle with decorative border 8¾ x 7 3/8 inches. Half-length, head to left, column and curtain in background.
Inscription: "DE WITT CLINTON / Drawn & Engd by V. Balch – from

a Portrait by E. Ames." (Stauffer, *Supplement*, No. 92.)
Note: Copies of this engraving are at the American Antiquarian Society, Worcester, Massachusetts, and NYHS.

[571] CLINTON, GEORGE (1739-1812).
Engraving: By John Chester Buttre.
Description: Line, vignette about 4½ x 3½ inches. Bust, head to right.
Inscription: "Painted by Ames – Engraved by Buttre / George Clinton [facsimile of signature]."
Publication: Allen C. Beach, *Centennial Celebrations of the State of New York*, Albany, 1879. Frontispiece.

[572] CLINTON, GEORGE (1739-1812).
Engraving: By Daggett, Hinman & Co.
Description: Line, vignette 4 3/8 x 3½ inches. Bust, head to right.
Inscription: "Ames Pinxt / Daggett, Hinman & Co. Sc. / GEORGE CLINTON."
Publication: Jabez D. Hammond, *The History of Political Parties in the State of New-York*, Albany, 1842, I, frontispiece.
Reproduction: *Kingston Daily Leader*, July 3, 1930.

[573] CLINTON, GEORGE (1739-1812).
Engraving: By J. B. Forest.
Description: Line, vignette 4 x 3¾ inches exclusive of inscription. Bust, head to right.
Inscription: "Ames / J. B. Forest / GOVERNOR GEORGE CLINTON / Printed by W. Pate / Geo Clinton [facsimile of signature] / New York G. P. Putnam & Co."
Publication: Washington Irving, *Life of Washington*, N.Y., 1857, II, facing 224. (Engraved title, 1857; printed title, 1856; one of 110 copies, quarto. The volume examined is at the Century Club, New York City.)

[574] CLINTON, GEORGE (1739-1812).
Engraving: By Peter Maverick.
Description: Line, rectangle 5¼ x 4¼ inches. Bust, head to right.
Inscription: "Painted by Ames. – Engraved by P. Maverick. / Published by Joseph Delaplaine. / George Clinton. / Printed by Porter & Harrison." Two states: (1) as given, (2) with publisher's line erased. (Stauffer, No. 2195.)
Publication: Joseph Delaplaine, *Delaplaine's Repository of the Lives and Portraits of Distinguished Americans*, Philadelphia, 1818, II, Pt. I, facing p. 19. Copy at FARL.
Reproduction: Justin Windsor, *Narrative and Critical History of America*, Boston and New York, 1888, VI, p. 308.

[575] CROLIUS, CLARKSON (1773-1843).
Lithograph: By F. D'Avignon.
Description: Vignette, bust, 4¾ x 3½ inches on oval, tan, 10 x 8 inches, with decorative border.
Inscription: "Lith. by D'Avignon / from Portrait by Ezra Ames / Clarkson Crolius [facsimile of signature] / Late Vice-President of the American Institute."
Note: The portrait after which this was engraved is probably No. 78. Copies of this lithograph are at NYHS.

[576] CUSHMAN, JOHN P. (1784-1848), lawyer, born in Pomfret, Connecticut, son of Isaac Cushman and Sarah (Paine) Cushman; moved to Troy, N.Y., in 1809; married the eldest daughter of Benjamin Tallmadge. Representative from New York, U.S. Congress, 1817-1819; Regent of the University of the State of New York, 1830-1834; and a Trustee of Union College (*BDAC*, and *Genealogy of the Cushmans*, pp. 318-334).
Lithograph: By F. D'Avignon. After an unlocated portrait by Ezra Ames, according to Irwin F. Cortelyou.
Description: Rectangle 5 x 4 inches. Bust, head slightly to right.
Inscription: "Lith. by F. D'Avignon / 80, Leonard St., N.Y. / HON. JOHN P. CUSHMAN / Aged 35 / Troy, N.Y. / See 894 / J.P. Cushman. [facsimile of signature].
Publication: Henry Wyles Cushman, *A Historical and Biographical Genealogy of the Cushmans*, Boston, 1855, facing p. 318.
Note: "The foregoing portrait was engraved from a daguerrotype taken from a portrait painted some years before his decease. It is said to be an excellent likeness of him in the prime of life." (*Ibid*,, 334.)

[577] HAMILTON, ALEXANDER (1757-1804).
Engraving: By William S. Leney.
Description: Stipple, rectangle 4 x 3 1/8 inches. Bust, head to right.
Inscription: "Ames Pinxt – Leney fct / Alexander Hamilton. / Printed by A.G. Reynolds / New York Publish'd according to act of Congress by Williams & Whiting Septr 14.1810." Two states: (1) as given, (2) with printer and publisher erased. (Stauffer, No. 1768.)
Publication: *The Works of Alexander Hamilton*, New York, Williams & Whiting, 1810, frontispiece.
Note: See entry No. 533 quoting a letter from Williams & Whiting to Ames requesting the drawing for the above-mentioned engraving.
[Illustrated p. 51]

[578] HAMILTON, ALEXANDER (1757-1804).
Engraving: By William Hoogland.
Description: Stipple, rectangle 3½ x 2 11/16 inches. Bust, head to right. Similar to the engraving (No. 577) by William S. Leney.
Inscription: "Painted by Ames. – Engraved by Hoogland. / Alexander Hamilton. / Published by Samuel Walker (Harlem Place) Washington Street Boston." (Stauffer, No. 1423.)
Note: Based on the engraving by Leney or on the drawing (No. 533) which is lost. A copy of this engraving is at FARL.
[Illustrated p. 51]

[579] LANSING, JOHN, JR. (1754-1829).
Etching: By Albert Rosenthal.
Description: Etching, rectangle. Bust, head to left.
Inscription: " Etched by Albert Rosenthal Phila. 1888."
Reproduction: Reynolds, facing p. [370].
Note: The caption under the reproduction states that the etching was made from the oil painting (No. 181) owned by Thomas Addis Emmet in 1885. A copy of this etching has not been located.

[580] LANSING, JOHN, JR. (1754-1829).
Etching: By Max Rosenthal.
Description: Etching, rectangle 6¾ x 4½ inches. Bust, head to left.
Inscription: "Max Rosenthal / JOHN LANSING, JR / Member of the Continental Congress. / John Lansing Jr. [facsimile of signature]."
Note: The portrait after which this was made is possibly No. 181. A copy of this etching is at The New York Public Library, Manuscript Division, Emmet Collection, No. 694.

[581] NOTT, ELIPHALET (1773-1866).
Engraving: By A. B. Durand.
First State: Description: Line, rectangle 4¾ x 3 7/8 inches. Bust, head to right. Inscription: "Painted by Ames / Eng by A. B. Durand. / Rev. Eliphalet Nott D. D. LL.D. / Engraved expressly for the Parthenon." (Stauffer, No. 625.)
Second State: Description: Same as First State. Inscription: Same as First State except for last line erased. (Stauffer, No. 625.) Publication: Gorham A. Worth, *Random Recollections of Albany*, Albany, 1866, facing p. 76.
Third State: Description: Same as First State. Inscription: "Painted by Ames 1820 / Eng. by A. B. Durand / E. Nott [facsimile of signature] / REV. ELIPHALET NOTT D.D. LL. D." Publication: Van Santvoord and Lewis, *Memoirs of Eliphalet Nott*, New York, 1876, facing p. [11].
Note: Based on the miniature, No. 486.

[582] STAFFORD, SPENCER (1772-1844).
Lithograph.
Description: Vignette 4 1/8 x 3¾ inches. Bust, head to left.
Inscription: "Ames, 1805 / Spencer Stafford [facsimile of signature]"
Publication: Henry Marvin Benedict, *A Contribution to the Genealogy of the Stafford Family in America,* Albany, 1870, frontispiece.
Note: The portrait on which this lithograph was based is No. 290.

[583] TALLMADGE, BENJAMIN (1754-1835).
Engraving: By George Parker.
Description: Line, rectangle 4½ x 3 3/8 inches. Bust, head to right.
Inscription: "Painted by E. Ames / Engd by G. Parker / COL. BENJAMIN TALLMADGE / Benj. Tallmadge [facsimile of signature]."
Publication: James B. Longacre and James Herring, *National Portrait Gallery,* Philadelphia, 1836, III, no pagination.
Note: This might be based on any one of the oil portraits (Nos. 310-312) of Benjamin Tallmadge.

[584] VAN BUREN, MARTIN (1782-1862).
Engraving: By H. W. Smith.
Description: Line, vignette in rectangle 7 1/8 x 6 inches. Bust, head to right.
Inscription: "Ezra Ames. Pinxt / H. W. Smith. Sc. N.Y. / M Van Buren [facsimile of signature]."
Note: This might be based on either No. 379 or No. 380. A copy of this engraving is at The New York Public Library, Manuscript Division, Emmet Collection, No. 1414.

[585] WATSON, ELKANAH (1758-1842).
Engraving: By V[istus] Balch.
Description: Line, oval 4 x 3 inches with decorative border. Bust, head to right.
Inscription: "ELKANAH WATSON / E. Ames Pinxt / V. Balch Sculpt Alb[an]y."
Publication: Elkanah Watson, *History of the Rise, Progress, and Existing Condition of the Western Canals in the State of New York,* Albany, 1820, frontispiece.
Note: Presumably based on an unlocated original recorded in Account Book, September 15, 1818. See No. 425.

[Illustrated p. 158]

[586] YATES, JOSEPH CHRISTOPHER (1768-1837).
Lithograph: By W. Sharp.
Description: Vignette 2¾ x 2½ inches. Bust, head to left.

Inscription: "W. Sharp delt / JOSEPH C. YATES. / J. C. Sharp's Lith. Boston."

Publication: Jabez D. Hammond, *The History of Political Parties in the State of New-York,* Albany, 1842, II, facing p. 101.

Note: Although the artist's name is not given, the head resembles that in the known portraits of Yates by Ezra Ames, Nos. 448-450.

XV

PICTURES MISATTRIBUTED TO EZRA AMES

THIS LIST includes only pictures which have been published or exhibited or are otherwise recorded as by Ezra Ames but which, in the opinion of the writers, have been misattributed to him. It does not include word-of-mouth misattributions by owners or others; nor does it include misattributed pictures once on record at FARL as by Ezra Ames, but now no longer recorded there as by him, unless they have been so recorded elsewhere.

[587] AKIN, WILLIAM (1769-1841). Panel. Half-length. Owner: Mrs. J. Chester Chamberlain, New York City. Attributed to Ezra Ames on FARL photomount. Photograph: FARL 15535. After examination of the portrait Irwin F. Cortelyou is of the opinion that it was not painted by Ezra Ames. Judging from the photograph, T. Bolton concurs with this opinion. (Probably by Julius Rubens Ames, the artist's son. – IFC.)

[588] BALDWIN, STEPHEN. Canvas. Full-length. Owner: Mr. David A. Turnure, Salisbury, Connecticut. Listed as by Ezra Ames in Historical Records Survey, *Preliminary Catalogue of Early American Portraits Found in New York*, typewritten, Boston, 1942 (?). The writers, after an examination of a photograph of this portrait, are of the opinion that it is not the work of Ezra Ames.

[589] CLINTON, DeWITT (1769-1828). Canvas. Full-length standing. Owner: Senate House Association, hanging in Senate House Museum, Kingston, N.Y., and there attributed to Ezra Ames. Photograph: Irwin F. Cortelyou, 1952. Reproduced: *A Century of Progress; History of the Delaware and Hudson Company 1823-1923*, Albany, 1925, p. 20, with no attribution as to the artist. Irwin F. Cortelyou, after an examination of this portrait, is of the opinion that it was not painted by Ezra Ames. Miss Hope Mathewson (FARL) concurs, judging from the photograph.

[590] CLINTON, DeWITT (1769-1828). Canvas. Bust. Formerly at NYSHA, Cooperstown, N.Y. Now owned by the Canajoharie Library

and Art Gallery, Canajoharie, N.Y. Photograph: Print at FARL. Reproduced: *Handbook of the Museum and Art Gallery of the NYSHA*, 1942, as by Ezra Ames. After studying a photograph, the writers are of the opinion that it is not the work of Ezra Ames.

[591] CLINTON, GEORGE (1739-1812). Watercolor on paper. Half-length, head to right. Owner: NYHS. Examined by IFC and TB. Photograph: NYHS 3374A. Since the writers have seen no watercolor undoubtedly by Ezra Ames painted in a technique similar to this watercolor, they are of the opinion that it is not the work of Ezra Ames. The signature is unlike any by Ezra Ames they have seen.

[592] DOUW, JOHN DE PEYSTER (1756-1835). Panel. Half-length. Owner: AIHA. There tentatively attributed to Ezra Ames. Photograph: AIHA; print at FARL. After examining the painting the writers are of the opinion that it is not the work of Ezra Ames.

[593] DOUW, MARGARET LIVINGSTON. Miniature on ivory. Owner: AIHA. Photograph: AIHA; print at FARL. Recorded in T. Bolton, *Early American Portrait Painters in Miniature*, New York, 1921, as by Ezra Ames following the attribution at AIHA. However, the writers in examining the miniature found a business card of "A[nson] Dickinson" inserted in the back of the miniature showing that it was painted by that artist, and not by Ezra Ames.

[594] GANSEVOORT, CATHERINE DOUW (1782-1848). Miniature on ivory. Owner: AIHA. Photograph: FARL 15760. Recorded in T. Bolton, *Early American Portrait Painters in Miniature*, New York, 1921, as by Ezra Ames following the attribution at AIHA. However, the writers, after an examination of the miniature, are of the opinion that it is not the work of Ezra Ames.

[595] HENRY, JOHN V. (1769-1829). Miniature on ivory. Owner: AIHA. Photograph: FARL 15737. Exhibited at AIHA in 1936 as by Ezra Ames. However, after an examination of the miniature, the writers are of the opinion that it is not by Ezra Ames.

[596] JAY, JOHN (1745-1829). Canvas. Full-length. Owner: American Bible Society, New York City. Photograph: FARL 18599. According to their minutes it was presented to the Society by Samuel Campbell, March 20, 1823, as by John Trumbull. Reproduced: J.J. Ide, *Portraits of John Jay*, New York, 1938, p. 49, and there attributed to Ezra Ames on the basis of a former record at

FARL. The writers, after examining this portrait, are of the opinion that it is not the work of Ezra Ames.

[597] KEARNEY, MRS. R. Miniature on ivory. Owner: Clapp and Graham, dealers, New York City. Exhibited at the Brooklyn Museum, 1936, as by Ezra Ames. The writers, after an examination of photograph FARL 21760, are of the opinion that it is not the work of Ezra Ames.

[598] LEVY, MAURICE. Miniature on ivory. Bust. Owner: Metropolitan Museum. Photograph: Metropolitan Museum 37019. Exhibited at Four Centuries of Miniature Painting, Metropolitan Museum, 1950, as by Ezra Ames. The writers, after an examination of the miniature, are of the opinion that it is not the work of Ezra Ames.

[599] LIVINGSTON, EDWARD (1764-1836), by Anson Dickinson. Miniature on ivory. Half-length. Owner: Metropolitan Museum (photograph: Metropolitan Museum 115513). Exhibited at Four Centuries of Miniature Painting, Metropolitan Museum, 1950, as "Portrait of a Man" by Ezra Ames. The sitter was identified as Edward Livingston by Irwin F. Cortelyou in February 1952, because of the striking resemblance of this miniature to that of Edward Livingston, by an unknown artist, in the collection of General John Ross Delafield, Barrytown, N.Y. (photograph: FARL 32151).

On the FARL photomount of the miniature owned by General Delafield, there also unattributed to any artist, appears a notation made September 2, 1938: "Compare with the work of Sarah Goodridge," and a notation made by Mrs. Thurman Rotan (FARL), November 1950: "Compare also with Anson Dickinson." Following the suggestion made in Mrs. Rotan's note, Irwin F. Cortelyou, with the aid of photographs at FARL of miniatures by Anson Dickinson, discovered the convincing similarity of both the Delafield and Metropolitan Museum miniatures in technique and composition to that of Stephen Van Rensselaer III, signed and dated, "A. Dickinson / Feb. 22, 1827," now owned by Mrs. James Gore King, New York City (photograph: FARL 20060), and thus was able to attribute both these miniatures of Edward Livingston to Anson Dickinson. The attributions were strengthened by entries for miniatures of this sitter in Mary Helen Kidder, *List of Miniatures Painted by Anson Dickinson*, 1803-1851, Hartford, 1937, pp. 35, 40.

FARL in their letter of March 5, 1952, to General Delafield, his letter to FARL of May 28, 1952, and the Metropolitan Museum in their letter of March 22, 1952, to Irwin F. Cortelyou, accepted these findings.

[600] REYNOLDS, LYDIA LOUISA (1817-1876), Mrs. Thomas Hun. Canvas. Bust. Owner: Mrs. Kenneth G. Reynolds, Albany, N.Y. Photograph: FARL 15437. Although once attributed by the family to Ezra Ames and exhibited as by him at AIHA in 1934, the writers in examining the portrait found it inscribed on the back of the canvas as having been painted by: "J.E. Freeman."

[601] STUART, GILBERT (1755-1828). Miniature on ivory. Bust. By Anson Dickinson. Owner: NYHS. Photograph: NYHS 320. Assigned to Dickinson in Donald A. Shelley, *Catalogue of American Portraits in NYHS*, 1941, p. 295. Incorrectly attributed to Ezra Ames in Harry B. Wehle, *American Miniatures*, Garden City, 1927, reproduced facing p. 50. After examining the miniature, the writers agree with the attribution to Anson Dickinson.

[602] TOWNSEND, JOHN FONDEY, M.D. (1810-1874). Miniature on ivory. Owner: AIHA. Photograph: FARL 15761. Recorded in T. Bolton, *Early American Portrait Painters in Miniature*, New York, 1921, as by Ezra Ames following the attribution at AIHA. However, after an examination of the miniature, the writers are of the opinion that it is not the work of Ezra Ames. (Probably by Julius Rubens Ames, the artist's son.–IFC.)

[603] TOWNSEND, MRS. JOHN FONDEY, née Catherine Louisa Douw (1817-1891). Miniature on ivory. Owner: AIHA. Photograph: FARL 15762. Recorded in T. Bolton, *Early American Portrait Painters in Miniature*, New York, 1921, as by Ezra Ames following the attribution of AIHA. However, after an examination of the miniature, the writers are of the opinion that it is not the work of Ezra Ames. (Probably by Julius Rubens Ames, the artist's son. –IFC.)

[604] UNIDENTIFIED WOMAN. So-called "Ellen Tree." Canvas. Photograph: FARL 15076. Brought $25.00 at the John F. Braun Collection Sale, January 16, 1942, New York City. Listed in the sale catalogue as of "Ellen Tree" painted by Ezra Ames. Now unlocated. After studying a photograph, the writers are of the opinion that it is not the work of Ezra Ames.

[605] WALSH, HUGH (1745-1817). Miniature on ivory. Bust, profile. Owner: Mrs. Helen N. Elderkin, Old Greenwich, Conn. Photograph, FARL 9549a. Exhibited at Metropolitan Museum, 1927, and attributed to Ezra Ames in the catalogue. After studying a photograph, the writers are of the opinion that it is not the work of Ezra Ames.

XVI

PICTURES OF QUESTIONABLE ATTRIBUTION. UNSETTLED MATTERS

THIS LIST includes: (1) those pictures which have been attributed to Ezra Ames, but about which the authors have been unable to form an opinion as to whether Ezra Ames did or did not paint them; (2) a few pictures attributed to him by others but which the authors have been unable to examine either directly or through a reproduction; and (3) unlocated pictures of which a doubtful record exists.

[606] AMES, EZRA (1768-1836). So-called self-portrait, on glass. Size: 8¼ x 5¼ inches. Owner: AIHA. Attributed to Ezra Ames by descendants. Examined by IFC and TB. The writers have not seen any certain early work of this type by Ezra Ames with which to compare this portrait and so must leave the matter of attribution an open question.

[607] BOGART, MRS. HENRY I., née Barbara Marselis (1727-1816). Canvas. Bust. Owner: Miss Eleanor H. Lovett, New London, N.H. Photograph: The owner. This portrait was tentatively attributed to Ezra Ames by Mrs. Haven Parker. After studying the photograph, the writers have formed no opinion as to whether Ezra Ames did or did not paint the portrait.

[608] CLINTON, GEORGE (1739-1812), so-called. Canvas. Bust. Owner: Historical Society of the Tarrytowns, hanging at the Philipse Castle Restoration, North Tarrytown, N.Y. Photograph: FARL 32809. On the back of a photograph of this portrait in the late William Sawitzky's file on Ezra Ames there is the following inscription in pencil: "Considered by Mr. Sawitzky and Mr. Rosen to be by Ezra Ames," and "per H.G. Rowell." After examining the picture, the writers have formed no opinion as to whether Ezra Ames did or did not paint this portrait.

[609] CLYMER, GEORGE (1739-1813). A portrait of George Clymer by "Ames" is listed in the catalogues of The Pennsylvania Academy of the Fine Arts, Philadelphia, 1837, p. 10; 1838, p. 10; 1840, p. 10; 1843, p. 6. T. Bolton is inclined to feel that these are errors

of cataloguing and that the portrait in question was probably the portrait painted by Charles Willson Peale. According to Mrs. Barbara S. Roberts, Registrar of the PAFA, in a letter to Irwin F. Cortelyou, 3/13/52, the Peale portrait was exhibited at the PAFA before and after the "Ames" portrait but not in the same years; however, it was always exhibited with a long title while the "Ames" portrait was listed with a short title; therefore: "Since the Academy owned the Peale portrait for so many years before the Ames was exhibited and since the longer title was always used to designate it, it seems likely that there were two portraits, even though they are not listed in the same catalogue together." The writers leave the matter an open question. The "Ames" portrait, if Ezra Ames painted it, is unlocated or was destroyed in the fire of 1845 at the PAFA.

[610] COAT OF ARMS OF THE CITY OF ALBANY. Canvas. Owner: AIHA. Photograph: By Irwin F. Cortelyou. This painting might possibly be the unlocated painting by Ezra Ames (No. 521) called BEAVER ASSIDUITY FOR STEAMBOAT. For details see pp. 59-60 herein. The writers, after examining this canvas, have come to no conclusion as to whether Ezra Ames did or did not paint it.

[611] COOPER, WILLIAM (1754-1809). Canvas. Bust. Owner: Dr. H.S. Fenimore Cooper, Cooperstown, N.Y. Stated by Mr. Theodore Sizer, in *Colonel John Trumbull*, New Haven, 1950, as possibly by Trumbull, but "more likely a copy" by Ames after a lost portrait by Trumbull. The writers have not seen this portrait, or a photograph of it.

[612] CUMMING, HOOPER (1787-1825). A portrait of him which was to have been painted for Joseph Delaplaine is recorded in Account Book, September 8, 1818, but it is crossed out, and is not reinstated in the apparently final list of portraits to be painted for Delaplaine. It is here assumed that the portrait was never painted. However, there is a possibility that it was painted and that the entry was crossed out when the portrait was paid for.

[613] DE GRAFF, JOHN I. Canvas. Half-length. Owner: AIHA. Reproduced: *Magazine of Art*, Albany Institute Edition, April 1946, as by Chester Harding. Now attributed at AIHA to Henry Inman. Examined by IFC. A portrait of John I. De Graff by Ezra Ames is listed as No. 26, in the handbill: *Catalogue Sale of Portraits*, 1842, in the Ezra Ames estate (No. 90 herein); but the writers simply record the fact for consideration, for they have been unable to form any opinion as to who painted the picture at AIHA.

[614] DEXTER, SAMUEL (1756-1825). Canvas. Bust. Formerly owned by Marcus Tullius Reynolds. Photograph: FARL 15723. Exhibited at AIHA, 1934, as by Ezra Ames. After studying the photograph, the writers have formed no opinion as to whether Ezra Ames did or did not paint this portrait.

[615] EGBERTS, CORNELIUS. Canvas. Bust. Oval. Owner: Miss Evelyn Newman, Albany, N.Y. Exhibited at AIHA, 1946, as by Ezra Ames. A portrait of a "Mr. Egberts" is recorded in Ezra Ames's Account Book, October 9, 1826 (No. 107 herein). However, after an examination of the present portrait, the writers have been unable to form an opinion as to whether Ezra Ames did or did not paint it.

[616] GANSEVOORT, LEONARD (1751-1810). Canvas. Bust. The sitter was a judge; brother of General Peter Gansevoort (1749-1812); cousin of Leonard Gansevoort (1754-1834); lived in his country house "White Hall" (*CAB;DAB*). A portrait of Leonard Gansevoort, listed as by Ezra Ames and as owned by Mrs. Abraham Lansing [grandniece of the sitter], in the *Catalogue of Albany's Bicentennial Loan Exhibition at the Albany Academy, July 5 to July 24, 1886*, pp. 114, 126 (62), is presumably the portrait listed as by Gilbert Stuart and as formerly owned by Mrs. Abraham Lansing, Albany, in Lawrence Park, *Gilbert Stuart*, New York, 1926, I, 335, reproduced, III, 183. Of the picture listed in Lawrence Park, Mr. William Sawitzky states: "The portrait of Leonard Gansevoort is in my opinion, an early work of Ezra Ames. The Albany painter, while in a general way influenced by Stuart, became later on a more competent portraitist then he is usually given credit for." (William Sawitzky, "Some Unrecorded Portraits by Gilbert Stuart," *Art in America*, June 1933, p. 89.) For the time being the writers prefer to leave the subject as open.
Notes: (a) This is possibly the portrait of Leonard Gansevoort mentioned in the extract of the will of Mrs. Peter Gansevoort (sister-in-law of the sitter), quoted in the note to No. 126. (b) Judging from a photograph, No. 617 appears to be almost identical to the portrait reproduced in Lawrence Park.
Examined by IFC and TB.

[617] GANSEVOORT, LEONARD (1751-1810). Canvas. Bust. Owners: (1) Mrs. Edgar Morris Griffiths; (2) Mr. Robert Ten Eyck, Albany. Hung originally at the sitter's country home "White Hall." Photograph: FARL 16716. Exhibited at AIHA 1936, as by Gilbert Stuart, lent by Mrs. Griffiths; and at AIHA 1946, as by Ezra Ames,

lent by Mr. Ten Eyck. Judging from the photograph, this portrait appears to be almost identical with the portrait reproduced in Lawrence Park, *Gilbert Stuart,* III, 183, which is probably the portrait listed as No. 616. The writers have not been permitted to see the portrait owned by Mr. Ten Eyck and can form no opinion from examining the photograph as to whether Ezra Ames did or did not paint it.

[618] KANE, MRS. JOHN, née Sybil Kent (1738-1806). Canvas. Half-length. Owner: Mr. R. Keith Kane, New York City. Photograph: FARL 15274. Attributed to Ezra Ames by family tradition. After an examination of this portrait, the writers have formed no opinion as to whether Ezra Ames did or did not paint it.

[619] LANDSCAPE. CAMPAGNA AND VOLCANO. Lettered at bottom: "INTERNO DEL VESUVIO DEL 1835." Gouache. Photograph: By Irwin F. Cortelyou. Presented in 1941 to AIHA by Miss Elizabeth S. Edwards and Mr. Henry Ames Edwards, Albany, great-grandchildren of Ezra Ames, as by Ezra Ames. After examining the picture, the writers have formed no opinion as to whether Ezra Ames did or did not paint it.

[620] LANDSCAPE. FARMING COUNTRYSIDE. Gouache. Presented in 1941 to AIHA by Miss Elizabeth S. Edwards and Mr. Henry Ames Edwards, Albany, great-grandchildren of Ezra Ames, as by Ezra Ames. The writers have not seen this painting nor a photograph of it.

[621] LIVINGSTON, JOHN (1750-1822). Miniature on ivory. Bust. Formerly owned by Herman Livingston, Greendale, N.Y., (died 1951.) Examined by TB. Photograph: FARL 30363. According to Mr. Theodore Sizer: copied after a portrait by John Trumbull. Attributed to Ezra Ames by the late John Marshall Phillips. The writers have formed no opinion as to whether Ezra Ames did or did not paint the miniature.

[622] MELVILLE, ALLAN (1782-1832). Panel. Bust. Formerly owned by the Melville family; later by Thomas B. Clarke, who listed it as by Ezra Ames; now by the Henry E. Huntington Library and Art Gallery, San Marino, California, where it is exhibited as by Ames. Photograph: The owner; print at FARL, where it is listed as *attributed* to Ames. Reproduced in Jay Leyda, *The Melville Log,* New York, 1951, II, plate I, as by Ames. After studying a photograph, the writers have been unable to form an opinion as to whether Ezra Ames did or did not paint this portrait.

[623] PAULDING, JOHN (1758-1818). Canvas. Bust. Owner: The Historical Society of the Tarrytowns; hanging at Philipse Castle Restoration, North Tarrytown, N.Y. Photograph: FARL 35663. Attributed to Ezra Ames by the late William Sawitzky in a brochure on the portrait. After examining the picture, the writers have formed no opinion as to whether Ezra Ames did or did not paint this portrait.

[624] QUACK DOCTOR, or STREET FAIR. Panel. Presented to AIHA by Miss Elizabeth S. Edwards and Mr. Henry Ames Edwards, Albany, great-grandchildren of Ezra Ames, as by Ezra Ames, copy after Vermeer. Photograph: By Irwin F. Cortelyou. After examining the picture, the writers have formed no opinion as to whether Ezra Ames did or did not paint it.

[625] TEN BROECK, ABRAHAM (1734-1810). Canvas. Three-quarter length. Owner: The City of Albany; on loan at the Ten Broeck mansion. Examined by IFC. Photograph: AIHA; print at FARL. Painted in 1799 for the Bank of Albany. Attributed to Ezra Ames in the *Magazine of Art*, AIHA Edition, March 1948, p. xliii, cover. The writers have not seen a sufficient number of portraits by Ezra Ames of the period in which this portrait was painted for them to form an opinion as to whether Ezra Ames did or did not paint it.

[626] TEN EYCK, HARMANUS (1749/50-1828). Canvas. Bust. Owner: AIHA, bought at a sale at Cazenovia, N.Y., May 1951. The head is very similar to that in No. 327. It was originally a bust with a hand, but the canvas has been restretched and the hand can be seen turned under and tacked to the stretcher. The exposed canvas is new but this may be a relining. However, there is no sign of the old canvas. The stretcher is old. After examining the picture, Irwin F. Cortelyou has formed no opinion as to whether Ezra Ames did or did not paint it. Not examined by T. Bolton.

[627] TEN EYCK, HARMANUS (1749/50-1828). Canvas. Bust. Very similar to No. 327. Owner: The Henry Francis Du Pont Winterthur Museum, Winterthur, Delaware. Of this portrait Mr. Joseph Downs, Curator of the Museum, says: "I think there is some reason to question the date of the portrait, and it too may be a copy, judging by the canvas and the pigment" (letter to IFC from Mr. Downs, 2/21/52). Inscribed on the stretcher in pencil is: "1825 H. Ten Eyck of Albany," and in a different handwriting, "Mr. S.E. Wendell 1873." After examining the portrait, Irwin F. Cortelyou has formed no opinion as to whether Ezra Ames did or did not paint it. Not examined by T. Bolton.

[628] UNIDENTIFIED MAN. Miniature on ivory. Oval. Bust, head to left. Dark-brown hair, brown eyes, black coat, pin in frill. Photograph: By Irwin F. Cortelyou. Owner: Presented to AIHA in 1951 by Miss Elizabeth S. Edwards, Albany, great-granddaughter of Ezra Ames, as by Ezra Ames or his son Julius Rubens Ames. After examining the ivory, the writers have formed no opinion as to whether Ezra Ames or his son painted this miniature.

[629] UNIDENTIFIED MAN (unfinished). Miniature on ivory. Oval. Bust, head and eyes to left. Brown hair, side burns, blue eyes. Photograph: By Irwin F. Cortelyou. Owner: Presented to AIHA in 1951 by Miss Elizabeth S. Edwards, Albany, great-granddaughter of Ezra Ames, as by Ezra Ames or his son Julius Rubens Ames. After examining the ivory, the writers have been unable to form any opinion as to who painted the miniature.

[630] UNIDENTIFIED WOMAN. Miniature on ivory. Oval. Bust, head to right, eyes crossed. Owner: Presented to AIHA in 1951 by Miss Elizabeth S. Edwards, Albany, great-granddaughter of Ezra Ames, as by Ezra Ames or his son Julius Rubens Ames. Photograph: By Irwin F. Cortelyou. The writers have formed no opinion as to whether Ezra Ames did or did not paint this miniature.

[631[VAN RENSSELAER, PHILIP SCHUYLER (*c.* 1766-1824). Canvas. Half-length. Owner: AIHA. There attributed to Ezra Ames. Photograph: AIHA. Reproduced: Without attribution as to artist in *DAR Magazine*, August 1917, p. 73; in May King Van Rensselaer, *The Van Rensselaers of the Manor of Rensselaerswyck*, New York, 1888, n. p. After studying a photograph, the writers have formed no opinion as to whether Ezra Ames did or did not paint this portrait.

[632] VAN SANTVOORT, ABRAHAM (1784-1858). Miniature. Support not given. Former owner: Mrs. J. Amory Haskell, Red Bank, N.J. Photograph: Print at FARL. Reproduced: Catalogue, Mrs. J. Amory Haskell Collection Sale, November 8-11, 1944, Parke-Bernet Galleries, New York City, as by Ezra Ames; described as having a manuscript inscription inside miniature frame which reads, "Pinxit Ezra Ames, Albany, 1805." However, after examining the photograph, the writers have fomed no opinion as to whether Ezra Ames did or did not paint this miniature.

[633] VAN SANTVOORT, MRS. ABRAHAM. Miniature on ivory. Owner: National Museum, Washington, D.C., presented by the late Mrs. Pepita Milmore. Photograph: Print at FARL. Reproduced:

Catalogue, Mrs. J. Amory Haskell Collection Sale, November 8-11, 1944, Parke-Bernet Galleries, New York City, as by Ezra Ames. After examining the photograph, the writers have formed no opinion as to whether Ezra Ames did or did not paint this miniature.

[634] WARD, AARON (1790-1867). Canvas. Bust. Owner: Mrs. Henry Bacon, Goshen, N.Y. Photograph: FARL 20369. Attributed to Ezra Ames on FARL photomount. The writers have formed no opinion from studying the photograph as to whether Ezra Ames did or did not paint this portrait.

CHRONOLOGY

BIBLIOGRAPHY

INDEX

CHRONOLOGY OF RESIDENCES AND PLACES VISITED

THE SOURCES for the dates of the birth, marriage, and death of Ezra Ames are given in the text. The sources for most of the remaining information in the Chronology are the artist's first Account Book (1790–1797) and his Expense Books (1799–1826). All other sources used in the Chronology are given by short title in parentheses after the entries to which they pertain and appear in full in the Bibliography.

The Chronology may not be taken as a complete record of Ames's movements except insofar as the sources cited in the text are complete. That is to say: it may be possible that Ames made trips of which the authors remain ignorant through failure to find any record of them.

Ames settled permanently at Albany in July 1793, and references to places after that date indicate trips of unspecified length but, presumably, of short duration. In other words: the spans between the dates should not be taken to indicate the time-spans of the artist's trips.

Used in conjunction with the Catalogue, this Chronology may help to determine the residences of some of the sitters whose addresses when painted were not found, as well as to suggest the places where as-yet-unlocated or undiscovered pictures by Ames may be found, or may have originated.

1768	May	5	Born, Framingham, Mass.
1778			Living in Sudbury, Mass., that portion which became East Sudbury in 1780, and in 1835 was renamed Wayland (*Wayland Vital Records*).
1790			East Sudbury, Mass.
1790	May		Moved to Worcester, Mass.
1792	Jan	27	Still at Worcester, Mass.
1792			Trips to Leicester and Lancaster, Mass.
1793	Jan	17	Still at Worcester, Mass.

1793	Apr	1	At Poughkeepsie, N. Y. (E. T. Reid, 11).
1793 *c.*	Apr		"From Poughkeepsie to Majr [Henry, Jr.?] Livingstons."
1793 *c.*	May	1	From Poughkeepsie to New York City.
1793 *c.*	May		From New York City to Long Island.
1793 *c.*	Jun	1	From New York City to Albany, N. Y.
1793	Jun	?	From Albany to Staatsburg, N. Y.
1793 *c.*	Jul	1	"Passage back again" to Albany.
1793	Jul	5	Now settled at Albany, N. Y.
1793	Aug	1	Studio in Mark Lane, Albany, N. Y. (Munsell, *Annals of Albany*, III, 157–8).
1794	Apr	1	Trip to Staatsburg, N. Y.
1794	Apr	13	Trip to Pittstown, N. Y.
1794	May	4	Trip to Troy, N. Y.
1794	May	24	Trip to Cohoes, N. Y.
1794	Sep	9	Trip to Boston, Mass.
1794	Oct	6	At Northbridge, Mass. (date of marriage).
1799	Nov	25	Moved from Mark Lane to Washington Street, Albany, N. Y. (*The Albany Register*, November 25, 29, and December 10, 1799).
1800	Jun	7	Trip to Framingham, Mass.
1803	Jun		Trip to New York City.
1805	Jul	16	Trip to New England, including Boston, and ending September 16, 1805.
1813			Living at 41 Washington Street (First *Albany Directory*, 1813).
1814			Living at 41 South Pearl Street, the name of Washington Street having been changed to South Pearl Street (*Albany Directory*, 1814).
1817	May		Trip to Schenectady, N. Y.
1817	Jul		Trip to Schenectady, N. Y.
1819	Jun		Trip to New York City.
1821	May		Trip to New York City.
1822	Jun		Trip to New York City.
1823	Jun		Trip to New York City and Philadelphia.

1823	Aug		Trip to Buffalo and Niagara, N. Y.
1823	Oct		Trip to Waterford, N. Y.
1824	Sep		Trip to New York City.
1826	Jun		Trip to Staatsburg, N. Y.
1826	Jul		Trip to New York City.
1826	Jul		Trip to Staatsburg, N. Y.
1827			Trip to Rochester, N. Y. (letter from Caroline Spencer to Julius Ames, 7/23/1827, at NYHS).
1836	Feb	23	Died, Albany, N. Y.

CIGAR STORE INDIAN

Repainted by Ezra Ames, 1823
for Caldwell & Solomons

(*Albany Gazette*, Jan. 13, 1820)

BIBLIOGRAPHY OF SOURCES CITED

THE FOLLOWING Bibliography lists the sources cited in this volume with the exception of the many references used only in the catalogue entries. These exclusively Catalogue sources are omitted here because, being pertinent only to individual sitters or pictures, they have no bearing on the work at large.

The source-entries below are divided into five groups: (1) Manuscript Sources; (2) Books and Brochures; (3) Articles in Periodicals; (4) Newspapers; and (5) Miscellaneous Sources. Within each group the entries are alphabetized by authors' names or by key words of citations in footnotes or text.

MANUSCRIPT SOURCES

Albany Institute of History and Art. Correspondence with Mr. Robert G. Wheeler, Director; and Mr. Ledyard Cogswell, Jr., President.

American Academy of the Fine Arts. Minutes. At NYHS.

Ames, Ezra. Account Book, No. 1, from May 1790 through July 8, 1797, including one entry for 1802. On a loose sheet are entries presumably for 1794 and a few for 1800. Records receipts and expenses as well as craft and art work. Not chronological. Wrappers. 25 leaves. No pagination. Size: width 4½ x height 7¾ inches. At NYHS.

Ames, Ezra. Account Book, No. 2, from August 2, 1797, through October 1802. Records receipts as well as craft and art work. Not chronological. No covers. 12 leaves. No pagination. Size: width 4¾ x height 8½ inches. At NYHS.

Ames, Ezra. Account Book, No. 3, from May 4, 1804, through December 28, 1834, ending on [p. 47]. No pagination. Records only craft and art work. Originally in boards, front board lacking. Size of pages: width 8 x height 9¾ inches. At AIHA. Presented anonymously, November 1946.

Ames, Ezra, Estate. No. I. Inventory.

Item 1. Copy. There is at the Albany Institute of History and Art an inventory presented in 1946 by Miss Elizabeth S. Edwards and Mr. Henry Ames Edwards (of which there is a photostat at The New York State Library) which begins: "Copy/A True and Perfect Inventory/Of all the personal property and effects of Ezra Ames/late of the city of Albany, in the county of Albany,/deceased, made by Julius R. Ames & Angelo Ames/the executors—/ of the last will of the said deceased, with the aid and in the presence of/Green Hall and James Merrifield, they having been previously appointed and sworn as Appraisers. . . ." April 19, 20, 1836. 15 pages. At the foot of page 3: "(Omissions. The following three items were accidentally omitted /on the list and therefore not appraised; Viz. Pew No. 36/in N. E. Corner of Gallery of S. Dutch Church; Rent/for One quarter from J. Whitney; and one share in/the Albany Library, total $35/the above note not on the Inventory as filed.)" Page 14 is: "A diagram of the Real Estate of Ezra Ames decd/With apportionments confirmed by the Chancellor May 27, 1839." Also: pages 10 and 11, inventory of paintings.

Item 2. Inventory, with Map of Real Estate owned by Ezra Ames, undated, filed at the Surrogate's Court, Albany County, Albany, New York.

Ames, Ezra, Estate. No. II. Documents relating to the Ames Estate. In folder inscribed: "Ezra & Zipporah Ames. Twenty Six Items." At The New York State Library, Albany, New York. Call number: CG 9862. These are all receipts as of the year 1836 for money received from the Ames Estate. Included are the following:

Item 1. February 24, 1836, for funeral expenses of "Mr. E. Eames." Richard Merrifield, $91.00.

Item 2. April 11, 1836, for funeral expenses of "Mrs. Eames." R. Merrifield, $64.00.

Ames, Ezra, Estate. No. III. Documents relating to the Ames Estate. In folder at The New York State Library, Albany, New York. Call number: CG 9864. Six receipts all dated as of 1836 for small sums paid out by the executors.

Ames, Ezra, Estate. No. IV. Executors' Account Book, Angelo Ames and Julius Ames in account with E. Ames and Estate, January 1, 1836 to May 1, 1836. 16 pages. At The New York State Library, Albany, New York.

Ames, Ezra, Estate. No. V. Documents relating to the Ames Estate. At the Surrogate's Court, Albany, New York. About 27 documents including the following items:

Item 1. The Inventory, with Map of Real Estate owned by Ezra Ames. (Cf. Ames, Ezra, Estate. No. I. Inventory.)

Item 2. Typewritten copy of the Will of Ezra Ames, dated January 6, 1836.

Item 3. Executors' accounts. 8 pages.

Item 4. Bills receipted by Dr. A. March for professional services to February 29, 1836, for $100; and to April 8, 1836, for $67.75.

Item 5. A document relating to pew No. 36, 2d floor, 2d Dutch Church, $5.

Item 6. Power of attorney given to J. R. Ames by A. Ames to act as sole executor, May 2, 1838.

Item 7. Decree granted to J. R. Ames to act as sole executor, May 28, 1838.

Item 8. Payment of Angelo Ames to Eloise Visscher for services during February, March, April, 1836, "as nurse and watcher to his parents."

Ames, Ezra, Expense Books. 16 booklets recording, intermittently, the artist's expenses from January 1, 1799, in Book 1, through August 1826 in Book 16. [Books numbered in chronological sequence 1 through 16 by the writers for convenience.] Wrappers. No pagination. 12 to 28 pages in each booklet. Average size: width 4 x height 6½ inches. At NYHS.

Ames, Ezra, and Others. No. I. Letters by or to Ezra Ames. 25 letters, the earliest dated August 25, 1792, Clinton, N. Y., the latest dated October 14, 1833, Albany, N. Y., including 13 letters relating to the artist's official duties as a Mason. At NYHS.

Ames, Ezra, and Others. No. II. Financial papers. 15 receipts, two undated; the earliest of the others dated August 14, 1797; the latest dated February 14, 1821. At NYHS.

Ames Exhibition. Albany, N. Y., November 1934. Exhibition of Paintings by Ezra Ames Owned by Albanians. At the Albany Institute of History and Art. Two typewritten sheets: "List of Portraits in the Ames Exhibition sent to the Frick Art Reference Library by the Curator of the Albany Institute of History and Art," in 1936.

Ames Exhibition. Albany, N.Y., November 1946. At the Albany Institute of History and Art. Card-labels used on pictures in the Ezra Ames Exhibition. At AIHA.

Ames Family. Genealogy Compiled in 1848 of the Family of Ezra Ames and his wife, Zipporah Wood. Anonymous. 5 leaves, bound. Size: width 7¾ x height 9½ inches. At NYHS.

Armitage, Benjamin. Letter dated September 27, 1816, to Ezra Ames. At AIHA.

Beekman, James William. Letter dated October 20, 1838, to Evert A. Duyckinck. In Manuscript Division, The New York Public Library.

Clinton, DeWitt. Diary. Manuscript in ledgers. At NYHS.

Dutchess County Clerk's Office, Poughkeepsie, New York. (1) Book Inventory, Mortgages, Vol. 4 or D, covering June 1776 to April 1887. Manuscript, page 116: Mortgage dated March 2, 1784. (2) Book Inventory, Deeds, Vol. 11 or K, covering 1788–1793. Typescript, page 301: Indenture dated August 28, 1790. (3) Book Inventory, Deeds,

Vol. 14. Typescript, page 569: Indenture dated April 20, 1791. (4) Transcript of an Indenture dated May 22, 1761, between Gertruyd Coejmans and Christian Bergh, recording the sale by the former to Christian Bergh, for 1,000 pounds, of a tract of land "Commonly called Staatsburgh or Paulings Purchase."

Emes, Jesse. Will. Typewritten transcript at the Surrogate's Office, Poughkeepsie, N.Y. Vol. H, pages 181–183.

First Presbyterian Church, Albany, N.Y. Register from 1785 to recent years. Typewritten. At The New York State Library, Albany, N.Y.

Gansevoort-Lansing Collection. Manuscript Division, The New York Public Library. Album in a box marked "Poets & Artists/1890–1899/A. L. & C. G. L."

James, Mrs. William, née Marcia Lucretia Ames. Letter to Angelo Ames, January 6, 1831, Albany, N.Y. At NYHS.

Mariners Museum, Norfolk, Virginia. Letter from Mr. Harold S. Sniffen, September 22, 1949, to Mrs. George B. Cortelyou, Jr.

Mechanics and Farmers' Bank. Minutes. At Mechanics and Farmers' Bank, Albany, N. Y.

Mechanics' Society, Albany, N.Y. (1) Register, and (2) Act of Incorporation, March 6, 1801. At The New York State Library, Albany, N.Y.

Meredith, William T. Letter to John Pintard, January 2, 1817. At NYHS.

Meredith, William T. Letter to David Hosack, January 18, 1817. At NYHS.

Merriam, John M. Letter to Mrs. George B. Cortelyou, Jr., April 16, 1951.

New-York Historical Society. Minutes. At NYHS.

Peale, Charles Willson. Letter to David Hosack, June 24, 1817. At NYHS.

Pennsylvania Academy of the Fine Arts. Letter dated March 22, 1949, from Mrs. Barbara S. Roberts, Registrar, to Dr. George Clinton Andrews, enclosing a sheet of "all the information we have on the portrait of George Clinton by Ames"; and a letter dated May 11, 1949, from Mrs. Roberts to Mrs. George B. Cortelyou, Jr., relating to the portrait of George Clinton by Ames exhibited at the Pennslyvania Academy in 1812.

Sawitzky, William. Letter file box of notes on and photographs of portraits by Ezra Ames. Owned by Mrs. William (Susan Clay) Sawitzky.

Sellers, Charles Coleman. Letters to Mrs. George B. Cortelyou, Jr., May 31, 1949, and October 30, 1950.

Society for the Promotion of Useful Arts, Albany, N.Y. Minutes. At AIHA.

Spencer, Caroline. Letter to Julius Ames, July 23, 1827. At NYHS.

Sully, Thomas. Letter to David Hosack, January 9, 1817. At NYHS.

Sully, Thomas. Register, 1801–1872. At Historical Society of Pennsylvania. Photostat copy at FARL.

Union College Portrait Index, June 1950. Typewritten.

Walker, Wendell. Letter to Miss Dorothy Barck, March 17, 1950.

BOOKS AND BROCHURES

Adams, James Truslow, editor, *Dictionary of American History* (New York: 1940), 5 vols., and index.

Albany Chronicles. See Reynolds, Cuyler.

Albany Directory, 1813–1886.

American Academy of the Fine Arts, *Catalogue of Paintings and Engravings* (New York: 1825–1827). Three pamphlets. At NYHS.

Ames, Wilmot Spofford, compiler, *Eames-Ames Genealogy, Descendants of Robert of Woburn and Thomas of Framingham, Massachusetts, 1634–1931* [Auburn, Maine: 1931].

Appletons' Cyclopaedia of American Biography (New York: 1887–1901), 7 vols.

Barry, William, *A History of Framingham, Massachusetts . . .* (Boston: 1847).

Beardsley, Levi, *Reminiscences; Personal and Other Incidents; Early Settlement of Otsego County . . .* (New York: 1852).

Biddle, Edward, and Mantle Fielding, *The Life and Works of Thomas Sully (1783–1872)* (Philadelphia: 1921).

Biographical Directory of the American Congress 1774–1927 . . . ([Washington, D.C.:] Gov't. Print. Office, 1928).

Bonney, Mrs. Catharina V. R., compiler, *A Legacy of Historical Gleanings* (Albany: 1875), 2 vols.

Bowen, Clarence Winthrop, editor, *The History of the Centennial Celebration of the Inauguration of George Washington . . .* (New York: 1892). Cited as: Bowen, *Centennial*.

Carlyle, Thomas, "Project of a National Exhibition of Scottish Portraits," letter to David Laing, dated May 3, 1854. In: *Critical and Miscellaneous Essays* (New York: 1872), VII: 129–130.

Carrick, Alice Van Leer, *Shades of Our Ancestors; American Profiles and Profilists* (Boston: 1928), plate facing p. 40.

Colden, Cadwallader D., *Memoir Prepared at the Request of a Committee of the Common Council of the City of New York, and Presented to the Mayor of the City at the Celebration of the Completion of the New York Canals* (New York: 1825).

Cowdrey, [Mary] Bartlett, compiler, *National Academy of Design Exhibition Record 1826–1860* (New York: 1943), 2 vols.

Cowdrey, Mary Bartlett, *American Academy of Fine Arts and American Art-Union 1816–1852*, Vol. I: *Introduction* [including a history of the American Academy and a listing of its members by Theodore Sizer]; Vol. II: *Exhibition Record* (New York: The New-York Historical Society, 1953), 2 vols.

Cummings, Thomas Seir, *Historic Annals of the National Academy of Design* (Philadelphia: 1865).

Delaplaine, Joseph, *Prospectus of Delaplaine's National Panzographia, for the Reception of the Portraits of Distinguished Americans* (Philadelphia: 1818). Pamphlet.

Dickson, Harold E., *John Wesley Jarvis, American Painter, 1780–1840, with a Checklist of His Works* (New York: The New York Historical Society, 1949).

Dictionary of American Biography (New York: 1928–1944), 21 vols. and index. Abbreviated as: *DAB*.

Dunlap, William, *History of the Rise and Progress of the Arts of Design in the United States* (New York: 1834), 2 vols. Also Bayley and Goodspeed edition (Boston: 1918), 3 vols., cited only in Catalogue.

First Annual Exhibition of the Society of Artists of the United States (Philadelphia: 1811). Catalogue. See also Pennsylvania Academy.

Flexner, James Thomas, *Steamboats Come True; American Inventors in Action* (New York: 1944).

Framingham, Massachusetts, *Memorial of the Bi-Centennial Celebration of the Incorporation of the Town of Framingham, Massachusetts, June, 1900* (South Framingham: [1900]).

Framingham, Massachusetts, *Vital Records of Framingham, Massachusetts, to the Year 1850 . . .* (Boston: New England Historic Genealogical Society, 1911).

Hamilton, Alexander, and others, *The Works of Alexander Hamilton . . ., an Improved Edition of the Federalist* . . . (New York: Williams and Whiting, 1810), 3 vols. Plate in Vol. I.

Howell, George Rogers, and Jonathan Tenney, *Bi-Centennial History of Albany. History of the County of Albany, N. Y., from 1609 to 1886* (New York: 1886).

Larkin, Oliver W., *Art and Life in America* (New York: 1949).

Mason, George C., *The Life and Works of Gilbert Stuart* (New York: 1894).

Massachusetts Soldiers and Sailors of the Revolutionary War. A Compilation from the Archives, Prepared and Published by the Secretary of the Commonwealth . . . (Boston: 1896–1908), 17 vols.

Matthiessen, Francis O., *The James Family* . . . (New York: 1947).

Mechanics and Farmers' Bank, *Span of a Century 1811–1911* (Albany: [1912?]). Pamphlet.

Morrison, John H., *History of American Steam Navigation* (New York: 1903).

Munsell, Joel, *The Annals of Albany* (Albany: 1850–1859), 10 vols; and Vol. 1 (1869).

Munsell, Joel, editor, *Collections on the History of Albany, from its Discovery to the Present Time* . . . (Albany: 1865–71), 4 vols.

New York City Directories, 1802–1806.

New-York Historical Society, *Catalogue of American Portraits*. See Shelley, Donald A.

New York State, *Laws of the State of New-York, comprising the Constitution, and the Acts of the Legislature, since the Revolution, from the First to the Fifteenth Session, Inclusive* (New York: Printed by Thomas Greenleaf, 1792), 2 vols. Covering the years 1777–1792.

New York State, *Laws of the State of New-York . . . From the First to the Twenty-Second Session, Inclusive* (Albany: Printed by Charles R. and George Webster, 1800), 3 vols. Covering the years 1777–1799.

New York State, *Laws of the State of New-York . . . Passed at the Second Meeting of the Twenty-Fourth Session of the Legislature, Begun and held at the City of Albany, the Twenty-Seventh Day of January, 1801* (Albany: Printed by Loring Andrews, Printer to the State, 1801).

New York State, *Laws of the State of New-York, Passed at the Twenty-Sixth Session of the Legislature: Begun and held at the City of Albany, the Twenty-Fifth Day of January, 1803 (Albany:* Printed by John Barber, Printer to the State, 1803).

New York State, *Laws of the State of New-York . . . Containing All the Acts Passed from the Revision of 1801, to the End of the 27th Session of the Legislature, 1804* (Albany: Printed by Charles R. and George Webster, 1804), 3 vols., Vol. III.

New York State, *Laws of the State of New-York, Passed at the Thirty-Sixth Session of the Legislature, Begun and held at the City of Albany, the Second Day of November, 1812* (Albany: Printed for S. Southwick, Printer to the State, 1813).

New York State Freedom Train, Official Document Book (Albany: New York State Freedom Train Commission, 1949).

Park, Lawrence, *Gilbert Stuart, An Illustrated Descriptive List of His Works* (New York: 1926), 4 vols., Vol. II: 854–855.

Pennsylvania Academy of the Fine Arts. [A photostat file of the catalogues of the annual exhibitions held at the Pennsylvania Academy is kept at the Frick Art Reference Library. The title varies in the earlier issues, and the first catalogue does not bear the name of the Pennsylvania Academy. The first three catalogues bear the following titles:]

1. *First Annual Exhibition of the Society of Artists of the United States* (Philadelphia: 1811).
2. *Second Annual Exhibition of the Society of Artists of the United States and the Pennsylvania Academy* (Philadelphia: 1812). 2 issues.
3. *Third Annual Exhibition of the Columbian Society of Artists and the Pennsylvania Academy* (Philadelphia: 1813).

Pennsylvania Academy of the Fine Arts, *Exhibition of Paintings, Statues and Casts, at the Pennsylvania Academy of the Fine Arts, Chestnut Street above Tenth, Founded in 1806* (Philadelphia: 1845). Catalogue.

Phelps, Henry P., *The Albany Rural Cemetery* (Albany and Chicago: 1893).

Poucher, J. Wilson, and Helen Wilkinson Reynolds, compilers, *Old Gravestones of Dutchess County, New York* (Poughkeepsie, N. Y.: 1924).

Raymond, Andrew Van Vranken, *Union University* (New York: 1907), 3 vols.

Reynolds, Cuyler, compiler, *Albany Chronicles, a History of the City Arranged Chronologically, from the Earliest Settlement to the Present Time . . .* (Albany: 1906).

Reynolds, Helen Wilkinson, compiler and editor, *Notices of Marriages and Deaths About 4,000 in Number Published in Newspapers Printed at Poughkeepsie, New York, 1778–1825* [Collections of the Dutchess County Historical Society, Volume IV] (Poughkeepsie, N. Y.: 1930).

Roosevelt, Franklin Delano, editor, *Records of the Town of Hyde Park, Dutchess County* [Collections of the Dutchess County Historical Society, Volume III] (Hyde Park, N. Y.: 1928).

Ross, Peter, *A Standard History of Freemasonry in the State of New York* . . . (New York and Chicago: 1901), 2 vols.

Sawitzky, William, *Catalogue, Descriptive and Critical, of the Paintings and Miniatures in the Historical Society of Pennsylvania* (Philadelphia: 1942), p. 112.

Scott, Joseph, *The United States Gazeteer: Containing an Authentic Description of the Several States* . . . (Philadelphia: 1795).

Shelley, Donald A., compiler, *Catalogue of American Portraits in The New-York Historical Society: Oil Portraits, Miniatures, Sculptures* (New York: 1941).

Sizer, Theodore, *The Works of Colonel John Trumbull, Artist of the American Revolution* (New Haven: 1950).

Smith, Edward M., *Documentary History of Rhinebeck, in Dutchess County, New York, Embracing Biographical Sketches and Genealogical Records of Our First Families and First Settlers, with a History of Its Churches and Other Public Institutions* (Rhinebeck, N. Y.: 1881).

Society of Artists of the United States and the Pennsylvania Academy, *Second Annual Exhibition* (Philadelphia: 1812). Catalogue. 2 issues. See also Pennsylvania Academy.

Sutliff, Mary Louisa, compiler, *A Record of the Ancestors and the Descendants of Betsy Mulford Sutliff* . . . (Albany: 1897).

Sweet, Frederick A., *The Hudson River School and the Early American Landscape Tradition, The Art Institute of Chicago, February 15 to March 25, 1945; Whitney Museum of American Art, New York, April 17 to May 18, 1945* (New York: 1945). Catalogue.

Temple, Josiah Howard, *History of Framingham, Massachusetts, Early Known as Danforth's Farms, 1640–1880* . . . (Published by the Town of Framingham, 1887).

Tenney, Jonathan, *New England in Albany* (Boston: 1883).

Terry, Garnet, engraver, *New & Allegorical Devices for Artists in General & Particularly for Jewlers & Enamel Painters* . . . (London: 1795). Pattern book.

United States [Department of Commerce and Labor], Bureau of the Census . . . *Heads of Families at the First Census of the United States taken in the Year 1790, Massachusetts* (Washington: 1908).

Watson, Elkanah, *Men and Times of the Revolution; Or, Memoirs of Elkanah Watson . . .*, edited by his son Winslow C. Watson (New York: 1856).

Wayland, Massachusetts, *Vital Records of Wayland, Massachusetts, to the Year 1850* (Boston: New England Historic Genealogical Society, 1910).

Wehle, Harry B., *American Miniatures 1730–1850. One Hundred and Seventy-three Portraits Selected with a Descriptive Account by Harry B. Wehle, and a Biographical Dictionary of the Artists by Theodore Bolton* (Garden City: 1927).

Weatherwise, Abraham, *The Book of Knowledge: or, Wheel of Fortune. Shewing The Signification of Moles, and the Interpretation of Dreams. The various and wonderful operations of the Signs & Planets on the Human Body. The Art of Physiognomy & Palmistry.—The Wheel of Fortune, and several Solutions in matters of Love . . .* (New York: 1806). 55th edition. Pamphlet. Copy at NYHS.

ARTICLES IN PERIODICALS

Barck, Dorothy C., "Ezra Ames (1768–1836) Painter," *The New-York Historical Society Quarterly Bulletin*, X, January 1927, pp. 131–134.

Bolton, Theodore, "Charles Loring Elliot," *The Art Quarterly*, V, Winter 1942, pp. 58–96.

Bolton, Theodore, "Charles Willson Peale," *The Art Quarterly*, II, Autumn 1939, pp. 354–385.

Bolton, Theodore, "Henry Inman," *The Art Quarterly*, III, Autumn 1940, pp. 353–374.

Bolton, Theodore, and George C. Groce, Jr., "John Hesselius," *The Art Quarterly*, II, Winter 1939, pp. 76–91.

Bolton, Theodore, and George C. Groce, Jr., "John Wesley Jarvis," *The Art Quarterly*, I, Autumn 1938, pp. 299–321.

Bresee, Wilmer E., "Masonry and the Erie Canal," *The Masonic Family Magazine*, IV, July–August 1950, pp. 11, 15.

Brown, Alexander Crosby, "Paddle Box Decorations of American Sound Steamboats," *The American Neptune*, III, January 1943, pp. 35–47.

Bullock, C. Seymour, "Anniversary of American Commerce," *The Journal of American History*, I, 1907, pp. 395–432.

Fortune, XLIII, February 1951, color plate of Alexander Hamilton by Ezra Ames, [p. 75].

Frankenstein, Alfred, and Arthur K. D. Healy, "Two Journeyman Painters," *Art in America*, XXXVIII, February 1950, pp. [7]–63, plate facing p. 21.

Groce, G[eorge] C[uthbert], Jr., "New York Painting Before 1800," *New York History*, XIX, January 1938, pp. 44–57.

Hart, Charles Henry, "Thomas Sully's Register of Portraits, 1801–1871," *The Pennsylvania Magazine of History and Biography, XXXII*, October 1908, pp. 385–432; XXXIII, January 1909, pp. 22–85; April 1909, pp. 147–215.

Harper's Weekly, IX, July 29, 1865, pp. 472–474: "Burning of Barnum's Museum."

Hastings, Mrs. Russel, compiler, "William James (1771–1832) of Albany, N. Y., and His Descendants . . . ," *The New York Genealogical and Biographical Record*, LV, April 1924, pp. 101–119; July 1924, pp. 222–236; October 1924, pp. 301–313. Reprinted with index.

Hatch, John Davis, Jr., "The Albany Institute of History and Art: A Sketch of Its Early Forerunners," *New York History*, XXV, July 1944, pp. 311–325.

Hatch, John Davis, Jr., "Isaac Hutton, Silversmith, Citizen of Albany," *The Magazine Antiques*, XLVII, January 1945, pp. 32–35.

Magazine of Art, Albany Institute of History and Art Edition, December 1946; April 1948.

McClinton, Katharine M., "Ezra Ames, Ornamental Painter," *The Magazine Antiques*, LX, September 1951, p. 194.

Medical Repository, Third Hexade, II, 1811, pp. 88–89: "Improvements in Albany," section for May, June, and July 1810.

Port Folio, n.s. VIII, July 1812, pp. 17–28; "Review of the Second Annual Exhibition" of the Society of Artists, and the Pennsylvania Academy United.

Port Folio, 3d series, II, August 1813, pp. 122–141: "Review of the Third Annual Exhibition of the Columbian Society of Artists and Pennsylvania Academy of Fine Arts."

Reid, E. T., "Ezra Ames, Ne Plus Ultra," *The Royal Arch Mason*, I, March 1943, pp. 9–14.

Sawitzky, William, "American Portraits," *Bulletin of the Associates in Fine Arts at Yale University*, VIII, June 1937, pp. 21–27.

Sawyer, Charles H., and Louisa Dresser, "The Salisbury Houses," *Worcester Art Museum Annual*, V, 1946, pp. 65–92.

Thomas, William S., "Henry Livingston," *Year Book, Dutchess County Historical Society*, V, 1919, pp. 30–45.

Union Alumni Monthly, XVII, January 1928, p. 71.

Wheeler, Robert G., "Ezra Ames of. Albany (1768–1836): Painter, Banker, Business Man," *American Collector*, XVI, August 1947, pp. 6–8.

Williams, Hermann Warner, Jr., "Extracts from the Memoranda of Ezra Ames of Albany," *Art in America*, XXX, October 1942, pp. 254–255.

NEWSPAPERS

[Albany] *Argus*

Albany Argus

Albany Argus and City Gazette

[Albany] *Balance and State Journal*

Albany Gazette

Albany Gazette and Daily Advertiser

Albany Evening Journal

Albany Register

Daily Albany Argus

New York Times

[Worcester] *Massachusetts Spy*

MISCELLANEOUS SOURCES

Albany Institute of History and Art, *Exhibition of American Portraits and Landscapes at the Albany Institute of History and Art, June 2 to September 20, 1936* ([Albany: mimeographed, 1936), [5] + 44 pp. Copy at AIHA and at FARL.

American Academy of the Fine Arts. [Invitation to Exhibit, December 12, 1831.] One-page leaflet. At NYHS.

[Ames, Ezra,] *Catalogue Sale of Portraits*, Albany, July 26, 1842. Handbill. At NYHS.

Gravestones and cards of the Ezra Ames family plot at the Albany Rural Cemetery.

Gravestones in the Jesse Emes family burying ground, Staatsburg, N. Y.

Inscribed portraits.

Middlesex County, Massachusetts, *Map of Middlesex County, Massachusetts* (Boston: Henry F. Walling, 1857). At NYHS.

Transcripts of records of Albany churches, at The New York State Library, Albany, N. Y.

INDEX

THE FOLLOWING index was prepared by David H. Wallace, Assistant Editor of The New-York Historical Society. It consists for the most part of a simple alphabetical listing of the names of all persons, places, and institutions mentioned in the Introduction, Life, transcript of the Account Books, and Catalogue. In addition to these there are a few entries in italics for books, prints, and paintings other than identified portraits, as well as a few subject entries such as those on Masonry, Masons, and Unidentified sitters.

The reader's attention is particularly drawn to the analytical entry on Ezra Ames, under which are grouped a number of sub-entries dealing, roughly, with the following aspects of his career: leading events in his life; likenesses of Ames himself; inventory of his estate; *Catalogue Sale of Portraits*, 1842; Ames as Mason; as banker; as craftsman, job painter, engraver, etc.; as artist (statistical and critical analysis); comparison of his work with that of other artists; Ames's work in varied media (oils, pencil, hair, etc.); Ames's paintings other than portraits and miniatures.

Numbers within parentheses refer to catalogue entries, *e. g.*, André, John, (5, 172, 310) means see entries [5], [172], and [310] of the catalogue.

Account Books (Ames's): repros., 174, 185; notes on, 3, 9, 13, 16, 36, 124, 147-75· transcript of, 176-90.

Adam and Eve, by Ames, (514).

Adams, John, portrait of, 56, 132, (1).

Aherne, Mrs. Madeline Clinton, owner, (71).

Akin, William, portrait of, (587).

Albany (N.Y.), xvii, xviii, 3, 11, 13, 16, 19, 20, 27, 31, 32, 60, 61, 100, 102, 109, 111, 112; Ames advertises in, 13, 16, 21, 29, 30; Ames's property in, 30-31; cemeteries of, 3, 27, 35, 126, 129; churches, 34, 107, 126, (22, 27, 79, 114, 153, 189, 222, 260, 297, 428, 486, 567); coat of arms of, 59-60, (521, 610); DeWitt's map of, repro., 31; harbormaster of, (432); taverns of, 19, 96; Aldermen, (35, 140); City Clerk, (26, 389); City Surveyor, (34); Common Council, 65, (37, 66, 87, 133, 145, 305, 326, 412, 440); Inspector of Revenue at, (34); Mayors, (32, 228, 284); Postmaster, (394); owner, 131, 140, 141 (55, 66, 160, 337, 341, 378, 448, 625); patron, 65, 80, 91-92, 184, (55, 66); view of, 17.

Albany Academy, *see* Albany's Bicentennial Loan Exhibition.

Albany Academy for Girls, owner, (170).

Albany County (N.Y.), 77; first judge of, (121); Clerk of, (389); Bible Society, (27); Historical Society, (478).

Albany Exchange Bank, (293).

Albany Gallery of Fine Arts, 56, 115, (420, 424).

Albany Historical and Art Society, Ames's work exhibited at, (169, 453, 454, 456, 459, 469, 486).

Albany Institute and Historical and Art Society, *see* Albany Institute of History and Art.

Albany Institute of History and Art, sketch of, 20; Ames manuscripts at, 147, 164; Ames's work exhibited at, 1934: (3, 11, 29, 115, 123, 124, 127, 129, 199, 200, 221, 248-250, 277, 394, 403, 409, 420, 424, 600, 614); Ames's work exhibited at, 1936: (29, 32, 127, 221, 449,

595, 617); Ames's work exhibited at, 1946: 55, (8-11, 13, 29, 55, 64, 66, 110-112, 115, 124, 156, 159-160, 169-170, 220-221, 228-229, 248-250, 337, 341, 366, 378, 394, 403, 411, 420, 424, 448, 460, 480, 485, 504-505, 534, 538, 554, 615, 617); owner or loanee, frontis., xvi, 2, 11, 17, 18, 20, 32, 35-36, 49, 55, 59, 65, 69-71, 75, 80, 97, 98, 138-140, 169, (8, 10, 55, 66, 110-11, 115, 124, 126-127, 131, 141, 160, 169, 173, 185, 193, 337, 341, 377, 403, 424, 448, 454, 484, 496-500, 503, 518, 525, 538, 543, 546, 554, 557, 592-595, 602-603, 606, 610, 613, 619-620, 624, 626, 628-631).
Albany Library, 20, (440).
Albany Mechanics' Society, 20, 33-34, (481).
Albany Regiment, patron, 96.
Albany Register, (21).
Albany Rural Cemetery, 3, 27, 35.
Albany Theater, 111-112.
Albany Young Men's Association, owner, (29).
Albany's Bicentennial Loan Exhibition at the Albany Academy, 1886, Ames's works exhibited in: (42, 71, 184, 208, 285, 287, 320, 328, 400, 501, 616).
Alden, Mrs. Charles, owner, (402).
Alethia, portrait of, (2).
Alexander, Ann, *see* Mrs. William Henry.
Alexander, Francis, Ames's work attributed to, 116, 143, (228).
Alexander, Joseph, portrait of, (3).
Allanson, Richard, patron, 35.
Allcott, Mr., 120.
Allegorical Landscape, see *Romantic Landscape*.
Allegorical Painting, by Ames, 71, 96, 186, (515).
Allegory of Faith & Death, by Ames, 71, (516).
Allegory present past & future, by Ames, 71, (15).
Allegory of Providence, by Ames, 71, (517).
Allen, Esquire, patron, 10.
Allen, Mrs. Frank, owner, (5, 227).
Allen, Nathaniel, portrait of, 154, 169, (4); patron, 183.
Allen, S. & M., patrons, 83, 87, 96, 99.
Allen, Solomon, (Sr.?), portrait of, 169, 182, (5); repro., 156; engraving of, 169 (564).
Allen, Solomon, (227); patron, 169, 182, (5).
Allen, Mrs. Solomon, *see* Priscilla Clark Paddock.
Allen, Tilly, portrait of, 188, (6).
Allen, Mrs. Tilly, portrait of, 188, (7).
Allen's Truly Lucky Lottery Office, *see* S. & M. Allen.
Alton, Ill.; (155).
Alvord, William, (207).
Amenia City (N.Y.), (249).
American Academy of the Fine Arts, Ames and, 84-85, 107-108,
American Bible Society, owner, (596).
American Institute, (575).
American Museum, *see* Barnum.
American Philosophical Society, owner, (524).
American Revolution, 5-7, 12; portraits of American officers of, (5, 31, 34, 81, 110, 125, 172, 305, 310, 352, 381); British officers of, (36, 243).
Ames, variant spellings of, 3.
Ames, ———, miniature of unidentified girl, 10, (495).
Ames, Angelo, 35-36, 115, 119, 123-124, 126, 129-130, 133, (2); portrait of, 39, (16); miniatures of, (453, 454); repros., 127; owner, (453-457, 459, 469, 484, 486, 495-500, 503).
Ames children, group portrait of, (16).
Ames, Ezra
birth and family, xvii, 3-8; in Worcester (Mass.), 8-13; moves to Albany (N.Y.), xvii, 13-16, 19-20; marriage and children, 23-24, 35-36; and Mechanics' Society, 33; exhibits at Philadelphia, 59-64; paintings collected by, 56; and Society for the Promotion of Useful Arts, 83; and American Academy, 85, 108; and Delaplaine's Gallery, 88, 91; and Erie Canal, 102, 109, 111; noticed in Dunlap's *Arts of Design*, 123; death and burial, xvii, 3, 124, 126, 129; will, 129; books owned by, 131; portrait gallery of, 56, 100 (*see* Albany Gallery of Fine Arts).
silhouette by Henry Williams, 40, 42; self-portraits in oils, 32, 53, 199, (8-12, 456-457); miniature self-portraits, 10-11, 32, 43, 127, (455-458, 565); self-portrait(?) on glass, (606); engraved portrait of, (565); repros., frontis., 8, 42, 75, 127.
Inventory of estate of: 50, 56, 71, 78, 88, 99, 129, 164, (1-2, 8, 10, 12, 14-15, 19, 39, 50, 57-58, 69-72, 78, 92-93, 98, 103, 105-106, 109, 111-

112, 114, 125, 138, 144, 159, 161-162, 166-167, 169, 183, 185, 189, 196, 198, 204-205, 213-214, 223-224, 234, 241, 242, 251, 254, 257, 258, 264, 266, 272, 279, 282, 304, 306, 308, 310, 323, 330, 379-380, 390, 396, 401, 420-421, 424, 428, 431, 433, 437, 442, 444-446, 451, 514, 516-517, 522-523, 532, 538-539, 541-545, 547-556, 558, 560-563).

Catalogue Sale of Portraits of, repro., 132; mentioned, 56, 78, 88, 99, 131-133, (1, 39, 57, 58, 69-72, 90, 92, 105-106, 114, 117, 125, 135, 138, 161, 166-167, 169, 179, 189, 194, 198, 213-214; 222-224, 234, 254-255, 266, 304, 306, 323, 331, 337, 363, 367-376, 379, 390, 396, 401, 420, 422, 424, 428, 431, 437, 444, 447, 451, 539, 547, 553, 555, 558, 563, 613).

Ames as Mason: xviii, 14, 24-25, 29, 33, 43-44, 58, 83, 95, 102-104, 109, 111, 114, 120, 129; as Masonic craftsman, 21, 25, 28, 30, 32, 39, 43, 58, 71, 87, 96, 171, 186, (515).

Ames as banker: xviii, 79, 120, 123-124.

Ames as craftsman and laborer: xviii-xix, 10-11, 13-14, 16, 22, 26-29, 34-35, 43-45, 58, 71, 77, 96, 162, 170-172, 178-184, 186; as job-painter, gilder, sign-painter, etc., 10-12, 21-22, 25-30, 32, 34-36, 39-40, 43, 45, 47, 49, 53, 58-60, 71, 77, 83, 87, 96, 100, 104, 170-173, 179, 181-184, 186, 304; as tradesman, 26-28, 35, 40, 43, 44, 58, 77, 176, 177; as engraver, 25, 28-30, 32, 171.

Ames as artist: table of paintings by, 150; Account Books of, 3, 9, 13-16, 36, 124, 147-190; analysis of technique, 53, 99, 105, 112, 114, 139-140, 164, and "Notes on the Catalogue"; criticisms of, xvii-xix, 36, 40, 49, 53-54, 63-64, 66, 71, 77, 79, 84, 95-96, 99, 112, 116, 119, 134-43.

Comparisons with other artists: Cole, 70-71; Copley, 55; Hudson River School, 71; Inman, xvii; Jarvis, xvii, 56, 95, 99; Jewett, 105; Morse, 99; Rembrandt Peale, 95; Ramage, 10; Rococo School (English) 77; Stuart, xvii, 55-56, 74, 104, 164; Vanderlyn, xvii, 78,95; Waldo, 72, 105.

Ames as portrait painter, xvii, 10-15, 21-22, 26, 28, 30, 32, 35-36, 39, 43-46, 49-58, 61, 63-67, 73, 78-79, (1-452); as portrait draftsman (518, 533, 557); as miniaturist, 10-13, 21-22, 26, 28, 30, 32, 36, 39, 43, 80, 83, 136-138, 149, 172, 176-177, (453-513); as hair-worker, 12-13, 21, 26, 30, 171-172, 176-177; as painter on glass, (542, 556, 561, 606); drawings by, 151, (518, 525, 533, 546, 557); gouaches by, (619-620).

Subjects, other than portraits: allegorical, 69-71, 96, 186, (15, 515-517, 538); birds, animals and fish, 91-92, 95, 99-100, 184, 186-187, (521, 523, 527-531, 540-541, 549-550); classical, (522, 542, 548, 562-563); figure compositions, (525, 541, 545, 556, 561, 624); historical, 53, 132, (520, 546-547); landscapes, 12, 67-71, 135, 140, 149, 170, 181-182, (524, 535-538, 619-620); literary, 132, (551, 554, 555); religious, 132, (514, 534, 539, 543, 544, 552, 553); still lifes, 100, 135, 149, 187, (519, 532).

Ames, Mrs. Ezra (née Zipporah Wood), 23, 119-120, 126, 129; silhouette of, 40, 42; miniature of, 43, 83, 137, (459); repros., 42, 137.

Ames, Fisher, pencil portrait of,(518).

Ames, Julius Rubens, 35, 115, 124, 126, 129, 130, 133, (269); portraits of, xvii, 39, 112, 114, (13, 16); repro., 125; miniatures by, 120, 123-124, (453 note, 587, 602, 603, 628-630).

Ames, Lucretia, 24.

Ames, Marcia Lucretia (Mrs. William James), 27, 105, 107, 115, 119-120, 133, (2, 156, 157); portraits and miniature of, 39, 137, (14-16, 159, 460); repro., 137; owner, (10,159).

Ames Mark Lodge (Schoharie, N.Y.), 43-44.

Amsterdam (N.Y.), (249-250).

André, John, (5, 172, 310).

Andrews, George Clinton, Sr., owner, (72).

Andrews, Dr. George Clinton, owner, 62, 65, 78, (68, 72).

Annesley, William(?), portrait of, (17); repro., 89.

Annesley, Mrs. William(?) (née Margaret La Casse), portrait of, (18); repro., 89.

Apple and a Pear, by Ames, 100, 187, (519).

Appleton, William Henry, 164.

Armitage, Benjamin, 72-73, 84-85,108.

Armstrong, General, portrait of, 77.
Artists' supplies, cost of, 13-14.
Assault of the Isle of (?), by Ames 53, (520).
Astor, John Jacob, 27, (333).
Astoria, Oregon, (333).
Astrology, book on, 15.
Aurora (N.Y.), sitters from, (43-44).

Bacon, Mrs., portrait of, (19).
Bacon, Mrs. Henry, owner, (634).
Bacon, John F., patron, 183, (20).
Baker, Charles E., attributions by, (104, 343a).
Balch, Vistus, engravings by, 158, (56, 425, 570, 585).
Baldwin, Stephen, portrait of, (588).
Ballston (N.Y.), (91, 239).
Bamman, H., patron, 96.
Bangs, Mr. Bleecker, owner, (31).
Bank of Albany, 19-20, (47, 199, 299, 388, 414); patron, (625).
Banyard, Mrs., patron, 45.
Baptist Church, at Albany (N.Y.), (428).
Barber, Catharine, *see* Mrs. William James.
Barber, John, of Barber & Southwick, portrait of, (21).
Barber, Robert, 49, 180, (21).
Barber, Thomas H., owner, (23).
Barclay, William, patron, 71, 186, (515).
Barnum, P.T., of the American Museum, 91, 166-167, (395); owner, (198a).
Barretto, Mrs. Laurence, attributions by, (29, 30, 343).
Barrey (or Barry), Thomas, patron, 43, 179, (22).
Bartlett, Mrs. Franklin, owner, (171).
Bartlett, Lydia, *see* Mrs. Stephen Reynolds.
Bartlett, Nathaniel, (250).
Bartlett, Mrs. Nathaniel (née Mercy Otis), (250).
Bassett, Miss, 53.
Bassett, N.B., patron, 28-29.
Bassett & Warford, patrons, 29.
Bayard, Harriet Elizabeth, (23).
Bayard, Leroy & McEvers, (23).
Bayard, William (23).
Bayard, William, 2d, portraits of, (23-24).
Beardsley, Levi, and the Erie Canal, 109,111.
The Beaver Assiduity for Steamboat, by Ames, 59-60, (521, 610).
Beck, Dr. Romeyn, patron, 182,(260).
Beekman, Cornelia, (Mrs. Gilbert Livingston), (382).
Beekman, Cuneira, portrait of, (25).
Beers, William P., patron, 43, 179, (26).
Benkard, Mrs. Harry Horton, owner, (171).
Bent, Betty (Mrs. Jesse Emes), mother of Ezra Ames, 3, 6.
Bent, Betty, elder sister of Betty (Bent) Emes, 3.
Bent, John, grandfather of Ezra Ames, 3.
Bent, Mrs. John (née Betty Read), grandmother of Ezra Ames, 3.
Bergh, Christian, 7, 8.
Bergh, John, 7.
Bessac, Miss Florence V., owner, (81, 82, 142, 143).
Betts, Mr. Frederick, owner, (265).
Binding of Samson, by Ames, (553).
Binnian, Mrs. Walter B., owner, (125).
Bisbee, John, artist, 108.
Blackford, *see* Blatchford.
Blanchard, Lillian, owner, (120).
Blanchard, Marcus L., owner, 197, (120).
Bland, Harry MacNeill, owner, (138).
Blatchford, E.H., patron, 158-159, 189 (225).
Blatchford, Dr. Samuel, portrait of, 99, 186, (27); engraving of, (566); patron, 187, (28).
Blatchford, Mrs. Samuel (née Alicia Windeatt), portrait of, 99, 187, (28).
Bleecker, Catherine Westerlo, (400).
Bleecker, Harmanus, (163, 267); portraits of, xvii, 95-96, 169, 186, (29-30); repro., 152.
Bleecker Library (Albany, N.Y.), owner, 95-96, 152, 169, (29).
Bleecker, James L., (31).
Bleecker, Leonard, portrait of, (31); repro., 37.
Bleecker, Margaret (Mrs. Harmanus Ten Eyck,) (327).
Bliss, Cornelius N., donor, (64).
Bloodgood & Follet's store (Albany, N.Y.), 21.
Bloodgood, Francis, (228); portrait of, xvii, 53, 56, 143, (32); repro., 142; owner, (32, 33).
Bloodgood, Mrs. Francis (née Eliza Cobham), portrait of, 53, (33).
Bloodgood, Mrs. Francis (née Anna Shoemaker Morris), (32).
Bloodgood, Lynot, patron, 183, (319).

Bloodgood, Robert Fanshaw, owner, (30).
Bogardus, Anna, *see* Mrs. George Provost.
Bogart, Henry I., portrait of, (34).
Bogart, Mrs. Henry I. (née Barbara Marselis), portrait of, (607).
Bogart, John, patron, 181, (35).
Bogart, William H., owner, (34).
Book of Knowledge...., by Abraham Weatherwise, 15.
Boston (Mass.), xix, 23, 144, (578, 586).
Boynton, Mrs. Theodore Vernon, owner, (24).
Box made and decorated by Ezra Ames, repro., 174.
Braintree (Mass.), sitter from, (172).
Brant, Joseph, portrait of, 44, 138, (36); repro., 37.
Braun, John F., owner, (604).
Brenauer, Joseph B., owner, (384, 502).
Brinckerhoff, John, patron, 189, (37).
Brinckerhoff, Mrs. John, portrait of, 189, (37).
Briton, Miss, 53.
Broadhead, Rev., patron, 186, (30).
Broadhead, Mrs. John Romeyn, owner, (30).
Brook Club, owner, (67).
Brooklyn Museum, Ames's works exhibited at, (68, 132, 173, 597).
Brown, Dorotha, *see* Mrs. Jesse Emes.
Brown, Maj. Gen. Jacob Jennings, portrait of, 132, (38-39); patron, 184, (40-41).
Brown, Mrs. Jacob Jennings (née Pamela Williams), portraits of, 95, 139, 143, 167, 184, (40-41); repro., 168.
Brown, S., patron, 53.
Brown, Mr. and Mrs. W. Harman, owners, (357-359, 365).
Bryan, Thomas J., owner, (198a).
Buckminster, Mr. Thomas (or Lawson), patron, 9, 10.
Buell, Elias, portrait of, (42).
Buell, Jesse, owner, (42).
Buffalo (N.Y.), 102, 108-109; sitter from, (73).
Bulkey, Mr., patron, 43, 178, (461).
Bulkley, Ellen, *see* Mrs. Philo Ruggles.
Bulkley, Capt. Joseph, (262).
Bulkley, Mrs. Joseph (née Ellen Hubbell), (262).
Bullard, Samuel, 6.
Bunnel, ________, Mason, 29.
Burdick, Horace, Ames's work formerly attributed to, (266).
Burgoyne's surrender, 7.
Burnham, Eleazer, portrait of, 12, (43); repro., 121.
Burnham, Mrs. Eleazer (née Urania Smith), (43).
Burnham, Mrs. Eleazer (née Caroline Matilda Wood), portrait of, (44); repro., 121.
Burr, George Lindsley, owner, (116).
Butler, Mrs. Arthur W., owner, (327).
Buttre, John Chester, engraving by, (571).

Cady, ________, of N.Y. State Assembly, 73.
Cady, Aaron, (45).
Cady, Mrs. Aaron (née Anna Palmer), (45).
Cady, David, portrait of, (45, 226).
Cady, Mrs. David (née Anna Schuler), portrait of, (46).
Caldwell, James, patron, 20, 43, 53, 67-69, 100, 179-180, 186-187, (47-49, 520, 535).
Caldwell & Solomon's Tobacco and Snuff Store (Albany, N.Y.), patron, 104, 304.
Caldwell Village, Lake George (N.Y.), 67-69, (47, 535).
Caldwell, William, patron, 44, 68, (36); owner, (535).
Callender, James H., attribution by, (139).
Cambridge (Mass.), 4, 6.
Campagna and Volcano, Interno del Vesuvio del 1835, gouache (619).
Campbell, Miss Catherine, owner, (23).
Campbell, Miss Marie, owner, (23).
Campbell, Samuel, owner, (596).
Canajoharie (N.Y.) Library and Art Gallery, owner, (590).
Canal Bank, (228).
Canfield, Laura, *see* Mrs. Ambrose Spencer.
Car of Neptune, Hudson River steamboat, 59.
Carey, Miss Eliza, portrait of, (50).
Caricatures of England and Scotland, prints, 172.
Carleton, (probably William T. Carlton), artist represented in Albany Gallery of Fine Arts, 115.
Carlyle, Thomas, on painting as history, xx, 135-136.
Carroll, Alida Van Rensselaer, owner, (168).

Cary, Mrs. Clarence, owner, (149-150).
Cary, Miss Elizabeth Luther, owner, (458).
Cary, Miss Lydia, owner, (458).
Catalogue Sale of Portraits, Albany 1842, *see* Ames, Ezra, *Catalogue*.
Cate, Mrs. William C., owner, (30).
Catholic Church, at Albany (N.Y.), (22).
Catlin, George, copy after Ames by, (36).
Causici, Enrico, 108.
Cazenovia (N.Y.) Public Library, owner, (71).
Century Association (N.Y.C.), Ames's work exhibited at, (211).
Ceracchi, Giuseppe, bust by, 50.
Chamberlain, George Agnew, owner, (17-18).
Chamberlain, Mrs. J. Chester, owner, (587).
Champlain Canal, 102.
Chapman, John Gadsby(?), artist represented in Albany Gallery of Fine Arts, 115.
Chapman, Mrs. Marie Weston, owner, (39, 69, 135, 223, 266, 360, 379, 401).
Cherubs, by Ames, 172.
Chester, Dr., 107.
Chester, Rev. John, patron, 96; portraits of, (51-52); engravings of, (567-568).
Chicago Art Institute, 69, (538).
Child, Abner, patron, 10.
Cigar store Indian, repainted by Ames (woodcut), repro., 356.
Clapp, Beulah, (Mrs. Solomon Allen), (5).
Clapp and Graham, owners, (597).
Clark, A., patron, 87.
Clark, Asahel, *see* Rawdon, Clark & Co.
Clark, Mary, (Mrs. John James), (155).
Clark, Stephen C., owner, 101, (70, 167).
Clarke, Mrs. Beulah Allen, portrait of, (53); engraving of, (569).
Clarke, Thomas B., owner, (211,622).
Clermont, see *North River*.
Clinton (N.Y.), 12.
Clinton, Catharine, *see* Mrs. Pierre Van Cortlandt II.
Clinton, Catherine, *see* Mrs. Ambrose Spencer.
Clinton, Cornelia Tappen, *see* Mrs. Edmond Charles Genet.
Clinton, DeWitt, (284, 285, 287); and Erie Canal, 103-104, 109, 111; patron, 91, 92, 95, 99, 100, 184, 186, 187, (59-62, 73, 519, 527-531); portraits of, 80, 91, 92, 112, 132, 140, 169, 184, (54-58); repro., 141; engraving of, (570); portraits of, misattributed to Ames, (589-590).
Clinton, Mrs. DeWitt (née Maria Franklin), portrait of, 91, 184, (59).
Clinton, Mrs. DeWitt (née Catherine Jones), (164, 165); portraits of, 99, 187, (60-61); repro., 98.
Clinton, Elizabeth, *see* Mrs. Matthias B. Tallmadge.
Clinton, Franklin, portrait of, 91, 184, (62).
Clinton, George, (72, 127, 318, 383, 384, 502); patron, 35; watercolor portrait of, (591); miniature of, 22, 177, (462); engravings of, (571-574); portraits of, by Ames, xvii, 61-66, 73-74, 77-79, 88, 91, 123, 132, 140, 146, 154, 157, 182, 184, (63-71, 608); repros., 62, 76, 146.
Clinton, Mrs. George (née Cornelia Tappen), (72); miniature of, 22, 177, (462-463).
Clinton, George, Jr., (72).
Clinton, George Washington, portrait of, 78-79, 132, 143, (72); repro., 78.
Clinton, Mrs. George Washington, (née Anna Floyd), (72).
Clinton, George William, portrait of, 91, 184, (73).
Clinton, James, (72).
Clinton, Mrs. George William (née Laura Catharine Spencer), (73).
Clinton, Mary, *see* Mrs. Ambrose Spencer.
Clymer, George, portrait of (609).
Coat of Arms of the City of Albany, by Ames, (610).
Cobham, Eliza, *see* Mrs. Francis Bloodgood.
Coeymans, Gertrude (née Staats), 7.
Coffee, William J., sculptor, 92.
Cohoes (N.Y.), 22.
Cole, Thomas, possible influence of Ames on, 70-71.
Collegiate Church (New York City), (189).
Colt, Betsey, *see* Mrs. Ebenezer Foot.
Columbia University (New York City), owner or loanee, 88, 93, 143, 159, 163, (215, 261, 262, 342).
Commercial Bank of Albany, (3).
Concord (Mass.). 5-6.

Cone, Mr. and Mrs. Bernard H., owners, (86).
Congregational Church, East Hartford (Conn.), (443).
Connolly, Mary Ann, *see* Mrs. William James.
Conover, Cornelia Fitzhugh, owner, (168).
Cook, Mrs. Seth W., owner, 89, (17-18).
Cooper, Dr. Charles DeKay, portraits of, 124, 190, (74-75).
Cooper, Mrs. Charles DeKay (née Margaret Tayler), portrait of, 124, (76); patron, 124, 190, (74-75).
Cooper, Cornelius V., DeWitt Clinton calls on, 92.
Cooper, Dr. H.S. Fenimore, owner, (611).
Cooper, Mrs. John Tayler, owner, (71, 320).
Cooper, William, portrait of, (611).
Cooperstown (N.Y.), 28, (30, 167, 235); *see also*, New York State Historical Association.
Copley, John Singleton, xix; influence on Ames, 55, 132, 138-139, (424); repro., 139.
de Coppet, Mrs. L. Casimir, owner, (332a, 333, 333a).
Corcoran Gallery of Art, Ames's works exhibited at, 74, (64, 215-216).
Corning, Cynthia, *see* Mrs. Elias Mather.
Cox, Eliza Abbey Hughes, 116, (15).
Craft work, *see under* Ames, Ezra.
Crane, Elisha, (208).
Crane, Mrs. Elisha (née Ruth Phelps), (208); portrait of, 186, (77).
Crane, Louisa, *see* Mrs. John Meads.
Crocker, ______, Mason of Albany, 29.
Crolius, Clarkson, portrait and engraving of, 112, (78, 575); repro., 86.
Crolius, Clarkson, Jr., owner, 86, (78).
Crosby, Stephen Van Rensselaer, owner, (402).
Cruikshank, *see* Alexander C. Gibson.
Cumming, Harriet, portrait of, (80).
Cumming, Rev. Hooper, portraits of, 91, 95, 143, 151, 184, (79, 612).
Cumming, Mrs. Hooper, (née Sophie Wright), portrait of, 95, 143, (80).
Curtis, Dora Lee, owner, (97).
Cushing, Thomas Humphrey, portrait of, xvii, 80, (81); repro., 81.
Cushing, Mrs. Thomas Humphrey (née Margaret Eleanor Norwood), 80, (143); portrait of, xvii, 80, (82); repro., 81.
Cushman, Isaac, (576); portrait of, 188, (83).
Cushman, Mrs. Isaac (née Sarah Paine), (576); portrait of, 188, (84)
Cushman, John P., lithographed portrait of, (85, 576); patron, 170, 188, (83-84, 310).
Cushman, Mrs. John P. (née Tallmadge), (576).
Cutting, William, portrait of, (86).
Cuyler, John C., patron, 181, (87).

D _____, A _____, patron, 176, (464).
Daggett, Hinman & Co., engraving by, (572).
Darby and Joan, picture or print sold by Ames, 40, 58, 87, 171; sign painted by Ames, 40, 87, 171-172; repro., 173.
D'Avignon, Francis, engravings by, (575-576).
Davinson, Mr., portrait of, 188, (88).
Davinson, Mrs., patron, 188, (88).
Davis, James, and son, portrait of, 184, (89).
Davis, Mary Frances, *see* Mrs. Guert Van Schoonhoven.
Davis, Richard, (405).
Dedham (Mass.), 4-5.
DeGraff, John Isaac, portrait of, 132, (90, 613).
DeKay, Helena, *see* Mrs. Absalom Townsend.
DeKay, Col. Thomas, (348).
Delafield, Elizabeth, estate of, owner, (311).
Delafield, Brig. Gen. John Ross, owner, (599).
DeLancey, Ann Elizabeth, *see* Mrs. Joseph Christopher Yates.
Delanoy, Abraham, portrait painter, xix.
Delaplaine, Joseph, commissions portraits by Ames, 88, 89, 91, 95, 154, 166, 169, 170, 184, 186, (59, 68, 191, 217, 278, 321, 395, 397, 574, 612).
Delaplaine's Gallery, *see* Joseph Delaplaine.
Dela Van, Mr., patron, 182, (91, 358, 365).
Dela Van, Mrs.(?), portrait of, (365).
Delavan family, sitter of, (358).
Delavan, Henry W., (91).
Delhi, (N.Y.), 115.
Denton, Rachel, *see* Mrs. Stephen Reynolds, the elder.

DePeyster, Anna (Mrs. Volckert Douw), (300).
DePeyster, Nicholas, 7.
De Rose, Anthony L., artist, 108.
De Rose, Mrs. Edward, owner, (408).
De Sherbinin, Michael, owner, (316, 318); attribution by, (361).
Dewett, M., patron, 22, 177, (465).
Dewey, Timothy, portrait of, 132, (92).
DeWitt Clinton, Erie Canal boat, 102.
DeWitt, Miss Sarah, owner, (94).
DeWitt, Simeon, (524); portraits of, 55, 164, (93-94); map by, 31.
Dexter, Katharine, *see* Mrs. Stanley McCormick.
Dexter, Samuel, (243); portrait of, (614).
Dexter, Mrs. Samuel, owner, (243).
Dexter, Mrs. Samuel (née Provost), (243).
Dexter, Wirt, owner, (243).
Dexter, Mrs. Wirt, owner, (243).
DeYoung Memorial Museum (San Francisco, Cal.), Ames's work exhibited at, (41).
Diamond, Thomas, patron, 22, 177, (95).
Diamond, Mrs., patron, 44, 179, (96).
Diana, by Ames, (522).
Dickerson, Mahlon, portrait of, (97).
Dickinson, Anson, miniatures by, (593, 599, 601).
Dietrich family, owners, (97).
Dixon, Polly, patron, 10, 176, (466).
Doane, Mr. Henry K., owner, (142, 143).
Doane, Miss Rachel A., owner, (142, 143).
Dole, John M., patron, 28, 177, (467).
Donhauser, Dr. J. Lewi, owner, 110, 167, 169, (228, 229, 449).
Donhauser, Mrs. J. Lewi, (née Eliza Paige), owner, (228, 229, 449).
Donnely, Captain, patron, 28.
Dotty, John T., patron, 87.
Douglass, James B., patron, 188, (98).
Douglass, Mrs. James B., and daughter, portrait of, 188, (98).
Douw, Catherine Louisa, *see* Mrs. John Fondey Townsend.
Douw, John DePeyster, portrait of, (592).
Douw, Magdalena, *see* Mrs. John Stevenson.
Douw, Margaret Livingston, miniature of, (593).
Douw, Volckert, (300).
Douw, Mrs. Volckert (née Anna de Peyster), (300).
Downer, Mrs. Delavan B., owner, (30).
Dox, ______, member of New York State Assembly, 73.
Draper, Mr., patron, 12, 176, (99).
Dreams, book on interpretation of, 15.
Duer, Mrs. J.G.K., owner, (77, 207, 208).
Duglass, *see* Douglass.
Dunbar, Robert, patron, 46, 170, 180, 188, (100, 101, 399).
Dunham, David, portrait of, (102).
Dunlap, William, 16, 92, 123.
Dunn, Mr., 120.
Dunn, Mary, *see* Mrs. Aaron Thorp.
Dupont Winterthur Museum (Winterthur, Del.), owner, (627).
Durand, A.B., 108, 115; engraving by, 158, (581).
Dusenbury, Miss, portrait of, (103).
Dutch Reformed Church, (189): Dutch Church, Albany, 34, 107, 126; North Dutch Church, Albany, (27); Third Reformed Protestant Dutch Church, Albany, (114); Dutch Reformed Church, Schenectady, (260).
Dutchess County (N.Y.), 7, (250, 261).
Duveen, Albert, owner, (398).
Dwight, Miss Frances H., owner, (404-405).
Dwight, Miss Laura, owner, (404-405).
Dwight, Theodore, portrait of, 183, (104); repro., 90.
Dwight, Rev. Dr. Timothy, portraits of, 132, (105-106).

Eagle, Portrait of an, by Ames, (523).
Eagle Tavern (Albany, N.Y.), patron, 96.
Eames, *see* Ames *and* Emes.
Eames, John, patron, 28.
Eamms, *see* Ames *and* Emes.
Eams, *see* Ames *and* Emes.
East Hartford (Conn.), (443).
East Sudbury (Mass.), 6-7, 9.
Easthampton (Long Island, N.Y.), (219).
Eclipse of the Sun, by Ames, (524).
Edgeall, Captain, patron, 12.
Edgel, Simon, 6, 12.
Edwards, Miss Elizabeth Seelye, owner, 8, 11, 32, 39, 42, 53, 69, 83, 127, 128, 137, (10, 16, 156,

159, 169, 453-457, 459, 469, 484, 486, 495-500, 503, 518, 525, 534, 538, 543, 554, 619, 620, 624, 628-630).
Edwards, Mr. Henry Ames, owner, (169, 453-457, 459, 469, 484, 486, 495-500, 503, 518, 525, 538, 546, 557, 619, 620, 624).
Edwards, Mrs. Isaac, 133; owner, (10, 159, 169, 453-457, 459, 469, 484, 486, 495-500, 503).
Edwards, Jonathan, (105).
Edwards, Mrs. Thomas, attributions by, (17, 18).
Egberts, Cornelius(?), portrait of, 189, (107, 615).
Ehrich Galleries, owner, 37, (31,67).
Eights, James, view of Albany by, 17.
Eights, Dr. Jonathan, patron, 28.
Elderkin, Mrs. Helen E., owner, (605).
Ellen Tree, portrait formerly attributed to Ames, (604).
Elliott, Charles Loring, xix, (408).
Ellis, Mr., patron, 26, 177 (108, 468).
Ellis, Mrs. John French, owner, (332a, 333, 333a).
Ellis, Dr. Samuel C., owner, 164-165, (254).
Emerson, Dr. Haven, owner, (343).
Emes, Bette, sister of Ezra Ames, 6.
Emes, Bette, half-sister of Ezra Ames, 6, 116.
Emes family, miniatures of, 43.
Emes, Henry, grandfather of Ezra Ames, 4-5.
Emes, Henry, half-brother of Ezra Ames, 6, 115-116; miniature and portrait of, 137, (109, 469); repro., 127.
Emes, Mrs. Henry, 115.
Emes, Mrs. Henry (née Ruth Newton), grandmother of Ezra Ames, 5.
Emes, Jesse, father of Ezra Ames, 3, 5-8, 12, 115-116; portraits of, 11, 96, 138, (110-111); repros., 2, 97.
Emes, Mrs. Jesse (née Betty Bent), mother of Ezra Ames, 3, 6.
Emes, Mrs. Jesse (née Dorotha Brown), step-mother of Ezra Ames, 6, 12-13, 116.
Emes, Mrs. Jesse (formerly Mrs. Fanny Parminter), step-mother of Ezra Ames, 96, 115; portrait of, 96, (112); repro., 97.
Emes, Jesse, Jr., brother of Ezra Ames, 6, 116.
Emes, John, 4-5.
Emes, Polly, sister of Ezra Ames, 6.
Emes, Polly or Polle, half-sister of Ezra Ames, 6, 115-116.
Emes, Sally, *see* Mrs. Ezekiel Mulford.
Emes, Thomas, 3-5.
Emes, Timothy, brother of Ezra Ames, 6, 116.
Emmes, Mary, *see* Mary (Emmes) James.
Emmes, *see* Emes *and* Ames.
Emmet, Thomas Addis, owner, (181, 579, 580).
Emms, *see* Emes *and* Ames.
Ems, *see* Emes *and* Ames.
England, xix, 4; sitters from, (17, 27, 28).
English-Speaking Union (New York City), Ames's works on exhibition at, 39, 80, (316-317).
Ennis, Mr., Ames's boarder, 29.
Erie Canal, Ames and, 100, 102-104; ceremonies at opening of, 102-104, 108-109, 111-112; transparency of, 112; Act of 1792, 19; Commission, (148).
Evertson, Bernardus, 33.

Fairley, Major, portrait of, 22, 177, (113).
Fairley, Mrs., patron, 22, 177, (113).
Fairlie, James, patron, 20.
Fairman, Caroline, *see* Mrs. Caroline (Fairman) Rodgers.
Fairman, Gideon, engraver, 56, 108, 132.
Fallington, Samuel, *see* Samuel Fullerton.
Family Group, by Ames, (525).
Farming Countryside, gouache, (620).
Feke, Robert, portrait painter, xix.
Ferargil Galleries (New York City), Ames's work exhibited at, (41).
Ferguson, Mrs. Van Rensselaer, owner, (122).
Ferris, Isaac, portrait of, (114).
Fess, Mrs. Le Roy E. (Margaret Richmond), owner, (155).
Field, Rev. G.F., owner, (41).
Figure of Hope, by Ames, 59-60, (526).
Fish, paintings of, 91, 92, 95, 99, 100, 184, 186, (527-531).
Fishkill (N.Y.), xix.
Fitch, Asa, Mason, 114.
Five Heads, by Ames, (558).
Flexner, James Thomas, attribution by, (311).
Floyd, Anna (Mrs. George Washington Clinton), (72).

Floyd, Mary (Mrs. Benjamin Tallmadge), (310).
Follet, Francis, patron, 21, 26, 177, (470).
Fondey, Cornelia, portrait of, 18, (115).
Fondey family, group portrait of, 36, 138, (115, 471); repro., 18.
Fondey, Isaac, portrait of, 18, (115).
Fondey, John, Jr., miniature of, 36, 137, (471); portrait of, 18, (115, 471).
Fondey, Maria, portrait of, 18, (115).
Fondey, Sarah, portrait of, 18, (115).
Fondey, Stephen, portrait of, 18, (115).
Fondey, William, portrait of, 18, (115).
Foot, Ebenezer, (116).
Foot, Mrs. Ebenezer, (née Betsey Colt), portrait of, 80, (116).
Forbs, Mr., Ames's boarder, 29.
Forest, J.B., engraving by, (573).
Forman, Rev. Dr., portrait of, 132, (117).
Forsyth, Dr. Russell, patron, 190, (118, 119).
Forsyth, sons of Dr. Russell, portraits of, 190, (118, 119).
Fort Astor, Oregon, (332a, 333).
Fort George (N.Y.), (47); Ames's view of, 67-68, (535-536).
Fowler, Samuel Stevenson, portrait of, xvii, 116, 119-120, 143, (120); repro., 197.
Fowler, Mrs. Samuel Stevenson (née Julia Frances Gregory), (120).
Framingham, (Mass.), xvii, 3-6, 9, 33.
France, U.S. Minister to, (214); French Minister to U.S., (127).
Franklin, Maria, *see* Mrs. DeWitt Clinton.
Fraser, Charles, 108.
Frazee, John, artist, 108.
Frazer, Mrs. James Carroll, owner, (402).
Freeman, J.E., portrait by, (600).
Frelinghuysen, Joseph S., owner, (126).
Frelinghuysen, Mrs. Joseph S., owner, owner, (125).
Frothingham, James, Ames's works formerly attributed to, (165, 343, 362).
Fruit Piece, by Ames, (532).
Fry, Joseph, patron, 87, 173.
Fryer, John W., patron, 34.
Fryer, William, patron, 34.
Fullerton, (or Fallington), Samuel, patron, 176, (472).
Fulton, steamboat, 112.
Fulton, Robert, (86); *see also* Livingston & Fulton Co.

Gansevoort, Catherine Douw, miniature of, (594).
Gansevoort, Harmen, owner, (126).
Gansevoort, Leonard (1751-1810), (122); patron, 36, 178, (121); Stuart's (?) portrait of, (122, 616); Ames's portraits of (?), (124, 616-617).
Gansevoort, Leonard (1754-1834), (616); patron of, 36, 178, (121); portraits of, (122-124).
Gansevoort, Maria, *see* Mrs. Allan Melville.
Gansevoort, Peter, the elder, (210, 616); portrait of, 56, 132, 187, (125).
Gansevoort, Mrs. Peter (née Catherine Van Schaick), (210, 616); portrait of, (126); repro., 98.
Gansevoort, Peter, the younger, patron and owner, 35, 187, (125-126).
Garvan Collection, Mabel Brady (Yale University), owner, 38, (316, 318).
Gazetteer of New York, by Horatio G. Spafford, (279).
Genesee County (N.Y.), (476).
Genesee River, 102.
Genet, Miss, *see* Mrs. Col. Le Mai.
Genet, Edmond Charles, 95, (184); portrait of, xvii, 49, 138, (127). repro., xvi.
Genet, Mrs. Edmond Charles (née Cornelia Tappen Clinton), (127).
Genet, Mrs. Edmond Charles (née Martha Brandon Osgood), (127).
Genet, George Clinton, owner, (127).
Genet, Mrs. George Clinton, owner, (127).
Gentleman, Portrait of a, see, Unidentified: *Portrait of a Gentleman.*
Germain, Mr., patron, 44, 179, (128).
Gerritse or Gerritsen, Marie, *see* Mrs. Wessel Van Schaick.
Gibson (James), of the Pennsylvania Academy, 64.
Gibson, Alexander C. (formerly Cruikshank), (129).
Gibson, Mrs. Alexander C. (née Marcia Phebe Reynolds), portrait of, (129).
Gilder, Miss Louise S., owner, 45, (290-291).
Gilder, Mrs. W. Howard, owner, (290-291).
Glen, Mr., portrait of, 22, 176, (130).

Glens Falls (N.Y.) Masonic Chapter, 87.
Goetze, ______, engraving by, (122).
Gold, Thomas Ruggles, portrait of, 187, (131).
Golden Chain of Salvation, print sold by Ames, 172.
Goodrich, Jesse W., 158-159; patron, 189, (225).
Goodridge, Sarah, miniaturist, (599).
Gordon, Archibald, (345).
Gordon, Mrs. Archibald, *see* Sarah Ann Tompkins.
Goshen (N.Y.), (435).
Gould, Phares, portrait of, (132).
Gourlay, James, patron, 180, 183, (133-134).
Graham, *see* Clapp & Graham.
Grand Central Art Galleries (New York City), Ames's work exhibited at, (193).
Green, Mrs. John, owner, (46).
Greenbush (N.Y.), (256).
Greene, Phillipse E.N., owner, (332a, 333, 333a).
Greene, Mrs. Phillipse E.N., owner, (332a, 333a).
Greene, Phillipse, E.N., Jr., owner, (333).
Gregory, Julia Frances, *see* Mrs. Samuel Stevenson Fowler.
Griffin, Edward Dorr, portrait of, 132, (135).
Griffiths, Mrs. Edgar Morris, owner, (617).
Group of Three Children, by Ames, (560).
Groups of Heads, by Ames, 132, (558-559).
Guest, Mr., patron, 26.
Gutowski, A.R., landscapes by, 132.

Hackley, Aaron, patron, 183, 188, (136-137).
Hackley, Mrs. Aaron, portrait of, 188, (137).
Hallenbake, Dorothea (Mrs. Spencer Stafford), (290).
Hallett, Maria, *see* Mrs. Benjamin Tallmadge.
Hall's Sons, H.B., engravers, (565).
Halpert, Mrs. Edith G., owner, (345).
Hamill, Mrs. Robert L., owner, (447a).
Hamilton, Alexander, portraits of, by Ames, 50, 52, 132, 157, 180, (138-139, 533); repro., 52; portraits, bust and engravings of, by artists other than Ames, 50, 51, (533, 577-578); repros., 51; *Works of*, 50.
Hamilton, Alexander, grandson of the above, owner, 157, (139).
Hamilton College, (307).
Hamilton, Isaac, patron, 183, (140-141).
Hamilton, Schuyler Van Cortlandt, owner, (381).
Hankinson, John, portrait of, 80, (142).
Hankinson, Mrs. John (née Frances McCrae), portrait of, 80, (143).
Hansen, Miss, portrait of, (144).
Hansen, Isaac, patron, 46, 50, 180, (145-146).
Harding, Chester, portrait by (?), (613).
Harris, Mr., patron, 176, (473).
Harris, Stephen, patron, 13, 176, (474).
Harrison, *see* Porter & Harrison.
Hart, Charles Henry, attribution by, (362).
Hart, (James M.), artist, 115.
Hart, Mrs. Theophilus Phillipse, owner, (332a, 333, 333a).
Hart, (William), artist, 115.
Haskell, Mrs. J. Amory, owner, (357-359, 365, 632).
Hatch, Mr., patron, (252).
Hawkins, Mrs. Samuel, patron, 26, 177, (475).
Hawley, Jesse, miniature of, 108, 137, (476); repro., 109.
Hayke, John, patron, 22, 177, (477).
Heath, William H., engraver, 74, (419).
Hecksher, E.E., owner, (211).
Height, Captain, patron, 28.
Henry, John V., 107; miniature of, (595).
Henry, Joseph, (478).
Henry, Mrs. William (née Ann Alexander), miniature of, (478).
Hesselius, Gustavus, portrait painter, xix.
Hesselius, John, portrait painter, xix.
Hill, Frederick, estate of, owner, 81, (81-82).
Hillhouse, John T.E., owner, (147).
Hillhouse, Mrs. John T.E., owner, 90, (147).
Hillhouse, Thomas, portrait of, xvii, (147); repro., 90.
Hillhouse, Mrs. Thomas (Harriet Hosmer), (147).
Hillhouse, Mrs. Thomas (Anne Van Schaick Ten Broeck), (147).
Hills, Mrs. John (née Huldah Mulford), miniatures of, 137, (479-480); repro., 136.

Hills, John Ames, owner, (111).
Hills, Miss Sally Huldah, owner, (111, 479).
Hinman, *see* Daggett, Hinman & Co.
Hirschl & Adler, owners, (81, 82).
Hitchcock, Warner F., patron, 87.
Hoadley, Mrs. Eliot Betts, owner, (265).
Hodge, James, patron, 34, 39, 178, (481).
Hoffman, Nicholas, 7.
Hoffman, Schuyler Van Vechten, owner, (406).
Hogeboom, Miss M.R., owner, (377).
Holley, Myron, portrait of, (148).
Holley, Miss Sallie, owner, (148).
Holy Family, by Ames, (534).
Hoogland, William, engraving by, 50, (578); repro., 51.
Hook, Mr. William C., owner, 121, (43-44).
Hooker, John, patron, 22, 177, (482).
Hooker, Philip, patron, 34.
Hooker & Putnam, patrons, 34.
Hope, Hudson River steamboat, 59-60, (388, 526).
Hopkins Grammar School (New Haven, Conn.), owner, (434).
Horton, Ruth, *see* Mrs. Benjamin Phelps.
Hosack, Dr. David, 161-163.
Hosmer, Harriet (Mrs. Thomas Hillhouse), (147).
The Hours: Past, Present and Future, miniature by Malbone, (15).
Howell, Silas W., patron, 28.
Hubbell, Ellen, *see* Mrs. Joseph Bulkley.
Huckley, *see* Hackley.
Hudson (N.Y.), 60 (167).
Hudson River, 7, 14, 16, 59-60, (388, 521, 526).
Hudson, Robert, portrait of, (149); repro., 94.
Hudson, Mrs. Robert (née Eliza ?), portrait of, (150); repro., 94.
Hughes, ——, English artist, (361).
Hughes, Angelo, Jr., 116, (15).
Hume, Mrs. John E.N., owner, (45).
Humphrey, F (or J., or G.), patron, 186, (151).
Hun, Mrs. Marcus T., owner, (123).
Hun, Miss Mary V., owner, (123).
Hun, Mrs. Thomas, *see* Lydia Louise Reynolds.
Hunter, James, portrait of, 189, (152).
Huntington Library and Art Gallery (San Marino, Cal.), owner, (622).
Hurlbert, Revd. G. (or J.), see Joseph Hurlbut.
Hurlbut, Joseph, portrait of, 188, (153).
Hutton, George, *see* I. & G. Hutton.
Hutton, I & G. patrons, 34, 53, 71.
Hutton, Isaac, 79; *see also* I. & G. Hutton.
Hyde Park (N.Y.), 7.

Ijams, Mrs. J. Horton, owner, (447a).
Ingersoll, Anne (Mrs. Joshua King), (173).
Ingham, Charles C., artist, 108.
Inman, Henry, xvii-xix, 108, 144, (360, 613); Ames's works formerly attributed to, 143, (32, 416-417).
Iselin, Mrs. Arthur, owner, (54, 105).

Jackson, Allan H., owner, (154).
Jackson, Samuel, portrait of, (154).
James, Anna, 119.
James, Daniel, (155).
James, Ellen, *see* Mrs. James King.
James, Mrs. Ellery S., owner, (265).
James, Henry, Sr., 27, (14, 159, 460).
James, Henry, Jr., novelist, 27, 133, (14, 157, 159, 460).
James, Dr. John, portrait of, (155).
James, Mrs. John (Mary Clark), (155).
James, Katharine Barber, portrait of, (156); repro., 128.
James, Mary (Emmes), (155).
James, William, Sr., 27, 105, 107, 120, (158, 171); portrait of, 104, 143, (157); repro., 106.
James, Mrs. William, Sr. (née Catharine Barber), (157); portrait of, 105, (158); repro., 106.
James, Mrs. William, Sr. (née Mary Ann Connolly), 105, (157).
James, Mrs. William, Sr. (née Elizabeth Tillman), 105, 107, (157).
James, Rev. William, Jr., 27, 105, 107, (14, 156, 157, 159, 460).
James, Mrs. William, Jr., *see* Marcia Lucretia Ames.
James, William, philosopher, 27, 133, (14, 157, 159, 460).
Jarvis, John Wesley, xvii-xix, 56, 92, 143, 144; Ames's works formerly attributed to, 95, 99, 143, 167, (41, 102, 167, 302, 303).
Jay, John, portraits of, 45, 140, (160, 361, 596); repro., 141.
Jay, Col. William, owner, (105).
Jee, Mrs. Edward A., *see* Harriet Cumming.
Jeffcott, Mr. and Mrs. Harry A., owners, (356).

Jefferson, Thomas, portraits of, 56, 132, (161-162).
Jenkins, Elisha, patron, 184, (55).
Jersey City (N.J.), 115.
Jerusalem, picture or print sold by Ames, 27, 172.
Jewell, Edward Alden, criticism of Ames's work by, 74, 77.
Jewett, William, 108; *see also* Waldo & Jewett.
Jocelyn, Nathaniel, 108.
Johnson, Mr. C.K., owner, 90, (104).
Jones, ———, New York State Assemblyman, 73.
Jones, Catherine, *see* Mrs. DeWitt Clinton.
Jones, Henry, portrait of, xvii, 53, 55, 61, (163, 354); repro., 54.
Jones, Henry T., (163).
Jones, Mrs. Julia C. Van Arsdale, owner, (80).
Jones, Philip Livingston, owner, (60).
Jones, Dr. Thomas, (60, 165); portrait of, (164).
Jones, Mrs. Thomas (née Margaret Livingston), (60, 164); portrait of, 99, (165).
Jones, Thomas P., portrait of, 132, (166).
Jones, W.R., engraver, (564).
Jordan, Ambrose Latting, portrait of, xvii, 99, 132, 143, (167); repro., 101.
Jordan, Ezra Ames, 42.
Jumel, Mme., (104).

Kane Brothers, (168).
Kane, Mr., patron, 36.
Kane, James, patron, 67, 181, (537).
Kane, John, 138; portrait of, 39-40, (168); repro., 41.
Kane, Mrs. John (née Sybil Kent), (168); portrait of, (618).
Kane, Maria, *see* Mrs. Joseph C. Yates.
Kane, Mr. R. Keith, owner, 41, (168, 618).
Kearney, Mrs. R., miniature of, (597).
Kent, James, (331); portraits of, xvii, 67, 132, (169-170); repro., 75.
Kent, Sybil, *see* Mrs. John Kane.
Kentucky, Ames's work owned in, 50.
Kernochan, Mrs. Edward L., owner, (287).
Kierstede, Maria, *see* Mrs. James Livingston.
Kilburn, Lawrence, portrait painter, xix.
King, Mr., 120.
King, James, (171).
King, Mrs. James (née Ellen James), portrait of, 105, (171); repro., 106.
King, Mrs. James Gore, (599).
King, Joshua, portrait of, 58, 181, (172-173).
King, Mrs. Joshua (Anne Ingersoll), portrait of, 58, 181, (173).
King Philip's War, 4-5.
King, Sophia (Mrs. William McHarg), (172).
Kip, Isaac L., patron, (190).
Kirkland, Miss Lucy, owner, (404-405).
Kline, Mathias, tobacconist, 88.
Knights Templar, 83.
Knoedler, M., & Co., owner, (41, 210, 325, 406).
Knower, Benjamin, patron, (176); portraits of, 45, 179, (174-175).
Knower, Mrs. Benjamin, portrait of, 45, 179, (176).
Krumbhaar, Dr. G. Douglas, owner, (320).
Krumbhaar, Dr. Louis, owner, (71, 320).
Krumbhaar, Mrs. Susan Cooper, owner, (71, 320).
Kühn, Engelhardt, portrait painter, xix.

La Casse, Margaret, *see* Mrs. William Annesley.
Ladu, Miss Gladys, owner, 136-137, (460, 479-480).
Lady in the Red Shawl, by Ames, (365).
Lady of the Lake, see *Romantic Landscape*.
Lafayette, Marquis de, (409).
La Grange, James, patron, 44, 179, (177-178).
Lake George (N.Y.), views of, 67-69, 71, 100, 170, 181-182, 187, (535-537); repros., 68, 69.
Lamb, Col., portrait of, 132, (179).
Lancaster (Mass.), 12.
Landis, Benjamin F., copy by, (64).
Lane, Louisa Greenough, *see* Mrs. William Bayard Van Rensselaer.
Lansing, Mr., owner, (181).
Lansing, Mrs. Abraham, owner, (403, 616).
Lansing, Charles B., owner, (180, 285).
Lansing, Mrs. Charles B., owner, (285, 287).
Lansing, Elizabeth (Mrs. Absalom Townsend), (347).
Lansing family, owners, (126).

Lansing, Gerrit Yates, (182); portrait of, 119, 167, 190, (180).
Lansing, Gerrit Yates (grandson), owner, (180, 285).
Lansing, Gerrit Yates (great-great-grandson), owner, 167, (180).
Lansing, Mrs. J. Townsend, owner, (124).
Lansing, John, (406).
Lansing, Chancellor John, Jr., (180); portraits and engravings of, 190, (181-182, 579-580).
Lansing, Sanders, patron, 35.
Lansingburgh (N.Y.), (27-28).
Lansingh, Chancellor, *see* Chancellor John Lansing, Jr.
Lansingh, Garret Y., *see* Gerrit Yates Lansing.
Lansingh, H., patron, 53.
Lanton, Dr. William, patron, 176, (483).
La Porte, Dr. G. L., owner, 169, (4).
Larned, Mrs., and child, portrait of, (183).
Larocque, Mr. Joseph, Jr., owner, 85, 192, (77, 207, 208).
Larocque, Mrs. Joseph, Sr., owner, (77, 207, 208).
Lassell, Mrs. Charles, owner, 155, 170, (312-313).
Last Supper, by Ames, 132, (539).
Lawton, *see* Lanton.
The Lawyer's Agent, print, 172.
Leake, Henry H., owner, (478).
Leavitt, Robert W., owner, (443).
Lebanon (Conn.), (250).
Lee, Lucinda, *see* Mrs. Elias Mather.
Leicester (Mass.), 12.
Le Mai, Mrs. Col. (née Genet), portrait of, (184).
Leney, William S. engravings by, 50, (533, 577-578); repro., 51.
Lennox (N.Y.), 100.
Leslie, Charles, artist, 108.
Levy, John, owner, (325).
Levy, Maurice, miniature of, (598).
Lewis, Col. Morgan, (34).
Lewis, Mrs. S., portrait of, (185).
Liberty, anti-slavery pamphlet by Julius R. Ames, 35.
Liberty, print, 172.
Lion, by Ames, 178, (540).
Lion and Lady, by Ames, (541).
Litchfield (Conn.) Historical Society, owner, (311).
Little, Miss, 53.
Livingston, Edward, miniature of, (599).
Livingston & Fulton Co., steamboat proprietors, 60.
Livingston, Gerald M., owner, (192).
Livingston, Gertrude (Mrs. William Cutting), (86).
Livingston, Gilbert, (382).
Livingston, Mrs. Gilbert (née Cornelia Beekman), (382).
Livingston, Henry (1714-1789), (189).
Livingston, Henry (1753-1823), portrait of, (188).
Livingston, Major Henry, Jr., (189); patron, 13-15, 151, 176, (186-187).
Livingston, Mrs. Henry, Jr. (née Jean McLean Paterson), portraits of, (186-187).
Livingston, Herman, owner, (621).
Livingston, James, (192).
Livingston, Mrs. James (née Maria Kurstede), (192).
Livingston, Joanna, *see* Mrs. Pierre Van Cortlandt I.
Livingston, John, miniature of, (621).
Livingston, John H. owner, (193, 484).
Livingston, Dr. John Henry, (186) ; portraits of, 32, 88, 186, (189-191).
Livingston, Margaret, *see* Mrs. Thomas Jones.
Livingston, Margaret, *see* Mrs. Peter Robert Livingston.
Livingston, Maria C., *see* Mrs. John Cox Stevens.
Livingston, Col. Peter Robert, (192).
Livingston, Mrs. Peter Robert (née Margaret Livingston), portrait of, (192).
Livingston, Philip, (60, 164-165).
Livingston, Mrs. Philip (née Christina Ten Broeck), (165).
Livingston, Robert, (188, 192).
Livingston, Mrs. Robert (née Maria Thong), (188, 192).
Livingston, Robert C., (297).
Livingston, Robert L., patron, 182, (297).
Livingston, Robert R., portraits and miniature of, 56, 80, 83, 132, (193-194, 484); *see also* Livingston & Fulton Co.
Livingston, Thomas, patron, 53, 188, (195).
Livingston, Walter, (86).
Livingston, Mrs. Walter (Cornelia Schuyler), (86).
"Locust Grove," near Poughkeepsie (N.Y.), 14, (186).
London (England), (254).
Long Island (N.Y.), xix, 15.
Long Island Historical Society, owner, 98, 99, (60).
Lotteries, *see* S. & M. Allen.
Loudonville (N.Y.), 67.

Lovett, Miss Eleanor H., owner, (34, 607).
Lovett, John, portrait of, (196).
Loyal Gazette, (254).
Lucretia, by Ames, (542).
Lyon, Mr. C.W., owner, (226).

Macaulay, Jr., artist, patron, 28.
Macauley (or Macauly), ____, Mason, 29.
Macbeth Gallery, owner, (36, 398).
McCormick, Mrs. Stanley, owner, 167, 168, (243).
McCrae, Frances, *see* Mrs. John Hankinson.
McCrae, Mrs. Margaret Eleanor (Norwood), (82).
McGourk, Mrs., patron, 39, 178, (197).
McHarg family, (357-359, 365).
McHarg, Harriette D., owner, (359).
McHarg, William, patron, 58, 181, (172-173).
McHarg, Mrs. William (Sophia King), (172).
Mackay, Clarence, owner, (97).
McQuade, Rev. Mr., (22).
Madison, James, portrait of, 56, 132, (198).
Madison, Mrs. James (née Dolly Payne), portrait of, (198a).
Madonna and Child, by Ames, (543).
Madonna and Infant, by Ames, (543).
Madonna of the Chair, by Raphael, (543).
Magdalen, by Ames, (544).
Main, William, artist, 108.
Malbone, Edward Greene, miniature by, (15).
Maley, John, patron, 20; portrait of, 67, (199).
Maley, Mrs. John (née Catharine Tremper), portrait of, 67, (200).
Mancius, Mr., portrait of, 188, (201).
Mancius, Mrs., patron, 188, (201, 202).
Mandevell, ______, portrait of, 189, (203).
Mandeville, Mrs., portrait of, (204).
Mann, Elias, patron, 10.
March, Dr. Alden, 124, (353).
Marchant, Edward D., artist, (215-216).
Marcy, Governor, (176).
Mark Lodges of New York State, 43-44.
Marselis, Barbara, *see* Mrs. Henry I. Bogart.
Marsiglia, Gerlando, artist, 108.
Marvin, Mr., 120.
Marvin, Mrs. Emma, portrait of, (205).
Maryland, art in, xix; sitter from, (305).
Mason, Mrs. William V., owner, 69, 82, 170, (36, 300, 382-386, 502, 535).
Masonic Temple (Albany, N.Y.), owner, 53, (9).
Masonry, xviii, 14, 21, 24-25, 28-30, 32-33, 39, 43-44, 58, 71, 83, 87, 95-96, 102-104, 109, 111, 114, 120, 124, 129, 171, 186, (30, 235, 305, 515).
Masons, *see:* Angelo Ames; Ezra Ames; Julius Rubens Ames; Bunnel; A. Clark; DeWitt Clinton; Crocker; John T. Dotty; John Eames; Jonathan Eights; Ennis; Asa Fitch; Warner F. Hitchcock; Macauley; Elijah H. Metcalf; Capt. Moullen; Penniman; Elihu Phinney; Samuel Stringer; Thomas Smith Webb; Charles White; C.C. Yates.
Massachusetts, Ames and, 3-8, 13, 22-23; Militia of, 5-6, (5, 408); Supreme Court of, (266).
Mather, Mr., 187, (436).
Mather, Capt. Elias, Sr., (206).
Mather, Mrs. Elias, Sr. (née Lucinda Lee), (206).
Mather, Elias, Jr., portrait of, (206); repro., 118.
Mather, Mrs. Elias, Jr. (née Cynthia Corning), (206).
Mathews, Miss Catharine Van Cortlandt, owner, 69, 82, 170, (36, 298, 300, 382-386, 502, 535).
Mathewson, Miss Hope, attributions by, 95, 167, (25, 32, 38-40, 45, 116, 229, 259, 260a, 307, 336, 347, 356, 359-360, 365, 379, 408, 444, 447a, 589).
Maverick, Peter, engravings by, (53, 569, 574).
Maynard, Ross H., owner, (325).
Meads, John, patron, 186, (77, 207, 208); portrait of, 84, 183, (207); repro., 85.
Meads, Mrs. John (née Louisa Crane), portrait of, xvii, 84, 143, 183, 192, (208); repros., 85, 192.
Meads, Orlando, owner, (77, 207-208).
Mechanics and Farmers' Bank (Albany, N.Y.), officers of, 45, 120, (174, 221, 238, 277, 290); Ames and, xviii, 79, 120, 123; owner, 39, 45, 75, 169 (11, 174, 277).
Mechanics' Society, see Albany Mechanics' Society.

Medford, (Mass.), 4.
Megs, *see* Meigs.
Meigs, Dr., 120; patron, 188, (209).
Meigs, Mrs., portrait of, 188, (209).
Mellon Educational and Charitable Trust, owner, (211).
Melville, Allan,(210); portrait of, (622).
Melville, Mrs. Allan (née Maria Gansevoort), portraits of, (210-211); repro., 82.
Melville, Herman, novelist, (210).
Melville, Mrs. Herman, owner, (125).
Mendon (Mass.), 23.
Merchants Club, N.Y.C., owner, (64).
Meredith, William T., 161-162.
Merle-Smith, Major Van Santvoord, owner, (347).
Merle-Smith, Mrs. Van Santvoord, owner, 152, 169, (347).
Merrifield, Richard, 126.
Metcalf, E., artist, 108.
Metcalf, Elijah H., patron, 28.
Metropolitan Museum of Art, owner, xvi, 49, (381, 598-599); Ames's work exhibited at, (458, 476, 598-599, 605); mentioned, (160).
Metropolitan Opera House (New York City), Ames's works exhibited at, (68, 215).
Mezzotints, sold by Ames, 172.
Middlesex County (Mass.), militia regiment of, 6.
Milbert, J., artist, 92, 108.
Milledgeville (Ga.), (256).
Miller, Mr. Clinton, owner, (70).
Miller, Margaret C. (Mrs. William Annesley), (17).
Miller, Sylvanus, patron, 73.
Mills, Mr., patron, 189 (212).
Mills, son of the above, portrait of, 189, (212).
Milmore, Mrs. Pepita, owner, (633).
Minaville (N.Y.), sitters from, (129, 154, 249-250, 409).
Minthorne, Hannah, *see* Mrs. Daniel D. Tompkins.
Minthorne, Mangle, (344).
Mitchill, Dr. Samuel Latham, 103; portrait of, 132, (213).
Moles, Ames's interest in, 15.
Montclair (N.J.) Art Museum, Ames's work shown at, (126).
Montgomery County (N.Y.), (250).
Montgomery County Historical Society (Fort Johnson, N.Y.), owner, (410).
Montreal (Canada), sitters from, (17-18).
Montville (Conn.), sitter from, (147).
Moore, Edward Small, owner, (138).
Moore, Mrs. Evelyn N., owner, (138).
Moore, Roland, owner, (126).
Morehouse, John, 100.
Morewood, Miss Helen Gansevoort, owner, (210).
Morris, Anna Shoemaker (Mrs. Francis Bloodgood), (32).
Morris, Gouverneur, portraits of, 88, 132, 143, 159-166, 183, 186, (214-217); repro., 160.
Morris, Mrs. Gouverneur, patron, 162, 183, (215).
Morris, Gouverneur, grandson of the above, owner, 159, (215).
Morse, Samuel F.B., 108; Ames's work attributed to, 99, 143, (167, 400).
Mother and Child, Likeness of a, by Ames, 132, (363).
Moullen, Capt., patron, 25.
Mounsey, Thomas, patron, 183, (218).
Mount Vernon Lodge No. 3 (Albany, N.Y.), 25.
Mount Wayte (Framingham, Mass.), 4-5.
Mourning Bride, by Ames, (545).
Mulford, Betsy, *see* Mrs. Henry Sutliff.
Mulford, Capt. David, 8.
Mulford, Delos W., (219).
Mulford, Ezekiel, 8, 12-13, 42, (309, 411, 479); portrait of, 49, 138, (219).
Mulford, Mrs. Ezekiel (née Sally Emes), 6, 8, 12.13, 116, (219, 309, 411, 479, 485, 505); portrait of, 39, (220); repro., 2.
Mulford, Ezra Ames, 42; miniature of, (485).
Mulford, Ezra Ames, Jr., 42; owner, (219).
Mulford family, miniatures of, 43, 136, (485, 505).
Mulford, Huldah, *see* Mrs. John Hills.
Mulford, Orren, owner, (219).
Mulford, Sally, *see* Mrs. James Wade.
Munson-Williams-Proctor Institute (Utica, N.Y.), owner, 95, 167, (38, 40).
Murder of the Princes in the Tower, by Ames, 132, (546-547).
Murray, Dr. Henry Alexander, owner, 82, (210).
Museum of the City of New York, owner, 80, 156, (5, 227, 384, 502); Ames's works shown at, (68, 86).
Musidora, by Ames, (548).
Mynderse, Mrs. Herman V., owner, (122).

Mynderse, Mrs. William Ten Broeck, owner, (192).

Nassau (Bahamas), (20).
Natchez (Miss.), sitter from, (142).
National Academy of Design, 108.
National Commercial Bank and Trust Company of Albany, owner, (3).
National Museum (Washington, D.C.), owner, (633).
New and Allegorical Devices for Artists..., engravings by Garnet Terry, 30.
New Brunswick (N.J.), Theological Seminary at, (189); sitter from, (114); *see also* Rutgers University.
New England, portrait painting in, xix; Ames in, 22, 23, 33, 40, 42.
New Haven (Conn.), (353); *see also* Yale University.
New Haven Colony Historical Society, owner, (102, 377).
New Jersey, portrait of governor of, (97).
New Jersey Historical Society, owner, 95, (79).
New Rochelle (N.Y.), sitter from, (31).
New York Academy of Medicine, (296).
New York City, xviii-xix, 7, 14-16, 19-20, 72, 91; Ames and, 13-16, 36, 50, 72-73, 84, 96, 100, 102, 114; sitters from, (23-24, 60, 78, 102, 102, 114, 254, 261, 445); Mayor of, (54); view of, 17.
New York County, Sheriff of, (86),
New York Genealogical and Biographical Society, owner, (361).
New-York Historical Society, xvii, 17, (54, 169, 214) ; owner of Ames manuscripts, 147, 153; owner of Ames portraits, xvii, 44, 47, 53-54, 61, 65-66, 79, 86, 88, 95, 108-109, 112, 146, 154, 157, 160-166, (65, 78, 80, 148, 163, 198a, 216, 254, 344, 354, 476, 591, 601).
New York Pocket Book, by Horatio G. Spafford, (279).
New York State, art in, xvii-xix, 84, 99; Emes Family in, 7, 13-16; owner, 76, (64, 419); governors of, 92, 131, 141, (55, 66, 160, 319, 337, 341, 377, 448, 462); lieutenant-governors of, (54, 76, 319, 337, 396); secretary of state of, (74); surveyor-general of, (93); attorneys-general of, (16, 406); treasurers of, (174, 236); chancellors of, (169, 181, 193, 484).
New York State Assembly, Acts of, 19, 33; patron, 73-74, (64, 419); members of, (4, 29, 78, 132, 136, 167, 476); clerk of, (388).
New York State Bank, 53, (302, 446).
New York State Capitol (Albany, N.Y.), Ames works at, 76, (64, 419).
New York State Historical Association (Cooperstown, N.Y.), owner or loanee, 37, 44, 86, 99, 101, 170, (36, 398, 590); Ames works exhibited at, (70, 167, 378).
New York State Historical Association Museum (Ticonderoga, N.Y.), 140; owner, 44, (36).
New York State Library (Albany), owner, (94).
New York State Medical Society, (296).
New York State Militia, (383, 394, 396, 435).
New York State Senate, members of, (131, 167, 296, 435); clerk of, (20).
New York Supreme Court, justices of, (169, 181, 248, 284, 390) ; clerk of, (228).
New York Tax Court, loanee, (381).
New York University, (114).
New York, University of the State of, Regents of (180, 576).
Newark,(N.J.), sitter from, (79).
Newark (N.J.),Museum, Ames works exhibited at, (79, 93).
Newman, Clarence E., owner, (221).
Newman, Miss Evelyn, owner, 57, (221, 615).
Newman, Henry, portrait of, xvii, 53, 56, (221); repro., 57.
Newman, John L., owner, (221).
Newton, Ruth (Mrs. Henry Emes), 5.
Newtown (Long Island, N.Y.), (31).
Niagara Falls, 102.
North River, (Clermont), Hudson River steamboat, 59-60.
Northampton (Mass.), sitter from, (5).
Northbridge (Mass.), 23.
Norton, Burrage, (284-285).
Norton, Mrs. Burrage, *see* Mrs. Ambrose Spencer.
Norton, Mary (Mrs. Alexander O. Spencer), (286).
Norton, Samuel, (284, 287).
Norton, Mrs. Samuel, *see* Mrs. Ambrose Spencer (née Clinton),
Norwood, Margaret Eleanor, *see* Mrs. Thomas Humphrey Cushing.
Nott, Dr. Eliphalet, portraits of, 119, 132, 158-159, 189, (222-225); repro., 156; miniature of, (486, 581); engravings of, (486, 581).
Nova Scotia, (168).

Noyes, Sarah, *see* Mrs. George Tibbits.

Oakey, Mr. and Mrs., of New York City, 85.
Ogden, Aaron, portrait of, (45, 226).
Olcott, Mrs. Eben Erskin, owner, (348).
Olcott, Miss Katharine, owner, (348).
Old South Association (Boston, Mass.), owner, 156, 158, (39, 69, 135, 223, 266, 360, 379, 401).
Onondaga County (N.Y.), sitter from, (132).
Ontario County (N.Y.), 77.
Oppenheimer, Dr. and Mrs. Frederick G., owners, (86).
Orange County (N.Y.), (302).
Osborn, Mrs. William H., owner, (188).
Osgood, Martha Brandon, *see* Mrs. Edmond Charles Genet.
Otis, Bass, 64-65; Ames work formerly attributed to, (68).
Otis, Mercy, *see* Mrs. Nathaniel Bartlett.
Otsego (N.Y.), Masonic lodges at, 28, (235).
Otsego (N.Y.) *Herald*, (235).
Otsego County (N.Y.) Historical Society, owner, (36).
Ovid (N.Y.), 100.
Owl, by Ames, (549).
Ox, by Ames, (550).

Paddock, Priscilla Clark, portrait of, (227).
Page, *see* Paige.
Paige, Alonzo W., owner, 142, (32-33).
Paige, Miss Clara Antoinette, owner, (32-33).
Paige, Eliza, *see* Mrs. J. Lewi Donhauser.
Paige, John Keyes, portrait of, xvii, 116, 143, 169, 189, (228); repro., 110.
Paige, Mrs. John Keyes (née Anna Maria Bloodgood), (228); owner, (32-33).
Paige, Mrs. John Keyes (née Helen Maria Yates), (228); portrait of, xvii, 116, 167, (228-229); repro., 110.
Paige, Joseph C.W., owner, (228-229, 449).
Paige, Joseph Yates, owner, (228-229, 449).
Pain, Mrs., of Troy, portrait of, 188, (230).
Paine, Sarah, *see* Mrs. Isaac Cushman.
Paine, Seth, (84).
Palmateer, Miss, *see* Mrs. Jesse Emes.
Palmer, Anna, *see* Mrs. Aaron Cady.
Palmistry, book on, 15.
Palmiter, Mr. Robert H., owner, (71, 320).
Paradise, John, artist, 108.
Pardee, Mrs. Harold E.B., owner, (447a).
Parisen, W.D., artist, 92.
Park, Lawrence, attribution by, (122).
Parke-Bernet Galleries, owner, (381, 384, 386, 415).
Parker, G.S., owner, (362).
Parker, George, engraving by, (583).
Parker, Mrs. Haven, attributions by, (34, 155, 607).
Parmature, Mrs., *see* Mrs. Jesse Emes.
Parminter, Mrs. Fanny, *see* Mrs. Jesse Emes.
Pate, W., (573).
Paterson, Jean McLean, *see* Mrs. Henry Livingston, Jr.
Patterson, Harold T., owner, 167-168, (41).
Paul and Virginia, by Ames, (551).
Paulding, John, portrait of, (623).
Payne, Dolly, *see* Mrs. James Madison.
Peale, Charles Willson, xix, 115; portraits by, (362, 609); Ames work formerly attributed to, 143, 159-160, 163, (215).
Peale, Rembrandt, Ames's work attributed to, 95, 143, (80, 198a, 260a).
Peale, Rubens, 91.
Peale's Museum, 91, (68).
Pearson, George, patron, 87-88, 173.
Peebles, Gerrit B., (403).
Peebles, Mrs. Gerrit B. (née Maria Van Schaick), (403).
Pelham's Farm (Sudbury, Mass.), 4.
Pell, Stephen H.P., owner, (168).
Peltz, John DeWitt, owner, 48, 158, 167, (284, 299, 301, 414).
Penniman, ———, Mason of Albany, 29.
Penniman, Mrs. Mary, owner, (175).
Penniman, Obadiah, patron, 58, 181, (231).
Penniman, Mrs. Obadiah, portrait of, 58, 181, (231).
Penniman, S., portrait of, 190, (232); patron, 190, (233).
Penniman, Mrs. S., portrait of, 190, (233).
Penniman, Sylvanus J., portrait of, 132, (234).

Pennsylvania, art in, xix, 84.
Pennsylvania Academy of the Fine Arts, owner, 61, 64-66, 123, 154, (63, 355, 609).
Penrose & Edgette, owners, (357-359, 365).
Penrose, Miss Helena, owner, (359).
Pepoon, Mrs., owner, (155).
Pequot War, 4.
Perseverance, Hudson River steamboat, 59-60, (388, 521).
Perspective Painting of Lake George, by Ames, 67-68, 182, (536).
Peters, Lt. Col. DeWitt Clinton, owner, (138).
Peters, John Rogers, owner,(138).
Petersham (Mass.), (112).
Pfeifer, F.W., owner, (97).
Phelps, Benjamin, (77).
Phelps, Mrs. Benjamin (née Ruth Horton), (77).
Phelps, Ruth, *see* Mrs. Elisha Crane.
Philadelphia (Pa.), xix, 16; art in, 59-61, 63-64, 66, 88, 91; Ames in, 102; sitters from, (416-417, 567).
Philadelphia Gazette, 64.
Philadelphia Museum, Ames work exhibited at, (211).
Philipse Castle Restoration (Tarrytown, N.Y.), Ames works at, 84, 169, (319, 608, 623).
Phillips, John Marshall, attribution by, (621).
Phillips, Jonathan(?), patron, 176, (487).
Phinney, Alexander S., owner, (235).
Phinney, Mrs. Alexander S., owner, 26, (235).
Phinney, Elihu, portrait of, 28, 79, 138, 178, (235); repro., 26.
Physiognomy, book on, 15.
Pike-fish, see Fish.
Pintard, John, 161.
Pittsfield (N.Y.), 77.
Pittstown (N.Y.), 22, 25.
Platt, Charles Z., patron, 53, 77, 180, (236).
Plum, David B., owner, (120).
Pocahontas, by Ames, 87; repro., 173.
Pocket Guide for Canals, by Horatio G. Spafford, (279).
Pomeroy, Dr., patron, 53, 180, (237).
Pomfret (Conn.), sitters and patron from, (83-85, 576).
Port Folio, 63-64.
Porter, Giles, (238).
Porter, Giles W., portrait of, (238).
Porter, Giles W. and Ira, (238-239).
Porter, H. Hobart, owner, (447a).
Porter & Harrison, printers, (574).
Porter, Ira, (238); patron, 34, 182, (239-240).
Portrait of a Lake Herring, see Fish.
Portrait of a White Lake Fish, see Fish.
Portrait painting, development of, in America, xviii-xix, 84.
Portraits of Seven Governors of New York, by Ames, 140, (55, 66, 160, 337, 341, 378, 448); repros., 131, 141.
Poughkeepsie (N.Y.), 13-14, 176, (186, 405).
Poughkeepsie Courthouse (N.Y.), 14.
Powers, T., portrait of, (241).
Presbyterian Churches: First, Albany, 107, (222, 292, 486); Second Albany, (567); Third, Albany, (79, 153); Second, Newark (N.J.), (79); First, Caldwell (N.Y.), (47); Lansingburgh (N.Y.), (27).
Preston, Mrs. Harry, owner, (154).
Price, Mrs. Edson C., owner, (435).
Prince, Kitty, *see* Katharine Barber James.
Prince, William Henry, (156).
Prince, Mrs. William Henry (Kitty Prince), *see* Katharine Barber James.
Princeton University Museum, (424).
Prints sold by Ames, 172.
Procter, Mrs. Rodney, owner, (238).
Proudfit, Miss, portrait of, (242).
Providence (R.I.), 187, (256).
Provost, George, patron, 43, 179, 243-244); portrait of, 138, 167, (243); repro., 168.
Provost, Mrs. George (née Anna Bogardus), (243).
Pyne, Percy Rivington, 164.

Quack Doctor (or *Street Fair)*, (624).
Quackenbush, Mr., patron, 21.
Queen's College, *see* Rutgers.

Randel, John, Sr., portrait of, 182,(245).
Randel, Mrs. John, Sr., and daughter, portrait of, 181, (246).
Randel, John, Jr., patron, 181, 182, (245, 246, 426).
Rankin, Edward E., owner, 86, 166, (394).
Rankin, Mrs. Edward W., owner,(394).
Rankin, Miss Emily W., owner, 86, 166, (394).
Raphael, (543).
Rathbone, ______, portrait of, 189, (247).

Rathbone, Valentine W., patron, 189, (247).
Rawdon, Clark & Co., engravings by, (51, 567).
Read, Betty (Mrs. John Bent), 3.
Redmond, Mrs. Geraldyn, owner, (188).
Reformed Church, *see* Dutch Church.
Rensselaer (N.Y.), (120).
Reynolds, A.G., (577).
Reynolds, Betsey, *see* Mrs. Samuel Voorhees.
Reynolds, Mr. Kenneth G., owner, 105, 118, (199, 200, 248-250, 409).
Reynolds, Mrs. Kenneth G., owner, (600).
Reynolds, Lydia Louisa (Mrs. Thomas Hun), portrait of, (600).
Reynolds, Marcia Phebe, *see* Mrs. Alexander C. Gibson.
Reynolds, Marcus Tullius, portrait of, xvii, 79, 104, (248); repro., 105.
Reynolds, Marcus Tullius, grandson of the above, owner, (129, 199, 200, 248-250, 409, 614).
Reynolds, Stephen, the elder, (249).
Reynolds, Mrs. Stephen (née Rachel Denton), (249).
Reynolds, Stephen, the younger, (248, 409); portrait of, 104, (249).
Reynolds, Mrs. Stephen (née Lydia Bartlett), (248, 409); portrait of, 104, (250) ; repro., 118.
Rhinebeck (N.Y.), (74).
Rice, Mr. and Mrs., of New England, 23.
Rice, Mrs., portrait of, (251).
Rice, Randel, portrait of, 189, (252).
Richmond (N.Y.), 87, 96.
Richmond, Mrs. Anna (James), owner, (155).
Richmond, George, owner, (155).
Richmond, Mrs. Mabelle (Jones), owner, (155).
Ridgefield (Conn.), (172).
Rivington, Mrs., portrait of, 46, 164, 180, (253).
Rivington, James, Sr., portraits of, 44, 56, 132, 163-166, (254); repro., 165.
Rivington, Mrs. James, Sr., (254).
Rivington, James, Jr., patron, 44, 164, 179, (254).
Robertson, Archibald, print by, 17.
Robertson, William, portrait of, 132, (255).
Robie, Mrs. H.B., owner, (334-336).
Rochester (N.Y.), 115.
Rockwell, Mr. and Mrs. Charles Spencer, owners, (256).
Rockwell, Samuel, (256).
Rockwell, Mrs. Samuel (née Sarah Ann Spencer), portrait of, (256).
Rodgers, Mrs. Caroline (Fairman), portraits of, (257-258).
Rogers, George, portrait of, (259).
Rogers, Judge Halsey, (259).
Rogers, Mrs. Halsey (née Deborah Wing), (259).
Rogers, James, patron, 26, 177, (488).
Rogers, N., artist, 108.
Roman Charity, by Ames, (552).
Romantic Landscape, by Ames, 69-71, (538); repro., 70.
Romeyn, Dr. Dirck, portrait of, 182, (260).
Romeyn, Harriet, *see* Mrs. Spencer Stafford.
Romeyn, Rev. James V.C., (291).
Romeyn, Miss Nina, owner, (17, 18).
Root, "General," portrait of, (260a).
Rose, Mrs. Reginald P., owner, 106, (171); attribution by, (158).
Rosen, Mr., attribution by, (608).
Rosenthal, Albert, etching by, (579).
Rosenthal, Max, etching by, (580).
Rotan, Mrs. Thurman, attributions by, (243, 256, 599).
Rowell, H.G., attribution by, (608).
Roxbury (Mass.), 6.
Roy, Mrs. Charles Peace, 170, (312, 313).
Royal Arch Masons, xviii, 25, (235).
Royal Gazette, (254).
Ruggles, Burnet Rathbone, owner, (261, 262).
Ruggles, Philo, portrait of, (261); repro., 93; owner, (261, 262).
Ruggles, Mrs. Philo (née Ellen Bulkley), portrait of, (262); repro., 93.
Rush, ______, New York State Assemblyman, 64.
Russell, Caleb, patron, 58, 181, (263).
Russell, Capt. Isaac, 7.
Rutgers College *and* University, (260, 307); owner, (93).
Rutland (Vt.), 187, (324).
Rutland County (Vt.), (325).

Saint Andrews Society, patron, 72.
Salisbury, Stephen, patron, 10.
Samson and the Philistines, by Ames, 132, (553).
San Antonio (Texas), *see* Witte Memorial Museum.
Sanford, ______, miniature of, 176, (489).
Sanger, Judge, portrait of, (264).
Saratoga Springs (N.Y.), (104).

Sartain, John, engravings by, (52, 568).
Sawitzky, William, attributions by, 95, 105, 162, 167, (3, 5, 29-31, 41, 54, 80, 102, 122, 132, 139, 157, 175, 180, 215, 226, 227, 284, 334, 335, 361, 364, 377, 381, 402, 404, 405, 434, 435, 449, 608, 616, 623).
Schagticoke (N.Y.), (404).
Schenectady (N.Y.), sitters from, (90, 129, 149, 150, 249, 260, 333, 333a, 416, 417, 448); *see* Union College.
Schermerhorn, A. Coster, owner, 106, (158).
Schermerhorn, Mrs. Alfred E., owner, (158).
Schoharie (N.Y.), 43-44.
Schuler, Anna, *see* Mrs. David Cady.
Schuyler, Cornelia (Mrs. Walter Livingston), (86).
Schuyler mansion (Albany, N.Y.), 31.
Scoville, John, portrait of, (265).
Sea Pieces, prints and picture, 172.
Sears, ——, New York State Assemblyman, 73.
Sedgwick, Mrs., patron, 186, (29); owner, (29).
Sedgwick, Miss Maria, owner, (29).
Sedgwick, Catharine Maria, (266, 267).
Sedgwick, Theodore (1746-1813), (267); portrait of, 56, 132, (266).
Sedgwick, Theodore (1780-1839), (29); patron, 49, 180, 182, (267, 268).
Selkreg, John, 116.
Selkreg, Mrs. John (née Bette Emes), 116.
Selkreg, John W., 116.
Selkreg, Mary L., 116.
Semple, Robert, *see* Robert Temple.
Senate House Association (Kingston, N.Y.), owner, (589).
Seneca Chief, canal boat, 109, 111.
Sera, ——, transparency by, 112.
Several Ages, mezzotint, 172.
Seymore, ——, patron, 9, 10, 176, (490).
Shakespeare's *The Tempest*, scenes from, by Ames, 132, (554, 555).
Sharliff, Hezekiah, patron, 26, 177, (491).
Sharp, W., lithograph by, (586).
Sharp's Lith., J.C. (Boston, Mass.), (586).
Shaw, Miss, portrait of, 190, (269).
Shaw, Henry, patron, 124, 190, (269).
Shaw, John, 7.
Shelburne (Vt.) Museum, owner, (345).
Sheppard, Thomas, patron, 12.
Sherborn (Mass.), 4, 5, 7.
Sherbrooke, Miles, 7.
Shipherd, Zebulon Rudd, patron, 43, 178, (270, 271).
Shoemaker, Anna (Mrs. Francis Bloodgood), (32).
Sign of Raphael's Bust, 30.
Silhouettes, 40, 42.
Silknegg, *see* Selkreg.
Silkregg, *see* Selkreg.
Silver Lake White Fish, *see* Fish.
Sizer, Theodore, (621); attributions by, (611).
Skinner, Dr., portrait of, (272).
Smibert, John, portrait painter, xix.
Smith, Miss, *see* Mrs. Gilbert Steward.
Smith, David Cady, owner, (46).
Smith, Ebenizer, patron, 182, (273, 274).
Smith, Frank Bulkeley, owner, (4, 362).
Smith, Mrs. Frank Sullivan, owner, (361).
Smith, Miss Gertrude Robinson, owner, owner, 118, (206).
Smith, H.W., engraving by, (584).
Smith, James Burnham, owner, (43, 44).
Smith, Luther L., owner, (43, 44).
Smith, Urania, *see* Mrs. Eleazer Burnham.
Smith, William D., engraver, (566).
Smithsonian Institution, (478).
Society of Artists of the United States, 59-64, (63, 354, 355).
Society of the Cincinnati, (31, 172).
Society for the Promotion of Agriculture, Arts and Manufactures, 20.
Society for the Promotion of Useful Arts, 80, 83, (193).
Solomans, *see* Solomon.
Solomon, Levi, Sr., 104, (275, 276).
Solomon, Mrs. Levi, Sr., patron, 189, (275, 276).
Solomon, Levi, Jr., portrait of, 189, (275).
Solomon, Samuel, portrait of, 189, (276).
Solomon's Lodge No. 1 (Poughkeepsie, N.Y.), 14.
Solomon's Temple, print, 27, 172.
Southerland, Judge, patron, 190, (182).
Southwick, Solomon, patron, 45, 49, 180, (21); portraits of, 39, 79, 91, 169, 178, 184, (277, 278).
Spafford, Horatio Gates, 74; portrait of, (279).
Spain, U.S. Minister to, (160).
Spalding, Mr., patron, 22, 177, (492).
Spencer, Miss, 95.

Spencer, Miss (daughter of Giles Spencer), portrait of, 186, (280).
Spencer, ______(son of Ambrose Spencer), portrait of, 187, (281).
Spencer, Mrs., portrait of, (282).
Spencer, Abby, *see* Mrs. John Townsend.
Spencer, Alexander O., patron, 187, (285, 286).
Spencer, Mrs. Alexander O. (née Mary Norton), (286).
Spencer, Ambrose, (281, 283, 285-287, 316); patron, 77, 96; portrait of, xvii, 56, 100, 167, 180, (284); repro., 158.
Spencer, Mrs. Ambrose (née Laura Canfield), (283, 284).
Spencer, Mrs. Ambrose (née Catharine Clinton), (284); portrait of, 96, (287).
Spencer, Mrs. Ambrose (née Mary Clinton), (284); portraits of, 187, (285, 286).
Spencer, Caroline, 115.
Spencer, Ezra Ames, 42.
Spencer, Frederick R., portrait painter, 100, (192).
Spencer, George B., patron, 183, (288, 289).
Spencer, Giles, patron, 186, (280).
Spencer, John Canfield, (73, 281).
Spencer, Laura Catharine, *see* Mrs. George William Clinton.
Spencer, Mrs. Polly (Emes), 6, 115, 116.
Spencer, Sarah Ann, *see* Mrs. Samuel Rockwell.
Spencer, Theodore, (281).
Spencer, Thomas (288).
Spencer, William Ambrose, (281).
Staats, Gertrude, 7.
Staatsburg (N.Y.), 3, 5, 7-8, 12, 14, 16, 22, 23, 114-116, (219).
Stafford, Samuel Spencer, owner, (290, 291).
Stafford, Spencer, (288, 291); portrait of, 45, 79, 138, (290); repro., 45; lithograph of, (582).
Stafford, Mrs. Spencer (née Dorothea Hallenbake), (290).
Stafford, Mrs. Spencer (née Harriet Romeyn), (290); portrait of, 45, 138, (291); repro., 45.
Stansbury, Mrs., portrait of, 186, (292).
Stansbury, Rev. Arthur J., patron, 186, (292).
Stanton, George W., patron, (294); portrait of, 187, (293).
Stanton, Mrs. George W., portrait of, 187, (294).
Starr, Mr., portrait of, 189, (295).
Starr, Chandler, patron, 189, (295).
Staten Island (N.Y.), (432).
Staten Island Institute of Arts and Sciences, owner, 46, 49, (343a, 346).
Steamboats, 59-60, (388, 521, 526).
Stearns, Dr. John, patron, 182, (296).
Stevens, Mrs. John Cox (née Maria C. Livingston), portrait of, 182, (297).
Stevens, Mrs. L.W., owner, (238).
Stevenson, Anne, *see* Mrs. Pierre Van Cortlandt II.
Stevenson, James, patron, (298).
Stevenson, John, (383); patron, 20; portrait of, (299).
Stevenson, Mrs. John (née Magdalena Douw), (383); portraits of, (300, 301).
Steward, Daniel Jackson, owner, (302, 303).
Steward, Gilbert, portraits of, 181, 190, (302, 302a).
Steward, Mrs. Gilbert (née Miss Smith), patron, 190, (302, 302a); portrait of, (303).
Steward, Miss Mary B., owner, (302, 303).
Stewart, Gilbert, *see* Gilbert Steward *and* Gilbert Stuart.
Stewart, Mrs. Weeks, owner, 68, (74, 76, 536).
Stone, William Leete, portrait of, 132, (304).
Stonington (Conn.), (45).
Street Fair (or *Quack Doctor*), (624).
Strickland, William, artist, 108.
Stringer, Dr. Samuel, patron, 44, 179, (305).
Strong, James, portrait of, 132, (306).
Strong, Theodore, portrait of, xvii, 104, (307); repro., 105.
Strong, Mrs. Theodore, owner, (400).
Strong, Theodore, Jr., owner, 105, (307).
Stuart, Mrs., portrait of, (308).
Stuart, Gilbert, *see* Gilbert Steward.
Stuart, Gilbert, xvii-xix, 15-16; and Ames, xvii-xviii, 15-16, 55-56, 115, 138, 143, 144, 164; portraits by, copied by Ames, 44, 56, 74, 80, 132, 141, 163-166, (1, 125, 160, 161, 193, 198, 254, 266, 360, 396, 419, 420, 484, 503, 518); Ames portraits formerly attributed to, 104, 143, (122, 157); portrait and miniature of, (362, 601); portrait by (?), (616).
Student, by Ames, (556).
Sturbridge (Mass.), 6.
Suczannet, Count Jean de, owner, (175).
Sudbury (Mass.), 3, 4, 6, 7.

Sullivan, Mrs. Cornelius, Jr., owner, (157).
Sully, Thomas, 115; Ames work formerly attributed to, 143, 159, 161-162, (215).
Sutliff, Ezra Ames, Sr. and Jr., 42.
Sutliff, Henry, (309).
Sutliff, Mrs. Henry (née Betsy Mulford), portrait of, (309).
Sutliff, Miss Mary L., owner, 2, 11, 32, (8, 110).
Sutliff, Mr. Walter H., owner, (309).
Sutliff, William Kirby, owner, (8).
Synge, Mrs. F.J., owner, (165).

Tallmadge, Col. Benjamin, (313, 315, 576); portraits of, 104, 116, 169, 170, 188, (310-312); repro., 155; engraving of, (583).
Tallmadge, Mrs. Benjamin (née Mary Floyd), (310).
Tallmadge, Mrs. Benjamin (née Maria Hallett), (310); portraits of, 169, 170, 188, (313-314); repro., 155.
Tallmadge, Lt. Benjamin, Jr., portrait of, 104, (315).
Tallmadge, George Clinton, owner, 146, 154, 157, (65).
Tallmadge, Matthias Burnett, patron, 154, 182, (65, 317); portraits of, xvii, 39, 80, 178, (316-317); repro., 38.
Tallmadge, Mrs. Matthias Burnett (née Elizabeth Clinton), portrait of, 39, 80, 178, (318); repro., 38.
Talmadge, *see* Tallmadge.
Tanner, B., engraver, (564).
Tappen, Cornelia, *see* Mrs. George Clinton.
Tarrytowns (N.Y.), Historical Society of the, owners, 78, 84, (319, 608, 623).
Taxes, 96.
Tayler, John, 91, 124, (76); owner, (536); patron, 67, 68, 182, 183, (321, 536); portraits of, 84, 91, 132, 169, 184, 189, (319-323); repro., 78.
Tayler, Margaret, *see* Mrs. Charles DeKay Cooper.
Taylor, ______, New York State Assemblyman, 73.
Taylor, Frank Beardsley, owner, (309).
Taylor, Capt. John, (383, 384, 502).
Taylor, Mrs. John (née Catharine Clinton), (383, 384, 502).
Teller, Jacobus, (512).
Teller, Willem, (512).
Teller, Mrs. Willem (Cornelia Yates), (512).
Temple, ______, portrait of, 187, (324).
Temple Chapter (Albany, N.Y.), 25, 33, 58, (235).
Temple Lodge (Albany, N.Y.), 25, 58, 71, 96, 124, 186, (515).
Temple, Robert, (324); portrait of, 187, (325).
Ten Broeck, Mrs., owner, (357-359, 365).
Ten Broeck, Abraham, (326); portrait of, (625).
Ten Broeck, Anne Van Schaick (Mrs. Thomas Hillhouse), (147).
Ten Broeck, Christina, *see* Mrs. Philip Livingston.
Ten Broeck, Dirck, patron, 12, 182, (326).
Ten Broeck family, (357-359, 365).
Ten Broeck mansion (Albany, N.Y.), (478, 625).
Ten Eyck, Abraham, patron, 35.
Ten Eyck, Harmanus, portraits of, 44, 190, (327-329, 626, 627).
Ten Eyck, Mrs. Harmanus (née Margaret Bleecker), (327).
Ten Eyck, Jacob H. (1781-1872), patron, 190, (329).
Ten Eyck, Jacob H. (1833-1898), owner, (328).
Ten Eyck, Jacob Hendrick, (327).
Ten Eyck, Mrs. Jacob Hendrick (née Annatje Wendel), (327).
Ten Eyck, Robert, owner, (617).
Terry, Garnet, *New and Allegorical Devices for Artists ....*, 30.
Thatcher, Margaret Ann, *see* Mrs. Jonathan Walton.
Thayendanegea, *see* Joseph Brant.
Thayer, Eunice, portrait of, (330).
Thayer, Margaret, *see* Mrs. Jonathan Wood.
Theological Seminary (New Brunswick, N.J.), (189).
Thomas, Elijah, patron, 157, 180, (139).
Thomas, Mrs. Henry B., owner, (125).
Thomas, J., patron, 172.
Thomas place (Wayland, Mass.), 5.
Thompson, Smith, patron, 43, 132, 178, (332, 493); portrait of, 133, (331).
Thompson, William, 100.
Thomson Hall (Princeton, N.J.), owner, 139, (424).
Thong, Maria, *see* Mrs. Robert Livingston.
Thorn, Eliza, *see* Mrs. John French Ellis.
Thorn, James Van Slyck, portrait of, (332a).

Thorn, Jonathan, portraits of, 44, 179, (333, 333a).
Thorn, Samuel, (333).
Thorp, Aaron, (336); portrait of, 116, 167, 189, (334); repro., 117.
Thorp, Mrs. Aaron (née Mary Dunn), (336); portraits of, 116, 167, 189, (334, 335) ; repro., 117.
Thorp, Frances Mary, portrait of, 116, 167, 189, (334, 336).
Thorp & Sprague, (334).
Throop, Enos T., portraits of, 132, 140, (337, 338) ; repro., 131.
Tibbits, George, portrait of, (339); repro., 122.
Tibbits, Mrs. George (née Sarah Noyes), portrait of, (340); repro., 122.
Tibbits, George Dudley, owner, 121, (339, 340).
Tibbits, Rev. John Knox, owner, (339, 340).
Tibbits, Miss Sarah Bleecker, (339, 340).
Ticonderoga (N.Y.), 140; *see also* New York State Historical Association Museum.
Tiffeny, Mr., patron, 20-21.
Tillman, Elizabeth, *see* Mrs. William James.
Tobacconists' Signs, 1817; woodcuts after work by Ezra Ames, repros., 174.
Todd, John, Jr., (198a).
Tompkins, Arietta, portrait of, (346).
Tompkins, Daniel D., (344, 345); portraits of, 140, (341-343a); repro., 141.
Tompkins, Mrs. Daniel D. (née Hannah Minthorne), portrait of, (344); repro., 47; family of, owners, (344).
Tompkins, Daniel D., children of, group portrait, 49, 55, 138, (346); repro., 46.
Tompkins, Griffen, portrait of, (346).
Tompkins, Hannah, portrait of, (346).
Tompkins, Minthorne, portrait of, (346).
Tompkins, Sarah Ann (later Mrs. Archibald Gordon), portrait of, (345, 346).
Tompkins, Mrs. Willard, owner, (346).
Tompson, Mrs. patron, 53.
Torrey, Joseph, 10.
Townsend, Absalom, Sr., (347).
Townsend, Absalom, Jr., (348); portrait of, xvii, 84, 95, 139, 169, 183, (347); repro., 152.
Townsend, Mrs. Absalom, Sr. (née Helena DeKay), (347); portrait of, (348).
Townsend, Mrs. Absalom, Jr. (née Elizabeth Lansing), (347).
Townsend, Charles, (302).
Townsend, Dr. Howard, owner, (398).
Townsend, Mrs. Howard (née Justine Van Rensselaer), owner, (398).
Townsend, John, (283); patron, 187, (281).
Townsend, Mrs. John (née Abby Spencer), (281); owner, (285, 287); portrait of, (283).
Townsend, John Fondey, miniature of, (602).
Townsend, Mrs. John Fondey (née Catharine Louisa Douw), miniature of, (603).
Townsend, Capt. Solomon, patron, 46, 180, (349).
Transparency celebrating opening of Erie Canal, 112.
Treat, Dr. D., miniature of, 22, 176, (494).
Tremper, Cantine, owner, (501).
Tremper, Catharine, *see* Mrs. John Maley.
Tremper, Jacob W., (200).
Trevor, Mr. John Bond, Jr., owner, (310, 315).
Trevor, Mrs. John Bond, Sr., owner, (310).
Trotter, John, patron, 189, (351); portrait of, 189, (350).
Trotter, John, son of, portrait of, 189, (351).
Trotter, Mathew, patron, 58, 181, (352).
Troy (N.Y.), 22; patrons and sitters from, 188, 189, (83, 147, 230, 252, 310, 339, 340, 576).
Trumbull, John, xix, 50, 92, (596, 611, 621); Ames work formerly attributed to, (105).
Tucker, Richard D., owner, (165).
Tucker, Mrs. Richard Sands, owner, (165).
Tucker, Samuel Auchmuty, owner, (165).
Tully, William, Jr., portrait of, xvii, 112-114, (353); repro., 113.
Turnure, David A. owner, (588).
Twitchell, Asa W., remarks on Ames, 143-144.

Unidentified sitters, portraits and miniatures of, (354-376, 495-501, 557-561, 604, 628-630); *Portrait of a Gentleman*, 63, (355); *Portrait of a Lady* (10 of them), 132, (367-376); *Portrait of a Youth*, 59-61, (354).
Union College (Schenectady, N.Y.),

(222, 260, 443, 486); owner or loanee, 50, 52, 104, 106, 119, 156-159, (139, 157, 223-225).
Union League Club (New York City), Ames's work shown at, (211).
Union Lodge No. 1 (Albany, N.Y.), 25.
United States:
House of Representatives, members of, (4, 29, 90, 131, 136, 180, 196, 213, 214, 270, 310, 339, 381, 394, 396, 408, 435, 576);
Senate, members of, (97, 213, 214, 408);
Continental Congress, members of, (214, 580).
Army, officers of, (31, 38, 62, 81, 125);
District Court for New York, (316);
Navy, officers of, (315, 333); Secretaries of, (97, 331);
Supreme Court, justice of, (160);
Treasury, Secretary of, (138);
Presidents, *see:* George Washington, John Adams, Thomas Jefferson, James Madison, Martin Van Buren;
Vice-Presidents, *see:* George Clinton, Daniel D. Tompkins.
Upton (Mass.), 23.
Utica (N.Y.), (569); *see also:* Munson-Williams-Proctor Institute.
Uxbridge (Mass.), 23.

Vail, Dr. R.W.G., attribution by, (94).
Vail, Mrs. Thomas, owner, (259).
Vallance, John, Keeper of the Pennsylvania Academy, 64.
Van Buren, Martin, portraits of, 132, 140, (377-380); repro., 131; engraving of, (584).
Van Cleek, *see* Van Kleeck.
Van Cortlandt, Miss Anne S., owner, (36, 300, 382-386, 502, 535).
Van Cortlandt House Museum (New York City), owner, (25).
Van Cortlandt, P., patron, 72.
Van Cortlandt, Philip, portrait of, xvii, 49, 138, (381); repro., xvi.
Van Cortlandt, Pierre I, (381-383).
Van Cortlandt, Mrs. Pierre I (née Joanna Livingston), (381, 383); portrait of, (382).
Van Cortlandt, Pierre II, (502); patron, 80, (384, 385); portrait of, 80, (383); repro., 82.
Van Cortlandt, Mrs. Pierre II (née Catharine Clinton), (383) ; portrait and miniature of, 80, (384, 502).
Van Cortlandt, Mrs. Pierre II (née Anne Stevenson), (383); portraits of, 80, (385, 386).
Van Cott, Joshua Marsden, owner, (138).
Van Cott, Dr. Joshua Marsden, Jr., owner, (138).
Van Dyke, John C., owner, (307).
Van Horne, Cornelius, 164, (254).
Van Horne, Mrs. Cornelius, (254).
Van Ingen, Mr., portrait of, 183, (388).
Van Ingen Company, 59-60.
Van Ingen, James, 73-74; patron, 20, 59, 181, 183, (388, 521, 526).
Van Kleeck, Mrs., patron, 46, 180, (253).
Van Kleeck, Lawrence L., patron, 58, 181, (389, 391).
Van Ness, Judge William W., portrait, 132, (390).
Van Rensselaer, Miss, portrait, 181, (391).
Van Rensselaer, Cornelius Glen, (400).
Van Rensselaer, Mrs. Cornelius Glen (née Catherine Westerlo), owner, (400).
Van Rensselaer, Harriet (Mrs. Solomon Van Rensselaer), (394).
Van Rensselaer, John S., portrait of, 190, (392); patron, 190, (393).
Van Rensselaer, Mrs. John S., portrait of, 190, (393).
Van Rensselaer, Katherine Westerlo, owner, (400).
Van Rensselaer, Philip, (394); patron, 77, 166.
Van Rensselaer, Philip Schuyler, patron, 71, 172; portrait of, (631).
Van Rensselaer, Gen. S., *see* Stephen Van Rensselaer III.
Van Rensselaer, Solomon, (396); portraits of, 88, 91, 96, 153, 166, 167, 184, 186, 188, (394, 395); repro., 86.
Van Rensselaer, Mrs. Solomon (née Harriet Van Rensselaer), (394).
Van Rensselaer, Stephen III, 111, 132, (100); patron, 20, 186, (396); owner, 160, 163, (216); portraits of, 91, 170, 186, (396-402a); repro., 86; minature of, (503, 599).
Van Rensselaer, Stephen IV, (23); patron, 170, 186, (398).
Van Rensselaer, Mrs. Stephen IV, (23).
Van Rensselaer, Sybilla Adeline Kane, owner, (168).
Van Rensselaer, William Bayard, owner, (402).

Van Rensselaer, Mrs. William Bayard (née Louisa Greenough Lane), owner, (402).
Van Santvoort, Abraham, miniature of, (632).
Van Santvoort, Mrs. Abraham, miniature of, (633).
Van Schaick, Anna (Mrs. John Gerritsen Van Schaick), (403).
Van Schaick, Catharine, *see* Mrs. Peter Gansevoort.
Van Schaick, John, patron, 46, 180, (403).
Van Schaick, John Gerritsen, (403).
Van Schaick, Mrs. John Gerritsen (née Anna Van Schaick), (403).
Van Schaick, Maria, portrait of, (366, 403).
Van Schaick, Wessel, (126).
Van Schaick, Mrs. Wessel (née Marie Gerritsen), (126).
Van Schoonhoven, Guert, patron, 187, (405) ; portrait of, (404).
Van Schoonhoven, Mrs. Guert (née Mary Frances Davis), portrait of, 187, (405).
Van Vechten, ______, New York State Assemblyman, 73.
Van Vechten, Abraham, portrait of, (406).
Van Vechten, Miss Frances K., owner, (334-336).
Van Veghten & Kline, 88.
Van Veghten, Walter, 88.
Van Wie, Gerrit W., patron, 46, 180, (407).
Van Wyck, Philip Van Cortlandt, owner, (381).
Van Zandt, Mrs. T. Kirby, owner, (184).
Vander Heyden, Jacob, patron, 43, 179, (387).
Vanderlyn, John, 92; Ames's work compared with, xvii, xviii, 144; Ames's works formerly attributed to, 78, 95, 143, (72, 79, 86, 447a, 449).
Varnum, Joseph Bradley, portrait of, (408).
Venus, by Ames, (562).
Venus and Cupid, by Ames, 132, (563).
Vermeer, copy after, (624).
Vermont, xvii, 187, (42, 324, 325).
Vermont Academy of Medicine, (353).
Verreau, Rev. l'Abbe, owner, (36).
View of Lake George, by Ames, 67, 181, (537).
View of Lake George and Caldwell Village, by Ames, 67-69, 100, 170, 187, (535).
Voorhees, Dr. Samuel, (409).
Voorhees, Mrs. Samuel (née Betsey Reynolds), portraits of, (409-410).
Voyage of Life, by Ames, see *Romantic Landscape*.
Voyage of Life, by Cole, 70-71.

Wade, Miss Edith Sutliff, owner, 2, 39, 97, 125, 136, (13, 112, 220, 366, 411, 485, 504, 505).
Wade, Ezekiel Mulford, miniature of, 136, (504).
Wade family, miniatures of, 43.
Wade, Dr. James, (485, 504); miniature of, 136, (505) ; repro., 136.
Wade, Mrs. James (née Sally Mulford), 136, (504, 505); portrait of, (411).
Wade, James S., owner, (366, 411).
Waldo, Daniel, patron, 10.
Waldo and Jewett, copy after, (135); Ames works formerly attributed to, 105, 143, (102, 157).
Waldo, Samuel Lovett, 72, 144; Ames work formerly attributed to, 143, (158); *see also* Waldo and Jewett.
Walker, Dr. Hiram, 23.
Walker, Samuel, (578).
Walker, Willard, portrait of, 190, (412) ; patron, (413).
Walker, Mrs. Willard, portrait of, 190, (413).
Wall, W.W., artist, 108.
Walsh, Ann, portrait of, (414); repro., 48.
Walsh, Dudley, (414); patron, (415).
Walsh, Hugh, minature of, (605).
Walton, Jonathan, portrait of, (416).
Walton, Mrs. Jonathan (née Margaret Ann Thatcher), portrait of, xvii, 143, (417); repro., 134.
War of 1812, 72.
Ward, Gen. Aaron, (423); portrait of, (634).
Ward, Mrs. Aaron, *see* Mary Lucia Watson.
Warford, Joseph, patron, 50, 180, (418).
Warner, Mr., Ames's boarder, 29.
Warrensburgh (N.Y.), (250).
Washington Benevolent Society, 53, 71, 77, (249).
Washington County (N.Y.), 71.
Washington, George, portraits of, 16, 56, 73-74, 77-78, 132, (419-421); repro., 76.
Waterford (N.Y.), 104, 189, (203).
Watertown (Mass.), 5.
Watervliet (N.Y.), (147).
Watervliet Center (N.Y.), (219).

Watkins, Mr., portrait of, 132, (422).
Watkins, Mrs. de Lancey W., (45).
Watkins, Miss Helen de Lancey, owner, 134, (416, 417, 450, 451).
Watkins, John de Lancey, owner, (443).
Watson, Elkanah, 19; patron, 184, (423); portraits of, 55-56, 132, 153, 186, (424, 425) ; repros., 139; engraving of, 169, (425, 585); repro., 158.
Watson, Miss Mary Lucia, portrait of, 183, (423).
Wayland (formerly East Sudbury, Mass.), 4, 6.
Weatherwise, Abraham, *The Book of Knowledge: or, Wheel of Fortune,* 15.
Webb, Thomas Smith, patron, 28.
Weed, Rev. Mr., 107.
Weeks, Mrs. (née Randel), portrait of, 181, (426).
Wegdon, Mr., patron, 181, (427).
Weir, Miss Eleanor B., owner, 117, 167, (334-336).
Weir, R.W., artist, 108, 115.
Welch, Bartholomew T., portraits of, (428, 429).
Wells, Ann Van Rensselaer Van Wyck, owner, (381).
Wells, I.M., patron, 182, (430).
Weltz, ______, owner, (157).
Wendel, Annatje (Mrs. Jacob Hendrick Ten Eyck), (327).
Wendell, Mrs. Burr, owner, (327).
Wendell, Mr. S.E., (627).
Wentworth, Thomas H., portrait of, 132, (431).
Westerlo, Catherine (Mrs. Cornelius Glen Van Rensselaer), (400).
Weybridge, Vt., sitter from, (155).
Whealer, *see* Theophilus Wheeler.
Wheeler, Joseph, patron, 10, 151, 176, (506, 507).
Wheeler, Robert G., 147-148; attribution by, (497).
Wheeler, Theophilus, patron, 10, 176, (508).
Whipple, Barnum, portrait of, 187, (432).
Whipple, Mrs. Barnum, portrait of, (433).
White, Alexander M., owner, (68).
White, Charles, patron, 87.
White, Miss Frances E., owner, (68).
White Hall (N.Y.), 102, (121, 616).
White, Winsor, owner, (406).
Whitehouse, William F., owner, (260a).
Whitestown (N.Y.), 28.
Whiting, *see* William & Whiting.
Whitney, Eli, portrait of, (434).
Whitney Museum of American Art (New York City), 69, (538).
Wilbraham (Mass.), sitter from, (296).
Wilde, Mrs. Frank, owner, (410).
Wilkin, James Whitney, portrait of, (435).
Wilkinson, William, portrait of, 187, (436).
Willard, Levi, patron, 22, 177, (509).
Williams, Col., portrait of, 132, (437).
Williams College, (135)
Williams, D., portrait of, 188, (438); patron, 188, (439).
Williams, Mrs. D. and child, portrait of, 188, (439).
Williams, E., New York State Assemblyman, 73.
Williams, Henry, silhouettist, 40, 42,
Williams, Capt. Judah, (40).
Williams, Pamela, *see* Mrs. Jacob Jennings Brown.
Williams, S.T., owner, (138).
Williams & Whiting, publishers, 50, (533, 577).
Windeatt, Alicia, *see* Mrs. Samuel Blatchford.
Wing, Deborah, *see* Mrs. Halsey Rogers.
Winne, Dr. Charles K., Jr., owner, 18, (115).
Witte Memorial Museum (San Antonio, Texas), owner, (86).
Wollaston, John, portrait painter, xix.
Wood, Caroline Matilda, *see* Mrs. Eleazer Burnham.
Wood, J. artist, 108.
Wood, Jonathan, 23.
Wood, Mrs. Jonathan (née Margaret Thayer), 23.
Wood, Josiah, 23.
Wood, Mrs. Josiah (née Zipporah Wheelock).
Wood, Zipporah, *see* Mrs. Ezra Ames.
Woodruff, Hunloke, patron, 20, 46, 49, 180, (441); portrait of, (440).
Wooldridge, John, 116, (15).
Worcester (Mass.), 8-13, 22, 176, (99, 464, 466, 472-474, 483, 487, 489, 490, 506, 508).
Wright, Charles C., artist, 108.
Wright, Sophie, *see* Mrs. Hooper Cumming.
Wunderlich, Mr. Hermann, attribution by, (72).
Wynkoop, Miss, portrait of, (442).
Wynkoop, S.R., patron, 158-159, 189, (225).

Yale College, (105).
Yale University Art Gallery, owner,

38, 39, 80, 113, (316, 317, 353).
Yates, Mrs., patron, 22, 176, (510, 511).
Yates, Rev. Dr. Andrew, portraits of, 132, (443, 444).
Yates, Dr. Christopher C., patron, 58, 157, 180, (139); portrait of, (445).
Yates, Miss Cornelia (Mrs. Willem Teller), patron, 22, 177, (512, 513).
Yates, Helen Maria, *see* Mrs. John Keyes Paige.
Yates, John Waters, portraits of, 132, (446, 447, 447a),
Yates, Joseph Christopher, portraits of, 102, 132, 140, (448-451); repro., 141; patron, 157, (139); lithograph of, (586).
Yates, Mrs. Joseph Christopher (née Ann Elizabeth de Lancey), portrait of, (452).
Yates, Mrs. Joseph C. (née Maria Kane), (229).
Yates mansion (Albany, N.Y.), 31.
Yates, Pieter, (512).
Yates, Winfield Scott, owner, 157, (139).
Young Galleries, owner, (41).
Youth, Portrait of a, see Unidentified Sitters.

Zabriskie, Christian, owner, (381).